ENDORSEMENTS

"Today, more than ever before, God's people need a fresh restoration of a moment-by-moment, first-love relationship with Christ Jesus. This book is a vital lifeline to knowing all who Christ is now! It is inspired by the Holy Spirit and biblically anchored to ensure that Jesus is squarely at the center of all believers' lives before it's too late. I'm praying that the whole Church will use it to meditate on Christ, cling to Him, and be authentically renewed in Him."

– Buzz Leonard, In God's Service, Seattle, WA

"In the U.S. we do not give much thought to names and we don't assume they carry much meaning. Not so in Scripture. Under the inspiration of the Holy Spirit, the biblical writers revealed much about God the Son through the many names they gave Him. Steve Hall scoured the pages of the Bible looking for those names-and unpacking much of the meaning they contain. All those experiencing an awakening to the Son in our day will profit from this gift from Steve."

*– Richard Ross, PhD, Professor of student ministry at Southwestern Seminary and author of **Student Ministry and the Supremacy of Christ***

"It has been a great joy spending time in the mornings starting my day 'with Christ.' Focusing on a name of Christ at the beginning of each day helps me carry Christ into my everyday world of work, family, and church."

– Dr. Jason Hubbard, Light of the World Prayer Center, Bellingham WA

"Steve Hall's passion for Christ is blatant and infectious. He has provided me with a daily scriptural reminder of who my Lord is, what He has accomplished for me, and how He is present, providing and protecting as we walk together into another day. Thank you Steve, for reintroducing me to my Lord and Savior!"

– Rev. Phil Miglioratti, National Facilitator Mission America Coalition, National Pastors' Prayer Network, Palatine, IL

"Steve Hall loves the Lord Jesus Christ as much as anyone I know. It's obvious that his favorite subject is Jesus. His prayers exalting our Lord will infect the reader with this kind of love too."

– Pastor Steve Ulmer, New Hope Church,
Shoreline WA

"I have known Steve Hall for many years and watched the Holy Spirit give him a passionate love for the Savior and an insatiable desire to reach the lost. Out of Steve's personal hunger for Jesus, this book is rich in God's Word, with a prayer and meditational flavor that will touch readers' hearts for our Coming King. I have personally been encouraged and moved to a deeper intimacy with our Living God. Steve has the insight and ability to produce on paper the yearnings of the soul. May the Lord use these efforts to further His Kingdom, strengthening believers and introducing many to His righteousness, love and glory."

– Dr. Richard Palmer, retired dentist and minister
to pastors, TX

"Steve Hall has provided a much-needed service in chronicling the many names and facets of the Lord Jesus Christ! You can never have a big enough concept of Jesus. Steve has certainly elevated us toward the true reality of all Christ is."

– Dr. Ron Boehme, Director YWAM US Renewal,
Port Orchard, WA

"I have seen Steve's heart for knowing Jesus just as Paul's was when he states in Philippians 3:5 that he counted everything a loss compared to the priceless privilege of knowing Christ Jesus his Lord, and of progressively becoming more deeply and intimately acquainted with Him. I see our Father saying over this devotional, as He did at Jesus' baptism, *"This is my beloved Son in whom I am well pleased."* Setting aside time to experience Christ's matchless names will be for the reader like finding a pearl of great price each day worth selling all we have.

– Dr. Dennis Crane, anesthesiologist and prayer facilitator,
Yakima, WA.

"I love reading Pastor Steve Hall's daily reminders of the all-sufficiency of Christ. It is refreshing how the Holy Spirit uses the Scripture and Steve's heartfelt words to give me an increased appreciation for the greatness of our Savior. The peace of Christ grows in me as I am encouraged to trust in the Perfect One, who loves me completely and provides for every aspect of my life."

– Katie Christine Rhodes, small business owner and
city prayer coordinator, Kenmore, WA

"I have known Steve Hall for over a decade. He is consumed with passion for Jesus. While Rector of St. Luke's, Seattle, I met with Steve regularly and our conversations always centered on the person of our wonderful Savior. I have been encouraged and stretched by Steve's daily reflections on Jesus Christ, calling me to a deeper, richer walk with Him. I know that those who engage Steve's book will be strengthened in their walk with Christ."

– The Rev'd. Dr. John Roddam, Atlantic Canada Church Relations
Coordinator, Campus Crusade for Christ

I WANT TO KNOW MORE OF CHRIST

A Daily Devotional on His Matchless Names

AUDIO Ink PUBLISHING

Published by AudioInk
P.O. Box 1775
Issaquah, WA 98027
www. AudioInk.com

Distributed by AudioInk Publishing

For ordering information, please contact AudioInk +14255266480

Cover Design by DeeDee Heathman
Interior Design by DeeDee Heathman

Library of Congress Cataloging-in-Publication Data

Hall, Steve
I Want to Know More of Christ: A Daily Devotional on His Matchless Names/ Steve Hall
p.cm.

ISBN: 978-1-61339-276-8

LCCN: 2012950529

1. RELIGION/Devotional   2. RELIGION /Christian Life/Spiritual Growth
3. RELIGION / Christian Life / Devotional

First Edition

Printed in the United States of America

For further information contact AudioInk +14255266480 or email support@AudioInk.com

Contents

FOREWORD

By David Bryant

My son and daughter-in-law spent months recently deciding on a name for their first child – while the eager grandparents grew increasingly impatient! After all, names are important.

How would you identify yourself to someone without using your name? Once we get to know someone, their name takes on a whole new meaning based on who we find them to be. "Albert Einstein" would have no magical ring to it if it were not for his achievements; now, to hear his name is to simultaneously think "scientific genius". My other daughter-in-law is from India. Her name is "Sasmita" which means "one who laughs and makes others laugh." With her, the name describes who the person is before you meet her.

Names are important – not only to us but also to God. Thus, whatever names He chooses for Himself we need to understand and celebrate. This is even more crucial in terms of the names the Father has given to His Son – the one of whom He says "that in everything Christ may have the supremacy" (Colossians 1:18). How many names for the Son could the average Christian recite? – 5? 20? How about 365? Whatever the number, do we really understand the claims behind His names?

Thankfully, we are not left to fend for ourselves. The Spirit of God has raised up Steve Hall, a life-long trainer of Christian leaders in the Pacific Northwest. He is the force behind the resource you hold. **I Want To Know More of Christ** began as an on-line, daily devotional e-blast, sent throughout an entire year to over 300 leaders. Each day, Steve took one name for God's Son from the Bible, quoted the passage it appeared in, highlighted the main focus of that name (or attribute) and then developed a brief prayer to expand on the claim in that name. Doing so, Steve created 365 separate devotionals – now brought together under one cover.

Having ministered with Steve in the Northwest USA for over three decades – as we created a bi-coastal traveling team spending days at a time serving Christian leaders from all backgrounds – I can attest that Steve is a man of God who is constantly, joyfully consumed with the vastness of God's Son. To spend time with him is to spend time in the presence of Christ, and no less. I can't think of anyone who is better qualified – by study and by experience – to help all of us "know more of Christ".

The Claims of His Names

Hebrews 13 summons us: "Through Jesus, therefore, let us continually offer to God a sacrifice of praise – *the fruit of lips that confess His name*." Or, as expressed in another translation: "Therefore, let us offer through Jesus a continual sacrifice of praise to God, *proclaiming our allegiance to his name*." (New Living Translation)

Scripture overflows with names for Christ. As you'll discover in this daily devotional, all Old Testament names and descriptions for Yahweh are fulfilled in and can be applied to God-in-the-flesh, including: the Holy One, First and Last, Living One, King of Kings, Bridegroom, Creator, Redeemer, Lord of Heaven's Armies.

But the New Testament greatly *expands* His titles. In John 1, for example, Jesus is called "The Word" meaning, among other things, that He has become to us God's voice – God's language, God's truth, God's final message to the world.

The apostle Paul designates Christ as "the Righteousness of God" (Romans 1 and 1 Corinthians 1). Many claims are implied by this phrase: His whole life was lived in perfect *obedience* to the Father. Due to His inherent nature as God, He remained *consistently true* to the character of God throughout His life and ministry. He was *loyal* to the purposes of God, extending all the way to the cross. Therefore, Jesus has secured God's forgiveness and eternal blessings for all who are alive in Him. He has become *our* righteousness – we are clothed with Him – as we live before God's face. Because He is God's perfect righteousness "in bodily form," one day God will judge the world in righteousness through this one Man appointed the *Judge* of all things (Acts 17). What claim lies in this one name alone – "the Righteousness of God"!

The puritan theologian and revival leader in the 1700's, Jonathan Edwards, took the dual names for Christ in Revelation – Lion and Lamb – and reasoned about the claims like this: As a *lion*, Jesus is a devourer. He excels in strength; in appearance and voice He rises up with majesty. Everything is His "prey", to do with as He pleases. As a *Lamb*, however, this same Jesus excels in meekness and patience. He is yielded to the Father's will and to our good – becoming our sacrifice and (like wool) our covering before the Court of Heaven. John's vision of Jesus in the throne room means that in Christ both of the "excellencies" come together in perfect harmony.

For some time now, as it was in Edward's generation even so today, I've become increasingly convinced we stand at the threshold of another mighty, Spirit-driven revival. I foresee what I term a coming, widespread *Christ Awakening Movement* throughout the Church, as God's people are "re-converted" back to God's Son for ALL He is. In light of that impending hope, **I Want To Know More of Christ** could not be better timed! It can help prepare the way and feed the flames of a Christ Awakening, beginning in your own life – starting right now.

Names are important. As you journey with Steve Hall over the next 365 days, you will be amazed again and again how the *fame* of Jesus' *name* ratifies His *claim* to fully carry out His *reign*, which is all to Heaven's *gain*...and, therefore, ours as well.

David Bryant
Metro New York City
www.ProclaimHope.org

I WANT TO KNOW MORE OF CHRIST

Acknowledgements

I acknowledge the Holy Spirit as the primary Person who has helped me write this book on the matchless Lord Jesus Christ. He has given me a consuming passion for Christ and an intense burden to help other believers know more of Christ. He inspired all the Scripture in this book, and I pray that He will use the book for His purposes.

From my earliest memories, my parents always demonstrated an awe of Jesus and an abiding love for Him. God has also put a number of other godly mentors in my life who have shared with me the Scriptures that proclaim the power and majesty of Christ, and of the necessity to live in all He is. David Bryant of Proclaim Hope has been the chief among mentors, with his extraordinary understanding of the vastness of Christ and his devotion to make Christ known to all believers. My "SIPS" group of Pastors Steve Ulmer, Ingolf Kronstad and Phil Nelson have consistently demonstrated the nature of Christ to me.

My wife, Johnie, has been my greatest moment-by-moment supporter. She has given me the complete freedom to pursue my passion for Christ, as well as invaluable, constructive insights on every part of the book, including a very helpful third editing of the book. My two children, Joe and Elizabeth, have also understood how important it is to make the names of Christ available in this book, and have cheered me on. I really appreciate Elizabeth's help in the editing of some Scripture passages.

Two other very special people, Pastor Steve Ulmer and Loretta Bennison, have provided exceptional help with the book. Steve was a "rock" with His strong understanding of the Bible, drafting of the "Significance" lines and attention to grammar. Loretta was our expert in grammar and in writing effectively.

Richard and Sally Palmer deserve my profound gratitude for their constant love of me and of Jesus. As part of that love for Jesus, they encouraged me to write this book on His names, and they generously funded the costs to bring the book to production.

Finally, I thank the many friends and relatives over the past 30 years who have talked to me about Christ, worshiped Him with me, read Scripture about Him with me, and prayed with and for me. What a magnificent treasure we have shared together!

INTRODUCTION

Do you hunger to know more of the matchless wonders of the Lord Jesus Christ? Do you hunger to know Him much more intimately? I do, with all my heart. The Apostle Paul says in Philippians 3:10 (Amplified version), that knowing Christ is the most significant purpose of his life: *"For my determined purpose is that I may know him [Christ] - that I may progressively become more deeply and intimately acquainted with him, perceiving and recognizing and understanding the wonders of his person more strongly and more clearly."*

I am earnestly praying that this book will help all who use it to *"understand the wonders of [Christ's] person more strongly and more clearly,"* and to *"become more deeply and intimately acquainted with him."* As I have studied the Bible for many years to discover all I can about Christ, I have been thrilled at how His names and attributes permeate all of Scripture, and display all He is (His supremacy). This devotional book is a collection of 365 of those names and attributes, arranged from Genesis to Revelation. Please note that the names from the Old Testament are ultimately fulfilled in Christ, and the names from the New Testament directly reveal His unique nature, authority and mission.

I pray that these names of Christ will impact you daily with the enormity of what Paul declared in Colossians 3:11 that *"Christ is all, and is in all."* May this ongoing focus on Christ's names inspire you to worship Him more, love Him more, abandon your life wholly to Him, speak of His greatness to everyone you know, and pray for His rule in your life and in all people.

I pray also that as you engage with the names of Christ, you will experience the same amazement over Christ that the Jewish people of His day did when they heard Him teach as one who had authority, and saw Him heal the sick, cast out demons, quiet the waters and forgive sins. As you read the daily Scripture passages in this book, may your heart "burn" just as those of the two disciples did on the Road to Emmaus when He opened the Old Testament Scriptures about Himself to them.

Each daily devotional consists of a **Name or Attribute** of Christ, the **Scripture passage** the name appears in, a **"Significance"** line (a brief summary of what that name reveals about Christ), a **"Prayer"** (which often includes worship and thanksgiving for the aspect of Christ the name represents, submitting of ourselves to Him through that name, and praying for His lordship), and **Lines** for you to write what the Holy Spirit has just impressed upon you about the greatness of Christ.

You will note that some of the names are similar. In other words, one name is "The Spring of Living Water," and another "The Living Water." Or one is "Christ the Lord," and another "The Lord Jesus Christ." I have tried to discover as many combinations of His names and attributes as I could from the New International Version (NIV) Bible, to present the fullest possible understanding of Christ. Someone has called this, "painting a complete portrait of Christ." It has also been exciting to discover how the names and attributes of Christ powerfully relate to the context of the Scripture passages in which they are found.

Some suggestions from my personal use of this devotional, which I hope will be useful to you (whether you are doing this silently, out loud by yourself or with a group) are:

1. Begin by **praying** that the **Holy Spirit** will reveal all of Christ that He has for you today.
2. **Read or say the daily name/attribute** a couple times to firmly implant it in your mind.
3. **Read through the Scripture** passage once to receive a general understanding of it. Then, read it one or more additional times for the Spirit to freshly show you more of the fullness of Christ in that passage.
4. **Read the "Significance"** line. It is a brief summary of what that name reveals about the Lord Jesus Christ in that Scripture. It is not "all there is" about that specific aspect of Christ, but it provides a "seed" thought on which to build more knowledge of Him.
5. The **Prayers** are all directed to the Father (like Jesus prayed). They are meant to be a beginning point, to help you pray throughout the day around that day's focus on the name of Christ.

I especially love the worship and thanksgiving for each name, including parts of old hymns in several of the prayers. This might prompt you to worship Christ with other hymns or songs. The prayers often include submitting to Christ or praying for His lordship according to the name of the day. May you stay engaged in this worship and prayer of Christ throughout each day!

After the prayer, there are lines for you to write down anything that has especially impacted you about the wonders, abilities, character or authority of the Lord Jesus Christ today. I am praying that as the days and weeks go by, you will be overwhelmed with all He is!

I really hope you will share what you discover and experience about the spectacular and precious Christ with others. We must not keep Him to ourselves. I urge you to pray that the Spirit will give you at least one person each day to share the fresh hope you have in Christ based on His name/attribute of the day. May speaking about Jesus be our fondest delight!

I also invite you to visit the Facebook page, **"Knowing More of Christ,"** or the website – www.knowingmoreofchrist.com. These are meeting places for "all who are thirsty" for more of Christ to come to, at any time, to worship Christ, tell of his mighty deeds, express our love for Him, and unite in prayer. And, I would love to talk in person with any individuals or groups who are hungry to know more of Christ.

I pray that **"I Want to Know More of Christ: A Daily Devotional on His Matchless Names"** will be used by individuals, families, small groups, congregations and gatherings of believers in whole communities, to help you experience each day what Habakkuk prophesied: *"For the earth will be filled with the knowledge of the glory of the Lord as the waters cover the sea."*

CHRIST IS ALL,
Steve Hall
www.KnowingMoreOfChrist.com
stevehall_irm@msn.com

JANUARY

*Genesis 9:12-17 And God said, "This is the **sign of the covenant** I am making between me and you and every living creature with you, a covenant for all generations to come: I have set my rainbow in the clouds, and it will be the **sign of the covenant** between me and the earth. Whenever I bring clouds over the earth and the rainbow appears in the clouds, I will remember my covenant between me and you and all living creatures of every kind. Never again will the waters become a flood to destroy all life. Whenever the rainbow appears in the clouds, I will see it and remember the everlasting covenant between God and all living creatures of every kind on the earth." So God said to Noah, "This is the **sign of the covenant** I have established between me and all life on the earth."*

Significance: The **LORD JESUS CHRIST** guarantees the sure promise of God's covenant with mankind. He is pictured by the everlasting rainbow.

Dear Father,

I rejoice that Jesus ultimately fulfills Your **covenant** of grace and mercy, as the final and eternal **Sign of the Covenant** from You to all mankind. I am deeply grateful for the promise in Romans 3:22-24, *"This righteousness is given through faith in Jesus Christ to all who believe. There is no difference between Jew and Gentile, for all have sinned and fall short of the glory of God, and all are justified freely by his grace through the redemption that came by Christ Jesus."* I pray that I and all other believers will bow in worship and humility before the **Sign of the Covenant**, and give Him every part of our lives. Please help us to be hungry (even famished) to know the depths and riches of the **Sign of the Covenant**. I pray that You will convict us of all ways we have taken Him for granted or given ourselves to other attractions. I pray these things in His most precious name. Amen.

What impacted me about Christ today...

_____

_____

_____

_____

_____

*<u>Genesis 28:10-15</u> Jacob left Beersheba and set out for Haran. When he reached a certain place, he stopped for the night because the sun had set. Taking one of the stones there, he put it under his head and lay down to sleep. He had a dream in which he saw a **stairway** resting on the earth, with its top reaching to heaven, and the angels of God were ascending and descending on it. There above it stood the L*ORD*, and he said: "I am the L*ORD*, the God of your father Abraham and the God of Isaac. I will give you and your descendants the land on which you are lying. Your descendants will be like the dust of the earth, and you will be spread out to the west and to the east, to the north and to the south. All people on earth will be blessed through you and your offspring. I am with you and will watch over you wherever you go, and I will bring you back to this land. I will not leave you until I have done what I have promised you."*

Significance: The LORD JESUS CHRIST is the way for mankind to God in the heavenlies.

Dear Father,

It is exciting to know that Jesus fulfills the role as Your eternal **Stairway** (or ladder). I rejoice that He is the connection between You in heaven and all of mankind on earth. John 1:51 says: *"He [Jesus] then added, 'Very truly I tell you, you will see heaven open, and the angels of God ascending and descending on the Son of Man.'"* I pray You will keep my feet and hands securely on the Son of Man, the **Stairway**, so I will always be completely dependent upon Him and connected with You. All my hope is in Him. I pray You will reveal to all believers their urgent need to continually ascend the **Stairway,** and that millions of us will enjoy a lifetime of climbing on Him towards You. Please help masses of unbelievers soon be willing to take the first step up that ladder too. I ask these things in His name. Amen.

What impacted me about Christ today...

_____

_____

_____

_____

_____

*Exodus 9:1-3 Then the LORD said to Moses, "Go to Pharaoh and say to him, 'This is what the LORD, the **God of the Hebrews**, says: "Let my people go, so that they may worship me. If you refuse to let them go and continue to hold them back, the hand of the LORD will bring a terrible plague on your livestock in the field—on your horses, donkeys and camels and on your cattle, sheep and goats.'"*

Significance: **The LORD JESUS CHRIST is the ultimate judge of all individuals and nations who defy Him, and the defender of all His people.**

Dear Father,
I am very grateful that You punished Pharaoh and the people of Egypt for not letting the Hebrew people go from slavery to worship You. I honor Jesus that He is the fulfillment of the **God of the Hebrews**, as the Supporter, Ruler, Protector, Defender and Judge for all who receive Him as their Savior, regardless of whether we are Jews or Gentiles. I praise the Lord Jesus that before the beginning of time, He had all the power, wisdom, authority, strength and righteousness to say to the powers of darkness, *"Let my people go,"* so that many of us can freely worship Him, follow Him, love Him, serve Him, obey Him and speak about His greatness. I pray that in all the situations today where Christians are being persecuted for their faith, the **God of the Hebrews** will punish all the persecutors, and cause them to submit to His Lordship. I pray that as Satan seems to be increasing his relentless attacks on many righteous people, that the whole Body of Christ will trust the **God of the Hebrews** with all of our hearts, and pray without ceasing for His will to be done. I ask these things in the victorious name of Jesus. Amen.

What impacted me about Christ today...

_____

_____

_____

_____

_____

Exodus 15:25-26 Then Moses cried out to the LORD, and the LORD showed him a piece of wood. He threw it into the water, and the water became fit to drink. There [at Marah] the LORD issued a ruling and instruction for them and [put them to the test. He said, "If you listen carefully to the LORD your God and do what is right in his eyes, if you pay attention to his commands and keep all his decrees, I will not bring on you any of the diseases I brought on the Egyptians, for I am the **LORD, who heals you.***"*

Significance: The LORD JESUS CHRIST brings the ultimate healing and safeguard for His people.

Dear Father,

I bless You for sending Jesus to fulfill Your promise of the **Lord Who Heals You** for me and all others who receive Him as our Savior. I exalt Him for the demonstration of His power in Matthew 4:23, *"Jesus went throughout Galilee, teaching in their synagogues, proclaiming the good news of the kingdom, and **healing** every disease and sickness among the people."* I rejoice that those people who saw Him heal 2000 years ago were amazed with His authority, and that today He continues to be the same perfect **healer** of my sin, my physical ailments, and my every other need. All glory to the Lord Jesus Christ! I pray You will help me, my family members and all other believers today to do what is right in His eyes, pay attention to His commands and keep all His decrees. I pray You will prevent and heal many diseases in our lives that are plaguing the lost around us. I ask these things in the name of the **Lord Who Heals You.** Amen.

What impacted me about Christ today...

_____

_____

_____

_____

_____

_____

_____

*Exodus 34:12-15 Be careful not to make a treaty with those who live in the land where you are going, or they will be a snare among you. Break down their altars, smash their sacred stones and cut down their Asherah poles. Do not worship any other god, for the LORD, whose name is **Jealous**, is a jealous God. Be careful not to make a treaty with those who live in the land; for when they prostitute themselves to their gods and sacrifice to them, they will invite you and you will eat their sacrifices.*

Significance: The LORD JESUS CHRIST, as God's Son, has the right to protect what is His and to expect that all praise and devotion be reserved for Him alone.

Dear Father,

I exalt Jesus, the Lord of the universe, Whose name is **Jealous**. He alone is worthy of all honor, glory, praise and **jealousy** about Himself. I pray You will help me and all His other believers to put no other gods before Him (the first of the Ten Commandments in Exodus 20). Please break all treaties, altars and allegiances we have with other gods and unrighteous people, so we will only love, serve, obey and devote ourselves to Him. I pray we will be deeply **jealous** (intensely desirous) that He is honored by all people, and we will constantly speak about His greatness. I pray that You will also reveal to many non-Christians (especially those You have put in leadership positions), how harmful it is for them to value and serve other gods, and that they will turn to Jesus in repentance and reverence. I ask these things in His matchless and exalted name. Amen.

What impacted me about Christ today...

_____

_____

_____

_____

_____

_____

_____

*Leviticus 16:6-10, 20-22 Aaron is to offer the bull for his own sin offering to make atonement for himself and his household. Then he is to take the two goats and present them before the LORD at the entrance to the tent of meeting. He is to cast lots for the two goats—one lot for the LORD and the other for the **scapegoat**. Aaron shall bring the goat whose lot falls to the LORD and sacrifice it for a sin offering. But the goat chosen by lot as the **scapegoat** shall be presented alive before the LORD to be used for making atonement by sending it into the wilderness as a **scapegoat**. . . . When Aaron has finished making atonement for the Most Holy Place, the tent of meeting and the altar, he shall bring forward the live goat. He is to lay both hands on the head of the live goat and confess over it all the wickedness and rebellion of the Israelites—all their sins—and put them on the goat's head. He shall send the goat away into the wilderness in the care of someone appointed for the task. The goat will carry on itself all their sins to a remote place; and the man shall release it in the wilderness.*

Significance: **The LORD JESUS CHRIST, like the scapegoat, has borne all sins and carried them far away.**

Dear Father,

I am so grateful that You sent Jesus to earth 2000 years ago to be the **Scapegoat** for me and all people. Thank You that like the **scapegoat** carried the sins of Israel far into the wilderness once a year to remove them from the people, Jesus, Your perfect **Scapegoat**, takes our sin completely and forever upon Himself and away from us *"as far as the east is from the west, so far has he removed our transgressions from us"* (Psalm 103:12). I am very humbled by Isaiah 53:6, *"We all, like sheep, have gone astray, each of us has turned to our own way; and the LORD has laid on him the iniquity of us all."* I rejoice over John 1:29, *"The next day John saw Jesus coming toward him and said, 'Look, the Lamb of God, who takes away the sin of the world!'"* I pray that Christians today will awaken to the greatness of the **Scapegoat** and devote themselves completely to Him. May large numbers of people who are currently lost in sin receive Him as their **Scapegoat**. In His sacrificial name I pray. Amen.

What impacted me about Christ today...

*Numbers 24:15-19 Then he [Balaam] spoke his message: "The prophecy of Balaam son of Beor, the prophecy of one whose eye sees clearly, the prophecy of one who hears the words of God, who has from the Most High, who sees a vision from the Almighty, who falls prostrate, and whose eyes are opened: I see him, but not now; I behold him, but not near. A **star** will come out of Jacob; a scepter will rise out of Israel. He will crush the foreheads of Moab, the skulls of all the people of Sheth. Edom will be conquered; Seir, his enemy, will be conquered, but Israel will grow strong. A ruler will come out of Jacob and destroy the survivors of the city."*

Significance: The LORD JESUS CHRIST embodies the fullness of the brilliance, splendor and radiance found in the universe.

Dear Father,

I understand that great rulers and deliverers in early Oriental culture were called "**stars**," and I assume King David was likely the near-term ruler that Balaam was referring to as a **star** that would come out of Jacob (Israel) in this prophecy. But, I praise Jesus that He is now, and will forever be, the ultimate **Star**. Glory to Jesus that all the attributes of this **Star** are in Him alone: He possesses the brilliance, brightness and splendor of the Godhead; He shines through the darkness and outshines all other lights; He radiates Your holiness, knowledge, grace, truth, guidance, wonder, consistency, beauty and much more; He is uncontainable and undiminishable; He is ever-present; He is the deliverer for Israel and all people. I pray that many believers will very soon awaken to the magnificence of the **Star**, and be hungry to live in all His brightness. May many non-believers "see the light" and come to Him too. I pray these things in His name. Amen.

What impacted me about Christ today...

_____

_____

_____

_____

*Numbers 24:15-19 Then he [Balaam] spoke his message: "The prophecy of Balaam son of Beor, the prophecy of one whose eye sees clearly, the prophecy of one who hears the words of God, who has knowledge from the Most High, who sees a vision from the Almighty, who falls prostrate, and whose eyes are opened: I see him, but not now; I behold him, but not near. A star will come out of Jacob; a **scepter** will rise out of Israel. He will crush the foreheads of Moab, the skulls of all the people of Sheth. Edom will be conquered; Seir, his enemy, will be conquered, but Israel will grow strong. A ruler will come out of Jacob and destroy the survivors of the city."*

Significance: **The LORD JESUS CHRIST, ascended on high, has become the everlasting sign of God's rule and authority.**

Dear Father,

I exalt Jesus, the **Scepter**, Who rose out of Israel to rule Israel and the nations! I love to picture scepters being held by monarchs as the symbol of their authority. I bow before the great **Scepter**, Who exceeds all the power and authority of all Israel's kings (including King David), and all the kings of the earth. Thank You that Jesus, the **Scepter,** conquers His enemies, protects and provides for His people, gives guidance and righteousness to His subjects, and builds hope into those who put their faith in Him. I pray that we who are His people will seek to know the vastness of the **Scepter**, and will give Him all our devotion, adoration, gratitude, obedience, will and trust. I pray that multitudes of unsaved people all around us will desperately turn to Him as their mighty **Scepter** too. May the reign and fame of Jesus spread like wildfire! I ask these things in His glorious name. Amen.

What impacted me about Christ today...

_____

_____

_____

_____

*<u>Deuteronomy 32:15-18</u> Jeshurun grew fat and kicked; filled with food, they became heavy and sleek. They abandoned the **God who made them** and rejected the Rock their Savior. They made him jealous with their foreign gods and angered him with their detestable idols. They sacrificed to false gods, which are not God—gods they had not known, gods that recently appeared, gods your ancestors did not fear. You deserted the Rock who fathered you; you forgot the God who gave you birth.*

Significance: **The LORD JESUS CHRIST is the Son of the Father. He created all people—and all things—for Himself.**

Dear Father,
I am grieved by this account of the wickedness and self-indulgence of Jeshurun (the people of Israel), and their abandonment of the **God Who Made Them**. I am very mindful that Your beloved Son, Jesus, made the people of Israel and all other people, as the Bible says in John 1:3, *"Through him [Jesus, the Word] all things were made; without him nothing was made that has been made."* I can only imagine how grieved You must be that the people of Israel and great numbers of other people throughout history, including now, have abandoned Jesus. I repent for all the ways I have abandoned Him, and I pray You will cleanse me and cause me to embrace Him and devote every part of my life to Him. I pray that You will so powerfully awaken Christians everywhere to the greatness of the **God Who Made Them**, that repentance, cleansing and devotion to Him will revive us to the depths of our being. I pray these things in Jesus' name and for His glory. Amen.

What impacted me about Christ today...

_____

_____

_____

_____

_____

_____

_____

*Deuteronomy 32:15-18 Jeshurun grew fat and kicked; filled with food, they became heavy and sleek. They abandoned the God who made them and rejected the **Rock their Savior**. They made him jealous with their foreign gods and angered him with their detestable idols. They sacrificed to false gods, which are not God—gods they had not known, gods that recently appeared, gods your ancestors did not fear. You deserted the Rock who fathered you; you forgot the God who gave you birth.*

Significance: The **LORD JESUS CHRIST** personifies true and righteous strength and security.

Dear Father,

I grieve also that the people of Israel and so many other people throughout history, including now, have rejected Jesus, the ultimate **Rock Their Savior**. Thank You for sending Jesus to be the **Rock** upon Which we can build our lives, if we receive Him as **Savior**. I shout, "Hallelujah," that I can depend upon Jesus, the **Rock**, for all strength, security, wisdom, power, firmness, safety, truth, righteousness and infinitely more. I stand on Him, lean against Him, depend upon Him, am protected by Him, hold on to Him, and have absolute assurance that I am saved from the penalty of my sins through Him. I pray You will put an insatiable hunger in me and all other believers to know everything we possibly can about the **Rock Their Savior**, and that we will become consumed in the matchless Person of Jesus. May such a passion for Jesus overflow to all unsaved people we know that they will cry out to the **Rock Their Savior** for a relationship with Him too. I pray these things in Jesus' name. Amen.

What impacted me about Christ today...

*<u>Deuteronomy 33:26-28</u> There is no one like the God of Jeshurun, who rides across the heavens to help you and on the clouds in his majesty. The **eternal God** is your refuge, and underneath are the everlasting arms. He will drive out your enemies before you, saying, "Destroy them!" So Israel will live in safety; Jacob will dwell secure in a land of grain and new wine, where the heavens drop dew.*

Significance: **The LORD JESUS CHRIST provides us the perfect refuge because He has no limitations.**

Dear Father,

I am so grateful that Jesus, the **Eternal God**, has always been God with You, and that You sent Him to earth to reveal Your infinite power and love to me and all mankind. When I think about His being my constant refuge, and that in all circumstances of my life His everlasting arms are underneath me, I am filled with joy, hope, peace and faith, because I know that when I am weak He is strong, and that nothing is too difficult for Him. I rejoice in Matthew 28:20b where He says to His disciples (and me): *"And surely I am with you always, to the very end of the age."* Thank You for affirming that confidence through Paul's words in Philippians 4:19, *"And my God will meet all your needs according to the riches of his glory in Christ Jesus."* Please help me, my family members and all other believers to know the glorious riches in Christ Jesus, the **Eternal God**, as we place every part of our lives in His everlasting arms. In His name I pray these things. Amen.

What impacted me about Christ today...

_____

_____

_____

_____

_____

_____

_____

*Deuteronomy 33:29 Blessed are you, Israel! Who is like you, a people saved by the LORD? He is your shield and helper and your **glorious sword**. Your enemies will cower before you, and you will tread on their heights.*

Significance: The LORD JESUS CHRIST has become for us our greatest offensive weapon, bringing assurance of victory for His people.

Dear Father,

I am very grateful that the Lord Jesus is the **Glorious Sword** Who saves me and all His people today just as You saved the ancient people of Israel. I bow before the **Glorious Sword**, the victorious and eternal conqueror, provider, protector, leader, ruler, master and lord. I sing the hymn, "Onward Christian Soldiers," by Sabine Baring-Gould, to celebrate the dominion of the **Glorious Sword:** (verse 1)"Onward, Christian soldiers, marching as to war, With the cross of Jesus, Going on before. Christ, the royal Master, Leads against the foe; Forward into battle, See, His banners go!" (verse 2)"Like a mighty army, Moves the Church of God. Brothers, we are treading, Where the saints have trod. We are not divided; All one body we: One in hope and doctrine, One in charity." (verse 3)"Crowns and thrones may perish, Kingdoms rise and wane; But the Church of Jesus, Constant will remain. Gates of hell can never, 'Gainst that Church prevail; We have Christ's own promise, Which can never fail." (verse 4)"Onward, then, ye people! Join our happy throng; Blend with ours your voices, In the triumph song. Glory, laud, and honor, Unto Christ, the King; This thro' countless ages, Men and angels sing." (chorus)"Onward, Christian soldiers! Marching as to war, With the cross of Jesus, Going on before." May I and all other followers of the **Glorious Sword** submit ourselves wholly to His rule, and may all our enemies cower before Him. I pray these things in His name. Amen.

What impacted me about Christ today...

_____

_____

_____

The Commander Of The Army Of The Lord

*Joshua 5:13-15 Now when Joshua was near Jericho, he looked up and saw a man standing in front of him with a drawn sword in his hand. Joshua went up to him and asked, "Are you for us or for our enemies?" "Neither," he replied, "but as **commander of the army of the LORD** I have now come." Then Joshua fell facedown to the ground in reverence, and asked him, "What message does my Lord have for his servant?" The commander of the LORD's army replied, "Take off your sandals, for the place where you are standing is holy." And Joshua did so.*

Significance: The LORD JESUS CHRIST stands before His Church as the commander-in-chief of heaven's armies.

Dear Father,

As Joshua did, I fall facedown to the ground in reverence of Jesus, the supreme **Commander of the Army of the Lord**. I worship Him, and in honor and humility, I take off my shoes in His holy presence. I am in awe of Him, with His sword drawn for battle. I wholly submit to His **command** of the universe and of every area of my life, and I pray that every other believer will be convicted by Your Spirit do so too. I pray that the **Commander of the Army of the Lord** and His heavenly host will defend me, my family, and all His people against the relentless attacks and plans of the enemy of our souls. In fact, just as the **Commander of the Army of the Lord** caused the walls of Jericho to fall, I pray the enemy all around us will be crushed and defeated now. May Christ's kingdom come and His will be done, so that all lost people will fall on their faces before Him and cry out to Him for salvation. May all people revere the name of Jesus, in Whose name I pray these things. Amen.

What impacted me about Christ today...

_____

_____

_____

_____

_____

The Guardian (Kinsman)-Redeemer

*Ruth 4:13-17 So Boaz took Ruth and she became his wife. When he made love to her, the LORD enabled her to conceive, and she gave birth to a son. The women said to Naomi: "Praise be to the LORD, who this day has not left you without a **guardian** [kinsman]-**redeemer**. May he become famous throughout Israel! He will renew your life and sustain you in your old age. For your daughter-in-law, who loves you and is better to you than seven sons, has given him birth." Then Naomi took the child in her arms and cared for him. The women living there said, "Naomi has a son!" And they named him Obed. He was the father of Jesse, the father of David.*

Significance: The LORD JESUS CHRIST is the only Person in the universe willing and able to pay the price for mankind's redemption.

Dear Father,
I bless You for bringing together Boaz and Ruth to show the powerful value of a **Guardian** (Kinsman)-**Redeemer**, and to be a significant part of the earthly lineage of King David, and thus, Jesus. Thank You for deciding in the council of the Godhead before the beginning of time that mankind would need Him (one of our earthly **"kin"**) from the line of David, to know our earthly temptations and needs, and to give His perfect, sinless life to **redeem** us from our sins. I rejoice that Jesus, the Savior, the only qualified **Guardian-Redeemer**, completely loves us, paid the price for our redemption, takes us into His family, provides for us, protects us, and gives us eternal life. What a privilege to be joint-heirs with Him and abide in Him forever! All my hope is in Him. I pray these things in His redeeming name. Amen.

What impacted me about Christ today...

_____

_____

_____

_____

_____

_____

1 Samuel 15:26-29 But Samuel said to him [King Saul], "I will not go back with you. You have rejected the word of the LORD, and the LORD has rejected you as king over Israel!" As Samuel turned to leave, Saul caught hold of the hem of his robe, and it tore. Samuel said to him, "The LORD has torn the kingdom of Israel from you today and has given it to one of your neighbors—to one better than you. He who is the Glory of Israel does not lie or change his mind; for he is not a human being, that he should change his mind."

Significance: **The LORD JESUS CHRIST, as the Father's Son, has become the Glory of All God's people throughout all the ages.**

Dear Father,

I rejoice that Jesus is the **Glory of Israel**. I think of how He created Israel (and all people and lands) in **glory**. I think of Him sustaining all He created, coming to earth in Your fullness, revealing You to the people of Israel, teaching and performing miracles, dying for our sins, rising from the dead, ascending to heaven, ruling at Your right hand, returning one day as King of all kings, and much more—all in total **glory**. I love John's declaration of Christ's **glory** in John 1:14, *"The Word became flesh and made his dwelling among us. We have seen his glory, the glory of the One and Only, who came from the Father, full of grace and truth."* I pray that Habakkuk 2:14 will very soon come to pass: *"The earth will be filled with the knowledge of the glory of the LORD as the waters cover the sea."* I also pray that followers of Christ will continually acknowledge His greatness and give Him all **glory** and honor now. I pray especially that multitudes of Jewish people around the world will receive a revelation of Who the supreme Jesus is, and fully accept Him as their Messiah. I pray all these things in the name of the **Glory of Israel**. Amen.

What impacted me about Christ today...

_____

_____

_____

_____

_____

*2 Samuel 23:1-4 These are the last words of David: "The inspired utterance of David son of Jesse, the utterance of the man exalted by the Most High, the man anointed by the God of Jacob, the hero of Israel's songs: The Spirit of the LORD spoke through me; his word was on my tongue. The God of Israel spoke, the **Rock of Israel** said to me: When one rules over people in righteousness, when he rules in the fear of God, he is like the light of morning at sunrise on a cloudless morning, like the brightness after rain that brings the grass from the earth."*

S**ignificance: The LORD JESUS CHRIST prevails forever as the great Rock of Ages, the strong and secure foundation of all His people.**

Dear Father,

I rejoice that Jesus was the **Rock of Israel** in King David's time, and that He is the **Rock** of all people, now and for all eternity. I love David's song of praise in 2 Samuel 22, which includes: *"The Lord lives! Praise be to my Rock! Exalted be God, the Rock, my Savior!"* (verse 47). I praise the **Rock of Israel** through some of the verses of Bishop S.M. Lockridge's poem about Christ, "That's My King": "He's the king of glory; He's enduringly strong; He's eternally steadfast; He's imperially powerful; He's unparalleled and unprecedented; He supplies strength for the weak; He guards and He guides; He delivers the captives; His reign is righteous; He's invincible; Death couldn't handle Him; You can't live without Him." I pray that You will continually remind me and a growing number of other Christian leaders today of this immeasurable and incomparable greatness of the **Rock of Israel**. Please help us to hear and obey the directions He gave to David to rule over men in righteousness and in the fear of God. And please remove all hindrances in the hearts and minds of current Israeli leaders to receive Christ as their Rock. I pray all these things in His righteous name. Amen.

What impacted me about Christ today...

_____

_____

_____

_____

*1 Chronicles 29:10-13 David praised the LORD in the presence of the whole assembly, saying, "Praise be to you, LORD, the God of our father Israel, from everlasting to everlasting. Yours, LORD, is the greatness and the power and the glory and the majesty and the splendor, for everything in heaven and earth is yours. Yours, LORD, is the kingdom; you are exalted as head over all. Wealth and honor come from you; you are the **ruler of all things**. In your hands are strength and power to exalt and give strength to all. Now, our God, we give you thanks, and praise your glorious name."*

Significance: **The LORD JESUS CHRIST, by His rights as God's risen Son, takes authority over everything in the universe.**

Dear Father,

As I read this praise by King David, I am reminded of what Paul wrote in Ephesians 1:19b-21 about Christ as **Ruler of All Things**: *"That power is the same as the mighty strength he exerted when he raised Christ from the dead and seated him at his right hand in the heavenly realms, far above all **rule** and authority, power and dominion, and every name that is invoked, not only in the present age but also in the one to come."* I pray that Your Spirit will contir ually remind me, my family members, and the whole Church of today of the supreme authority, power and dominion of the **Ruler of All Things**. I pray we will revere Him, love Him, bow before Him, exalt Him, bless Him, adore Him, submit to His rule, serve Him and spread His fame wherever we go. Please convict us to repent of giving our allegiance to anything or anyone else above Christ. I pray also that You will put an urgent desire in the hearts and minds of many unsaved people to give their lives today to the **Ruler of All Things**. I pray these things in His majestic name. Amen.

What impacted me about Christ today...

_____

_____

_____

_____

_____

*Job 16:18-21 Earth, do not cover my blood; may my cry never be laid to rest! Even now my **witness** is in heaven; my advocate is on high. My intercessor is my friend as my eyes pour out tears to God; on behalf of a man he pleads with God as one pleads for a friend.*

Significance: The LORD JESUS CHRIST bears witness in Heaven on behalf of His people as our perfect advocate to the Father.

Dear Father,

I cannot adequately express my gratitude that, like Job, Jesus is my **Witness** in heaven, my Advocate on high. I rejoice that He is one with You and is a completely trustworthy and true **Witness**. I bless Him that His **witness** about me, and all of His followers, has the highest credibility and impact with You. I am glad He knows everything about us, loves us infinitely, and knows exactly what is best to plead on our behalf. What a Friend we have in Jesus! I pray Your Spirit will reveal to us more and more of the depths of Who the **Witness** is, and that we will place all our love, trust and hope in Him today, tomorrow and forever. I pray for Your will to be completely done regarding us, and that You will compel us to **witness** about the greatness of the **Witness** to everyone You bring into our lives. Please put an overwhelming longing in the hearts and minds of every person who has not yet received Jesus as their Savior and **Witness**, that they urgently need Him as their only hope too. I ask these things in the name and for the honor of Jesus. Amen.

What impacted me about Christ today...

_____

_____

_____

_____

_____

_____

_____

_____

_____

*Job 19:25-27 I know that my **redeemer** lives, and that in the end he will stand on the earth. And after my skin has been destroyed, yet in my flesh I will see God; I myself will see him with my own eyes—I, and not another. How my heart yearns within me!*

Significance: The LORD JESUS CHRIST, as the eternal liberator from all bondages, brings to fulfillment God's redemptive purposes.

Dear Father,

I praise Jesus that Job knew that the **Redeemer** (his **Redeemer**) would one day rise in resurrection life and stand on the earth. I rejoice that Job was certain, even in the midst of his darkest hour, that regardless of what happened to him in his earthly circumstances, he could ultimately trust the resurrected **Redeemer** to resurrect him into His presence. I know with total certainty that Jesus has already redeemed me and all others who have received Him as our Savior, and that one day we will be with Him too. Hallelujah! I pray we will trust the **Redeemer** with every part of our lives now, and that our hearts will always yearn within us to know and love Him more. I joyfully sing some of the hymn, "Redeemed," by Fanny Crosby: (verse 1) "Redeemed—how I love to proclaim it! Redeemed by the blood of the Lamb! Redeemed thro' His infinite mercy, His child, and forever I am. (chorus) Redeemed, redeemed, redeemed by the blood of the Lamb. Redeemed, redeemed, His child and forever I am. (verse 3) I think of my blessed Redeemer; I think of Him all the day long. I sing, for I cannot be silent; His love is the theme of my song." I give these things to You in Christ's precious name. Amen.

What impacted me about Christ today...

_____

_____

_____

_____

_____

*Psalm 4:1-3 Answer me when I call to you, my **righteous God**. Give me relief from my distress; have mercy on me and hear my prayer. How long will you people turn my glory into shame? How long will you love delusions and seek false gods? Know that the LORD has set apart his faithful servant for himself; the LORD hears when I call to him.*

Significance: The LORD JESUS CHRIST manifests the righteous character of the living God for all mankind to see.

Dear Father,

I rejoice that King David was ultimately addressing this conversation to Christ, his **Righteous God**, the God of his **righteousness**. I bless Christ that He is the author, witness, maintainer, judge and rewarder of all **righteousness**. Glory to Him, that all my **righteousness** is in Him, as Paul says in Romans 5:19, *"For just as through the disobedience of the one man the many were made sinners, so also through the obedience of the one man the many will be made **righteous**."* I am very grateful that living in the **Righteous God** includes relief from distress, receiving His tender mercy, and His inexhaustible purity, freedom, peace, truth, justice and goodness. I am filled with hope that He has set me, and all of His children, apart for Himself; and that when we call on Him He answers us. I pray that You will convict us to repent of all ways we have loved delusions and sought false gods. Please help us to become **righteous** as He, our great Lord and King, is **righteous**. I pray these things in His holy name. Amen.

What impacted me about Christ today...

_____

_____

_____

_____

_____

_____

_____

_____

The Refuge For The Oppressed

*Psalm 9:7-10 The LORD reigns forever; he has established his throne for judgment. He rules the world in righteousness and judges the people with equity. The LORD is a **refuge for the oppressed**, a stronghold in times of trouble. Those who know your name trust in you, for you, LORD, have never forsaken those who seek you.*

Significance: The LORD JESUS CHRIST provides the grandest sanctuary of all for everyone in need.

Dear Father,

I am immensely grateful that Jesus Christ the Lord reigns forever, and that all judgment, righteousness, justice and strength are in Him. I thank You that He is the defense and refuge of His people at all times, especially when we are in trouble. I worship Him that He alone has Your power and authority to stand against and overcome all oppression from man and Satan. Truly, Jesus is the **Refuge for the Oppressed**. I rejoice that, like the cities of refuge in ancient times, the **Refuge for the Oppressed** is our source of life, now and for all eternity. Christ is life. Christ is peace. Christ is hope. Christ is safety. Christ is rest. Christ is freedom. I pray that Your Spirit will help us to know Him more and trust Him more, for He has never forsaken us. These truths vividly remind me of the wonderful old hymn by Civilla Martin, "His Eye Is On The Sparrow": (verse 1) "Why should I be discouraged, Why should the shadows come, Why should my heart be lonely, And long for heaven and home, When Jesus is my portion? My constant friend is He: His eye is on the sparrow, and I know He watches me; His eye is on the sparrow, and I know He watches me. (chorus) I sing because I'm happy, I sing because I'm free, For His eye is on the sparrow, And I know He watches me." All glory to the **Refuge for the Oppressed**. I bring these things to You in Christ's strong and faithful name. Amen.

What impacted me about Christ today...

_____

_____

_____

_____

_____

*Psalm 10:12-18 Arise, L*ORD*! Lift up your hand, O God. Do not forget the helpless. Why does the wicked man revile God? Why does he say to himself, "He won't call me to account?" But you, God, see the trouble of the afflicted; you consider their grief and take it in hand. The victims commit themselves to you; you are the **helper of the fatherless**. Break the arm of the wicked man; call the evildoer to account for his wickedness that would not otherwise be found out. The L*ORD* is King for ever and ever; the nations will perish from his land. You, L*ORD*, hear the desire of the afflicted; you encourage them, and you listen to their cry, defending the fatherless and the oppressed, so that mere earthly mortals will never again strike terror.*

Significance: The LORD JESUS CHRIST lives and reigns today, ready to help all the oppressed, especially the fatherless.

Dear Father,

I am deeply grateful that Jesus is the great **Helper** (Father) **of the Fatherless** (helpless). I exalt Him that He has ALL Your power to help the helpless, ALL knowledge to know what the helpless need, ALL mercy to comfort and care for us; and He hears ALL our cries. I love what the prophet Hosea says in chapter 14 verse 3, *"Assyria cannot save us; we will not mount warhorses. We will never again say 'Our gods' to what our own hands have made, for in you **the fatherless find compassion**."* Thank You that Christ is filled with Your unfathomable love and goodness towards the fatherless, and, in His perfect time, He also calls wicked and evil people to account for oppressing the helpless. I give myself wholly to the **Helper of the Fatherless**, resting in His arms as a little child. I pray that the whole Church will become completely dependent upon Him, and may all the **fatherless** everywhere find their way to Him. I pray these things in His protective name. Amen.

What impacted me about Christ today...

_____

_____

_____

_____

_____

Psalm 18:1-6 I love you, LORD, my **strength**. *The LORD is my rock, my fortress and my deliverer; my God is my rock, in whom I take refuge, my shield and the horn of my salvation, my stronghold. I called to the LORD, who is worthy of praise, and I have been saved from my enemies. The cords of death entangled me; the torrents of destruction overwhelmed me. The cords of the grave coiled around me; the snares of death confronted me. In my distress I called to the LORD; I cried to my God for help. From his temple he heard my voice; my cry came before him, into his ears.*

Significance: The LORD JESUS CHRIST embodies all the might and power of the Godhead available for His people.

Dear Father,

I really love the Lord Jesus Christ, my **Strength**! I praise Him that all the **strength** (might, force, power, resolve and endurance) of the Godhead dwells in Him. I worship Him that He has always been all the **strength** of the entire cosmos, that He is all the **strength** of all things today, and that for all eternity He will be all the **strength** of everything! I am very grateful that I and all His followers can live in the total certainty of Philippians 4:13, *"I can do all this through him who gives me* **strength**.*"* Please help us to grow much more in our knowledge of and trust in Jesus, our **Strength**, and be willing to stop depending so much upon our own strength. I pray we will regularly tell one another and many other people You bring into our lives about the One Who is all **Strength**. I pray these things in His powerful name, and for His glory. Amen.

What impacted me about Christ today...

_____

_____

_____

_____

_____

_____

_____

*Psalm 18:1-3 I love you, LORD, my strength. The LORD is my rock, my **fortress,** and my deliverer; my God is my rock, in whom I take refuge, my shield and the horn of my salvation, my stronghold. I called to the LORD, who is worthy of praise, and I have been saved from my enemies.*

Significance: The LORD JESUS CHRIST, by the full extent of His saving work, provides complete protection of all Who trust in Him.

Dear Father,
I am so glad the Lord Jesus is my **Fortress**! I think of all that a **fortress** represents—a stronghold, a fortified town, a source of refuge, a high place, and many more settings that provide me and all others who reside there with complete and eternal safety, security, protection, deliverance and rest. I rejoice that our bodies, minds and souls are under His all-powerful lordship, and that we can put our trust in Him at all times. I exalt Jesus that He combines all there is of strength, rock, fortress, deliverer, refuge, shield, horn of my salvation, and stronghold. I agree with King David in calling out to the **Fortress** to save me, my family, the whole Church, and all people. I join with Martin Luther in singing some of "A Mighty Fortress Is Our God": (verse 1) A mighty **fortress** is our God, A bulwark never failing: Our helper He, amid the flood, Of mortal ills prevailing. For still our ancient foe, Doth seek to work us woe; His craft and power are great, And, armed with cruel hate, On earth is not his equal. (verse 2) Did we in our own strength confide, Our striving would be losing, Were not the right Man on our side, the Man of God's own choosing. Dost ask who that may be? Christ Jesus, it is He; Lord Sabaoth His Name, From age to age the same, And He must win the battle." Jesus, the mighty **Fortress**, is worthy of praise! In His name I pray these things. Amen.

What impacted me about Christ today...

_____

_____

_____

_____

_____

Psalm 18:16-19, 29 *He reached down from on high and took hold of me; he drew me out of deep waters. He rescued me from my powerful enemy, from my foes, who were too strong for me. They confronted me in the day of my disaster, but the LORD was my **support**. He brought me out into a spacious place; he rescued me because he delighted in me. . . . With your help I can advance against a troop; with my God I can scale a wall.*

Significance: The LORD JESUS CHRIST fulfills God's promise to be the willing-and-able champion of His people.

Dear Father,

I am forever grateful that the Lord Jesus came down from on high to take hold of me, physically and spiritually. Truly, He drew me out of deep water and rescued me from my powerful enemy. I praise Him that He is the only One Who can and will be my all-encompassing **Support**, today and forever. I marvel that the Lord Jesus has the power and the authority to sustain, provide for, assist, preserve, strengthen, comfort, defend, advocate for, and redeem all who put our faith in Him. I love the picture of His **support** in Psalm 94:18, *"When I said, 'My foot is slipping,' your unfailing love, LORD, **supported** me."* Please help me to become totally dependent upon Jesus, my **Support**. I pray that Your Spirit will remind believers everywhere of all Who Christ is, and that in the desperate times in which we live, we must trust our **Support** to rescue us and all the rest of the world. I pray all these things in the name of our supreme Rescuer. Amen.

What impacted me about Christ today...

_____

_____

_____

_____

_____

_____

_____

_____

*Psalm 18:46-50 The LORD lives! Praise be to my Rock! Exalted be **God my Savior**! He is the God who avenges me, who subdues nations under me, who saves me from my enemies. You exalted me above my foes; from a violent man you rescued me. Therefore I will praise you, LORD, among the nations; I will sing the praises of your name. He gives his king great victories; he shows unfailing love to his anointed, to David and to his descendants forever.*

Significance: **The LORD JESUS CHRIST, as our Savior God, delivers people into abundant life in Him.**

Dear Father,

I rejoice with all my heart that the Lord Jesus Christ lives, and is the solid Rock for all eternity! I highly exalt Christ that He has always been **God,** and that He has all the power, authority and grace to rescue all who believe in Him from the penalty of their sins. Blessed be **God my Savior**! Blessed be the **God** of **my Salvation**! Hallelujah! All hope is in Him; all freedom is in Him; all righteousness is in Him; all love is in Him; all peace is in Him; and all victory is in Him! I pray that all of us who have received Him as our **Savior** will be so grateful and devoted to Him that we will praise Him continually, hunger to know all we possibly can about Him, invite Him to rule and reign over every part of our lives, and joyfully speak of His wonders whenever we are together. This reminds me of the first stanza of "Joyful, Joyful We Adore Thee," by Henry van Dyke: "Joyful, joyful, we adore Thee, God of glory, Lord of love. Hearts unfold like flow'rs before Thee, Op'ning to the sun above. Melt the clouds of sin and sadness; Drive the dark of doubt away. Giver of immortal gladness, Fill us with the light of day!" May Your Spirit very soon cause multitudes of unsaved people to become desperate to know **God my Savior** too. I pray these things in His blessed name. Amen.

What impacted me about Christ today...

_____

_____

_____

_____

*Psalm 18:46-50 The LORD lives! Praise be to my Rock! Exalted be God my Savior! He is the **God who avenges me**, who subdues nations under me, who saves me from my enemies. You exalted me above my foes; from a violent man you rescued me. Therefore I will praise you, LORD, among the nations; I will sing the praises of your name. He gives his king great victories; he shows unfailing love to his anointed, to David and to his descendants forever.*

Significance: **The LORD JESUS CHRIST, just as Jehovah promised, ensures justice for His people forever.**

Dear Father,

This Scripture reminds me of what the prophet says in Nahum 1:2-3 about the anger of the Lord: *"The LORD is a jealous and avenging God; the LORD takes vengeance and is filled with wrath. The LORD takes vengeance on his foes and vents his wrath against his enemies. The LORD is slow to anger but great in power; the LORD will not leave the guilty unpunished. His way is in the whirlwind and the storm, and clouds are the dust of his feet."* I continue to rejoice that the Lord Jesus Christ ultimately fulfills all the attributes and purposes of the Godhead, including being the **God Who Avenges Me**. I am very grateful that the enemies of His people are His enemies too. I thank Him that He saves and rescues me and all of David's descendants from our enemies forever. He is completely wise, good, just and kind to us! I pray that You will constantly remind us to praise Him among the nations for all He is, and for all He does for us. I pray that whenever our enemies are trying to subdue us, the **God Who Avenges Me** will do whatever is necessary to avenge us and eventually transform them. At the same time, I pray Your Spirit will cleanse our hearts of all sin that is hindering that avenging and transforming process. In the righteous name of Jesus I plead these things. Amen.

What impacted me about Christ today...

_____

_____

_____

_____

_____

Psalm 22:2-8 My God, I cry out by day, but you do not answer, by night, but I find no rest. Yet you are enthroned as the Holy One; you are the one Israel praises. In you our ancestors put their trust; they trusted and you delivered them. To you they cried out and were saved; in you they trusted and were not put to shame. But I am a worm and not a man, scorned by everyone, **despised by the people.** *All who see me mock me; they hurl insults, shaking their heads. "He trusts in the* LORD," *they say, "let the LORD rescue him. Let him deliver him, since he delights in him."*

S ignificance: The LORD JESUS CHRIST, like the Psalmist pre-dicted, became an object of contempt when He suffered for our salvation.

Dear Father,

My heart is broken that the Lord of the universe (my beloved Lord Jesus Christ) could be considered a worm and not a man, and be scorned by men and **Despised by the People**. What a contrast it is that the One Who is the great "I AM" could be compared to a helpless, passive worm that is without strength, protection or relative value to us. Truly, this is a heart-wrenching, but accurate, portrayal of Christ when His body and soul suffered so tragically during His trial and crucifixion. Oh, how totally the Savior emptied Himself of all glory, and was willing to become of no reputation for our sakes! The gratitude I am able to express to Jesus for His willingness to become **Despised by the People** will never be adequate; but, with all my heart I thank Him, love Him and honor Him. I pray You will continually remind me and all others who have received Him as our Savior, of every part of His life that caused Him to be **Despised by the People**. Please help us to love Him so much, and be devoted to Him so much, that we would also be willing to be **despised** by others for His glory. I pray these things in the precious name of Jesus. Amen.

What impacted me about Christ today...

_____

_____

_____

_____

*Psalm 23:1-6 The LORD is my **shepherd**, I lack nothing. He makes me lie down in green pastures, he leads me beside quiet waters, he refreshes my soul. He guides me along the right paths for his name's sake. Even though I walk through the darkest valley, I will fear no evil, for you are with me; your rod and your staff, they comfort me. You prepare a table before me in the presence of my enemies. You anoint my head with oil; my cup overflows. Surely your goodness and love will follow me all the days of my life, and I will dwell in the house of the LORD forever.*

Significance: The LORD JESUS CHRIST was sent to the world to become the lead pastor and caregiver of the congregation of His saints.

Dear Father,

Today's name of Christ, the **Shepherd**, is one of His most amazing and reassuring names! I bless the **Shepherd** that He is the great Pastor, as well as the Redeemer and Preserver of men. I am deeply grateful that He completely guides, guards, provides for and lays down His life for me and all people who receive and follow Him. I rejoice that we can unquestionably say with King David, *"The Lord is **MY Shepherd**,"* and know with all certainty that because of His absolute authority and His absolute love for us, *"I [we shall] lack nothing."* I marvel at the full magnitude of the **Shepherd's** provision for us: *"He makes me lie down in green pastures, he leads me beside quiet waters, he refreshes my soul. He guides me along the right* [righteous] *paths for his name's sake. Even though I walk through the darkest valley [of the shadow of death], I will fear no evil, for you are with me; your rod and your staff, they comfort me. You prepare a table before me in the presence of my enemies. You anoint my head with oil; my cup overflows. Surely your goodness and love will follow me all the days of my life, and I will dwell in the house of the LORD forever."* I pray that I and all His sheep will follow our **Shepherd** wherever He leads. I ask these things in His beloved name. Amen.

What impacted me about Christ today...

_____

_____

_____

*Psalm 24:7-10 Lift up your heads, you gates; be lifted up, you ancient doors, that the **King of glory** may come in. Who is this **King of glory?** The LORD strong and mighty, the LORD mighty in battle. Lift up your heads, you gates; lift them up, you ancient doors, that the **King of glory** may come in. Who is he, this **King of glory?** The LORD Almighty—he is **the King of glory**.*

Significance: The LORD JESUS CHRIST fulfills the vision of Psalm 24, entering into our lives as the most resplendent ruler of all.

Dear Father,

I join all heaven in honoring the most **glorious King** at His triumphant entrance through the ancient gates into the eternal city. What a wonderful progression I see in Your holy Word: Psalm 22 is "The Psalm of the Cross" and Psalm 23 is "The Psalm of the Shepherd"; then, in Psalm 24, "The Song of the Ascension," the crucified Savior, our Shepherd, is the ascended Head and Crown of the universe, and the matchless **King of Glory**! I rejoice that such **glory** means that this mediator **King** is the weightiest of all kings, the most worthy of **glory**, the **King of** ALL **glory**! I marvel that the **King of Glory** is proclaimed five times in just the closing stanza of Psalm 24. Hallelujah! The Lord Jesus Christ is the **King of Glory**, the **King of Glory**, the **King of Glory**, the **King of Glory**, the **King of Glory**! I pray He will very soon fulfill His kingship in His Church, and over His Church, and over all things on behalf of His Church. I ask these things in His majestic name and for His **glory**. Amen.

What impacted me about Christ today...

_____

_____

_____

_____

_____

_____

_____

The Lord Strong And Mighty, The Lord Mighty In Battle

Psalm 24:7-10 Lift up your heads, you gates; be lifted up, you ancient doors, that the King of glory may come in. Who is this King of glory? The LORD strong and mighty, the LORD mighty in battle. Lift up your heads, you gates; lift them up, you ancient doors, that the King of glory may come in. Who is he, this King of glory? The LORD Almighty—he is the King of glory."

Significance: The LORD JESUS CHRIST has become for us the omnipotent victor Who fights and wins all of our battles.

Dear Father,

I am thrilled that the **Lord** Jesus Christ is the answer to the question: *"Who is this King of glory?"* He is resoundingly the eternal **Lord** (Owner and Master) of all heaven and earth! I am humbled that He is the self-existent and supreme Almighty God and Lord Jehovah. I exalt Him that ALL the strength, authority, power and might of the Godhead dwells in Him! I join again with the heavenly host in worshiping Him as the **Lord Strong and Mighty, the Lord Mighty in Battle**, Who is over all powers, death and sin. I am reminded of the third stanza of Chester Allen's "Praise Him! Praise Him," which says: "Praise Him! praise Him! Jesus, our blessed Redeemer! Heav'nly portals loud with hosannas ring! Jesus, Savior, reigneth forever and ever. Crown Him! crown Him! Prophet, and Priest, and King. Christ is coming! Over the world victorious; Pow'r and glory unto the Lord belong." I pray that You will reveal more and more of Christ's lordship (including His strength and might in battle) to me and many, many other believers, so that we will be in captivated awe of His greatness. Please remove the obstacles in the hearts and minds of the vast number of unsaved people around us, which have kept them from realizing their desperate need to give their lives to the **Lord Strong and Mighty, the Lord Mighty in Battle**. In His victorious name I plead these things. Amen.

What impacted me about Christ today...

FEBRUARY

Psalm 25:6-11 Remember, LORD, your great mercy and love, for they are from of old. Do not remember the sins of my youth and my rebellious ways; according to your love remember me, for you, LORD, are good. **Good and upright** *is the LORD; therefore he instructs sinners in his ways. He guides the humble in what is right and teaches them his way. All the ways of the LORD are loving and faithful toward those who keep the demands of his covenant. For the sake of your name, LORD, forgive my iniquity, though it is great.*

Significance: The LORD JESUS CHRIST is righteous, and He lovingly leads sinners and all who are humble in His righteousness.

Dear Father,

I am wholeheartedly grateful that You and Jesus are totally **good**! I delight in what King David says about You in Psalm 34:8, *"Taste and see that the LORD is* **good***; blessed is the one who takes refuge in him."* I am also strengthened by the Apostle Peter's statement in 1 Peter 2:2 that Christ is **good** and that His followers should "grow up" in His **goodness**: *"Like newborn babies, crave pure spiritual milk, so that by it you may grow up in your salvation, now that you have tasted that the Lord is* **good***."* I rejoice that Scripture and all of creation testify to the **goodness** of the Lord Jesus Christ! I am in awe that, at the same time the Lord is all-**good**, He is also all-**upright** (righteous, honest and just)! I praise Christ that He ultimately fulfills verses 12-15 in King David's wonderful Psalm 92, *"The righteous will flourish like a palm tree, they will grow like a cedar of Lebanon; planted in the house of the LORD, they will flourish in the courts of our God. They will still bear fruit in old age, they will stay fresh and green, proclaiming, 'The LORD is* **upright***; he is my Rock, and there is no wickedness in him.'"* I pray that You will help me and my family members to know all we possibly can of the incomparable **Good and Upright** One, and humbly live in all His righteous ways. Please forgive all of our iniquity, and answer these prayers in Jesus' name. Amen.

What impacted me about Christ today...

_____

_____

_____

The Stronghold Of My Life

*Psalm 27:1-3 The LORD is my light and my salvation—whom shall I fear? The LORD is the **stronghold of my life**—of whom shall I be afraid? When the wicked advance against me to devour me, it is my enemies and my foes who will stumble and fall. Though an army besiege me, my heart will not fear; though war break out against me, even then will I be confident.*

Significance: The LORD JESUS CHRIST has become the eternal, impregnable fortress in which all believers find refuge.

Dear Father,

I am very grateful for the endless security, hope and comfort I have since the Lord Jesus Christ is the impregnable **Stronghold** (the Strength) **of My Life**! I exalt the **Stronghold of My Life** that He is MY Light and MY Salvation, so I do not have to fear anyone! Hallelujah! He **holds** every part of my life **strongly**, now and forever, against all forces of darkness! I give Him all glory that, according to Colossians 2:15, *"And having disarmed the powers and authorities, he made a public spectacle of them, triumphing over them by the cross."* I worship His supreme strength and power, and His unwavering faithfulness to His people. I pray You will give us an ardent desire to know the **Stronghold of My Life** more, so we will put all of our hope in Him, be absolutely confident in Him, abandon ourselves to Him, speak more about His pre-eminence with one another, and intercede day and night for all the lost people around us to receive Him as their **Stronghold** too. Please cause the relentless evil men of our day to stumble and fall as they come against the **Stronghold**. I pray all these things in the strong name of Jesus. Amen.

What impacted me about Christ today...

_____

_____

_____

_____

_____

_____

Psalm 31:1-8 In you, LORD, I have taken refuge; let me never be put to shame; deliver me in your righteousness. Turn your ear to me, come quickly to my rescue; be my rock of refuge, a strong fortress to save me. Since you are my rock and my fortress, for the sake of your name lead and guide me. Keep me free from the trap that is set for me, for you are my refuge. Into your hands I commit my spirit; deliver me, LORD, my faithful God. I hate those who cling to worthless idols; as for me I trust in the LORD. I will be glad and rejoice in your love, for you saw my affliction and knew the anguish of my soul. You have not given me into the hands of the enemy but have set my feet in a spacious place.

Significance: The LORD JESUS CHRIST reigns over us in a totally faithful and dependable way.

Dear Father,

I praise Jesus that He abundantly fulfills the wonderful name, **Lord, My Faithful God**. I honor Him that He is THE **Lord**, the divine master, administrator, leader and ruler of all creation, because He was and is and always will be Almighty **God**! I love to state a bedrock truth of Christianity that, "Jesus Christ is **Lord**." And, I rejoice that today's name of Christ combines His infinite **lordship** with His infinite **faithfulness**. I exalt Him that He is all-sufficient and all-dependable in revealing all You are, in paying the price for the sins of mankind (delivering people through His righteousness), and in all the ways described in today's Scripture passage: turning His ear to His people, coming quickly to our rescue, being our rock of refuge, leading and guiding us, and so much more! I pray that You will reveal the vast riches of the **Lord, My Faithful God** to me and to the rest of His people, so that we will commit our bodies, minds and spirits completely into His hands. I celebrate Christ's **faithfulness** by singing the first verse of "Praise To The Lord," by Joachim Neander: "Praise to the Lord, the Almighty, the King of creation! O my soul, praise Him, for He is thy health and salvation! All ye who hear, now to His temple draw near; Praise Him in glad adoration." I pray these things in the **faithful** name of the **Lord** Jesus. Amen.

What impacted me about Christ today...

_____

_____

*Psalm 32:6-7 Therefore let all the faithful pray to you while you may be found; surely the rising of the mighty waters will not reach them. You are my **hiding place**; you will protect me from trouble and surround me with songs of deliverance.*

Significance: The LORD JESUS CHRIST offers Himself as the place of complete peace and security for all who belong to Him.

Dear Father,

I am exceedingly grateful that I can always depend upon my Savior to be my **Hiding Place**. I praise Him that He has all the power and love to be the perfect **Hiding Place** for me and all others who are saved through His blood. I am so glad for Psalm 27:4-5, which describes the protection He is as we dwell in Him: *"One thing I ask from the LORD, this only do I seek: that I may dwell in the house of the LORD all the days of my life, to gaze on the beauty of the LORD and to seek him in his temple. For in the day of trouble he will keep me safe in his dwelling; he will **hide** me in the shelter of his sacred tent and set me high upon a rock."* I rejoice greatly in what Paul declares to us in Colossians 3:3, *"For you died, and your life is now **hidden** with Christ in God."* I delight that part of "He Hideth My Soul," by Fanny Crosby, further echoes these assurances about Christ's power and love: (verse 1) "A wonderful Savior is Jesus my Lord, A wonderful Savior to me; He hideth my soul in the cleft of the rock, Where rivers of pleasure I see." (chorus) "He hideth my soul in the cleft of the rock, That shadows a dry, thirsty land; He hideth my life with the depths of His love; And covers me there with His hand." Please help us to forsake even the best of man's "hiding places," to devote ourselves to living under the full protection of the **Hiding Place**. In His victorious name I ask these things. Amen.

What impacted me about Christ today...

_____

_____

_____

_____

_____

*Psalm 34:17-18 The righteous cry out, and the LORD hears them; he delivers them from all their troubles. The LORD is **close to the broken-hearted** and saves those who are crushed in spirit.*

Significance: **The LORD JESUS CHRIST, by His Spirit, dwells with His children, especially those who are brokenhearted.**

Dear Father,

I am deeply grateful that the Spirit of Christ dwells in me and in each of Your children. What precious closeness we have with Him. I am comforted and strengthened that He never leaves us; He always has complete love and compassion for us; He knows all our needs and fears; and He is absolutely able to handle whatever is breaking us. I am also very grateful that Christ is always interceding to You for us. I rejoice in the certainty we have that He is **Close to the Brokenhearted** through His continual presence with us and His tender heart toward us when we are broken and humble. I love King David's testimony in Psalm 51:17 which strongly portrays the closeness and compassion that Christ has for His followers today: *"My sacrifice, O God, is a **broken** spirit; a **broken** and contrite heart you, God, will not despise."* I pray You will immerse us in all Jesus is, so we will depend upon more and more of His all-embracing **closeness**. May we be filled with hope as we worship Him, abide in Him, love Him, trust Him, and have broken and contrite spirits toward Him. Please draw many unsaved people around us **close** to the One Who is **Close to the Broken-hearted**. I pray all these things in Christ's blessed, saving name. Amen.

What impacted me about Christ today...

_____

_____

_____

_____

_____

_____

_____

*Psalm 36:5-9 Your love, LORD, reaches to the heavens, your faithfulness to the skies. Your righteousness is like the highest mountains, your justice like the great deep. You, LORD, preserve both people and animals. How priceless is your unfailing love, O God! People take refuge in the shadow of your wings. They feast on the abundance of your house; you give them drink from your river of delights. For with you is the **fountain of life**; in your light we see light.*

Significance: **The LORD JESUS CHRIST pours out His Spirit upon His people, becoming for us the source and wellspring of life.**

Dear Father,

I love how a **fountain** enables life-giving water to flow through it. I exalt Christ because I and all His followers have the certain assurance that He is the divine **Fountain of Life**, the **Fountain** of our **lives**! I praise Him that according to John 1:4, He was with You in the beginning and that: *"In him was **life**, and that **life** was the light of mankind."* Glory to Him that He is the self-sufficient, ever-flowing, perfect source of all physical, intellectual, emotional and spiritual **life**, and that He holds together and governs all the **life** He has created. As I look at the parts of today's Scripture passage, I am exceedingly grateful that Christ is the **Fountain** of Your love, faithfulness, righteousness, justice, preservation, refuge, abundance, delight, light and immeasurably more! I pray You will help me, my family members and the whole Church to have an unquenchable thirst for the **Fountain of Life**, so that every part of our lives flows from Him. I also pray that as we share about the **Fountain of Life** with our unsaved friends and relatives, they will become so thirsty for Him that they will eagerly receive Him as their Savior too. I ask these things in Jesus' name. Amen.

What impacted me about Christ today...

_____

_____

_____

_____

_____

_____

My Help And My Deliverer

*Psalm 40:13-17 Be pleased to save me, LORD; come quickly, LORD, to help me. May all who want to take my life be put to shame and confusion; may all who desire my ruin be turned back in disgrace. May those who say to me, "Aha! Aha!" be appalled at their own shame. But may all who seek you rejoice and be glad in you; may those who long for your saving help always say, "The LORD is great!" But as for me, I am poor and needy; may the Lord think of me. You are my **help and** my **deliverer**; you are my God, do not delay.*

Significance: **The LORD JESUS CHRIST triumphs as God's ulti-mate redeemer and emancipator of His people.**

Dear Father,

When I read this powerful testimony of King David's dependency upon You, my passion to be wholly dependent upon Jesus greatly increases. As David says to You, *"May those who long for your saving help always say, 'The LORD is great,'"* I say that I deeply love the complete physical and spiritual salvation I have in Jesus, and I exalt His greatness with all my heart! I also confess that I am poor and needy, and I am very grateful that Jesus thinks of me unceasingly! I rejoice that He is the divine, eternal and complete **Help and Deliverer** for me and all who receive Him as our Savior and Lord. I am confident that Jesus has all the strength and author-ity, and at the same time, all the love and compassion, to **help** and **deliver** us at all times and in all circumstances, just as He has delivered us from the kingdom of darkness into His glorious light. I pray that You will help us to know Jesus and trust Him more and more each day, and that You will remind us to always beseech Him, "**Help** me and **deliver** me, Jesus." I pray these things in His saving name. Amen.

What impacted me about Christ today...

_____

_____

_____

_____

_____

*Psalm 42:1-5 As the deer pants for streams of water, so my soul pants for you, my God. My soul thirsts for God, for the **living God**. When can I go and meet with God? My tears have been my food day and night, while people say to me all day long, "Where is your God?" These things I remember as I pour out my soul: how I used to go to the house of God under the protection of the Mighty One with shouts of joy and praise among the festive throng. Why, my soul, are you downcast? Why so disturbed within me? Put your hope in God, for I will yet praise him, my Savior and my God.*

Significance: The LORD JESUS CHRIST supplies rivers of life to all who thirst for Him and drink of Him.

Dear Father,

I am very humbled by the deep love King David expresses for You in today's Scripture passage, and by David's all-consuming passion to be with and communicate with You. With all my heart, I want to have that same thirsting within my soul for Your beloved Son, the **Living God**. I worship and honor Him, Who has been **God with You, and all Life with You,** for all eternity past, <u>AND</u>, Who created all **life** at the beginning of time, and is sustaining all **life**—now and for all eternity future! Further-more, I worship and honor the **Living God** for coming to earth to give His physical life, so that He could be raised back to eternal **life**, and provide the way for all who receive Him to have eternal **life** in Him. Hallelujah! Jesus is the **God of Life**! And, as David said, all of our hope is in Him. O Father, I pray that David's insatiable cry, *"When can I go and meet with [the **Living**] God?"* will burn in the hearts of the Body of Christ today. I pray these things in His living name. Amen.

What impacted me about Christ today...

_____

_____

_____

_____

_____

_____

*Psalm 42:8-11 By day the LORD directs his love, at night his song is with me—a prayer to the **God of my life**. I say to God my Rock, "Why have you forgotten me? Why must I go about mourning, oppressed by the enemy?" My bones suffer mortal agony, as my foes taunt me, saying to me all day long, "Where is your God?" Why, my soul, are you downcast? Why so disturbed within me? Put your hope in God, for I will yet praise him, my Savior and my God.*

Significance: **The LORD JESUS CHRIST is the King, Savior and Lord of our entire existence.**

❧

Dear Father,

I am so glad for Your constant reminders of the priceless truth that Jesus is the **God of my Life**. I praise His holy name that He is not just a God of part of my life, but THE one and only **God** of every part **of my life**, now and forever! I marvel that Jesus always has been and always will be the God of **ALL life**: He is the foundation and source of all **life**, the protector and keeper of all **life**, the beauty and hope of all **life**, the sustenance and refreshment of all **life**, the Lord and ruler of all **life**, the Redeemer of all eternal **life,** and far more than I can imagine. JESUS IS LIFE! I exalt Him that He is the **God** of His Church, and, thus, the **God of my Life**, as the Apostle Paul says in Ephesians 1:22-23, *"And God placed all things under his [Jesus'] feet and appointed him to be head over everything for the church, which is his body, the fullness of him who fills everything in every way."* I pray You will help me, my family members and the whole Church to know the **God of my Life** so thoroughly and intimately that we will put our full hope in Him and praise Him, regardless of the circumstances we are facing. I pray these things in the name of Jesus, our Savior and our **God**. Amen.

What impacted me about Christ today...

_____

_____

_____

_____

_____

*Psalm 45:1-2 My heart is stirred by a noble theme as I recite my verses for the king; my tongue is the pen of a skillful writer. You are the **most excellent of men** and your lips have been anointed with grace, since God has blessed you forever.*

Significance: The LORD JESUS CHRIST fulfills God's desire to be a Husband for His Bride.

Dear Father,

My heart too is thoroughly *"stirred"* as I read this portion of the Psalm 45 "wedding song" to King Jesus from His bride. I love to join in this unreserved admiration of the **Most Excellent of Men** (which another translation calls "fairer than the children of men"). I experience abounding hope and joy in thinking about the unrivaled and perfect beauty, fairness and **excellence** of EVERY aspect of Jesus! I delight that the Person of Jesus is **so lovely** that the most splendid words of man are exhausted before He is adequately described. All praise to Him that He is most lovely (and **most excellent**) in union with His beloved bride, the Church. I also rejoice that You blessed Jesus forever by anointing His lips (and all of Him) with the fullness of Your grace. Oh, thank You, precious Father, that I and all people who receive the **Most Excellent of Men** as our Savior are blessed beyond our wildest imaginations through His grace-filled teachings, promises, invitations, prayers, exhortations, commands, deeds, prophecies and all of His life in us. I pray that You will "stir our hearts" with wholehearted affection for, and devotion to, the **Most Excellent of Men**. In His beautiful name I ask these things. Amen.

What impacted me about Christ today...

_____

_____

_____

_____

_____

_____

_____

An Ever-Present Help In Trouble

*Psalm 46:1-3 God is our refuge and strength, an **ever-present help in trouble**. Therefore we will not fear, though the earth give way and the mountains fall into the heart of the sea, though its waters roar and foam and the mountains quake with their surging.*

Significance: **The LORD JESUS CHRIST presides over His people to provide us with our ultimate rescue.**

Dear Father,

I praise the Lord Jesus Christ, our **Ever-Present Help in Trouble**. I exalt Him that He has always had all power, all knowledge, all wisdom, all love, all mercy, all faithfulness and all compassion. In my mind's eye, I see Him speaking the heavens and the earth into existence; I see Him holding the world in His hands now and forevermore; I see Him enduring the testing of Satan in the wilderness, commanding wind and waves to be calm, and calling Lazarus from the tomb; I see Him revealing the ancient mysteries about the Godhead and sacrificing His life on the cross; I see Him coming out of the grave, ascending to sit at Your right hand and judge the earth; and, I see Him returning to earth to establish His eternal kingdom. Hallelujah! All things are possible for Him! Even though *"the earth may one day give way and the mountains fall into the heart of the sea,"* because of all Jesus is, I am confident that He knows what I need before I ask for help, and that He will continually be present as my refuge and strength, regardless of the circumstances. I pray You will help me and many, many other believers give ourselves totally to our **Ever-Present Help in Trouble**, trust Him more and more, and cast all our fears on Him. I place all these things before You in the name of our Savior. Amen.

What impacted me about Christ today...

_____

_____

_____

_____

_____

_____

The Lord Most High, The Great King Over All The Earth

*Psalm 47:1-6 Clap your hands, all you nations; shout to God with cries of joy. For the LORD Most High is awesome, **the great King over all the earth**. He subdued nations under us, peoples under our feet. He chose our inheritance for us, the pride of Jacob, whom he loved. God has ascended amid shouts of joy, the LORD amid the sounding of trumpets. Sing praises to God, sing praises; sing praises to our King, sing praises.*

Significance: The LORD JESUS CHRIST manifests in Himself and His saving work that God holds the highest rank in the universe.

Dear Father,

I join with people from all the nations in clapping my hands and shouting with cries of joy about how awesome the ascended Jesus, the **Lord Most High**, the **Great King Over all the Earth**, is! I exalt Him that He alone is most great in power, most high in lordship, most esteemed in wisdom, most exalted in glory, and most magnificent in all His other capabilities and authority. I praise Him that He is triumphant over all the kingdoms of the earth and the enemy of our souls; His dominion and sovereignty are absolute and forever; His justice is righteous and final; and His majesty surpasses the excellence of the whole universe. I pray that I and multitudes of other believers across the world will become immersed in the supremacy of the **Lord Most High**, the **Great King Over all the Earth**, and ceaselessly praise Him, submit all of ourselves to His lordship, speak of His greatness to everyone we know, and pray with great urgency that unsaved people everywhere will receive Him as their Savior, Lord and King too. May we truly become one Church under Him. I pray these things in the name and for the glory of Jesus. Amen.

What impacted me about Christ today...

_____

_____

_____

_____

_____

_____

*Psalm 48:10-14 Like your name, O God, your praise reaches to the ends of the earth; your right hand is filled with righteousness. Mount Zion rejoices, the villages of Judah are glad because of your judgments. Walk about Zion, go around her, count her towers, consider well her ramparts, view her citadels, that you may tell of them to the next generation. For this God is our **God for ever and ever**; he will be our guide even to the end.*

Significance: **The LORD JESUS CHRIST reveals how God will be supreme for His people at all times.**

Dear Father,

I am immensely grateful for today's reminder of the countless reasons that I and all other believers have to praise You and Jesus for all You are and all You do! I worship Jesus that He is magnificent in all ways! I pray that we followers will unite in praise of Him that reaches to the ends of the earth. I exalt Him that He is not our God for a moment, or until we experience earthly physical death, but that He is our all-loving, all-mighty, all-beautiful, all-holy, all-secure and all-glorious **God For Ever and Ever**! I pray that You will convict us to repent of the times we become so self-focused or world-focused that we forget Christ's never-changing, eternal supremacy. And, just as the inhabitants of Zion intentionally learned more about their city, I pray that multitudes of Christians today will earnestly devote ourselves to learning more about Jesus, so that we will completely trust Him and regularly tell of His greatness to the next generation. I rest in the certain hope we have in our **God For Ever and Ever**, and pray these things in His blessed name. Amen.

What impacted me about Christ today...

_____

_____

_____

_____

_____

_____

_____

Psalm 48:10-14 *Like your name, O God, your praise reaches to the ends of the earth; your right hand is filled with righteousness. Mount Zion rejoices, the villages of Judah are glad because of your judgments. Walk about Zion, go around her, count her towers, consider well her ramparts, view her citadels, that you may tell of them to the next generation. For this God is our God for ever and ever; he will be our **guide even to the end**.*

Significance: **The LORD JESUS CHRIST is appointed by God to go before His people into all of eternity.**

Dear Father,

It is a great joy to continue praising Christ, now focusing on Him as our **Guide Even to the End**. Thank You for the blessed assurance of knowing that He is the perfect Person to **guide** me (lead me, control the course of my life, supervise and instruct me, direct my steps, and advise and influence me) and all other people who receive Him as their Savior and Lord. How privileged we are to be under the infallible **guidance** of the One Who is fully God and fully man! I honor Him that He knows everything; He is all powerful; He has experienced all I will ever experience (and more); He loves me completely; He paid the price for my eternal life; He prays for me continually; and I will be with Him forever. I praise Him that, not only is He the **Guide** of His people until death, but He **guides** us **THROUGH** death to resurrection as the Apostle Paul says in 1 Corinthians 15:54b, *"Death has been swallowed up in victory."* I pray that You will help us become completely devoted to following the **Guide Even to the End**, just as He said in John 5:19 that He followed You: *"Very truly I tell you, the Son can do nothing by himself; he can only do what he sees his Father doing, because whatever the Father does the Son also does."* I pray these things in His wise name. Amen.

What impacted me about Christ today...

_____

_____

_____

_____

The Rock That Is Higher Than I

*Psalm 61:1-5 Hear my cry, O God; listen to my prayer. From the ends of the earth I call to you, I call as my heart grows faint; lead me to the **rock that is higher than I**. For you have been my refuge, a strong tower against the foe. I long to dwell in your tent forever and take refuge in the shelter of your wings. For you, God, have heard my vows; you have given me the heritage of those who fear your name.*

Significance: The LORD JESUS CHRIST, as God's preeminent refuge for His people, is so much more than adequate.

Dear Father,

I am greatly strengthened and secure because **anytime**, **anywhere**, in **any condition** I can call to Jesus, the **Rock That is Higher Than I**, and He is listening. I am so grateful that He is always higher and stronger and wiser than me or anyone or anything that threatens to overcome me. He cleansed me of ALL my sin and hopelessness. He is all-powerful, all-knowing, all-present and eternal. I confess that sometimes I have not been willing or able to cry out to Him in times of need, so I pray that Your Spirit will always lead me to the **Rock That is Higher Than I**, and help me climb upon Him and cling to Him. Please help me, my family members and an increasing number of His other followers to know more and more about the Solid Rock, so we will become completely dependent upon Him. And, I pray that You will lead millions of unbelievers—who really have nothing for their faint hearts—to Jesus. I ask these things in His "more-than-able" name. Amen.

What impacted me about Christ today...

_____

_____

_____

_____

_____

_____

_____

A Strong Tower Against The Foe

*Psalm 61:1-5 Hear my cry, O God; listen to my prayer. From the ends of the earth I call to you, I call as my heart grows faint; lead me to the rock that is higher than I. For you have been my refuge, a **strong tower against the foe**. I long to dwell in your tent forever and take refuge in the shelter of your wings. For you, God, have heard my vows; you have given me the heritage of those who fear your name.*

Significance: The LORD JESUS CHRIST is God's promised impregnable stronghold for all who dwell in Him.

Dear Father,

I praise Jesus that He has all the strength, power and might, as well as all the love, of the Godhead. I rejoice that Jesus has consistently been the refuge of all people who come to Him for shelter and protection. He is the supreme life-giver and life-sustainer. I exalt the omnipotent Jesus that He consistently demonstrates that He alone is the **Strong Tower Against the Foe**. I think of His immeasurable strength to separate the sky, land and seas; His strength to raise up mountains and carve out great valleys; His strength to keep the sun, moon and all the stars in their perfect orbits; His strength to push back the waters of the Red Sea; His strength to command heaven's armies to permanently defeat Satan and his forces; and countless other ways He rules His creation by His strength. I marvel at how Jesus surrounds His people as a **tower** surrounds its inhabitants. I praise Him that we are encircled by Him with all comfort, safety, peace and security against the enemy. I praise Jesus that He can see all advancements from our foes, just as a person who stands high in a **tower** has an excellent view of what is happening around him. I pray that You will continually remind me and all believers to dwell in the **Strong Tower Against the Foe**, and to invite everyone else we know to join us. I pray these things in Jesus' **strong** name. Amen.

What impacted me about Christ today...

_____

_____

_____

_____

_____

Thunders With Mighty Voice

*Psalm 68:32-35 Sing to God, you kingdoms of the earth, sing praise to the Lord, to him who rides across the highest heavens, the ancient heavens, who **thunders with mighty voice**. Proclaim the power of God, whose majesty is over Israel, whose power is in the heavens. You, God, are awesome in your sanctuary; the God of Israel gives power and strength to his people. Praise be to God!*

Significance: The LORD JESUS CHRIST upholds the whole universe by His powerful word, and speaks with authority to His people.

Dear Father,
I join with multitudes of believers throughout the earth in singing praises to the Lord Jesus Christ, Who triumphantly rides the ancient skies, and Who **Thunders With Mighty Voice**. His **mighty voice thundered**, creating the universe out of nothing; His **mighty voice thundered**, bringing judgment and eternal destruction or eternal life for men and nations; His **mighty voice thundered**, raising the dead, causing wind and waves to obey Him, forcing demons to come out of people, healing bodies and minds, and forgiving sin while He was living on earth. His **mighty voice thundered**: *"proclaiming good news to the poor, binding up the brokenhearted, proclaiming freedom for the captives, releasing from darkness the prisoners, and comforting all who mourn"* (Isaiah 61:1-2). Hallelujah! His **mighty voice** will **thunder** once again when He returns to earth to establish His eternal kingdom. All glory to Jesus, Whose **mighty voice thunders** as the Lord of all! What a mighty voice! I pray that I and all who have received Him as our Savior will revere and submit to the power of the **Mighty Voice**, and I pray that scores of unsaved people will soon hear the irresistible **Voice** and be radically saved. All these things I pray in Jesus' **thundering** name. Amen.

What impacted me about Christ today...

_____

_____

_____

*Psalm 71:3-8 Be my rock of refuge, to which I can always go; give the command to save me, for you are my rock and my fortress. Deliver me, my God, from the hand of the wicked, from the grasp of those who are evil and cruel. For you have been my **hope**, Sovereign Lord, my confidence since my youth. From birth I have relied on you; you brought me forth from my mother's womb. I will ever praise you. I have become a sign to many; you are my strong refuge. My mouth is filled with your praise, declaring your splendor all day long.*

Significance: **The LORD JESUS CHRIST, by dying, rising and ascending on high guarantees everything God has promised for His people.**

Dear Father,

This passage points me to Paul's opening declaration in 1 Timothy 1:1, *"Paul, an apostle of Christ Jesus, by the command of God our Savior and of Christ Jesus our **Hope**."* Yes, Jesus Himself is THE enduring **Hope** of the world. I praise Him that ALL **hope** for His followers is in Him! I pray that I and all other believers in our region and beyond will be convinced of this incomparable truth, that Paul also states in Colossians 1:27, *"To them God has chosen to make known among the Gentiles the glorious riches of this mystery, which is Christ in you, the **hope** of glory."* Please urge us moment by moment to be messengers of all that our glorious **Hope** is to one another, and to every lost person You bring into our lives. Help us to *"hold unswervingly to the **hope** we profess"* (Hebrews 10:23). May our *"mouths be filled with praise of him, declaring his splendor all day long."* I pray these things in Jesus' **hope-filled** name. Amen.

What impacted me about Christ today...

_____

_____

_____

_____

_____

_____

The Royal Son

*Psalm 72:1-7 Endow the king with your justice, O God, the **royal son** with your righteousness. May he judge your people in righteousness, your afflicted ones with justice. May the mountains bring prosperity to the people, the hills the fruit of righteousness. May he defend the afflicted among the people and save the children of the needy; may he crush the oppressor. May he endure as long as the sun, as long as the moon, through all generations. May he be like rain falling on a mown field, like showers watering the earth. In his days may the righteous flourish and prosperity abound till the moon is no more.*

Significance: The LORD JESUS CHRIST, God's divine Son, by becoming one of us has become the King of all.

Dear Father,

I rejoice that Christ is the true **Royal Son**. I love to think about how He is Your one and only divine **Son**, and the final earthly **son** (descendant and heir) in the line of King David and all the other Biblical patriarchs under Your eternal covenant with Abraham. I humbly praise Jesus, the **royal Son** of God and **Son** of Man. I exalt Christ that He is endowed with all the powers and attributes of You, His **Royal** Father, and that all things are possible with Him. I praise Him that His kingdom has no limits, and no end. All glory to Jesus that He will reign through all generations with perfect justice, righteousness, prosperity, defense of the afflicted, salvation of the needy, crushing of all oppressors, and endurance. I rejoice that His government and His rule bears much fruit. I pray that You will rise up within me and the whole Church, a burning passion to know the vastness of the **Royal Son**, and to subject ourselves to Him without limit. In that spirit, I commit to a pledge to King Jesus that is similar to the U.S. Pledge of Allegiance: "I pledge my highest allegiance to the **Royal Son**, and to the kingdom which He rules, one Church under Him, with liberty and justice for all." In His righteous name I pray these things. Amen.

What impacted me about Christ today...

Rain Falling On A Mown Field

*<u>Psalm 72:1-7</u> Endow the king with your justice, O God, the royal son with your righteousness. May he judge your people in righteousness, your afflicted ones with justice. May the mountains bring prosperity to the people, the hills the fruit of righteousness. May he defend the afflicted among the people and save the children of the needy; may he crush the oppressor. May he endure as long as the sun, as long as the moon, through all generations. May he be like **rain falling on a mown field**, like showers watering the earth. In his days may the righteous flourish and prosperity abound till the moon is no more.*

Significance: The LORD JESUS CHRIST blesses His people with Himself, in the same way that rain refreshes the fields.

Dear Father,
I am very grateful that King Jesus, Your royal Son, is the **Rain Falling on a Mown Field**. Truly, He does for His people all of the things this Scripture passage says, including showering us with nourishment when we are like a field that has just been cut and is desperately needing to be refreshed and restored. Thank You that Christ has all Your love, healing, strength, grace, tenderness, forgiveness, encouragement, and much, much more to **"rain"** on us, in fulfillment of what You say through the prophet Ezekiel in chapter 34, verses 26a-27, *"I will send down showers in season; there will be showers of blessing. The trees will yield their fruit, and the ground will yield its crops; the people will be secure in their land. They will know that I am the Lord, when I break the bars of their yoke and rescue them from the hands of those who enslaved them."* Hallelujah! Jesus is our ALL. I pray that I, my family members and all Christ's followers will grow in our esteem and trust of Him, and in total dependency upon Him. May we flourish and abound in Him, and joyfully speak of His greatness to every person You bring into our lives. I pray these things in the life-giving, hope-fulfilling name of Jesus. Amen.

What impacted me about Christ today...

_____

_____

_____

_____

My King From Long Ago

*Psalm 74:12-17 But God is my **King from long ago**; he brings salvation on the earth. It was you who split open the sea by your power; you broke the heads of the monster in the waters. It was you who crushed the heads of Leviathan and gave it as food to the creatures of the desert. It was you who opened up springs and streams; you dried up the ever-flowing rivers. The day is yours, and yours also the night; you established the sun and moon. It was you who set all the boundaries of the earth; you made both summer and winter.*

Significance: **The LORD JESUS CHRIST has ruled His creation magnificently from the beginning of creation.**

Dear Father,

I praise the Lord Jesus Christ that He is the majestic, glorious and mighty **King From Long Ago**. I exalt Him that out of His limitless, eternal power and authority, He has performed all the ancient works and ruled the heavens and the earth. I bow before the Sovereign **King From Long Ago**, Who is able to deliver me and all His people today and forever. He is our great **King**; He is our Defender; He is our Lord; He is our Savior and Deliverer. Thank You that He will never forsake us! I pray You will immerse us in the knowledge and awe of our **King From Long Ago**, and give us an increasing trust in His amazing faithfulness and grace. I pray that He will release His overcoming power now to save us from all attacks, schemes, plans and temptations of the enemy of our bodies, minds and souls. And, I pray that we will be so captivated by our **King** that we will speak of His greatness to everyone around us, so that they will intensely desire to receive Him as their **King From Long Ago** too!! I pray these things in the name of the immortal **King**. Amen.

What impacted me about Christ today..

_____

_____

_____

_____

_____

_____

The God Who Performs Miracles

*Psalm 77:12-15 I will consider all your works and meditate on all your mighty deeds. Your ways, God, are holy. What god is as great as our God? You are the **God who performs miracles**; you display your power among the peoples. With your mighty arm you redeemed your people, the descendants of Jacob and Joseph.*

Significance: **The LORD JESUS CHRIST displays His love and power through His mighty works for us, in us and through us.**

Dear Father,

I praise Jesus, the supreme **God Who Performs Miracles**. I exalt Him that all the greatness of the Godhead dwells in Him, that He continually displays His power among the people, and that with His mighty arm He redeems people everywhere. I repent for the lack of faith I sometimes have in Him, and I pray that You will help me to know Him so well that my faith in His matchless power and authority will become increasingly strong and sure. Please convince me and many other believers to tell one another, and as many lost people around us as possible, of Jesus' mighty works. Compel us to pray for exceeding abundantly more displays of His power in people, places and situations, here and throughout the world. I pray that soon millions more men, women and children will be amazed with the **God Who Performs Miracles**. May their wonderment of Him be as powerful as when Jesus walked the earth more than 2000 years ago. May they fervently cry out to Him for salvation. I ask these things in the name of the **miracle**-working Jesus. Amen.

What impacted me about Christ today...

_____

_____

_____

_____

_____

_____

_____

_____

Your (God's) Anointed One

*Psalm 84:5-9 Blessed are those whose strength is in you, whose hearts are set on pilgrimage. As they pass through the Valley of Baka, they make it a place of springs; the autumn rains also cover it with pools. They go from strength to strength, till each appears before God in Zion. Hear my prayer, LORD God Almighty; listen to me, God of Jacob. Look upon our shield, O God; look with favor on **your anointed one**.*

Significance: **The LORD JESUS CHRIST is God's chosen vessel to bring about the fulfillment of all His purposes and promises.**

Dear Father,

I dearly love all of Psalm 84, which the great theologian Charles Spurgeon calls "The Pearl of Psalms." I rejoice that what makes this Psalm the "Pearl" is that it focuses so strongly on Your beloved Son, Jesus, upon Whom You look with utmost favor. My heart and mind soar as I meditate on the limitless attributes and abilities of Your Son, the infinite love You and He have for each other, and the plans You are fulfilling in heaven and on earth through Him as **Your Anointed One**. I am eternally grateful that I and all other believers are saved through His sacrifice and obedience to You. He is our blessed Savior, our Lord, our Shield, and our All. I pray that You will give us an increasing passion to know and adore **Your Anointed One**, and please help us to live under His lordship at all times. May our knees bow and our tongues confess that **Your Anointed One** is Lord, to Your glory. I pray that all You **anointed** Him to do on earth, will soon be done as it is in heaven. In His holy name I ask these things. Amen.

What impacted me about Christ today...

_____

_____   _____

_____

_____

_____

_____

_____

<u>*Psalm 89:14-18*</u> *Righteousness and justice are the foundation of your throne; love and faithfulness go before you. Blessed are those who have learned to acclaim you, who walk in the light of your presence, LORD. They rejoice in your name all day long; they celebrate your righteousness. For you are their glory and strength, and by your favor you exalt our horn. Indeed, our shield belongs to the LORD, our king to the* **Holy One of Israel***.*

Significance: **The LORD JESUS CHRIST, like Jehovah was to Israel, is the Holy One Who reigns in the midst of His Church.**

Dear Father,

I exalt the all-**holy** Father, Son and Spirit. I rejoice that the Lord Jesus Christ created the universe out of His perfect **holiness**, and He lives and rules in pure **holiness**, now and forevermore. I praise Him that His **holiness** undergirds His abounding righteousness, justice, love, faithfulness, and all His other glorious attributes. I exalt Jesus that He spent His earthly life demonstrating Your **holiness** to His chosen people of Israel, then He rose from Israel to offer the fullness of His **holiness** to me and the whole world. Hallelujah! Jesus is the **Holy One of Israel**. I earnestly pray that You will reveal much more of the **Holy One of Israel** to me and to all other believers in all nations, so that we will constantly live in His **holiness** and praise His **holy** name all day long. I pray that multitudes of unsaved people all around us will be touched to the core of their spirits with longing for the **Holy One**, and will very soon receive Him as their **holy** Savior and Lord. And, may vast numbers of people in Israel today receive their **holy** Messiah and King too. I pray all these things in His sacred name. Amen.

What impacted me about Christ today...

_____

_____

_____

_____

_____

_____

Our Dwelling Place

*Psalm 90:1-2 Lord, you have been our **dwelling place** throughout all generations. Before the mountains were born or you brought forth the whole world, from everlasting to everlasting you are God.*

Significance: The LORD JESUS CHRIST invites us to abide in Him as the ultimate residence of His people.

Dear Father,

I have great joy and security that throughout all generations You have been the **Dwelling Place** of Your people. I love to be reminded often of the conclusion of King David's prayer in Psalm 23: *"And I will **dwell** in the house of the LORD forever."* I am exceedingly grateful that Jesus fulfills all Your promises in the Bible, including being the **Dwelling Place** for all who receive Him as our Savior. I am especially strengthened and comforted by His promise in John 15:4, *"Remain in me, as I also remain in you."* I desire more than anything else to always remain (live, abide or **dwell**) in Jesus, the Vine. As I think of the magnitude of all Christ is, and what it means to *"live and move and have our being in him"* (Acts 17:28), I am engulfed in hope, peace, love and utter contentment! I pray You will put the firm conviction in me and all other believers that Peter expressed in John 6:68, *"Lord, to whom shall we go? You have the words of eternal life. We have come to believe and know that you are the Holy One of God."* May we live so completely in the **Dwelling Place** that many men, women and children we know will fervently ask "what must we do?" to join us. I pray these things in the abiding name of Jesus. Amen.

What impacted me about Christ today...

_____

_____

_____

_____

_____

_____

_____

*Psalm 90:1-4 Lord, you have been our dwelling place throughout all generations. Before the mountains were born or you brought forth the whole world, from **everlasting to everlasting** you are God. You turn people back to dust saying, "Return to dust, you mortals." A thousand years in your sight are like a day that has just gone by, or like a watch in the night.*

Significance: **The LORD JESUS CHRIST, as God's Son, is the Lord of time, but exists beyond the bounds of time.**

Dear Father,

My security and hope are strengthened even greater through this powerful declaration that the Godhead existed before all creation! I worship Jesus, that as part of that Godhead, He is fully God, and therefore He is **Everlasting to Everlasting**. I exalt Jesus that as well as existing before time, He is beyond all constraints of time. All glory to the immortal Jesus! I exalt Him that He brought forth the earth and all the rest of the universe out of the vast pre-creation expanse, and that He continues to rule and reign over His creation forever. I pray that I and all others who are meditating about Him as the **Everlasting to Everlasting** will be in such profound awe of Him that we will bow before Him, and place every part of our lives and the world around us into His everlasting and almighty hands. **Nothing is too difficult for Jesus**! I pray that You will fuel a widespread grassroots awakening of the whole Church to the fullness of Your Son, the **Everlasting to Everlasting**. Thank You that those of us who have put our trust in Jesus have the complete assurance of dwelling with Him forever! In His most excellent name I pray these things. Amen.

What impacted me about Christ today...

_____

_____

_____

_____

_____

_____

The Rock In Whom I Take Refuge

*Psalm 94:20-23 Can a corrupt throne be allied with you—a throne that brings on misery by its decrees? The wicked band together against the righteous and condemn the innocent to death. But the LORD has become my fortress, and my God the **rock in whom I take refuge**. He will repay them for their sins and destroy them for their wickedness; the LORD our God will destroy them.*

Significance: The LORD JESUS CHRIST is the protection and safety for His people.

Dear Father,

I am extremely glad that I and all others who receive Jesus as our Savior have full assurance that He is the **Rock in Whom I Take Refuge**. I praise Him, the omnipotent Lord of the universe, that He is our unmovable protector, defender and provider. I am very grateful that His immeasurable strength and power are combined with His unconditional grace, compassion and love. I rejoice that no matter how the world around us is in turmoil, we can put ourselves wholly in His care. I pray too that He will repay those who are determined to bring misery to us. I ask that Your Holy Spirit will reveal much more of the greatness of the **Rock in Whom I Take Refuge** to believers, and that we will urgently tell many lost people all we know about Him. As I think about the wicked coming against the innocent, my heart especially breaks for the innocent children that desperately need to have **refuge** in Jesus from wicked influences. I pray that You will draw millions upon millions of children to the **Rock in Whom I Take Refuge** at this hour in history. Please compel me and unprecedented numbers of believers to be the part in that process that You created us to be. I pray these things in Jesus' secure name. Amen.

What impacted me about Christ today...

_____

_____

_____

_____

_____

*Psalm 95:1-7a Come, let us sing for joy to the LORD; let us shout aloud to the **Rock of our salvation**. Let us come before him with thanksgiving and extol him with music and song. For the LORD is the great God, the Great King above all gods. In his hand are the depths of the earth, and the mountain peaks belong to him. The sea is his, for he made it, and his hands formed the dry land. Come, let us bow down in worship, let us kneel before the LORD our Maker; for he is our God and we are the people of his pasture, the flock under his care.*

Significance: **The LORD JESUS CHRIST provides us with God's one true and secure source of our deliverance.**

Dear Father,

I certainly do sing for joy to the Lord Jesus, and shout aloud to Him as the **Rock of Our Salvation**. Once again, I am wonderfully reassured through Scripture that Jesus is my strong, mighty and complete shelter. I rejoice that just as the pure water poured out from the **rock** in the wilderness to refresh and sustain the ancient Jews, my salvation and all of my life pours out from the **Rock of Our Salvation**. Please convince me and the whole Church to come wholeheartedly to Jesus, the great King and great God above all gods. Hallelujah! Everything is His! Please incite us to *"come to him alone, bow down to him in worship, and kneel before him, for he is our God and we are the people of his pasture, the flock under his care."* I pray that an awe of the **Rock of our Salvation** will fill the Church, and that He will become the highest focus of all our thoughts, actions, words, delights, hopes, prayers and passions. May Your Spirit help us to pray for vast numbers of lost people across the nations, especially their leaders, to cry out to the **Rock of our Salvation** for salvation, so they will give all their allegiance and praise to Him, and govern under His lordship. I ask all these things in Jesus' mighty and merciful name. Amen.

What impacted me about Christ today...

_____

_____

_____

_____

_____

MARCH

THE FRUIT OF THE LAND
A WALL OF FIRE
ANOINTED ONE
THE MESSIAH
SON OF THE LIVING GOD
OUR MIGHTY ONE
Savior, Prince of Peace
The eternal
the
THE SF
MY CHOSEN ONE
THE MOST HOLY THE DELIVERER
A GREAT LIGHT
guardian
MMANUEL
THE ROCK OF ISRAEL
THE SON OF MAN
redeer
THE FOUNTAIN OF LIFE GOD WITH US
MY HIDING PLACE
MY STREN
WONDERFUL COUNSELOR SON OF DAVID
THE COMMANDER A STRONG TOWER
TEACHER
MY STRONG DELIVERER
PRINCE OF PEACE THE KING OF GLORY
THE REFUGE FOR THE OPPRESSED
GOD, WHO RAISES THE DE
THE LORD THE KING
THE MIGHTY SCEPTER
A SHELTER FROM THE STORM
A Witness to
the People

*Psalm 96:7-9 Ascribe to the LORD, all you families of nations, ascribe to the LORD glory and strength. Ascribe to the LORD the glory due his name; bring an offering and come into his courts. Worship the LORD in the **splendor of his holiness**; tremble before him, all the earth.*

Significance: **The LORD JESUS CHRIST displays the grandeur of God's holy character.**

Dear Father,

I worship the Lord Jesus, Who is the beauty of all **holiness** (of the Godhead), and the **Splendor of His Holiness**. I marvel at how all the attributes of the **Splendor of His Holiness** proceed from and converge into the dazzling white radiance of His holiness! Oh, the glorious purity, clarity, luster and perfection of His nature, like a most precious diamond without flaw or stain. I am in awe that He shines brightly as the only sinless One. I join the writer of this Psalm in trembling before Him. Please flood my life, and the lives of all His people, with constant demonstrations of His **holiness**, so that we will cry out to Him day and night, "**Holy, Holy, Holy** is Jesus, the Lord God Almighty." I pray that You will convince us to repent of all unholiness in our lives, and immerse our thoughts, motives, actions and words in His **splendid holiness** too. May we continually ascribe to the **Splendor of His Holiness** all the glory due His name. I pray that many lost people around us will also become captivated and transformed by that **holiness**. In the beautiful name of Jesus I ask these things. Amen.

What impacted me about Christ today...

*Psalm 97:1-7 The LORD reigns, let the earth be glad; let the distant shores rejoice. Clouds and thick darkness surround him; righteousness and justice are the foundation of his throne. Fire goes before him and consumes his foes on every side. His lightning lights up the world; the earth sees and trembles. The mountains melt like wax before the LORD, before the **LORD of all the earth**. The heavens proclaim his righteousness, and all peoples see his glory. All who worship images are put to shame, those who boast in idols—worship him, all you gods!*

Significance: The LORD JESUS CHRIST rules among the nations as the Lord of all creation.

Dear Father,

I exalt Jesus, the great Master and **Lord of All the Earth**! As I read today's Scripture passage, I am again in awe of the power and majesty that He alone possesses. All glory to Him that He rules and reigns over all heaven and earth, and that His righteousness and justice are displayed before all people. Hallelujah! His dominion is universal, and His power is felt everywhere! I pray that You will reveal much more of the magnificent **Lord of All the Earth** to me and to many other believers at this crucial hour in history, and that we will tremble before Him and repent for all the ways we have put other gods before Him. May we be filled with ceaseless reverence and praise of Him. I pray that countless numbers of unsaved people (including those who are aggressively opposing Him) will see Him as they never have before, and their hearts will melt like wax under His authority and righteousness. I pray these things in the name of the **Lord of All the Earth**. Amen.

What impacted me about Christ today...

_____

_____

_____

_____

_____

Psalm 98:1-9 Sing to the LORD a new song, for he has done marvelous things; his right hand and his holy arm have worked salvation for him. The LORD has made his salvation known and revealed his righteousness to the nations. He has remembered his love and his faithfulness to Israel; all the ends of the earth have seen the salvation of our God. Shout for joy to the LORD, all the earth, burst into jubilant song with music; make music to the LORD with the harp, with the harp and the sound of singing, with trumpets and the blast of the ram's horn—shout for joy before the LORD, the King. Let the sea resound, and everything in it, the world, and all who live in it. Let the rivers clap their hands, let the mountains sing together for joy; let them sing before the LORD, for he comes to judge the earth. He will judge the world in righteousness and the peoples with equity.

Significance: The LORD JESUS CHRIST, sitting at the right hand of God the Father, serves as ruler and judge of everything and everyone.

Dear Father,

I love this "Coronation Hymn," which was probably written by King David. All glory to the conquering Messiah, the supreme Monarch over all the nations! He is the great **Lord,** the **King**! I praise Him for the marvelous Person He is, and for the marvel of salvation, and all the other marvelous works that He gives to the world. He is worthy of all praise and adoration. I pray that I and all of His followers will bow down before Him, submit to His rule and reign, serve Him, live in His righteousness, and proclaim His fame to all people. As the sea resounds, as the rivers clap, and as the mountains sing about Him, may we, His people, resound, and clap and sing about Him. I fervently pray that You will remove all obstacles in the hearts and minds of multitudes of unsaved people we know, so that they too will receive Him as the **Lord,** the **King** of their lives. In the majestic name of Jesus, I ask these things. Amen.

What impacted me about Christ today...

_____

_____

_____

*Psalm 104:1-4 Praise the LORD, my soul. LORD my God, you are **very greatt**; you are clothed with splendor and majesty. The LORD wraps himself in light as with a garment; he stretches out the heavens like a tent and lays the beams of his upper chambers on their waters. He makes the clouds his chariot and rides on the wings of the wind. He makes winds his messengers, flames of fire his servants.*

Significance: **The LORD JESUS CHRIST and His Kingdom ways display for us just how great God really is.**

Dear Father,

I joyfully praise the Lord Jesus, my God, Who alone is **Very Great**. I love this Psalm's wonderful testimony of Christ's awesome creative and sustaining power and authority! An endless number of "**very greats**" to describe Christ would still be inadequate to describe how **great** He is. I can only imagine the vast splendor and majesty that He is clothed with. I marvel at the thought of Him wrapping Himself in light, and stretching out the heavens like a tent, and on and on. I pray that all His people throughout the earth will clearly see His eternal **greatness**, and praise Him continually. Please help us to trust His greatness completely, and submit every part of our lives to His lordship. And, please urge us to testify that Jesus is **Very Great** to the lost friends, relatives, neighbors, work associates and everyone else we know who so desperately need Him, so that they too will be eager to live in His **greatness**. I pray these things in the preeminent name of Jesus. Amen.

What impacted me about Christ today...

_____

_____

_____

_____

_____

_____

_____

*Psalm 110:1-7 The LORD says to my lord: "Sit at my right hand until I make your enemies a footstool for your feet." The LORD will extend your **mighty scepter** from Zion, saying, "Rule in the midst of your enemies!" Your troops will be willing on your day of battle. Arrayed in holy splendor, your young men will come to you like dew from the morning's womb.*
*   The LORD has sworn and will not change his mind: "You are a priest forever, in the order of Melchizedek." The Lord is at your right hand; he will crush kings on the day of his wrath. He will judge the nations, heaping up the dead and crushing the rulers of the whole earth. He will drink from a brook along the way, and so he will lift his head high.*

Significance: The LORD JESUS CHRIST by His reign could be called the Royal Rod in God's hand.

Dear Father,
I am humbled and thrilled that in this Psalm You declare that Your Son is the glorious priestly King. I rejoice that the ascended King is the Messiah and the **Mighty Scepter**, Who is sitting at Your right hand, ruling over all His followers, as well as over all His enemies. Hallelujah! You will not change Your mind about Christ's supreme might and position. Hallelujah! He is forever omnipotent and victorious, and cannot be overcome by any force or power. I exalt Him that His rule and authority extend through the Church to make Him known to unsaved people around us who urgently need freedom in Him! I give all my allegiance to Him. And, I pray that my family members and all of His people will submit to His rule and reign. Please awaken us so stunningly to all the **Mighty Scepter** is that we must speak to everyone about His greatness. I am eager for the day when Christ's enemies will be a footstool for His feet. I pray these things in His majestic name. Amen.

What impacted me about Christ today...

_____

_____

_____

_____

_____

A Priest Forever In The Order Of Melchizedek

*Psalm 110:1-7 The LORD says to my lord: "Sit at my right hand until I make your enemies a footstool for your feet." The LORD will extend your mighty scepter from Zion; you will rule in the midst of your enemies. Your troops will be willing on your day of battle. Arrayed in holy majesty, from the womb of the dawn you will receive the dew of your youth. The LORD has sworn and will not change his mind: "You are a **priest forever, in the order of Melchizedek**." The Lord is at your right hand; he will crush kings on the day of his wrath. He will judge the nations, heaping up the dead and crushing the rulers of the whole earth. He will drink from a brook beside the way; therefore he will lift up his head.*

Significance: The LORD JESUS CHRIST serves in the Temple of the universe as both High Priest and sacrifice.

Dear Father,

I am greatly in awe that, at this one and only time, You swore the solemn oath and command that Your Son is the **Priest Forever, in the Order of Melchizedek**. I praise Him that His life and His priesthood have no beginning and no end. I rejoice that the foundation of all Christ does in and for the Church is laid in His priestly office, whereby He made atonement and reconciliation for sin. I am so grateful for the absolute assurance that we believers have of eternal life through the **Priest Forever**, from many Scripture passages like Hebrews 6:19-20, *"We have this hope as an anchor for the soul, firm and secure. It enters the inner sanctuary behind the curtain, where our forerunner, Jesus, has entered on our behalf. He has become a high priest forever, in the order of Melchizedek."* I think of how Melchizedek was referred to as the "King of Salem," or the "King of Peace." I pray that You will help me and all Christ's followers today to live in the fullness of righteousness and peace we have through our beloved Jesus, the **Priest Forever, in the Order of Melchizedek**. I pray these things in His holy name. Amen.

What impacted me about Christ today...

Psalm 111:1-10 *Praise the LORD. I will extol the LORD with all my heart in the council of the upright and in the assembly. Great are the works of the LORD; they are pondered by all who delight in them. Glorious and majestic are his deeds, and his righteousness endures forever. He has caused his wonders to be remembered; the LORD is gracious and compassionate. He provides food for those who fear him; he remembers his covenant forever. He has shown his people the power of his works, giving them the lands of other nations. The works of his hands are faithful and just; all his precepts are trustworthy. They are established for ever and ever, enacted in faithfulness and uprightness. He provided redemption for his people; he ordained his covenant forever—**holy and awesome** is his name. The fear of the LORD is the beginning of wisdom; all who follow his precepts have good understanding. To him belongs eternal praise.*

Significance: **The LORD JESUS CHRIST provides the full and final display of God's awesome righteousness.**

Dear Father,

I rejoice in this marvelous testimony of Your all-encompassing greatness, that is ultimately fulfilled in the Lord Jesus Christ. I join the Psalmist in extolling Christ for His innumerable great works, His glorious and majestic deeds, and His righteousness that endures forever! Please help me and all His people to continually remember His wonders, and to praise Him with all our hearts that He is the gracious, compassionate, powerful, faithful, just, trustworthy and steadfast Lord of the universe. I am filled with gratitude that He has provided redemption for all people to fulfill Your covenant forever. I bow before Him as I exclaim, *"Holy and Awesome is his name!"* I pray that a widespread, **holy** fear and **awe** of Christ will rise within the Church and that we will speak without restraint of His authority and righteousness. I pray these things in His most **holy** name. Amen.

What impacted me about Christ today...

_____

_____

_____

_____

_____

The Stone The Builders Rejected

<u>*Psalm 118:22-24*</u> *The **stone the builders rejected** has become the corner-stone; the LORD has done this, and it is marvelous in our eyes. The LORD has done it this very day; let us rejoice today and be glad.*

Significance: The LORD JESUS CHRIST, although initially rejected, is the Source and Foundation of all God's kingdom.

Dear Father,
I grieve deeply that when You sent Jesus, the mighty Creator and Lord of the Universe, to earth to represent all that You are and to provide the only way for sinful man to receive redemption, the religious leaders You entrusted to **build** Your kingdom intently rejected, humiliated and killed Him. Shamefully, He was then, as He is often now, the contemptible **Stone the Builders Rejected**. I earnestly repent for the times when I and other believers today reject Him. But, then I shout "Hallelujah" that You raised the **Stone the Builders Rejected** up from the dead, and anointed Him to be the victorious corner**stone** (head **stone** of the corner) of the whole Church of the Living God! I rejoice that He is the solid, righteous, tried, true, firm, precious and strong **Stone** that has joined the two walls of Jews and Gentiles into one holy temple. Oh, how marvelous He is in our eyes! Please help the Church to build our lives solely upon Jesus, and devote ourselves to giving Him all the glory and honor He is due. I pray that many unsaved people we know will watch us live firmly upon the great **Stone**, and eagerly seek to receive Him too. I pray these things in His marvelous name. Amen.

What impacted me about Christ today...

_____

_____

_____

_____

_____

_____

_____

My Portion

*Psalm 119:57-58, 62-64 You are my **portion**, LORD; I have promised to obey your words. I have sought your face with all my heart; be gracious to me according to your promise. . . . At midnight I rise to give you thanks for your righteous laws. I am a friend to all who fear you, to all who follow your precepts. The earth is filled with your love, LORD; teach me your decrees.*

Significance: **The LORD JESUS CHRIST provides us *"immeasurably-more-than-all-we-can-ask-or-imagine"* straight from His riches in glory.**

Dear Father,

I am very grateful that in Jesus, the fullness of the Godhead dwells, and that He is my all-sufficient **Portion**. I marvel at all He is, and at how much He loves and cares for me! He is the all in all for the whole world, and certainly He is my all in all too. My thoughts quickly return to Psalm 23:1 where King David testifies: *"The Lord is my shepherd, I lack nothing."* I rejoice that praying today's Scripture helps me live in my blessed **Portion**. I promise to obey Jesus' words; I desire to seek His face with all my heart; I need His grace according to His promise; I give thanks for His righteous laws; I am a friend to all who fear Him and follow His precepts; I rejoice that the earth is filled with His love; and, I eagerly want Him to teach me His decrees. I also state my longing to be totally dependent upon Jesus like David's music director, Asaph, expressed to You in Psalm 73:26, *"My flesh and my heart may fail, but God is the strength of my heart and my **portion** forever."* I forsake dependence upon all other people and resources, so that I may rely only on Jesus. In His preeminent name I pray these things. Amen.

What impacted me about Christ today...

_____

_____

_____

_____

_____

_____

*Psalm 121:1-8 I lift up my eyes to the mountains—where does my help come from? My help comes from the LORD, the **Maker of heaven and earth**. He will not let your foot slip—he who watches over you will not slumber; indeed, he who watches over Israel will neither slumber nor sleep. The LORD watches over you—the LORD is your shade at your right hand; the sun will not harm you by day, nor the moon by night. The LORD will keep you from all harm—he will watch over your life; the LORD will watch over your coming and going both now and forevermore.*

Significance: The LORD JESUS CHRIST, as God's eternal Son, was and is the sole architect and builder of the whole universe.

Dear Father,

I am infinitely grateful that anywhere and anytime I can lift up my eyes, my voice and my spirit to Jesus, Who is the One and Only **Maker of Heaven and Earth**. I am in awe of Jesus that He thought about heaven and earth, designed them, spoke every cell and component of them into existence, and keeps them in His perfect order. I marvel that everything is under His dominion, and available for His plans and purposes. I praise Him that He has all the power, mercy, love, wisdom and authority to help me, and all people in the world when we call upon Him. A poem by Frances Ridley Havergal expresses such dependency upon Jesus very well: "Look away to Jesus, Look away from all! Then we need not stumble, then we shall not fall. From each snare that lures, Foe or phantom grim. Safety this ensures, Look away to him!" Please help me not to trust in my own abilities or in other people to guide or help me, but to place every part of my life in the **Maker of Heaven and Earth's** fully capable hands. I pray these things in His creative name. Amen.

What impacted me about Christ today...

_____

_____

_____

_____

_____

He Who Watches Over Israel

*Psalm 121:1-8 I lift up my eyes to the mountains—where does my help come from? My help comes from the LORD, the Maker of heaven and earth. He will not let your foot slip—He who watches over you will not slumber; indeed, he **who watches over Israel** will neither slumber nor sleep. The LORD watches over you—the LORD is your shade at your right hand; the sun will not harm you by day, nor the moon by night. The LORD will keep you from all harm—he will watch over your life; the LORD will watch over your coming and going, both now and forevermore.*

Significance: The LORD JESUS CHRIST stands guard over His people without wavering in fear or forsaking His post.

Dear Father,

I thank You for the steadfast assurance that Jesus is forever **He Who Watches Over Israel**, **over** me and **over** His whole Church. I am exceedingly grateful that He has all power to help us; He sees everything about us; He is all wise; and He loves us beyond measure. I rejoice also that He never sleeps, or gets distracted or exhausted in **watching** over us. I am excited as I remember that today's name/attribute of Christ refers back to Your conversation with Jacob in Genesis 28:15, where You promised him: *"I am with you and will **watch over** you wherever you go, and I will bring you back to this land. I will not leave you until I have done what I have promised you."* I rejoice that Christ does not even blink in **watching** and keeping us. Please help me, my family members and all of His people to know **He Who Watches Over Israel** so deeply and so intimately that we will readily place **every** part of our lives in His mighty hands. I pray that Jesus will **watch** and rule **over** all of the United States of America, Israel and all other countries of the world. All people and all nations desperately need Him! I ask these things in the name of Jesus, the Great Protector. Amen.

What impacted me about Christ today...

*Psalm 121:1-8 I lift up my eyes to the mountains—where does my help come from? My help comes from the LORD, the Maker of heaven and earth. He will not let your foot slip—he who watches over you will not slumber; indeed, He who watches over Israel will neither slumber nor sleep. The LORD watches over you—the LORD is your **shade at your right hand**; the sun will not harm you by day, nor the moon by night. The LORD will keep you from all harm—he will watch over your life; the LORD will watch over your coming and going, both now and forevermore.*

Significance: The LORD JESUS CHRIST protects us from everything the world, the flesh or the Devil might throw at us.

Dear Father,

I continue to be immensely grateful that the omnipotent Lord Jesus watches over every part of my life, and His whole Church. I marvel when I think of all the people and influences that can harm us (physically, mentally, emotionally and spiritually), and that Jesus alone has the power and love to **always** be our full shield of protection. I rejoice that not even the sun or the moon, or other forces that are blazing and relentless against us, can prevail over the Lord, Who is the **Shade at Your Right Hand**. Hallelujah! Our strength is in Jesus Who even guards our most favored and precious side (typically our right hand). This name of Jesus reminds me again of His prayer to You in John 17:12, *"While I was with them [His disciples], I protected them and kept them safe by that name you gave me. None has been lost except the one doomed to destruction so that Scripture would be fulfilled."* I humbly repent for the times I have rejected Jesus as my **shade**, and I now put myself completely under His powerful, everlasting cover. I receive His life-giving **shade**, and I pray that all the rest of His people will do so too. I ask these things in the name of Jesus, my faithful Keeper and Preserver. Amen.

What impacted me about Christ today...

_____

_____

_____

_____

Psalm 136:1-4, 26 Give thanks to the LORD, for he is good. His love endures forever. Give thanks to the God of gods. His love endures forever. Give thanks to the Lord of lords: his love endures forever. To him who alone does great wonders, his love endures forever. . . . Give thanks to the **God of heaven**. *His love endures forever.*

Significance: The LORD JESUS CHRIST demonstrates His eternal love as the ruler of all heaven and earth.

Dear Father,

I honor the Lord Jesus, the **God of Heaven**, Who deserves continual thanks. I am very grateful that His love endures forever, and that because of His enduring love, He created the heavens and the earth, including me and all mankind, and that He came to earth to demonstrate Your love and His love for us. As I read all of Psalm 136, I am in awe of His abounding greatness as the **God of Heaven**. A few of those aspects of His greatness that are stated in this passage declare that He is: *"the God of gods;"* Who *"alone does great wonders;"* Who *"spread out the earth upon the waters;"* Who *"struck down the firstborn of Egypt;"* Who *"divided the Red Sea asunder;"* Who *"led his people through the desert;"* Who *"freed us from our enemies;"* and much more. This also reminds me of what the prophet Jonah said in Jonah 1:9 to the people who were asking who he was: *"I am a Hebrew and I worship the LORD, the* **God of heaven**, *who made the sea and the dry land."* I pray that You will increasingly reveal all the glories, attributes, promises and power of the **God of Heaven** to me and all believers, so we will fully live in His enduring love. May our passion for Him be so consuming that we must tell every lost person we can about Him. All my hope is in Jesus, in Whose name I pray these things. Amen.

What impacted me about Christ today...

_____

_____

_____

_____

_____

*Psalm 140:6-8 I say to the LORD, "You are my God." Hear, LORD, my cry for mercy. Sovereign LORD, my **strong deliverer**, you shield my head in the day of battle. Do not grant the wicked their desires, LORD; do not let their plans succeed.*

Significance: The LORD JESUS CHRIST continues to deliver and liberate a people for His glory from all other people and nations.

Dear Father,

I praise the Sovereign Lord Jesus that He is my **Strong Deliverer**, and the **Strong Deliverer** of all who have received Him as their Savior. I think of the unlimited **strength** He has always possessed, and of the greatness of all His other attributes! Truly, Jesus is the all-**strong**, awesome God! I am forever grateful that His **strength** that created and sustains the whole world, has already **delivered** me countless times from the devil's attacks, and from the eternal penalty of my sins. I give Him all thanks that He shields my head (and my whole body, mind and spirit) in all battles, far beyond what all man's armor bearers could conceive. Like King David, who wrote this Psalm, without my **Strong Deliverer** I would have perished many times. I also rejoice at the amazing example in David's life when he confidently faced Goliath with these words recorded in 1 Samuel 17:47, *"All those gathered here will know that it is not by sword or spear that the LORD saves; for the battle is the LORD's and he will give all of you into our hands."* I pray that You will regularly remind me and the whole Church of the **Strong Deliverer's** fathomless **strength**, so we will continually praise Him, thank Him, trust Him and cry for His mercy in all our battles. I pray these things in His almighty name. Amen.

What impacted me about Christ today...

_____

_____

_____

_____

_____

The One Who Gives Victory To Kings

*Psalm 144:9-11 I will sing a new song to you, God; on the ten-stringed lyre I will make music to you, to the **One who gives victory to kings**, who delivers his servant David. From the deadly sword deliver me; rescue me from the hands of foreigners whose mouths are full of lies, whose right hands are deceitful.*

Significance: The LORD JESUS CHRIST rescues His anointed leaders and uses them to lead His people into His victory.

Dear Father,

I exalt the Lord Jesus Christ that He is the ultimate and eternal **King** of all kings, Ruler of all rulers, Lord of all lords, and Governor of all governors. I praise Him that He has always had all the wisdom and authority to raise up kings and take down kings. I place all leaders, in all walks of life (including in the Church), of all cities and nations, in the hands of Jesus, the **One Who Gives Victory to Kings**. I pray that You will put in each of these leaders a fear and respect for the **One Who Gives Victory to Kings**, and a resolute submission to and dependency upon Him. I pray Proverbs 1:7 for each of the Christian leaders: *"The fear of the LORD is the beginning of knowledge, but fools despise wisdom and instruction."* I pray that Christ will save and deliver them from sin, ungodly alliances, the devil's deceptions, wrong decisions, financial problems, strongholds, destructive habits and all other "battles." I pray that an unprecedented number of them will live under Christ's wisdom, righteousness, love, grace, truth, justice and courage that will impact great numbers of their followers. May unceasing glory go to the **One Who Gives Victory to Kings**, in Whose name I pray these things. Amen.

What impacted me about Christ today...

_____

_____

_____

_____

_____

_____

_____

The Friend Who Sticks Closer Than A Brother

Proverbs 18:24 _One who has unreliable friends soon comes to ruin, but there is a_ ***friend who sticks closer than a brother.***

Significance: **The LORD JESUS CHRIST, alive forever more, calls us to abide in Him as the best companion anyone can ever have.**

Dear Father,

When I think about the perfect **friend** for me and all people, the only person Who can truly fill that role is Jesus. A couple of dictionary definitions of "**friend**" are helpful to me: (1) "a person you know well and regard with affection and trust;" (2) "an associate who provides cooperation or assistance." I rejoice that Jesus, the **Friend Who Sticks Closer Than a Brother**, far exceeds those descriptions of "**friend**." I praise Him that He is Almighty God, with all Your power and love to minister as the **Friend** of all friends. I praise Him that He will never leave nor forsake those who trust in Him, and that nothing can separate us from His love. Hallelujah! He is completely faithful to His teaching in John 15:13, _"Greater love has no one than this: to lay down one's life for one's friends,"_ through His dying on the cross for us, protecting us, providing for us, forgiving us, teaching us, encouraging us, giving us His strength, taking our burdens upon Himself and much, much more. I love to sing part of the first verse of Joseph Scriven's hymn, "What A Friend We Have in Jesus": "What a Friend we have in Jesus, All our sins and griefs to bear! What a privilege to carry, Everything to God in pray'r!" I pray that I and all the followers of the **Friend Who Sticks Closer Than a Brother** will crave an intimate love relationship with Him, and will abide in the fullness of His **friendship**. And, please give us a deep burden to introduce all of our unsaved earthly friends to our best **Friend**, Jesus. In His blessed name I pray these things. Amen.

What impacted me about Christ today...

_____

_____

_____

_____

*Isaiah 4:2-3 In that day the **Branch of the Lord** will be beautiful and glorious, and the fruit of the land will be the pride and glory of the survivors in Israel. Those who are left in Zion, who remain in Jerusalem, will be called holy, all who are recorded among the living in Jerusalem.*

Significance: The LORD JESUS CHRIST, risen from the dead, has become like a sapling growing tall and filling the earth with Himself.

Dear Father,

I am saddened that in today's Scripture passage You had to warn the people of Israel of the coming day of judgment for their disobedience of You. But, I rejoice that You were also reminding them that the **Branch of the Lord** (or the **Branch** of Jehovah), Who is a descendent of King David, would come to those who escaped Your wrath. I am glad that the people of Israel knew that the **Branch of the Lord** would be the Messiah. I am eternally grateful that He was willing to sacrifice Himself on the cross, and that You raised Him from the dead, to grow into a strong new tree of righteousness, that would fill the earth with life in Himself. I praise Jesus that He was the hope of those who were left as the remnants in Zion, and that He is my strong hope, and the hope of the world. I exalt Him as the source of all life. Please help me and the whole Church to live in total dependence upon Him, and to be faithful conduits of His beauty, glory and all the rest of who He is, to one another and to all the people around us who are currently "life-less" without Him. Oh, I pray that You will do whatever is necessary in their hearts and minds to cause them to become grafted onto the **Branch of the Lord**. I ask these things in His holy name. Amen.

What impacted me about Christ today...

_____

_____

_____

_____

_____

_____

<u>Isaiah 4:2-3</u> *In that day the Branch of the L*ORD *will be beautiful and glorious, and the **fruit of the land** will be the pride and glory of the survivors in Israel. Those who are left in Zion, who remain in Jerusalem, will be called holy, all who are recorded among the living in Jerusalem.*

Significance: The LORD JESUS CHRIST produces a fruitful people for the glory of God.

Dear Father,

I marvel that by being the **Fruit of the Land**, Jesus' body came out of the earth as a man to fulfill all the purposes of the beautiful, glorious Branch of the Lord. He is the super-abundant, fragrant, lush, and sacrificial provider of all physical and spiritual goodness for His people. I rejoice that there are many references in the Bible to Your complete provision for Your people (ultimately through Jesus). One of my favorites is Ezekiel 34:23-27, *"I will place over them [the people of Israel] one shepherd, my servant David, and he will tend them; he will tend them and be their shepherd. I the L*ORD *will be their God, and my servant David will be prince among them. I the L*ORD *have spoken. I will make a covenant of peace with them and rid the land of savage beasts so that they may live in the wilderness and sleep in the forests in safety. I will make them and the places surrounding my hill a blessing. I will send down showers in season; there will be showers of blessing. The trees will yield their fruit and the ground will yield its crops; the people will be secure in their land. They will know that I am the L*ORD*, when I break the bars of their yoke and rescue them from the hands of those who enslaved them."* I pray that I and all believers will be overwhelmingly grateful for all You give us in the **Fruit of the Land**, and that we will have an insatiable hunger to be filled with Him only. May He be our *"pride and glory"* at all times. I pray these things in His blessed name. Amen.

What impacted me about Christ today...

_____

_____

_____

_____

_____

*Isaiah 4:5-6 Then the LORD will create over all of Mount Zion and over those who assemble there a cloud of smoke by day and a glow of flaming fire by night; over everything the glory will be a **canopy**. It will be a shelter and shade from the heat of the day, and a refuge and hiding place from the storm and rain.*

Significance: **The LORD JESUS CHRIST, by His righteousness and His reign before God's throne, has become the sufficient covering for His people.**

Dear Father,

I praise Jesus that He is the **Canopy** over all His people, now and forever. I am very grateful that He is our constant cloud of smoke by day, and our flaming fire by night. I marvel that He covers us with His glory. As I read today's Scripture passage, I think of what the Apostle John said in John 1:14 about Christ, the One and Only, revealing this glory: *"The Word became flesh and made his dwelling among us. We have seen his glory, the glory of the one and only Son, who came from the Father, full of grace and truth."* I thank You that Christ reveals His glory to us moment by moment as He covers us with His all-inclusive love, power, holiness, wisdom, mercy and the rest of Who He is! I am thrilled that we are able to continually dwell in Him and under Him as the transcendent priest, prophet, guide, shepherd, king, lord, leader, and much more, regardless of all trials that may come against us. Hallelujah! Our salvation and every part of our lives are hidden under the **Canopy**. I pray that You will help us to fully embrace the **Canopy** and always stay under His cover, and invite all other people we know to join us. I pray these things in Christ's name and for His glory. Amen.

What impacted me about Christ today...

_____

_____

_____

_____

_____

_____

*Isaiah 7:10-14 Again the LORD spoke to Ahaz, "Ask the LORD your God for a sign, whether in the deepest depths or in the highest heights." But Ahaz said, "I will not ask; I will not put the LORD to the test." Then Isaiah said, "Hear now, you house of David! Is it not enough to try the patience of humans? Will you try the patience of my God also? Therefore the LORD himself will give you a **sign**: The virgin will conceive and give birth to a son, and will call him Immanuel."*

Significance: The LORD JESUS CHRIST, by His miraculous birth, guarantees the tangible presence of God among His people forever.

Dear Father,

I am in awe of Your wonderful revelation of the Lord Jesus Christ through the prophet Isaiah in today's Scripture passage. I am exceedingly grateful that You gave King Ahaz, and thereby all people for all time, an understanding of Your sovereign intervention in the affairs of man, through Jesus, the **Sign**. I rejoice that Isaiah clearly knew You were foretelling that one day You would send the Messiah, Immanuel, to earth through a virgin. I exalt the **Sign**, that He came among us exactly as was foretold, and that He was and is the total manifestation of Your greatness, majesty, love, holiness, mercy and life! All glory and honor to Jesus, the eternal King from the lineage of David. I pray that the whole Church of today will: *"Hear now, you house of David,"* by knowing all we possibly can about Jesus, believing in Him completely, living in all of Him, loving Him unabashedly, and surrendering our all to Him. I pray that You will draw countless numbers of broken, unsaved people to the **Sign** whose hearts Your Spirit is preparing to receive as their Savior and Lord. All these things I pray in the name of Jesus. Amen.

What impacted me about Christ today...

_____

_____

_____

_____

_____

*<u>Isaiah 9:2-4</u> The people walking in darkness have seen a **great light**; on those living in the land of deep darkness a light has dawned. You have enlarged the nation and increased their joy; they rejoice before you as people rejoice at the harvest, as warriors rejoice when dividing the plunder. For as in the day of Midian's defeat, you have shattered the yoke that burdens them, the bar across their shoulders, the rod of their oppressor.*

Significance: **The LORD JESUS CHRIST has penetrated this dark world with the light of the glory of God.**

Dear Father,

I give the Lord Jesus Christ all praise that He enlightens people who are walking in the darkness of sin and hopelessness, like the people of Israel who were living under the darkest misery of captivity by becoming their **Great Light** of salvation and freedom. I rejoice that Jesus is THE **Light** that consumes and dispels the darkness. I honor Him, that no other power can put out or diminish His brightness. I thank You that today, all people who are without the **Great Light** can come to Him anytime, to receive Him as their **Light**, to allow Him to cleanse them of all darkness, and to live in the fullness of His joy. I want to live in the brilliance, glory, holiness and victory of the **Great Light**. I pray that You will help me and an increasing number of other believers to live so much in Jesus, living in all of the **Great Light**, that we will continually reflect Him to one another and to every unsaved person You bring into our lives. Oh, my Father, may we all see the **Great Light**, and may **light** dawn here and now as never before. Let there be **Light**! I pray these things in Christ's transforming name. Amen.

What impacted me about Christ today...

---

*Isaiah 9:5-7 Every warrior's boot used in battle and every garment rolled in blood will be destined for burning, will be fuel for the fire. For to us a child is born, to us a son is given, and the government will be on his shoulders. And he will be called **Wonderful Counselor**, Mighty God, Everlasting Father, Prince of Peace. Of the greatness of his government and peace there will be no end. He will reign on David's throne and over his kingdom, establishing and upholding it with justice and righteousness from that time on and forever. The zeal of the LORD Almighty will accomplish this.*

Significance: **The LORD JESUS CHRIST, by His Spirit, counsels people with uncommon wisdom and guides us into the purposes of God.**

Dear Father,

I rejoice greatly in this portion of Isaiah's amazing prophecy which proclaimed that the Messiah would be born, and would one day govern His people in righteousness. I further rejoice that all the implements which sinful leaders had been using to oppress the people of Israel were prophesied to be burned and destroyed under the Messiah's forthcoming, peaceful rule. Thank You for sending Your beloved Son to earth 2000 years ago to fulfill this prophecy! I praise Him that He alone possesses all the power, wisdom, justice, authority and love to be Your gift of salvation and freedom to all Jews and Gentiles. I exalt Him that He is the **Wonderful Counselor**. I say "Hallelujah," that there is no more **wonderful** Person than Jesus, Who is fully God and fully man! I love to think of the heavenly hosts being **full** of **wonder** of Him as Lord of the whole universe. I honor Jesus that He is the perfect, all-knowing, totally good, peace-making and impartial **Counselor**, Who for all eternity has known the full counsel of the Godhead. I am so grateful that the **Wonderful Counselor** is always available to counsel me and all His people, and that He ever lives to intercede for us. Please help us to know Him intimately, seek Him, hear Him, obey Him and give all glory to Him. I pray this in His wise name. Amen.

What impacted me about Christ today...

_____

_____

_____

*Isaiah 9:6-7 For to us a child is born, to us a son is given, and the government will be on his shoulders. And he will be called Wonderful Counselor, **Mighty God**, Everlasting Father, Prince of Peace. Of the greatness of his government and peace there will be no end. He will reign on David's throne and over his kingdom, establishing and upholding it with justice and righteousness from that time on and forever. The zeal of the LORD Almighty will accomplish this.*

Significance: **The LORD JESUS CHRIST, as God the Son, is co-equal in might and power with God the Father.**

Dear Father,

I praise Jesus that another aspect of His being able to carry the government of His people on His shoulders is that He is the **Mighty God**. I exalt Him that He is fully God, and, thus He is all-**mighty** to conquer all the forces of darkness, set every captive free from sin, rule and reign over all the universe, bear all of our burdens, answer every question, resolve any conflict, calm every storm, raise the dead to life, transform people and nations, judge the world in righteousness, and countless more expressions of His power and authority. I am greatly encouraged by the many other places in Scripture that also affirm His **might**, including Psalm 147:4-5, *"He determines the number of the stars and calls them each by name. Great is our Lord and **mighty** in power; his understanding has no limit."* I pray that You will help me and many other believers to regularly meditate on His **might**, notice displays of His awesome **might**, worship Him for His **might**, and pray for His **mighty** rule over our lives, over His Church and over all people and circumstances, here and now. I give all these things to You in Jesus' name. Amen.

What impacted me about Christ today...

_____

_____

_____

_____

_____

*Isaiah 9:6-7 For to us a child is born, to us a son is given, and the government will be on his shoulders. And he will be called Wonderful Counselor, Mighty God, **Everlasting Father**, Prince of Peace. Of the greatness of his government and peace there will be no end. He will reign on David's throne and over his kingdom, establishing and upholding it with justice and righteousness from that time on and forever. The zeal of the LORD Almighty will accomplish this.*

Significance: The LORD JESUS CHRIST, Who said that to see Him is to see the Father, will always govern His people the way a Father would do.

Dear Father,

Today, it is a joy to focus on Jesus governing His people through all the aspects of Him as the **Everlasting Father**. I bless Him for the complete assurance He gives in John 14:9b that He has all the fatherly power and attributes of You, the heavenly **Father**: *[Jesus said] "Don't you know me, Philip, even after I have been among you such a long time? Anyone who has seen me has seen the **Father**. How can you say, 'Show us the **Father**?'"* I marvel that Jesus, the **Everlasting Father**, is at the same time: (1) Eternal and never-ending (**Everlasting**), and (2) The perfect Head, Guide, Mentor, Leader, Provider, Protector, Shepherd, Lord, Priest, Hero, Advocate, Life-Giver, and every other role that could possibly be fulfilled as a **Father**. I am so glad that I am a child of the **Everlasting Father**! I pray that You will help me to know everything I possibly can about Him, and to live in wholehearted love of, respect for, and devotion to Him. Please help me and all His other children to say as He did to You in Matthew 26:39b, *"My Father, if it is possible, may this cup be taken from me. Yet not as I will, but as you will."* I pray that multitudes of people who are currently lost and **fatherless** without Him, will soon receive Him as Savior and **Everlasting Father** too. I ask all these things in His loving name. Amen.

What impacted me about Christ today...

_____

_____

_____

_____

*Isaiah 9:6-7 For to us a child is born, to us a son is given, and the government will be on his shoulders. And he will be called Wonderful Counselor, Mighty God, Everlasting Father, **Prince of Peace**. Of the greatness of his government and peace there will be no end. He will reign on David's throne and over his kingdom, establishing and upholding it with justice and righteousness from that time on and forever. The zeal of the LORD Almighty will accomplish this.*

Significance: The LORD JESUS CHRIST brings peace, wholeness and justice wherever God's Kingdom comes.

Dear Father,

I especially rejoice that Jesus governs His people through Him being the **Prince of Peace**. I marvel how His vast attributes, nature and abilities are all part of Him as the supreme **Peace**giver. I honor the **Prince of Peace** that He completely lives out the Beatitudes (of peace) that He taught His followers in Matthew 5:3-10: He is poor in spirit; He mourns; He is meek; He hungers and thirsts for righteousness; He is merciful; He is pure in heart; He is a peacemaker; and He is persecuted because of righteousness. I exalt Jesus that He is the giver of **peace** in all our relationships: (1) between You and man through sacrificing His life on the cross; (2) in the hearts and minds of each individual follower as they surrender more and more of themselves and every life situation to His lordship; and (3) between man and man as they live in His great love and humility with each other. I am very grateful that in John 14:27 He left never-ending **peace** with all His followers through the Holy Spirit: *"**Peace** I leave with you; my **peace** I give you. I do not give to you as the world gives. Do not let your hearts be troubled and do not be afraid."* I pray that I and believers everywhere will awaken to all the **Prince of Peace** is, and submit to His governance of our lives, so we will continually be ambassadors of **peace** in Him. And, I pray that very soon, *"Of the greatness of his government and **peace** there will be no end"* in America and around the world. In His name I ask these things. Amen.

What impacted me about Christ today...

_____

_____

_____

A Shoot . . . From The Stump Of Jesse

*Isaiah 11:1-6a, 6b, 9 A **shoot** will come up **from the stump of Jesse**; from his roots a Branch will bear fruit. The Spirit of the LORD will rest on him—the Spirit of wisdom and of understanding, the Spirit of counsel and of might, the Spirit of the knowledge and fear of the LORD—and he will delight in the fear of the LORD. He will not judge by what he sees with his eyes, or decide by what he hears with his ears; but with righteousness he will judge the needy, with justice he will give decisions for the poor of the earth. He will strike the earth with the rod of his mouth; with the breath of his lips he will slay the wicked. Righteousness will be his belt and faithfulness the sash around his waist. The wolf will live with the lamb . . . and a little child will lead them. . . . They will neither harm nor destroy on all my holy mountain, for the earth will be filled with the knowledge of the LORD as the waters cover the sea.*

Significance: The LORD JESUS CHRIST was dead but is alive forevermore, as out from His grave came a whole New Creation.

Dear Father,
What an amazing prophecy this is about the Messiah! I am in awe that King David (with whom You made a covenant that his descendants would always sit on his throne), descended from the humble Jesse. All glory to Jesus that David's descendents had fallen from power, and You sent Him, as a humble **Shoot** from the roots of the **Stump of Jesse**, to grow into a Branch to bear the complete reign and fruit of Your kingdom. I rejoice that the Holy Spirit came to rest upon Jesus (in the form of a dove) as He was baptized in the Jordan River, and that He has all the fullness of the Godhead abiding in Him. I am so grateful that Jesus governs His kingdom with absolute justice and righteousness, and that one day *"the earth will be filled with the knowledge of the LORD"* and His perfect peace. I pray that I and all believers will worship the **Shoot Who will come up From the Stump of Jesse**, and submit every part of our lives to His sovereign rule. I pray these things in the name of King Jesus. Amen.

What impacted me about Christ today...

_____

_____

_____

*Isaiah 11:10 In that day [Christ's return] the Root of Jesse will stand
as a **banner for the peoples**; the nations will rally to him, and his place
of rest will be glorious.*

Significance: The LORD JESUS CHRIST fulfills God's promise to
reconcile and rally people from all nations back to Himself.

Dear Father,

I bless Jesus that He is the Root that came from King David and his father,
Jesse, and He stands prominently as the supreme **Banner for the Peoples**
(Jews and Gentiles). I praise Him that all the magnificent character traits,
attributes, names, teachings and works He has displayed irrefutably confirm that He is the Messiah to Whom believers from all the nations will
rally. All our freedom, victory, revelation, truth, righteousness, trust and
hope are in Him. I rejoice that this impending rallying of Christ's people to
Himself fulfills many Biblical promises and prophesies, including Isaiah
5:26, *"He lifts up a **banner** for the distant nations, he whistles for those at
the ends of the earth. Here they come, swiftly and speedily!"* I come speedily to the **Banner for the Peoples**, and swear my complete allegiance to
Him. I pray that You will put a growing passion in believers everywhere to
know all they possibly can about the **Banner for the Peoples**, so that they
will follow Him unreservedly. I must also pray that at this crucial end time
of history, the lost of all nations will see the magnificence of the **Banner
for the Peoples**, and urgently rally to Him too. Thank You so much that
all who come to Him will dwell in His glorious place of rest. I pray these
things in His name. Amen.

What impacted me about Christ today...

_____

_____

_____

_____

_____

_____

_____

*Isaiah 12:1-6 In that day you will say: "I will praise you, LORD. Although you were angry with me, your anger has turned away and you have comforted me. Surely God is my salvation; I will trust and not be afraid. The LORD, the LORD himself, is my strength and my **defense**; he has become my salvation." With joy you will draw water from the wells of salvation. In that day you will say: "Give praise to the LORD, proclaim his name; make known among the nations what he has done, and proclaim that his name is exalted. Sing to the LORD, for he has done glorious things; let this be known to all the world. Shout aloud and sing for joy, people of Zion, for great is the Holy One of Israel among you."*

Significance: **The LORD JESUS CHRIST protects and cares for the many needs of His people.**

Dear Father,

I rejoice in how Jesus fulfills this whole Scripture passage, including that He is the impenetrable **Defense** of the people who are trusting in Him as our Savior. I am in awe that the sentence which our **Defense** is in, begins with *"The LORD, the LORD,"* to doubly emphasize the matchless lordship of Him Who is ALL the *"strength, **defense** and salvation"* of His people. I praise Jesus that throughout history He has demonstrated His magnificent strength, all the way from parting the seas and conquering nations, to saving individual souls and caring for individual needs, and much more. Truly, Christ our **Defense** is Lord of all! I pray that I and believers everywhere will continually praise our **Defense** for all He is, submit fully to His strength and **defense**, and speak of His power and mercy to everyone You bring into our lives. I repent for any ways I have not lived under the lordship of Jesus, my **Defense**. And, at this time in history, when there is so much chaos in neighborhoods, cities and nations, I pray that great numbers of believers and unbelievers will cry out to Jesus our **Defense** to save them spiritually and all other ways. May we join King David's plea in Psalm 35:23, *"Awake, and rise to my **defense**! Contend for me, my God and Lord."* In His strong name. Amen.

What impacted me about Christ today...

*Isaiah 12:1-6 In that day you will say: "I will praise you, LORD. Although you were angry with me, your anger has turned away and you have comforted me. Surely God is my salvation; I will trust and not be afraid. The LORD, the LORD himself, is my strength and my defense; he has become my salvation." With joy you will draw water from the **wells of salvation**. In that day you will say: "Give praise to the LORD, proclaim his name; make known among the nations what he has done, and proclaim that his name is exalted. Sing to the LORD, for he has done glorious things; let this be known to all the world. Shout aloud and sing for joy, people of Zion, for great is the Holy One of Israel among you."*

Significance: The LORD JESUS CHRIST, as God's Son, offers us the replenishing of God's saving power.

Dear Father,

I am deeply grateful that salvation comes from Your great love and grace for mankind that **wells** up within Jesus and pours out from Him. I praise Him that He is the true fountain of salvation, or the pure, free-flowing, refreshing, life-giving, inexhaustible **Wells of Salvation**. I love what Jesus promised to the people of Israel, and to all people of all times, in John 7:37b, *"Let anyone who is thirsty come to me and drink."* How wonderful it is that every need, craving, hope and thirst of those who put their trust in the **Wells of Salvation** can be met through His life, death and resurrection. This powerfully reminds me of what will soon take place in Christ's eternal kingdom, as declared in Revelation 7:15-17, *"Therefore, they are before the throne of God and serve him day and night in his temple; and he who sits on the throne will shelter them with his presence. Never again will they hunger; never again will they thirst. The sun will not beat down on them, nor any scorching heat. For the Lamb at the center of the throne will be their shepherd; he will lead them to springs of living water. And God will wipe away every tear from their eyes."* I pray that You will help me and all believers to come continually to the **Wells of Salvation** and drink deeply of Him. May we shout aloud and sing together about the glorious things He has done. I pray these things in His saving name. Amen.

What impacted me about Christ today...

*Isaiah 22:20-24 In that day I will summon my servant, Eliakim son of Hilkiah. I will clothe him with your robe and fasten your sash around him and hand your authority over to him. He will be a father to those who live in Jerusalem and to the people of Judah. I will place on his shoulder the key to the house of David; what he opens no one can shut, and what he shuts no one can open. I will drive him like a **peg into a firm place**; he will become a seat of honor for the house of his father. All the glory of his family will hang on him; its offspring and offshoots—all its lesser vessels, from the bowls to all the jars.*

Significance: The LORD JESUS CHRIST fulfills the vision of an unfailing handle to which God's people can cling with confidence that He will not fail.

Dear Father,

I honor Jesus, Who so powerfully fulfills this prophecy about Eliakim as the **Peg Into a Firm Place** (or what some translations call a *"nail in a sure place."*) I exalt Jesus that He is the ultimate King Who is clothed in the royal robe and has all the authority of the house (kingdom) of His father David, now and forever. I praise Him that the key to the house of David is placed on His shoulder. Truly, the government is solely upon His shoulders! I rejoice with all my heart that His power is unlimited and His authority is supreme; what He opens no one can shut, and what He shuts no one can open. Hallelujah, that You have driven Him as the **Peg Into a Firm Place** upon Whom I and all of His people can securely hang our faith in our salvation and every part of our lives. I am in awe of Jesus, the seat of honor for You, and the One upon Whom all the glory of the Church hangs. I submit my life wholly to Him. I am His subject and live to do His will. Oh, may millions of other believers, and those who have not yet received Him as their Savior, very soon completely hang on the **Peg Into a Firm Place**. I pray these things in His firm, trustworthy and unmovable name. Amen.

What impacted me about Christ today...

_____

_____

_____

_____

A Refuge For The Needy In Their Distress

*Isaiah 25:1-5 LORD, you are my God; I will exalt you and praise your name, for in perfect faithfulness you have done wonderful things, things planned long ago. You have made the city a heap of rubble, the fortified town a ruin, the foreigners' stronghold a city no more; it will never be rebuilt. Therefore strong peoples will honor you; cities of ruthless nations will revere you. You have been a refuge for the poor, a **refuge for the needy in their distress**, a shelter from the storm and a shade from the heat. For the breath of the ruthless is like a storm driving against a wall and like the heat of the desert. You silence the uproar of foreigners; as heat is reduced by the shadow of a cloud, so the song of the ruthless is stilled.*

Significance: The **LORD JESUS CHRIST**, offered to us by God as a permanent place of safety, is especially available for the overwhelmed.

Dear Father,

Just as Isaiah expresses praise for the deliverance of the Jews out of captivity, I want to exalt, praise and honor the Lord Jesus for His glorious victories over the enemies of His people today. I thank Him that in perfect faithfulness, He does marvelous things. I thank Him that He humbles the strong and proud, and gives strength to the needy and humble. I am deeply grateful that You sent Him to earth as the **Refuge For the Needy in Their Distress**. When I think of the dire needs of so many in our region and around the world, I tend to be overwhelmed. But, I know that all things are possible through Jesus, and that He is never overwhelmed! All glory to Jesus that He alone is willing and able to be the **Refuge** of ALL **the needy in** whatever their **distress**. Please draw them to Him, open their hearts to Him, and help them to put all their distress in His hands. May they find complete **refuge** in Him! I pray especially that You will reveal the greatness of the **Refuge For the Needy in Their Distress** to me and to all the Church today, so that we will abide in Him as a testimony of hope to the world. In the overcoming name of Jesus I pray these things. Amen.

What impacted me about Christ today...

APRIL

*Isaiah 25:1-5 LORD, you are my God; I will exalt you and praise your name, for in perfect faithfulness you have done wonderful things, things planned long ago. You have made the city a heap of rubble, the fortified town a ruin, the foreigners' stronghold a city no more; it will never be rebuilt. Therefore strong peoples will honor you; cities of ruthless nations will revere you. You have been a refuge for the poor, a refuge for the needy in their distress, a **shelter from the storm** and a shade from the heat. For the breath of the ruthless is like a storm driving against a wall and like the heat of the desert. You silence the uproar of foreigners; as heat is reduced by the shadow of a cloud, so the song of the ruthless is stilled.*

Significance: The LORD JESUS CHRIST provides us with God's maximum refuge in the midst of all life throws at us.

Dear Father,

I thank You that You always provide Your people with a **Shelter From the Storm**. When I think of all the spiritual, physical, financial, mental and emotional storms of life, I am so grateful that You sent Your Son, Jesus, to be the complete **Shelter From the Storm** that I and every one of His followers desperately need. I praise Him that He possesses all Your wisdom, power, love and mercy to know about all the storms that come into our lives, and to provide us with the perfect **shelter** from them. I rejoice that Jesus also knows the good purposes that You want to accomplish through the storms, and He is constantly working in and through us to give us victory, freedom, peace, faith, strength, and all His other *"plans to prosper you and not to harm you, plans to give you hope and a future"* (Jeremiah 29:11b). I honor Jesus that He is the Master of the storms, and all parts of our lives. I pray that You will help us to submit to His will for every part of our lives, (including in our storms), and that we will grow stronger and stronger in Him, and more like Him. May the many lost people around us see the **Shelter From the Storm** working in us, and quickly flee to Him as their **Shelter** too. All these things I pray in the mighty name of Jesus. Amen.

What impacted me about Christ today...

_____

_____

_____

*Isaiah 28:5-6 In that day the LORD Almighty will be a **glorious crown**, a beautiful wreath for the remnant of his people. He will be a spirit of justice to the one who sits in judgment, a source of strength to those who turn back the battle at the gate.*

Significance: **The LORD JESUS CHRIST, crowned by Heaven as the King of kings, reigns among us in the beauty of His majesty.**

Dear Father,

I praise Jesus as the only One Who could possibly be the **Glorious Crown**. I honor Him that He is worthy of all **glory** in heaven and earth, and that He is **crowned** with ALL majesty and righteousness. I worship the **Glorious Crown** in the splendor of all His attributes and powers. I exalt Him that His **glory** is everlasting and never-fading, and that He is more magnificent and precious than all earthly rulers of the people of Israel, and all other rulers who have ever lived. I rejoice that the **Glorious Crown** provides the fullness of life to me and all His people. In praise of the **gloriously crowned** King Jesus, I joyfully sing the first verse of "Crown Him With Many Crowns" by Matthew Bridges: "Crown Him with many crowns, The Lamb upon His throne. Hark! How the heavenly anthem drowns, All music but its own! Awake, my soul and sing, Of Him who died for thee, And hail Him as thy matchless King, Thro' all eternity." May He rule every part of my life and His whole Church, now and forever. May His glory crown us. I pray these things in His holy and exalted name. Amen.

What impacted me about Christ today...

_____

_____

_____

_____

_____

_____

_____

_____

_____

_____

*Isaiah 28:5-6 In that day the LORD Almighty will be a glorious crown, a **beautiful wreath** for the remnant of his people. He will be a spirit of justice to him who sits in judgment, a source of strength to those who turn back the battle at the gate.*

Significance: The LORD JESUS CHRIST is God's promised adornment for His people.

Dear Father,

I honor Jesus that He has all the **beauty** and royalty of the Godhead. I praise Him that He is the **Beautiful Wreath** for those who have given their lives to Him. I think of how **wreaths** of flowers, berries and other parts of tree branches are put on people's heads or doors to celebrate special occasions, and I am so grateful that Jesus continually covers us with His resplendent **beauty**, fragrance and color. I exalt Jesus that His **beauty** is beyond all imagination and compare. I pray You will reveal so much more of the **Beautiful Wreath** to us that we will forsake all other attractions and allegiances for Him. Please put in us the consuming passion for the **Beautiful Wreath** that King David expresses in Psalm 27:4, *"One thing I ask from the LORD, this only do I seek: that I may dwell in the house of the LORD all the days of my life, to **gaze upon the beauty of the LORD** and to seek him in his temple."* Please help us to talk about the **Beautiful Wreath** continually with one another and to live in all His beauty. I pray that You will do whatever is necessary in the unsaved people all around us so they will urgently seek Him too. I ask these things in Jesus' precious name. Amen.

What impacted me about Christ today...

_____

_____

_____

_____

_____

_____

_____

_____

_____

*Isaiah 28:5-6 In that day the L*ORD *Almighty will be a glorious crown, a beautiful wreath for the remnant of his people. He will be a **spirit of justice** to him who sits in judgment, a source of strength to those who turn back the battle at the gate.*

Significance: **The LORD JESUS CHRIST administers God's justice among His own people and to the ends of the earth.**

Dear Father,

I am deeply grateful that the Lord Jesus is the only One Who fulfills the high and holy role of the **Spirit of Justice**. I exalt Him that He has all the truth, wisdom, knowledge, mercy, compassion, courage, patience, discernment, peace and righteousness that are necessary for the administration of His perfect **justice**. I honor Jesus that He is completely fair and impartial. I pray that You will reveal more and more of the character and authority of the **Spirit of Justice** to me and to all His followers, so that we will become increasingly devoted to Him as our Lord and to living according to His **justice**. I pray that the men and women He places in positions of judging the affairs of the Church and the rest of our society will fear Him and judge according to His ways. May Your "liberty and justice for all" prevail for every person, place and situation across our nation, especially for those who are in the midst of severe physical and spiritual battles. I pray that many people who have resisted giving their lives to the **Spirit of Justice** will very soon cry out to Him as their only hope. I ask these things in Jesus' name. Amen.

What impacted me about Christ today...

_____

_____

_____

_____

_____

_____

_____

A Source Of Strength

*Isaiah 28:5-6 In that day the LORD Almighty will be a glorious crown, a beautiful wreath for the remnant of his people. He will be a spirit of justice to him who sits in judgment, a **source of strength** to those who turn back the battle at the gate.*

Significance: The LORD JESUS CHRIST is the One Who God has sent to be the fountainhead of all fortitude to us.

Dear Father,

When I think of the Lord Jesus Christ being the **Source of Strength** of the entire world, I stand in awe of Him. I praise Him that He has demonstrated His physical, mental and spiritual **strength** countless times in Scripture accounts and in every conceivable way throughout history. I shout "Hallelujah" that His limitless **strength** surrounds and undergirds His people in all situations and at all times. I rejoice that He spoke the world into existence with His **strength**, and that He maintains every atom of the world with His **strength**. I pray that You will help me and all believers in the **Source of Strength** to: *"Be strong in the Lord and in his mighty power,"* (Ephesians. 6:10), as we *"turn back the battle [against the enemies of our souls] at the gate"* (of their stronghold). I delight that in Him alone we have courage, endurance and hope, as the Apostle Paul powerfully confirms in Philippians 4:13, *"I can do all this [everything] through him who gives me **strength**."* I pray that we will be so dependent upon the strong Christ that all who know us will be anxious to know Him like we do. I pray these things in the name of Jesus, the all-mighty **Source of Strength**. Amen.

What impacted me about Christ today...

_____

_____

_____

_____

_____

_____

_____

_____

*Isaiah 28:16-17 So this is what the Sovereign LORD says: "See, I lay a stone in Zion, a **tested stone**, a precious cornerstone for a sure foundation; the one who relies on it will never be stricken with panic. I will make justice the measuring line and righteousness the plumb line; hail will sweep away your refuge, the lie, and water will overflow your hiding place."*

Significance: The LORD JESUS CHRIST remains forever the absolutely crucial building block of God's kingdom.

Dear Father,

I praise You that You laid the resurrected Lord Jesus, the **Tested Stone**, as the precious cornerstone of the whole Church. What a marvelous gift You have given to us! I am very grateful that before the beginning of time the Godhead decided to send the **Tested Stone** to earth to reveal Your grace and truth, and to lay down His life for mankind. I praise the **Tested Stone** that He possesses all the abilities, powers and understandings to be the strongest and most central part of the Church's foundation. I rejoice that Jesus has been **tested** with all kinds of trials, temptations, attacks and burdens, and He has ALWAYS been faithful and victorious. Hallelujah! Jesus never fails or falters! I want to be faithful in my times of testing too. I repent for not trusting Jesus when I have been tested. I pray You will help me and all other Christians to know much more of Who the **Tested Stone** is, so that we will become wholeheartedly dependent upon Him, and increasingly like Him. I pray that You will prepare us to be faithful in times of testing, and use us to radically demonstrate the character of Christ to people around us who are hopeless without Him. In the **tested** and secure name of Jesus I ask these things. Amen.

What impacted me about Christ today...

_____

_____

_____

_____

_____

_____

*Isaiah 28:16-17 So this is what the Sovereign LORD says: "See, I lay a stone in Zion, a tested stone, a precious cornerstone for a **sure foundation**; the one who relies on it will never be stricken with panic. I will make justice the measuring line and righteousness the plumb line; hail will sweep away your refuge, the lie, and water will overflow your hiding place."*

Significance: The LORD JESUS CHRIST has been placed by God as the unshakable understructure of creation, of the Church and of all our lives.

Dear Father,

I continue exalting Jesus that He is the tested stone and precious cornerstone, which is the key building block of His being the **Sure Foundation** upon which His Church is built. I praise the **Sure Foundation** that He is 100% trustworthy, steadfast, certain, unchanging, firm, unmovable and secure. I am very grateful that You designed the Church to be built upon His inexhaustible love, wisdom, mercy, holiness, truth and peace. I rejoice that our salvation and every other part of our lives are **sure** through His divine sacrifice, promises, teachings, prayers, prophesies and powers. Please help me and all other believers to know more and more about the **Sure Foundation**, so we will cement our lives totally to Him, and build straight and true character, values, mindsets, lifestyles and priorities upon Him alone. I pray that we will trust in Him so completely, that we will never be dismayed, regardless of any circumstances which come into our lives. I pray that in this desperate, unsure world in which we live, great numbers of lost people will urgently desire to build their lives on the **Sure Foundation** too. In the unfailingly **sure** name of Jesus I pray these things. Amen.

What impacted me about Christ today...

_____

_____

_____

_____

_____

A God Of Justice

*<u>Isaiah 30:15-18</u> This is what the Sovereign LORD, the Holy One of Israel, says: "In repentance and rest is your salvation, in quietness and trust is your strength, but you would have none of it. You said, 'No, we will flee on horses.' Therefore you will flee! You said, 'We will ride off on swift horses.' Therefore your pursuers will be swift! A thousand will flee at the threat of one; at the threat of five you will all flee away, till you are left like a flagstaff on a mountaintop, like a banner on a hill." Yet the LORD longs to be gracious to you; therefore he will rise up to show you compassion. For the LORD is a **God of justice**. Blessed are all who wait for him!*

Significance: **The LORD JESUS CHRIST enacts perfect justice for His people.**

Dear Father,

I am very grateful that You gave Your beloved Son Jesus the authority to **judge** the world, as He states in His teaching in John 5:27, *"And he [the Father] has given him [the Son] authority to **judge** because he is the Son of Man."* Thank You that Jesus has all Your knowledge, wisdom, under-standing, patience, truth, love, grace, mercy and righteousness to know everything there is to know about every person and circumstance, and to render perfect **justice** with perfect timing. I exalt Jesus that He is the **God of Justice**, and that He desires to be gracious, compassionate, merciful, just, good and wise with all people, without preference to anyone. I praise Him that the **judgments** He makes are all in accordance with all Scripture, and are to draw all people to the fullness of righteousness in Him. I praise Jesus that His motives in enacting **justice** are always pure; He is never disinterested or busy elsewhere; and His plans and purposes are always for our highest and best, and for His great glory. Please help me and all His people to know how great and **just** He is, and to wait for Him with every part of our lives. May the **God of Justice** bring full **justice** to the Church and to all people around the world. In His blessed name I pray these things. Amen.

What impacted me about Christ today...

_____

_____

_____

*Isaiah 33:20-22 Look on Zion, the city of our festivals; your eyes will see Jerusalem, a peaceful abode; a tent that will not be moved; its stakes will never be pulled up, nor any of its ropes broken. There the LORD will be our **Mighty One**. It will be like a place of broad rivers and streams. No galley with oars will ride them, no mighty ship will sail them. For the LORD is our judge, the LORD is our lawgiver, the LORD is our king; it is he who will save us.*

Significance: The LORD JESUS CHRIST has all of the abilities of the Godhead to completely take care of His people.

Dear Father,

I am greatly encouraged and strengthened by this Scripture passage, where the **Mighty One** is the complete caretaker of His people. I rejoice that all the **might**, power, excellence, faithfulness, authority and all the other infinite attributes of the Godhead are vested in Jesus. He is thus the only **One** Who could be this **Mighty One**. I note that some translations of the Bible refer to this name of Jesus as the "Glorious Lord." I rejoice that the **Mighty One**, the Glorious Lord, provides all the cleansing, freedom, defense, love, hope, refreshment and provision His people need. I praise Him that He constantly provides, *"a place of broad streams; a peaceful abode; a tent that will not be moved"* for His people. I shout "Hallelujah" that He is our judge, lawgiver and king, and *"it is he who will save us."* Please help us to have an insatiable desire to know Him, meditate on Him, praise Him, talk about Him and trust every part of our lives to His **might**. And, I pray that You will release the broad streams of Jesus into the lives of great numbers of lost people all around us, so they will be in awe of Him and eagerly receive Him as their Savior and Lord too. All glory and honor to our **Mighty One**, in Whose matchless name I pray these things. Amen.

What impacted me about Christ today...

_____

_____

_____

_____

_____

Isaiah 35:1-2 The desert and the parched land will be glad; the wilderness will rejoice and blossom. Like the crocus, it will burst into bloom; it will rejoice greatly and shout for joy. The glory of Lebanon will be given to it, the splendor of Carmel and Sharon; they will see the glory of the LORD, *the* **splendor of our God.**

Significance: The LORD JESUS CHRIST reveals to the world the magnificence and wonder of Almighty God.

Dear Father,

I rejoice that in the midst of all spiritual and physical *"desert, parched land and wilderness,"* the Lord Jesus is the source of all hope, refreshment, cleansing and restoration. I marvel that in Him all Your magnificence, brilliance, grandeur, grace, love and glory dwells. I resoundingly praise Jesus that He is the amazing excellence of the Godhead. I delight that in all circumstances, at all times, He is the **Splendor of our God**. I pray that I and multitudes of believers today will unite in praising Jesus as King David praised You in Psalm 145:3-5, *"Great is the* LORD *and most worthy of praise; his greatness no one can fathom. One generation commends your works to another; they tell of your mighty acts. They speak of the glorious* **splendor** *of your majesty, and I will meditate on your wonderful works."* Please help us to turn to Him, submit to Him and completely *"live and move and have our being in him"* (Acts 17:28), so there will be an unprecedented *"bursting into bloom," "rejoicing greatly and shouting for joy,"* and releasing of *"the glory of Lebanon and the splendor of Carmel and Sharon"* into the Church and all people in this generation. May the **Splendor of our God** receive all glory and honor. I pray these things in His beautiful name. Amen.

What impacted me about Christ today...

_____

_____

_____

_____

_____

The Way Of Holiness

Isaiah 35:8-10 And a highway will be there; it will be called the Way of Holiness; it will be for those who walk on that Way. The unclean will not journey on it; wicked fools will not go about on it. No lion will be there, nor any ravenous beast; they will not be found there. But only the redeemed will walk there, and those the LORD has rescued will return. They will enter Zion with singing; everlasting joy will crown their heads. Gladness and joy will overtake them, and sorrow and sighing will flee away.

Significance: The LORD JESUS CHRIST laid down His life to create a way that is holy to lead us straight into God's presence.

Dear Father,

I praise Jesus that He is completely **holy**. I exalt Him that He rules, leads and ministers in perfect **holiness**, and that the only **way** I can know You and be reconciled to You, is through the life, death and resurrection of the **Way of Holiness**. I am grateful that one day Jesus will return for me and all people who have received Him as their Savior, and lead them in His eternal **way**, as the prophet declared in Isaiah 52:10, *"The LORD will lay bare his holy arm in the sight of all the nations, and all the ends of the earth will see the salvation of our God."* With all my heart I want to be holy as the **Way of Holiness** is **holy**. I thank You that all spiritual and physical safety and security are in the **Way of Holiness**. I also pray that You will keep me, my family members and all of Christ's other followers always living in the **Way of Holiness**, so that all our thoughts, words and actions are **holy** in Him. I pray that *"gladness and joy will overtake"* us, and that *"sorrow and sighing will flee away"* from us. Please draw many sinners all around us irresistibly toward the **Way of Holiness** so they too might soon be redeemed. I ask these things in Jesus' holy name. Amen.

What impacted me about Christ today...

_____

_____

_____

_____

_____

The Everlasting God

Isaiah 40:27-29 *Why do you complain, Jacob? Why do you say, Israel,
"My way is hidden from the LORD; my cause is disregarded by my God?"
Do you not know? Have you not heard? The LORD is the **everlasting God**,
the Creator of the ends of the earth. He will not grow tired or weary, and
his understanding no one can fathom. He gives strength to the weary and
increases the power of the weak.*

Significance: **The LORD JESUS CHRIST, as God's Son, is the timeless master of all circumstances.**

Dear Father,

I admit that sometimes I question You like the people of Israel did in today's Scripture passage while they were in exile in Babylon. I repent for thinking and saying, *"My way is hidden from the LORD; my cause is disregarded by my God."* Without a doubt, I have heard, and I know for certain, that the Lord Jesus is the **Everlasting God**. I praise Him that He has always been, and always will be, the great and mighty I AM. Glory to Him that there is no One beyond Him or before Him, nor will there be any One after Him. I rejoice that my salvation in Him is **everlasting**, and that His love, goodness, power, majesty, wisdom, patience, mercy and all the rest of His infinite characteristics endure forever! Hallelujah! Nothing is hidden from Him; and my hope in Him is completely secure. I pray that You will reveal much more of the **Everlasting God** to me and to many other believers, so we will completely trust Him in all circumstances and speak of His **everlasting** faithfulness. I pray these things in the strength of His name. Amen.

What impacted me about Christ today...

_____

_____

_____

_____

_____

_____

_____

*Isaiah 40:27-29 Why do you complain, Jacob? Why do you say, Israel,
"My way is hidden from the LORD; my cause is disregarded by my God?"
Do you not know? Have you not heard? The LORD is the everlasting God,
the **Creator of the ends of the earth**. He will not grow tired or weary,
and his understanding no one can fathom. He gives strength to the weary
and increases the power of the weak.*

Significance: The LORD JESUS CHRIST is the architect and builder of the world.

Dear Father,

I praise Jesus that He was with You before the foundation of the earth, and that He has all wisdom, creativity and power. I know, and I have heard, that He is absolutely the **Creator of the Ends of the Earth**. I honor Jesus that all things are in Him, through Him, by Him, for Him, to Him, about Him and under Him. I rejoice that my way is **not** hidden from Him, and my cause **not** disregarded by Him, because He knows everything, He is everywhere, He loves me completely, and He has all authority over everything. I marvel that Jesus will not grow tired or weary, and His understanding no one can fathom! I am often weary and weak, and I thank Him that He gives strength to me and He increases my power. I pray that You will help me and the whole Church to know the all-mighty Jesus so well that we will continually praise Him for **creating** and sustaining the whole earth, and submit every part of our lives to His lordship. I pray that countless more people, to the ends of the earth, will very soon cry out to the **Creator** to be their Savior and Lord too. I ask these things in His name and for His glory. Amen.

What impacted me about Christ today...

_____

_____

_____

_____

_____

_____

_____

My Chosen One

*<u>Isaiah 42:1</u> Here is my servant, whom I uphold, my **chosen one** in whom I delight; I will put my Spirit on him, and he will bring justice to the nations.*

Significance: The **LORD JESUS CHRIST** was chosen before the foundation of the world to be the Savior of the world.

Dear Father,

I praise Jesus that He completely fulfills today's prophetic Scripture. I worship Him that He alone is Your beloved Son, Whom You **chose** before the foundation of the world as the Messiah, Savior, Redeemer and Servant to the world. I can only imagine how much You delight in Him, and I rejoice that You totally uphold Him with Your divine love, wisdom and power. Thank You for providing a number of Scriptures which affirm that Jesus is Your **Chosen One**, including the Apostle Paul's closing words to the Church of Rome in Romans 16:25-27, *"Now to him who is able to establish you in accordance with my gospel, the message I proclaim about Jesus Christ, in keeping with the revelation of the mystery hidden for long ages past, but now revealed and made known through the prophetic writings by the command of the eternal God, so that all Gentiles might come to the obedience that comes from faith—to the only wise God be glory forever through Jesus Christ! Amen."* I marvel at how You powerfully revealed Jesus as Your **Chosen One** when the Spirit descended upon Him after His baptism, and You said from heaven: *"This is my Son, whom I love; with him I am well pleased"* (Matthew 3:17). Please help His people to love the **Chosen One** with all their hearts, souls, minds and strength, and to tell everyone else You put into their lives about Him. May He bring unprecedented redemption and justice to the nations in our day. I pray these things in name of the **Chosen One**. Amen.

What impacted me about Christ today...

_____

_____

_____

_____

_____

A Light For The Gentiles

*Isaiah 49:5-7 And now the LORD says—he who formed me in the womb to be his servant to bring Jacob back to him and gather Israel to himself, for I am honored in the eyes of the LORD and my God has been my strength—he says: "It is too small a thing for you to be my servant to restore the tribes of Jacob and bring back those of Israel I have kept. I will also make you a **light for the Gentiles**, that my salvation may reach to the ends of the earth." This is what the LORD says—the Redeemer and Holy One of Israel—to him who was despised and abhorred by the nation, to the servant of rulers: "Kings will see you and stand up, princes will see and bow down, because of the LORD, who is faithful, the Holy One of Israel, who has chosen you."*

Significance: **The LORD JESUS CHRIST was sent by the Father to be the light of salvation to all earth's peoples.**

Dear Father,

I am very grateful that the One You chose to restore the tribes of Jacob and Israel to Yourself, You also chose to be the glorious **Light for the Gentiles**. I praise Jesus that **He** is the **light** in the midst of darkness and despair Who brings Your *"salvation to the ends of the earth."* It is amazing beyond all imagination that *"to him who was despised and abhorred by the nation [of Israel] . . . Kings will see you [him] and rise up, and princes will see and bow down."* I am thrilled with what the prophet further says about the **Light** in Isaiah 60:2-3, *"See, darkness covers the earth and thick darkness is over the peoples, but the LORD rises upon you and his glory appears over you. Nations will come to your **light**, and kings to the brightness of your dawn."* I am so glad that Jesus' salvation, hope, mercy, love and peace are available for me and anyone else who receives Him as their Savior. Please help me and multitudes of other believers to be faithful conduits of the **Light** to our family members, neighbors, friends, work associates and all others He gives us relationships with. May the people of Israel today receive the **Light** as never before in history. I ask these things in His all-illuminating name. Amen.

What impacted me about Christ today...

_____

_____

_____

*Isaiah 49:24-26 Can plunder be taken from warriors, or captives be rescued from the fierce? But this is what the LORD says: "Yes, captives will be taken from warriors, and plunder retrieved from the fierce; I will contend with those who contend with you, and your children I will save. I will make your oppressors eat their own flesh; they will be drunk on their own blood, as with wine. Then all mankind will know that I, the LORD, am your Savior, your Redeemer, the **Mighty One of Jacob**."*

Significance: The LORD JESUS CHRIST is the great warrior coming out of Israel.

Dear Father,

I exalt the Lord Jesus, the Savior and Redeemer of the world, that He is the awesome **Mighty One of Jacob**. I praise Him that He has all the power and **might** of the Godhead, Who has been the **Mighty One** of all our ancestors; He is the **Mighty One** now; and He will be the **Mighty One** for all eternity to come. I rejoice that He is greater than the devil and **mightier** than all others who try to oppress me and the rest of His followers. He is our Rescuer from their most fierce intentions. I am exceedingly grateful that Jesus the **mighty** Conqueror, continually contends for us, and that He will save our children from spiritual and physical bondage. I say "Hallelujah" that Jesus is our Deliverer and our life. I love how Hebrews 2:14-15 confirms Jesus' **might** in our lives: *"Since the children have flesh and blood, he [Christ] too shared in their humanity so that by his death he might break the power of him who holds the power of death—that is, the devil—and free those who all their lives were held in slavery by their fear of death."* May all His people, and multitudes who are currently lost without Him, freshly know of His supreme **might**, and live wholly under His lordship. I pray these things in the conquering name of the **Mighty One of Jacob**. Amen.

What impacted me about Christ today...

_____

_____

_____

_____

_____

Isaiah 53:1-4, 12 Who has believed our message and to whom has the **arm of the LORD** *been revealed? He grew up before him like a tender shoot, and like a root out of dry ground. He had no beauty or majesty to attract us to him, nothing in his appearance that we should desire him. He was despised and rejected by mankind, a man of suffering, and familiar with pain. Like one from whom people hide their faces he was despised, and we held him in low esteem. Surely he took up our pain and bore our suffering, yet we considered him punished by God, stricken by him, and afflicted. . . . Therefore I will give him a portion among the great, and he will divide the spoils with the strong, because he poured out his life unto death, and was numbered with the transgressors. For he bore the sin of many, and made intercession for the transgressors.*

Significance: **The LORD JESUS CHRIST not only reigns at God's right hand, but is, in a sense, the very arm of God at work among the nations.**

Dear Father,
I am saddened that today's prophecy states that the Jews in Jesus' time on earth would not believe in Him as the Messiah. I am more saddened that many people on earth today still do not believe in Him as Savior and Lord. But, I praise Jesus that He is the **Arm of the Lord**, Who has Your full strength, power, might, rule and justice. I worship Him that He is eternally sovereign over all the people and nations His **arm** created. I also rejoice that even though the **Arm of the Lord** grew up humbly *"like a tender shoot,"* He has all power to save mankind's souls, as Paul says in Romans 1:16, *"For I am not ashamed of the gospel, because it is the power of God for the salvation of everyone who believes: first for the Jew, then for the Gentile."* Oh, thank You so much for revealing that **Jesus is able** to conquer the forces of darkness, raise up and take down the kings of the earth, rule the wind and the waves, heal the sick, achieve victory over death, forgive mankind of our sins, fulfill all Your promises, strengthen the weak, and infinitely more. I repent for the many times I have lacked faith in the **Arm of the Lord**. Please help me and all His followers to become utterly dependent upon Him. I pray these things in His strong name. Amen.

What impacted me about Christ today...

*Isaiah 53:1-4, 12 Who has believed our message and to whom has the arm of the Lord been revealed? He grew up before him like a tender shoot, and like a root out of dry ground. He had no beauty or majesty to attract us to him, nothing in his appearance that we should desire him. He was despised and rejected by mankind, a **man of suffering**, and familiar with pain. Like one from whom people hide their faces he was despised, and we held him in low esteem. Surely he took up our pain and bore our suffering, yet we considered him punished by God, stricken by him, and afflicted. . . . Therefore I will give him a portion among the great, and he will divide the spoils with the strong, because he poured out his life unto death, and was numbered with the transgressors. For he bore the sin of many, and made intercession for the transgressors.*

Significance: The LORD JESUS CHRIST endured incredible suffering so that God might offer all mankind the gift of eternal life.

Dear Father,

I am very grateful that the exalted Son of God left His heavenly glory to become the **Man of Suffering** (Sorrows). I think of what Henry Gariepy says in *"The 100 Portraits of Christ,"* that Christ is: "The Prince of martyrs, the Lord of anguish, the King of **suffering**." My heart aches that the Lord Jesus willingly *"had no beauty or majesty . . . was despised and rejected by men . . . was familiar with **suffering** . . . took up our infirmities . . . carried our sorrows";* and was even *"stricken by God, smitten by him, and afflicted."* Oh, the unimaginable **suffering** and sorrows that He unjustly endured! I love Him so much for the precious spirit in which He bore those **sorrows** for us. I pray that You will help me to join the Apostle Paul in his response to Christ's suffering in Philippians 3:10-11, *"I want to know Christ—yes, to know the power of his resurrection and participation in his **sufferings**, becoming like him in his death, and so, somehow, attaining to the resurrection from the dead."* Please help me to be a clear witness of Him in whatever sufferings I have. I pray these things in the victorious name of the **Man of Sufferings**. Amen.

What impacted me about Christ today...

_____

_____

_____

Pierced For Our Transgressions

*Isaiah 53:4-6 Surely he took up our pain and bore our suffering, yet we considered him punished by God, stricken by him, and afflicted. But he was **pierced for our transgressions**, he was crushed for our iniquities; the punishment that brought us peace was on him, and by his wounds we are healed. We all, like sheep, have gone astray, each of us has turned to our own way; and the LORD has laid on him [Christ] the iniquity of us all.*

Significance: The LORD JESUS CHRIST, so horribly wounded, shed His blood not only for our sins but for the sins of the whole world.

Dear Father,
I want to give my deepest gratitude to Jesus that He came to earth as the completely sinless Son of God to be the One Who is **Pierced for our Transgressions**. I praise Jesus, the blessed Messiah, that He gave up His unlimited power and glory to allow His hands, feet and side to be **pierced** with nails and a spear. I thank Him for allowing Himself to be beaten and otherwise *"crushed"* for my iniquities and the iniquities of all people. I can only imagine the crushing weight of those iniquities that You laid upon Him. I love Him so much for being our substitute, fulfilling our payment, receiving our shame and much more, to pardon us from Your justice, and to make available to us a restored relationship with You. I think of the precious words of Paul in Romans 4:25, *"He was delivered over to death for our sins and was raised to life for our justification."* I rejoice with all my heart that by the wounds Jesus took on for us, all the ways we have gone astray from You are healed when we receive Him as our Savior. Hallelujah! The punishment that was upon Him has brought us everlasting peace. I pray these things in the name of the **Pierced One**. Amen.

What impacted me about Christ today...

_____

_____

_____

_____

_____

My Righteous Servant

*<u>Isaiah 53:7-11</u> He [Jesus] was oppressed and afflicted, yet he did not open his mouth; he was led like a lamb to the slaughter, and as a sheep before its shearers is silent, so he did not open his mouth. By oppression and judgment he was taken away. Yet who of his generation protested? For he was cut off from the land of the living; for the transgression of my people he was punished. He was assigned a grave with the wicked, and with the rich in his death, though he had done no violence, nor was any deceit in his mouth. Yet it was the LORD's will to crush him and cause him to suffer, and though the LORD makes his life an offering for sin, he will see his offspring and prolong his days, and the will of the LORD will prosper in his hand. After he has suffered, he will see the light of life and be satisfied; by his knowledge my **righteous servant** will justify many, and he will bear their iniquities.*

Significance: **The LORD JESUS CHRIST, in humility and obedience to the Father, fully served us by dying for us.**

Dear Father,

I am in awe of the **Righteous Servant**. I bless Jesus that He is the only Person Who is completely **righteous** and completely a **servant**. I exalt Him that He is holy and righteous as You are holy and righteous. I am deeply grateful that You sent Him to earth to **serve** all people through His suffering (a suffering servant). I rejoice that by His supreme knowledge of You, His supreme knowledge of His role of suffering, and His supreme knowledge of the condition of all people, He is justifying countless numbers of people for all of eternity! I rejoice that Your perfect will is magnificently *"prospering in his hand,"* and that He is absolutely satisfied that His suffering is bearing the fruit that You and He knew it would before the beginning of time. I am reminded of Isaiah 52:13 which confirms that Jesus fulfilled the role You gave Him as the **Righteous Servant**: *"See, my servant will act wisely; he will be raised and lifted up and highly exalted."* I pray that You will put a consuming passion in me and in great numbers of other believers to intimately know the **Righteous Servant**, so we will become devoted servants in His image. I ask these things in His righteous name. Amen.

What impacted me about Christ today...

A Witness To The Peoples

*Isaiah 55:3-5 Give ear and come to me; listen, that you may live. I will make an everlasting covenant with you, my faithful love promised to David. See, I have made him a **witness to the peoples**, a ruler and commander of the peoples. Surely you will summon nations you know not, and nations you do not know will come running to you, because of the LORD your God, the Holy One of Israel, for he has endowed you with splendor.*

Significance: **The LORD JESUS CHRIST reveals the entire nature of God and the whole purpose of God to all who have eyes to see.**

Dear Father,

I want to come to You and hear You completely, so that my *"soul may live"* in all of what another translation calls Your certain and *"sure mercies."* I am exceedingly grateful that You made an everlasting covenant with me and all believers that is marvelously fulfilled through King David's descendent, Your beloved Son. I rejoice that You sent Jesus as Your perfect **Witness to the Peoples**. I praise Him that He has been with You for all eternity and knows You fully, so He is the only One Who can be an absolutely truthful **eyewitness** about all You are through His words and actions. I love how Hebrews 1:1-2 confirms that You speak (**witness**) through Jesus: *"In the past God spoke to our ancestors through the prophets at many times and in various ways, but in these last days he has spoken to us by his Son, whom he appointed heir of all things, and through whom also he made the universe."* I honor Jesus that He was willing to lay down His life for **witnessing** the whole truth about You and about Himself as Messiah and King. I pray that I and all of Jesus' other followers will receive all He has **witnessed**, and will devote ourselves to knowing Him, worshiping Him, loving Him, submitting to Him, and joyfully **witnessing** about Him to one another and everyone else You bring into our lives. May the Holy Spirit open the hearts and minds of countless people to His truths now. I pray these things in the faithful name of the **Witness to the Peoples**. Amen.

What impacted me about Christ today...

_____

_____

_____

_____

A Ruler And Commander Of The Peoples

*Isaiah 55:3-5 Give ear and come to me; listen, that you may live. I will make an everlasting covenant with you, my faithful love promised to David. See, I have made him a witness to the peoples, a **ruler and commander of the peoples**. Surely you will summon nations you know not, and nations you do not know will come running to you, because of the LORD your God, the Holy One of Israel, for he has endowed you with splendor.*

Significance: The LORD JESUS CHRIST is the Commander-in-Chief Who triumphantly leads His redeemed ones from every people group of the earth.

Dear Father,

I eagerly come to You and listen, so that my soul may live according to Your highest and best for me. I exalt Jesus, Whom You sent to earth as the divine **Ruler and Commander of the Peoples**. I praise Him that He has all the eternal power, wisdom, courage, truth, authority, knowledge and righteousness of the Godhead to be the supreme **Ruler and Commander of the Peoples**! I continue to hold onto the magnificent proclamation Jesus made about Himself in Matthew 28:18-20a, *"All authority in heaven and on earth has been given to me. Therefore go and make disciples of all nations, baptizing them in the name of the Father and of the Son and of the Holy Spirit, and teaching them to obey everything I have **commanded** you."* I rejoice that Jesus perfectly **rules** and leads His followers in knowing You intimately, being totally dependent upon You, being holy, giving His life for others, serving out of compassion, speaking and living the truth, having sacrificial love and unquenchable hope, victoriously rising from death to life, and possessing wisdom and courage. I also rejoice that His **commands** are sure and will result in overwhelming victory for those who obey Him. I pray that ALL His people will unconditionally follow and obey the supreme **Ruler and Commander of the Peoples**. I pray that You will convincingly summon the hopeless, rulerless unsaved people all around us to Him. In the splendid name of Jesus I ask these things. Amen.

What impacted me about Christ today...

_____

_____

*Isaiah 57:14-15 And it will be said: "Build up, build up, prepare the road! Remove the obstacles out of the way of my people." For this is what the **high and exalted One** says—he who lives forever, whose name is holy: "I live in a high and holy place, but also with the one who is contrite and lowly in spirit, to revive the spirit of the lowly and to revive the heart of the contrite."*

Significance: The LORD JESUS CHRIST was exalted by His Father to the place of highest honor and supremacy in the universe.

Dear Father,

Once again I grieve with the prophet Isaiah that the people of Israel had given themselves to idols and turned away from a relationship of love and obedience with You. But, I am very grateful that You reminded Isaiah that the **High and Exalted** (Lofty) **One** is always willing to *"remove the obstacles out of the way of my people,"* so they can return to Him. I praise Jesus that He is the **High and Exalted One** for all His people, now and forever. I exalt Him Whom You raised from the dead and seated at Your *"right hand in the heavenly realms, far above all rule and authority, power and dominion, and every name that can be invoked, not only in the present age but also in the one to come. And God placed all things under his feet and appointed him to be head over everything for the church, which is his body, the fullness of him who fills everything in every way"* (Eph. 1:20b-23). I praise Him that He lives in and rules the highest and most exalted place, but He also lives in wonderful and continuous intimacy with every believer *"who is contrite and lowly in spirit."* What a wonderful Savior and Lord He is to us. I pray that You will please help me and multitudes of His other believers to be in complete awe of Him as the **High and Exalted One**, submit every part of our lives to Him, and trust Him to remove all the obstacles in our relationship with Him. And, I pray that great numbers of unsaved people will very soon receive this One Who is great over all other gods. I pray everything in the matchless name of Jesus. Amen.

What impacted me about Christ today...

_____

_____

*Isaiah 57:14-15 And it will be said: "Build up, build up, prepare the road! Remove the obstacles out of the way of my people." For this is what the high and exalted One says—he who lives forever, whose name is **holy**: "I live in a high and holy place, but also with the one who is contrite and lowly in spirit, to revive the spirit of the lowly and to revive the heart of the contrite."*

Significance: The LORD JESUS CHRIST is the embodiment of all the purity and righteousness of God.

Dear Father,

I bow before Jesus, Who lives forever and Whose name is **Holy**. I am in awe of Jesus as I think of some of the other words that help me understand His limitless **holiness**: consecrated, sacred, hallowed, sanctified, divine and pure. I exalt Jesus that He alone is the source and the finisher of all of those attributes, and much more. All glory and honor to Him. I exalt Him that He lives in a high and **holy** place, yet You sent Him to earth to reveal the magnificent **holiness** of the Godhead, and to give His life that I and all others who receive Him as our Savior might be **holy** in Him! I repent that, like the people of Israel to whom Isaiah spoke today's Scripture passage, I tend to be proud and follow unholy ways. I pray You will cleanse me of every obstacle that is keeping me from being contrite and lowly in spirit, and of all unholy thoughts, words and actions. There is nothing I need and want more than to live completely in Jesus, and to be fully revived in my spirit and heart. I further pray that You will put a compelling desire in the whole Church to intimately know the **holiness** of Jesus, and to become more and more holy as He is **Holy**. May the unsaved people all around us who are desperate to be released from unholy bondage into eternal life in the **Holy** One, turn to Him before it is too late. I pray these things in His blessed name. Amen.

What impacted me about Christ today...

_____

_____

_____

_____

_____

*Isaiah 60:19-20 The sun will no more be your light by day, nor will the brightness of the moon shine on you, for the LORD will be your **everlasting light**, and your God will be your glory. Your sun will never set again, and your moon will wane no more; the LORD will be your **everlasting light**, and your days of sorrow will end.*

Significance: The LORD JESUS CHRIST shines with the full brilliance of God, helping us to see all things through His eyes.

Dear Father,
I delight in the full assurance that Jesus is the **Everlasting Light** of everyone who receives Him as their Savior. I rejoice that for all eternity, He is far superior to all other forces in the universe. I praise Him that He is infinitely radiant and brilliant, beyond our imagination; He will never diminish; He consumes all darkness and sorrow; He is the perfect provider; and He illumines and reveals all Your righteousness, joy, truth, peace, love, hope and mercy. I shout, "Hallelujah," that we can live without limits in the **Everlasting Light**, and be enveloped in all of Him. I am thrilled that we can draw closer and closer to Him, to see more and more clearly the glorious Person He is. I pray that You will help me, my family members and all of His other followers to live fully in the **Light** now. May all darkness in us be exposed and burned away by Him completely, so that we will become dependent upon Him for all our sustenance. I am so grateful that Jesus is all our hope and joy. I pray that unprecedented numbers of lost people we know will see the **Everlasting Light** in us, and be irresistibly drawn to Him to receive all of Him too. In His splendid name I ask these things. Amen.

What impacted me about Christ today...

_____

_____

_____

_____

_____

_____

_____

*<u>Isaiah 63:7-9</u> I will tell of the kindnesses of the LORD, the deeds for which he is to be praised, according to all the LORD has done for us—yes, the many good things he has done for Israel, according to his compassion and many kindnesses. He said, "Surely they are my people, children who will be true to me"; and so he became their Savior. In all their distress he too was distressed, and the **angel of his presence** saved them. In his love and mercy he redeemed them; he lifted them up and carried them all the days of old.*

Significance: The LORD JESUS CHRIST is the Word Who was with God and is God, and is Heaven's Ambassador from God to the nations.

Dear Father,

I am glad that some of the ancient Jewish people realized that the many good and kind deeds You had done for the house of Israel were because of Your great compassion. I rejoice that after they had suffered many generations for their hard hearts, You empathized with their distress, and sent Your beloved Son as the **Angel of His** (Your) **Presence** to demonstrate Your enduring love for them. I like how one person describes Christ being the **Angel of His** (Your) **Presence** as His being the "**Angel** Who stands before His (Your) face continually." What an amazing reality it is that Jesus stands before Your face continually, and was Your faithful messenger of love, compassion, kindness, mercy and redemption to the Jews 2000 years ago, and is to all who come to Him today. I am very saddened that many of the early Jews who the **Angel of His Presence** came to save rejected and crucified Him, and that billions of people of all languages, nations and ethnicities still reject Him. He is the only Savior of the world, and we all desperately need Him. I pray that His followers across the globe today will exalt Him for all He is, and place every part of our lives in His hands to carry us all of our days. Please inspire each of us to tell many lost people we know about the merciful **Angel of His Presence** so they might very soon receive Him as their Redeemer too. I pray these things in Jesus' name. Amen.

What impacted me about Christ today...

_____

_____

*Isaiah 64:6-9 All of us have become like one who is unclean, and all our righteous acts are like filthy rags; we all shrivel up like a leaf, and like the wind our sins sweep us away. No one calls on your name or strives to lay hold of you; for you have hidden your face from us and have given us over to our sins. Yet you, LORD, are our Father. We are the clay, you are the **potter**; we are all the work of your hand. Do not be angry beyond measure, LORD; do not remember our sins forever. Oh, look upon us, we pray, for we are all your people.*

Significance: **The LORD JESUS CHRIST, as Lord of all, shapes the lives and destinies of people and nations, especially those who are His own.**

Dear Father,

I am so glad that Jesus is the **Potter** of the whole world, and I am the work of His skilled, loving, creative and perfect hand. I marvel how Jesus, the Lord and Master of the universe, Who has all the power and wisdom to create and rule everything, foreknew me, fashioned me with perfect precision in His image, and has good plans for me. I confess that sometimes I am like the people of Israel in being unclean, having unrighteous acts, not calling on Your name nor striving to lay hold of You. I humbly pray that You will do whatever is necessary in my life to make me the most usable clay for the **Potter**. I submit wholly to His molding, fashioning, purifying, firing and all other steps He knows I need. I want to become the pure vessel He desires, so I can best serve Him and others. I sing some of Adelaide Pollard's "Have Thine Own Way," for myself and for all the **Potter's** followers: "(verse 1) Have Thine own way, Lord! Have Thine own way! Thou art the Potter; I am the clay. Mold me and make me, After Thy will, While I am waiting, yielded and still. (verse 4) Have Thine own way, Lord! Have Thine own way! Hold o'er my being, Absolute sway! Fill with Thy Spirit, Till all shall see, Christ only, always, Living in me. " Please help us be fresh, cleansed clay in His expert hands. We are His people for His glory. I pray all these things in His merciful name. Amen.

What impacted me about Christ today...

_____

_____

*Jeremiah 8:18-22 You who are my Comforter in sorrow, my heart is faint within me. Listen to the cry of my people from a land far away: "Is the LORD not in Zion? Is her King no longer there?" Why have they aroused my anger with their images, with their worthless foreign idols? The harvest is past, the summer has ended, and we are not saved. Since my people are crushed, I am crushed: I mourn, and horror grips me. Is there no **balm in Gilead**? Is there no physician there? Why then is there no healing for the wound of my people?*

Significance: The LORD JESUS CHRIST brings full restoration and healing for the body, soul and spirit to us from the Father.

Dear Father,

I join the prophet Jeremiah in being crushed that so many people have chosen to be *"far away"* from You spiritually. *"I mourn, and horror grips me."* But, I rejoice that Jesus is the **Balm in Gilead**, Whom You sent to save lost and dying people from their sin. I think of how Gilead was, for many years, a region that was known to produce **balms** and other fragrant and healing products. I praise Jesus that **He** is the fragrant oil that all people who are desperate for healing from their sin and sorrow can receive. I bless Jesus that through His life, death and resurrection He is the all-sufficient remedy that can be poured out on the spiritually needy to give them life, and that life abundantly. I pray that I and all believers will be so immersed in the **Balm in Gilead** that we will be able: *"to grasp how wide and long and high and deep is the love of Christ, and to know this love that surpasses knowledge—that we may be filled to the measure of all the fullness of God"* (Eph. 3:18b-19). Please urge us to tell all the lost people in our lives about our loving, saving and healing Jesus. May many of them believe that He is the only medicine that heals the soul and the body, and eagerly receive Him as their **Balm in Gilead**. In Jesus' healing name I pray these things. Amen.

What impacted me about Christ today...

_____

_____

_____

Jeremiah 17:13 L<small>ORD</small>, *you are the hope of Israel; all who forsake you will be put to shame. Those who turn away from you will be written in the dust because they have forsaken the* L<small>ORD</small>, *the **spring of living water**.*

S**ignificance: The LORD JESUS CHRIST quenches the deepest thirst of all who "drink" of Him by faith.**

Dear Father,

I am forever grateful that the Lord Jesus is the hope of Israel, and of all people who put their trust in Him. I never want to forsake Him or turn away from Him Who is the eternal **Spring of Living Water**. I marvel that in Him is all Your comfort, cleansing, purity, healing, love, saving mercy and peace. I delight that He is the cool, clear, ever-flowing, ever-refreshing source and sustainer of all life. I love Him because my unquenchable spiritual thirst can only be satisfied by Him. Please forgive me for all the times I have tried to be satisfied by anything or anyone else. As I sing the first verse of "Come Thou Fount of Every Blessing" by Robert Robinson, I feel like I am being immersed in the **Spring of Living Water**: "Come thou Fount of every blessing, Tune my heart to sing Thy grace. Streams of mercy, never ceasing, Call for songs of loudest praise. Teach me some melodious sonnet, Sung by flaming tongues above. Praise the mount! I'm fixed upon it, Mount of God's unchanging love." I pray that You will strongly urge me and the rest of Jesus' followers to joyfully speak to one another about the wonders of the **Spring of Living Water**, and that we will overflow about Him to the many others we know who have not yet received Him. In the refreshing name of Jesus I ask these things. Amen.

What impacted me about Christ today...

_____

_____

_____

_____

_____

_____

_____

*Jeremiah 32:17-19a Ah, **Sovereign LORD**, you have made the heavens and the earth by your great power and outstretched arm. Nothing is too hard for you. You show love to thousands but bring the punishment for the parents' sins into the laps of their children after them. Great and mighty God, whose name is the LORD Almighty, great are your purposes and mighty are your deeds.*

Significance: The LORD JESUS CHRIST has no limits as He accomplishes the will of the Father.

Dear Father,

I rejoice that even though the prophet Jeremiah lacked full understanding of some of Your ways with the people of Israel, he was certain that he could depend upon Your commands and Your power. With that same assurance, I am in awe of Your Son, the **Sovereign Lord** Who *"made the heavens and the earth, by your [His] great power and outstretched arm."* I praise Him that He completely fulfills all definitions of "**sovereign**" and "**lord**": "monarch, ruler or permanent head of a state, one who exercises supreme authority, person of high rank, and master and owner." I worship Him, that He is the royal, all-powerful, preeminent, indisputable, most excellent, **Lord Jehovah**. I honor Him that nothing is too hard for Him, and that He fulfills what the writer said about You in Psalm 71:5-6, *"For you have been my hope, **Sovereign LORD**, my confidence since my youth. From birth I have relied on you; you brought me forth from my mother's womb. I will ever praise you."* I pray that Your Spirit will convict me and all of Jesus' followers of the many ways we take His **sovereignty** for granted, and cause us to repent and to devote ourselves to knowing and trusting Him. I pray all these things in the name of the One and Only **Sovereign Lord**. Amen.

What impacted me about Christ today...

_____

_____

_____

_____

_____

MAY

Jeremiah 32:17-19a Ah, Sovereign LORD, you have made the heavens and the earth by your great power and outstretched arm. Nothing is too hard for you. You show love to thousands but bring the punishment for the parents' sins into the laps of their children after them. **Great and mighty God**, *whose name is the LORD Almighty, great are your purposes and mighty are your deeds.*

Significance: The LORD JESUS CHRIST is the highest One in all ways, and His purposes and deeds fill the heavens and the earth.

Dear Father,

I worship Jesus, the **Great and Mighty God**. I am again reminded of what Paul says in Colossians 1:19, that You are pleased to have all Your fullness dwell in Jesus. I can barely imagine the boundless **fullness of the greatness and mightiness** that dwells in Jesus. Hallelujah! He alone is all-**great** and all-**mighty**, now and forever! I am in awe of the inexhaustible **greatness** of Jesus' love, wisdom, justice, grace, authority, holiness, leadership and every other aspect of His being. I further praise Him that He is the LORD **Almighty**, Whose purposes are **great** and deeds are **mighty**— especially the saving of mankind's souls from the kingdom of darkness, and His absolute lordship of the heavens and the earth! Please "stir up" me and countless other believers to continually worship the **Great and Mighty God**; devote ourselves to knowing all we possibly can of His incomparable **greatness** and **might**; trust Him completely; speak about His **greatness** and **might** to everyone we have relationships with; and pray for His **greatness** and **might** to be manifested in every part of our families, congregations, communities and nation. Oh Father, please reveal to our Christian youth how great and mighty Jesus is! I pray these things in His incomparable name. Amen.

What impacted me about Christ today...

_____

_____

_____

_____

_____

*Jeremiah 50:6-7 My people have been lost sheep; their shepherds have led them astray and caused them to roam on the mountains. They wandered over mountain and hill and forgot their own **resting place**. Whoever found them devoured them; their enemies said, "We are not guilty, for they sinned against the LORD, their verdant pasture, the LORD, the hope of their ancestors."*

Significance: The LORD JESUS CHRIST opens up His heart to us, and invites us to abide in Him and rest in Him.

Dear Father,
I am saddened that we, Your people, are often lost, and we spend much of our lives wandering around trying to find peace, joy, hope, rest, comfort, satisfaction and relief apart from depending upon You. At the same time, I am deeply grateful that You have given us our own perfect **Resting Place**, the Lord Jesus. I pray we will wholly receive the invitation He gives in Matthew 11:28-30 to all His followers: *"Come to me, all you who are weary and burdened, and I will give you rest. Take my yoke upon you and learn from me, for I am gentle and humble in heart, and you will find **rest** for your souls. For my yoke is easy and my burden is light."* Glory to Jesus that He has always had ALL the strength, love and other abilities to be the **place** of complete **rest** for our souls and bodies. May we joyfully sing together "My Faith Has Found A Resting Place," by Eliza Hewitt: (verse 1) "My faith has found a resting place, Not in device or creed; I trust the ever living One, His wounds for me shall plead. (chorus) I need no other argument, I need no other plea, It is enough that Jesus died, And that He died for me." Please help us to **never** again be led astray from Him by anything or anyone, and to **never** forget Him or roam away from Him. I fervently pray that in this world of turmoil and pain, many millions of unsaved, eternally lost sheep will give their lives to the **Resting Place** too. I ask all these things in His **restful** name. Amen.

What impacted me about Christ today...

_____

_____

_____

_____

*Jeremiah 50:6-7 My people have been lost sheep; their shepherds have led them astray and caused them to roam on the mountains. They wandered over mountain and hill and forgot their own resting place. Whoever found them devoured them; their enemies said, "We are not guilty, for they sinned against the LORD, their **verdant pasture**, the LORD, the hope of their ancestors."*

Significance: The LORD JESUS CHRIST is God's pure, perfect and prosperous habitat for all people who turn to Him.

Dear Father,

I love to think about Jesus as the **Verdant Pasture** for me and for all who have received Him as our Lord. I am so grateful that He far exceeds a dictionary definition of **verdant pasture**: "a place where animals feed or graze on lush, green growth." I praise Jesus that every characteristic, attribute, word, action, promise and command of His is **verdant**, or lush and full of life. What a wonderful privilege we followers of His have to **pasture** in Him, as it says in Psalm 100:3, *"Know that the LORD is God. It is he who made us, and we are his; we are his people, the sheep of his **pasture**,"* and in Psalm 95:7, *"He is our God and we are the people of his **pasture**, the flock under his care."* I Worship Him that He is our all-sufficient hope, as He has been for all of our ancestors in the faith. I am very sorry that the people of Israel, and so many of His followers today (me included), have at some time turned away from Him and been *"devoured"* by our enemies. I repent for our sins against the **Verdant Pasture**, and pray that You will cleanse us and keep us constantly living in His ceaseless righteousness, justice, peace, rest, security, provision and love. I pray that You will help many unsaved people in our spheres of influence to become completely dissatisfied with the false pastures they have been depending upon, so they can find refreshingly **verdant** life in Jesus. I pray these things in His hope-filled name. Amen.

What impacted me about Christ today...

_____

_____

_____

_____

_____

*Jeremiah 51:17-19 Everyone is senseless and without knowledge; every goldsmith is shamed by his idols. The images he makes are a fraud; they have no breath in them. They are worthless, the objects of mockery; when their judgment comes, they will perish. He who is the **Portion of Jacob** is not like these, for he is the Maker of all things, including the people of his inheritance—the LORD Almighty is his name.*

Significance: The LORD JESUS CHRIST is the full supply for all of the needs of God's people.

Dear Father,

I honor Jesus that He is far beyond all others who have ruled the people of Israel, and anywhere else in the world. I praise Him that He is *"the Maker of all things, including the people of his inheritance."* I exalt Him that He alone is the glorious **Portion of Jacob**, and *"the LORD Almighty."* I am totally in awe of Him that He has all power, all wisdom, all grace and mercy, all righteousness, and all other attributes as the full **Portion** of all people who seek Him! I am exceedingly grateful that He is willing and able to receive me and all others who have been senseless, without knowledge, and shamed by idols when we come to Him for His mercy and redemptive power. Father, I pray that You will cleanse us from all worthless influences that have falsely claimed to be our **portion**, and help us to live completely in the **Portion of Jacob**. I pray that we will follow Jeremiah's words in Lamentations 3:22-24 with all of our hearts: *"Because of the LORD's great love we are not consumed, for his compassions never fail. They are new every morning; great is your faithfulness. I say to myself, 'The LORD is my **portion**; therefore I will wait for him.'"* As an old song says, "He's every-thing to me." I ask these things in His blessed name. Amen.

What impacted me about Christ today...

_____

_____

_____

_____

_____

_____

*Daniel 2:19-23 During the night the mystery was revealed to Daniel in a vision. Then Daniel praised the God of heaven and said: "Praise be to the name of God for ever and ever; wisdom and power are his. He changes times and seasons; he deposes kings and raises up others. He gives wisdom to the wise and knowledge to the discerning. He reveals deep and hidden things; he knows what lies in darkness, and light dwells with him. I thank and praise you, **God of my ancestors**: You have given me wisdom and power, you have made known to me what we asked of you, you have made known to us the dream of the king."*

Significance: The LORD JESUS CHRIST, as the second Person of the eternal Godhead, was involved in God's people's lives from the beginning.

Dear Father,

I am excited to think about how Your Son, Jesus, ultimately fulfills all that Daniel is giving You praise and gratitude for in today's Scripture passage. I praise Jesus that all wisdom and power are in Him. I am grateful that He gives all wisdom, knowledge and revelation to those whom He chooses, and He causes the rise and fall of all rulers according to His perfect will. I worship Him that all light dwells in Him, and I honor Him that all of creation depends upon His authority, mercy, love, justice, understanding, goodness and holiness. I exalt Him that He has always been the faithful **God of My Ancestors**, and that I can completely trust His unchanging character and abilities. I am reminded of verses 54-55 of the praise that Jesus' mother, Mary, sang in Luke 1: *"He has helped his servant Israel, remembering to be merciful to Abraham and his descendents forever, just as he promised our **ancestors**."* I join the millions of our Christian forefathers and mothers in thanking and praising the **God of My Ancestors** for all He is and all He does! I pray that I and a growing number of believers today will abandon ourselves to Him as Daniel did, and that He will reveal deep and hidden things to us, and draw us into His marvelous light. Please irresistibly draw many unsaved and hopeless people to the **God of My Ancestors** too. I pray these things in His excellent name. Amen.

What impacted me about Christ today...

Daniel 4:37 Now I, Nebuchadnezzar, praise and exalt and glorify the **King of heaven**, *because everything he does is right and all his ways are just. And those who walk in pride he is able to humble.*

Significance: The LORD JESUS CHRIST rules from the highest place in the universe.

Dear Father,
I praise and exalt and glorify Jesus, Whom You have crowned **King of Heaven** forever. I honor Jesus, the **King** of all the vast domain He created in heaven, on earth and under the earth. I joyfully sing the first two stanzas of "Praise, My Soul, the **King of Heaven**" that Henry Lyte wrote from Psalm 103 to praise **King** Jesus: "Praise, my soul, the **King of heaven**; To His feet your tribute bring. Ransomed, healed, restored, forgiven, Who like me His praise should sing: Praise Him, praise Him, Praise Him, praise Him, Praise the everlasting **King**. Praise Him for His grace and favor, To our fathers in distress. Praise Him still the same as ever, Slow to chide, and swift to bless. Alleluia! Alleluia! Glorious in His faithfulness." As King Nebuchadnezzar did, I humbly acknowledge that everything the **King of Heaven** does is right and all His ways are just. I pray that the Holy Spirit will cleanse me, my family members and all believers of all pride and vanity. I earnestly plead that the Spirit will convict believers around the world of everything we have been exalting above the **King of Heaven**, so that we will repent, and devote ourselves to continually proclaiming His spectacular greatness and our total dependency upon Him. He is worthy of all praise and adoration. In His majestic name I ask these things. Amen.

What impacted me about Christ today...

_____

_____

_____

_____

_____

_____

*<u>Daniel 7:8-10</u> While I [Daniel] was thinking about the horns, there before me was another horn, a little one, which came up among them; and three of the first horns were uprooted before it. This horn had eyes like the eyes of a human being and a mouth that spoke boastfully. As I looked, thrones were set in place, and the **Ancient of Days** took his seat. His clothing was as white as snow; the hair of his head was white like wool. His throne was flaming with fire, and its wheels were all ablaze. A river of fire was flowing, coming out from before him. Thousands upon thousands attended him; ten thousand times ten thousand stood before him. The court was seated, and the books were opened.*

Significance: **The LORD JESUS CHRIST, is God in the flesh, the Lord of history, Whose kingdom will have no end.**

Dear Father,

I am profoundly in awe of the Lord Jesus Christ, Who is the **Ancient of Days**. I praise Him that He has existed for all eternity; He is timeless and ageless. I rejoice that His kingdom has no end, and that no empires or rulers are able to withstand or overcome the blazing fire of His absolute judgment. I revere Him for the authority You have given Him to judge, as He states in John 5:22-23a, *"Moreover, the Father judges no one, but has entrusted all judgment to the Son, that all may honor the Son just as they honor the Father."* I join the vast multitudes that Daniel prophesies will one day *"**attend**"* the **Ancient of Days** and *"**stand before him**,"* and that John proclaims in Revelation 5:11-12 will soon acknowledge His greatness: *"Then I looked and heard the voice of many angels, numbering thousands upon thousands, and ten thousand times ten thousand. They encircled the throne and the living creatures and the elders. In a loud voice they were saying: 'Worthy is the Lamb, who was slain, to receive power and wealth and wisdom and strength and honor and glory and praise!'"* As I bow down before the exalted **Ancient of Days**, I pray that unprecedented numbers of His people around the world today will humble themselves before Him. I pray these things in His esteemed name. Amen.

What impacted me about Christ today...

_____

_____

_____

Daniel 9:24 *Seventy sevens are decreed for your people and your holy city to finish transgression, to put an end to sin, to atone for wickedness, to bring in everlasting righteousness, to seal up vision and prophecy and to anoint the* ***Most Holy*** *Place.*

Significance: The LORD JESUS CHRIST has established God's standard of righteous perfection, the fulfillment of the Law.

Dear Father,

I exalt the Lord Jesus Christ, Who fulfills the ministry of the Old Testament **Holy** of **Holies**. All hail to Jesus, the Messiah, that He is the **Most Holy**, in Whom dwells all Your holiness and righteousness. I honor Him that He cannot be moved, improved or defeated, so our righteousness in Him is **holy**, steadfast and complete! Thank You that You anointed Him to overthrow the works of evil, break the power of cancelled sin, and set up His kingdom of everlasting righteousness! I love to meditate on the reality that Jesus came to *"lead captivity captive"* (Ephesians 4:8) in Him, and to permanently seal up the enemy of our souls. I join the scene of praise in Rev. 4:8, which acknowledges His victory of absolute **holiness**: *"Each of the four living creatures had six wings and was covered with eyes all around, even under its wings. Day and night they never stop saying:* ***'Holy, holy, holy*** *is the Lord God Almighty, who was, and is, and is to come.'"* I pray that the **Most Holy** will govern every part of my life and His whole Church. May many unsaved people around us become acutely aware that they too can receive cleansing from their transgressions, and cry out to Him for freedom. I eagerly look forward to the highest revelation of His **holiness** in the consummation of all things. In His **holy** name I pray these things. Amen.

What impacted me about Christ today...

_____

_____

_____

_____

_____

*Joel 3:14-16 Multitudes, multitudes in the valley of decision! For the day of the LORD is near in the valley of decision. The sun and moon will be darkened, and the stars no longer shine. The LORD will roar from Zion and thunder from Jerusalem; the earth and the heavens will tremble. But the LORD will be a refuge for his people, a **stronghold for the people of Israel**.*

Significance: The LORD JESUS CHRIST is God's ultimate protection for His own in times of judgment.

Dear Father,

I am exceedingly grateful that I can have complete faith and trust in Jesus at the time of final judgment, and right at this very moment as well, because He is my One and Only refuge and **Stronghold for the People of Israel**. As I read scores of passages in the Bible about His might and authority, I am convinced that He is the unconquerable **Stronghold for the People of Israel** (and for me and all His followers). I am especially assured by the "Great Commandment" He gave His early disciples in Matthew 28:18-20, *"Then Jesus came to them and said, 'All authority in heaven and on earth has been given to me. Therefore go and make disciples of all nations, baptizing them in the name of the Father and of the Son and of the Holy Spirit, and teaching them to obey everything I have commanded you. And surely I am with you always, to the very end of the age.'"* Hallelujah! Our salvation and our hope are in Jesus, the **Stronghold for the People of Israel**. I pray that the Christian Church of the world, and all Messianic believers in Israel and everywhere else today, will proclaim Him as their **Stronghold**. I pray that many multitudes of people, who would be eternally doomed if they were to face the valley of decision today, will decide to receive Him before that happens. In the **strong** name of Jesus I ask these things. Amen.

What impacted me about Christ today...

_____

_____

_____

_____

_____

*Amos 9:5-6 The Lord, the LORD Almighty—**he who touches the earth and it melts**, and all who live in it mourn; the whole land rises like the Nile, then sinks like the river of Egypt; he builds his lofty palace in the heavens and sets its foundation on the earth; he calls for the waters of the sea and pours them out over the face of the land—the LORD is his name.*

Significance: **The LORD JESUS CHRIST will one day bring down God's judgments upon the whole earth, especially on those who have refused Him.**

Dear Father,

I am sorry that the people of Israel were refusing to turn from their evil ways during Amos' time. I am in awe that You appointed the Lord Jesus to administer justice to His people during that era, and for all time. I revere Him for the many ways His omnipotence is described throughout the Book of Amos, like Amos 4:13, *"He who forms the mountains, who creates the wind, and who reveals his thoughts to mankind, who turns dawn to darkness, and treads the heights of the earth—the Lord God Almighty is his name."* I praise Him that today's name, **He Who Touches the Earth and it Melts**, is one of Amos' most fearsome names or attributes of the Lord Jesus. All glory and honor to the One Who can **touch any part of the earth and cause it to melt** in judgment, or do anything else He determines. I exalt the almighty creator and judge of the universe. I pray that You will continually remind me and Christ's other followers about His vast Lordship, so that we will repent of all confidence we have had in ourselves, and give our bodies, minds, souls and strength wholly to Him. At the same time, I pray that He will touch huge numbers of unsaved people everywhere with His redeeming love and power, and that they will quickly turn from refusing Him and being subject to melting under His eternal judgment. I pray these things in His almighty name. Amen.

What impacted me about Christ today...

_____

_____

_____

_____

_____

Micah 4:6-8 *"In that day," declares the LORD, "I will gather the lame; I will assemble the exiles and those I have brought to grief. I will make the lame my remnant, those driven away a strong nation. The LORD will rule over them in Mount Zion from that day and forever. As for you,* **watchtower of the flock,** *stronghold of Daughter Zion, the former dominion will be restored to you; kingship will come to Daughter Jerusalem."*

Significance: The LORD JESUS CHRIST is a caring shepherd Who never ceases to watch and protect those who belong to Him.

Dear Father,

I am grateful to You that the people of Israel, and all people around the world who have received Jesus as their Savior, have the wonderful promise of Him caring for us as the **Watchtower of the Flock**. I rejoice that we are the beloved sheep whom He gave His life for on the cross, so that we can have eternal life in Him. I exalt Him that His inexhaustible power, love, mercy, wisdom, compassion, peace and nourishment are constantly available to protect us from all our enemies and meet all of our needs, even when we are too feeble and broken to ask. I praise the **Watchtower of the Flock** that He is gigantically high and has perfect vision, so He is continually **"watching"** out for us, and He knows precisely what our needs are. I praise Him that He is all-wise to know exactly when and how to provide the shelter, rest and defense to all who are *"weary and burdened"* (Matthew 11:28). I am thrilled that we have the complete assurance of living in the dominion of His kingship forever. I pray that You will build a complete reliance upon the **Watchtower of the Flock** within me and multitudes of His other sheep. All our hope is in Him. I pray these things in His restoring name. Amen.

What impacted me about Christ today...

_____

_____

_____

_____

_____

*Micah 5:1-5a Marshal your troops now, city of troops, for a siege is laid against us. They will strike Israel's ruler on the cheek with a rod. But you, O Bethlehem Ephrathah, though you are small among the clans of Judah, out of you will come for me one who will be **ruler over Israel**, whose origins are from of old, from ancient times. Therefore Israel will be abandoned until the time when she who is in labor bears a son, and the rest of his brothers return to join the Israelites. He will stand and shepherd his flock in the strength of the LORD, in the majesty of the name of the LORD his God. And they will live securely, for then his greatness will reach to the ends of the earth. And he will be our peace.*

Significance: **The LORD JESUS CHRIST is the ultimate ruler of God's people; He shepherds us in the fulfillment of God's purposes.**

Dear Father,

I am delighted how this prophecy describes Jesus, Your chosen Messiah, the supreme and eternal **Ruler Over Israel**. I praise Him that out of lowly Bethlehem, the ancient One came to completely fulfill Your plan for King David's line to **rule over Israel** and all people. All glory to Jesus that the government of His kingdom is upon His shoulders, and that He is our security and our Prince of Peace. I exalt Him that He stands in all Your majesty and strength to shepherd His flock. I am forever grateful that He is my ruler, hope, deliverer, master, king, lord, peace and infinitely more! I pray that the whole Church will have a strong desire to know all we can about the **Ruler Over Israel**, and that we will become single-mindedly devoted to praising Him, loving Him, serving Him, and speaking with one another about His magnificence. Please remove all hindrances that are keeping us from such radical abandonment to Him. May His greatness very soon reach to the ends of the earth. I pray these things in His name and for His fame. Amen.

What impacted me about Christ today...

_____

_____

_____

_____

*Nahum 1:7-8 The LORD is good, a **refuge in times of trouble**. He cares for those who trust in him, but with an overwhelming flood he will make an end of Nineveh; he will pursue his foes into the realm of darkness.*

Significance: The LORD JESUS CHRIST has become God's supreme sanctuary to Whom we run for protection and victory.

Dear Father,
I rejoice that Your limitless goodness dwells in the Lord Jesus. I whole-heartedly follow King David's advice to believers in Psalm 34:8 to: *"Taste and see that the LORD is good; blessed is the one who takes **refuge** in him."* I want to taste and see all of Jesus' goodness, and to continually take **refuge** in Him. I am very grateful that He is the all-powerful, and, at the same time, the all-caring **Refuge in Times of Trouble.** I marvel that Jesus, the great Lord of the universe (Who holds all He has created in His mighty hands) cares unconditionally about me and all other people who trust in Him. I repent for my tendency to try and handle attacks by the enemy, other crises, and just daily life situations, by myself. I really want to trust Him, run to Him and cast ALL my cares upon Him, in times of trouble, and **at all times**. I praise Him that ALL my hope is in Him. I pray that I, my family members and millions of other believers will resoundingly state with the writer of Psalm 91:2, *"I will say of the Lord, 'He is my refuge and my fortress, my God, in whom I trust.'"* I pray that great numbers of lost people who are currently in desperate trouble without Him will come to the **Refuge in Times of Trouble** right away. Please convince them of His limitless love and lordship. I give all these things to You in Jesus' all-sufficient name. Amen.

What impacted me about Christ today...

_____

_____

_____

_____

_____

_____

*Zephaniah 3:15-17 The LORD has taken away your punishment, he has turned back your enemy. The LORD, the King of Israel, is with you; never again will you fear any harm. On that day they will say to Jerusalem, "Do not fear, Zion; do not let your hands hang limp. The LORD your God is with you, the **Mighty Warrior who saves**. He will take great delight in you; in his love he will no longer rebuke you, but will rejoice over you with singing."*

Significance: The LORD JESUS CHRIST is God's mighty warrior Who fights to rescue His people in all situations.

Dear Father,

Just as it was very reassuring for the people of Israel in Zephaniah's time to hear that You were going to take away their punishment from sin and turn back their physical enemy, it is a wonderful reassurance for me and every other believer today that Jesus greatly delights in taking away the punishment of **our** sins and turning back the enemy of **our** souls. Hallelujah! He even rejoices over us with singing! I praise Jesus that He is always with us through His Spirit, and that He is the **Mighty Warrior Who Saves** His followers. I marvel that You love us so much that You sent Jesus to dwell with us constantly. Thank You that the **Mighty Warrior Who Saves** has all the **might** and power of the Godhead to **save** me and all others who receive Him as our Savior in **every** spiritual and physical way we need Him. I pray that You will fill all believers with joy, freedom from fear, and a deep trust in all that the **Mightiest Warrior** is, and in all He does in His kingdom. I pray that You will disciple us into mighty warriors in Christ who will *"not let our hands hang limp"* about leading every lost person we possibly can to the **Mighty Savior**. I give all these things to You in His saving name. Amen.

What impacted me about Christ today...

_____

_____

_____

_____

_____

_____

*Zechariah 2:3-5 While the angel who was speaking to me was leaving, another angel came to meet him and said to him: "Run, tell that young man 'Jerusalem will be a city without walls because of the great number of people and animals in it. And I myself will be a **wall of fire** around it,' declares the LORD, 'and I will be its glory within.'"*

Significance: **The LORD JESUS CHRIST surrounds His people and defends them, even as He dwells within them by His Spirit.**

Dear Father,

I rejoice that Your Church (the "Jerusalem") is so large and inclusive that there is plenty of room for all the people who choose to receive Jesus as their Savior and Lord. I am grateful that He makes it possible for His Church to have no manmade walls or limits to its number of inhabitants, yet we are as safe as if we had the very strongest of walls because He is a **Wall of Fire** around us. I praise Jesus that He is the all-powerful and insurmountable protection against all our enemies, and that He consumes and purifies all darkness and sin for those who are within Him. I exalt the **Wall of Fire** that all of His promises, prayers, teachings, commands and works surround us and can consume us. May we join today in the prophet's praise in Isaiah 26:1-3, *"In that day this song will be sung in the land of Judah: 'We have a strong city; God makes salvation its walls and ramparts. Open the gates that the righteous nation may enter, the nation that keeps faith. You will keep in perfect peace those whose minds are steadfast, because they trust in you.'"* I pray that the whole Church of today will be hungry to know the whole Christ, and we will steadfastly trust Him as the supreme **Wall of Fire** around every part of our lives. Oh, may we be filled with His glory. I earnestly pray that great numbers of lost people will begin running to live in Him. I pray these things in Jesus' glorious name. Amen.

What impacted me about Christ today...

_____

_____

_____

_____

<u>*Zechariah 3:8-9*</u> *"Listen, High Priest Joshua, you and your associates seated before you, who are men symbolic of things to come: I am going to bring my **servant, the Branch**. See, the stone I have set in front of Joshua! There are seven eyes on that one stone, and I will engrave an inscription on it," says the LORD Almighty, "and I will remove the sin of this land in a single day. In that day each of you will invite your neighbor to sit under your vine and fig tree," declares the LORD Almighty.*

Significance: **The LORD JESUS CHRIST gave His life that all fruitfulness from the Father might be available to those who abide in Him.**

Dear Father,

I marvel how in this Scripture passage, two words that refer to the Messiah—the **Servant** and the **Branch**—are brought together. I bless Jesus, the supreme **Servant**, Who obeys and **serves** You with His whole being, and Who serves me and all of mankind, by giving His life *("in a single day")* for our sins. This reminds me of what Hebrews 9:26b says about Christ's **servanthood**: *"But he has appeared once for all at the culmination of the ages to do away with sin by the sacrifice of himself."* At the same time, I am deeply grateful that Jesus is the original **Branch** through Whom His followers receive all Your beauty, excellence, fragrance, fruit, life and promises. Thank You so much that You sent Your beloved **Servant, the Branch** to earth, and set (placed) Him as the most precious foundation stone of the Church. I am excited to know that the perfect number of eyes (including Yours) will be focused on Him for all time. I pray that You will help me and increasing numbers of His followers die to ourselves and live fully in Him. May so much fruit burst forth from our lives that when we *"invite our neighbors"* to consider Him, they will eagerly desire to *"sit under your vine and fig tree."* I ask these things in His bountiful name. Amen.

What impacted me about Christ today...

_____

_____

_____

_____

Zechariah 4:7-9 *"What are you, mighty mountain? Before Zerubbabel you will become level ground. Then he will bring out the* **capstone** *to shouts of 'God bless it! God bless it!' Then the word of the LORD came to me: 'The hands of Zerubbabel have laid the foundation of this temple; his hands will also complete it. Then you will know that the LORD Almighty has sent me to you.'"*

S **ignificance: The LORD JESUS CHRIST brings to culmination all of God's purposes for His people as well as for the whole universe.**

Dear Father,

It is very encouraging to know that one day all mountain-like obstacles will be leveled, so that Christ's work in the Church and the whole world can be completed. I eagerly look forward to that day, when Christ the **Capstone** (high point, crowning achievement, culmination and pinnacle) will return to earth to receive the full acknowledgement of His greatness and victories (including the saving of Israel), to shouts of *"God bless it! God bless it!"* This culmination in Christ, the **Capstone**, reminds me of Revelation 7:9-10, *"After this I looked, and there before me was a great multitude that no one could count, from every nation, tribe, people and language, standing before the throne and before the Lamb. They were wearing white robes and were holding palm branches in their hands. And they cried out in a loud voice: 'Salvation belongs to our God, who sits on the throne, and to the Lamb.'"* I rejoice that Jesus is the beginning, or Foundation-Stone, of the salvation of the Church, as well as the finishing, or **Capstone**, of the salvation of the Church. I fervently pray that You will awaken believers everywhere to all the **Capstone** is, so that we will give ourselves completely to living under His all-encompassing lordship. I give all these things to You in the name of the Messiah. Amen.

What impacted me about Christ today...

_____

_____

_____

_____

_____

Zechariah 12:10-11 *"And I will pour out on the house of David and the inhabitants of Jerusalem a spirit of grace and supplication. They will look on me, **the one they have pierced**, and they will mourn for him as one mourns for an only child, and grieve bitterly for him as one grieves for a firstborn son. On that day the weeping in Jerusalem will be as great as the weeping of Hadad Rimmon in the plain of Megiddo."*

Significance: The LORD JESUS CHRIST paid the ultimate price for us, even though it was our sins that nailed Him to the cross.

Dear Father,

I am exceedingly grateful that one day Your Spirit is going to pour out grace-filled salvation and prayer on the Jewish people, and on all people. I honor the Messiah that the Jews especially will think about Him, the **One They Have Pierced**, and mourn and grieve for Him with all their hearts. I am thankful that they will weep in bitter repentance for the suffering the Savior did for them. I think of what King David prophesied about Christ's horrible **piercing** in Psalm 22:16, *"Dogs surround me, a pack of villians encircles me; they **pierce** my hands, and my feet."* And, I rejoice that the suffering Christ will return to earth, as John speaks of in Revelation 1:7, *"Look, he is coming with the clouds, and every eye will see him, even those who **pierced** him; and all the peoples of the earth will mourn because of him. So shall it be! Amen."* I humbly repent for the part that my sins have contributed to the suffering of the **One They Have Pierced**. I pray that You will continually search my heart and cleanse me of all unrighteousness. I pray You will bring a spirit of repentance, and at the same time, gratitude, into the whole Body of Christ. Please open the hearts and minds of millions of unsaved people around the world to repent for their sins and receive the freedom that the **One They Have Pierced** gave Himself for. In His name I ask these things. Amen.

What impacted me about Christ today...

_____

_____

_____

_____

_____

The Man Who Is Close To Me (The Father)

*Zechariah 13:7 "Awake, sword, against my shepherd, against the **man who is close to me!**" declares the LORD Almighty. "Strike the shepherd, and the sheep will be scattered, and I will turn my hand against the little ones."*

Significance: The LORD JESUS CHRIST, is the most intimate Person to the Father, and at the same time, He draws close to His people.

Dear Father,
I am deeply moved by the severity of today's Scripture verse. I am stunned at how You commanded the sword of justice to awaken, so it could be used against Your Son: Who is the Shepherd of Your flock, and the **Man Who is Close to Me** (You). I can only imagine the unparalleled **closeness** that You have had for all eternity with Your most beloved companion and co-equal. I think of John's proclamation in John 1:1 that: *"In the beginning was the Word [Jesus], and the Word was with God, and the Word was God."* I am filled with awe of the majesty of Jesus, and at the same time, an intense gratitude for Your sacrifice and His sacrifice, for me and the rest of humanity. The words of verse 3 of Charles Wesley's hymn, "And Can It Be" flood into my mind: "He left His Father's throne above, So free, so infinite His grace—And bled for Adam's helpless race: 'Tis mercy all, immense and free, For O my God, it found out me." Jesus is my hope, my love and my life. He is my ALL. I pray that the Holy Spirit will give me and all believers an all-consuming desire to dwell in the perfect **closeness** that You and Jesus have with each other. I pray that the people all around us who have not yet known Jesus as their Savior/Shepherd will very soon see Him as He really is and come into His flock. In the name of the **Man Who is Close to Me** I pray these things. Amen.

What impacted me about Christ today...

_____

_____

_____

_____

_____

<u>Malachi 3:1</u> "I will send my messenger, who will prepare the way before me. Then suddenly the LORD you are seeking will come to his temple; the **messenger of the covenant***, whom you desire, will come," says the LORD Almighty.*

Significance: The LORD JESUS CHRIST, by His Spirit, proclaims God's promised redemption for all who believe.

Dear Father,
I am amazed at all that You prophesied about Your Son, the Messiah, through today's single verse in Malachi! I love to see how You summed up John the Baptist and all the prophets who foretold about the Messiah, as being the *"****messenger****, who will prepare the way for me."* I rejoice in Your declaration that suddenly, the One Whom the people of Israel (and all people) have been earnestly seeking (the divine "LORD" Jehovah), has come, and will one day come back to earth to **His** temple. I praise the Messiah that He is God as You are God! I bow before Him that He is the same Jehovah Who appeared to Abraham and Jacob in Genesis, to Moses in the burning bush, and as the Shekinah in Exodus. I worship Him that He alone is the **Messenger of the Covenant** (the fulfillment of the New Covenant and every other covenant You have given to mankind). With all my being, I desire to know all I can about this incomparable **Messenger of the Covenant**. I pray that Your Spirit will give multitudes of other believers that fervent passion to know more of Him, and that we will eagerly "tell the world" about Him. In Christ's splendid name I ask these things. Amen.

What impacted me about Christ today...

_____

_____

_____

_____

_____

_____

_____

_____

*Malachi 3:2-4 But who can endure the day of his [Christ's] coming? Who can stand when he appears? For he will be like a refiner's fire or a launderer's soap. He will sit as a **refiner and purifier of silver**; he will purify the Levites and refine them like gold and silver. Then the LORD will have men who will bring offerings in righteousness, and the offerings of Judah and Jerusalem will be acceptable to the LORD, as in days gone by, as in former years.*

Significance: **The LORD JESUS CHRIST comes among His people to refine and purify us to serve His Kingdom purposes together.**

Dear Father,

I worship Jesus, Who is the consummate **Refiner and Purifier of Silver**. I honor Him that He is the holy and righteous Judge, and the only One Who is able to take people through the **refining** and **purifying** fire to remove the impurities of our lives (before He soon comes again). I am very grateful that He never destroys us through this **refining**, but that He perfectly cleanses, redeems and **purifies** us into the most precious **silver** and gold for His use. With all my heart, I want to live in complete truth and righteousness, and to bring honor to His holy name. I repent of all sin in my life, and submit myself to the **Refiner and Purifier of Silver** to do whatever He knows I need. I pray that I and all believers will continually practice 1 John 1:7-9: *"But if we walk in the light, as he is in the light, we have fellowship with one another, and the blood of Jesus, his Son, **purifies** us from all sin. If we claim to be without sin, we deceive ourselves and the truth is not in us. If we confess our sins, he is faithful and just and will forgive us our sins and **purify** us from all unrighteousness."* May every part of our lives be an offering to Him in righteousness. May the cleansing presence of the **Refiner and Purifier of Silver** sweep through the whole world. In His **refining** name I ask these things. Amen.

What impacted me about Christ today...

_____

_____

_____

_____

Malachi 4:2-3 *"But for you who revere my name, the* **sun of righteousness** *will rise with healing in its rays. And you will go out and frolic like well-fed calves. Then you will trample on the wicked; they will be ashes under the soles of your feet on the day when I act," says the* LORD *Almighty.*

Significance: **The LORD JESUS CHRIST, Who is the Son of God, radiates the virtues of God.**

Dear Father,

I revere Your name and Your Son's name, the **Sun of Righteousness**! Like the multitudes of people who experienced His authoritative teachings and miraculous healings when He walked among them 2000 years ago, I am in awe that He is the source and giver of inexhaustible light, perfect righteousness, absolute truth, all-sufficient heat, incomparable revelation and complete healing today. I praise Jesus again for what Paul declares about Him in Colossians 1:18b-19, *"And he is the head of the body, the church; he is the beginning and the firstborn from among the dead, so that in everything he might have the supremacy. For God was pleased to have all his fullness dwell in him."* Hallelujah, that the **Sun of Righteousness** is supreme **righteousness**, and that the fullness of Your **righteousness** dwells in Him. I pray that He will rise up with His healing rays to cleanse me and my family members of all unrighteousness and afflictions, so that we will live in His holiness, radiance, light, truth, warmth, joy, victory, hope and grace. I pray that we will *"go out and frolic like well-fed calves,"* to give Him all the glory He deserves, and to be witnesses of His light to the world around us. I pray that the **Sun of Righteousness** will shine so brilliantly in His people, that many unsaved people will come to watch us "shine" for Him. In His holy name I pray these things. Amen.

What impacted me about Christ today...

_____

_____

_____

_____

_____

_____

The Son Of Abraham

*Matthew 1:1 This is the genealogy of Jesus the Messiah the son of David, the **son of Abraham**.*

Significance: **The LORD JESUS CHRIST is the promised Jew to bless all people.**

Dear Father,
I praise You that Jesus Christ is the **Son of Abraham** (and the Son of David). It is exciting to know that Abraham was the first Jewish leader (the great ancient prophet and priest) from whom it was prophesied that the Messiah would descend, according to Genesis 22:15-18, *"The angel of the LORD called to Abraham from heaven a second time and said, 'I swear by myself, declares the LORD, that because you have done this and have not withheld your son, your only son, I will surely bless you and make your descendants as numerous as the stars in the sky and as the sand on the seashore. Your descendants will take possession of the cities of their enemies, and through your offspring all nations on the earth will be blessed, because you have obeyed me.'"* Hallelujah, that Jesus is that offspring Who would *"bless all nations on the earth,"* as Messiah and Savior. I thank You for the perfect plan You and He had before Abraham was born, before the beginning of time, to sow the seed of the God-Man into the royal line of the Jewish nation, then to fulfill Your plan through His life, death, resurrection and ascension many generations later. I devote myself totally to Him and to His advancing kingdom. May His followers of our day eagerly know Him more, love Him with all our hearts, speak of His greatness with one another, and worship Him without ceasing. I ask these things in the name of the blessed **Son of Abraham**. Amen.

What impacted m e about Christ today...

_____

_____

_____

_____

_____

_____

*Matthew 1:21 She [Mary] will give birth to a son, and you
[Joseph] are to give him the name **Jesus,** because he will save
his people from their sins.*

Significance: The LORD JESUS CHRIST is "The Lord is salvation."

☙

Dear Father,

The name **Jesus** fills my whole being with joy and life. I marvel that one translation of this name in Hebrew means "Jehovah (God) the Savior." I rejoice that Jesus is the name You gave Your Son when You sent Him to earth to fulfill His unique role as Savior from my sins, and Savior of all people who receive Him! All glory to **Jesus**, the name above all names. I exalt **Jesus**, that very soon *"at the name of Jesus [my knee and] every knee should bow, in heaven and on earth and under the earth, and every tongue acknowledge that Jesus Christ is Lord, to the glory of God the Father"* (Philippians 2:10-11). I think of the many times I have worshiped **Jesus,** cried out **"Jesus"** in times of need, meditated on how precious and magnificent **Jesus** is, been comforted and strengthened by **Jesus**, told others about **Jesus'** marvelous attributes, and much more. I pray that You will help me and all other followers of **Jesus** to be in absolute awe of, and love for, Jesus. May we be devoted to living Colossians 3:17, *"And whatever you do, whether in word or deed, do it all in the name of the Lord **Jesus,** giving thanks to God the Father through him."* I also express my love to Jesus through Frederick Whitfield's hymn: "There is a Name I love to hear, I love to sing its worth; It sounds like music in my ear, The sweetest Name on earth. (chorus) Oh, how I love **Jesus**, Oh, how I love **Jesus**, Oh, how I love **Jesus**, Because He first loved me!" I fervently pray that today You will reveal the full truth about **Jesus** to unsaved people everywhere, and remove all hindrances to them receiving Him as their Savior. I pray all these things in the beautiful name of **Jesus**. Amen.

What impacted me about Christ today...

_____

_____

_____

_____

_____

Immanuel (God With Us)

*Matthew 1:22-23 All this took place to fulfill what the Lord had said through the prophet [Isaiah]: "The virgin will conceive and give birth to a son, and they will call him **Immanuel**" (which means "**God with us**").*

Significance: The LORD JESUS CHRIST is the veritable presence of God.

Dear Father,
I am excited that today's Scripture passage states that all of the aspects of the birth of Jesus fulfill Isaiah's prophecy 700 years earlier, that one day a virgin would give birth to a son Who would be called "**Immanuel**" (**which means "God with us"**). I am in awe that even in the midst of King Ahaz's wicked rule of the kingdom of Judah, You were giving him assurance (a sign) that You would ultimately preserve the line of David through sending **Immanuel**, Who is God manifested in the flesh. I say "Hallelujah," that You sent Jesus, Your Son, Who eternally was and is fully God, to reside on earth with us as fully man. Thank You that I and all His people can know all Your thoughts, Your heart, Your desires, Your plans, Your mercy, Your love, Your compassion, Your power, Your righteousness, and the whole of Your nature through watching, hearing, touching, reading about and living in **Immanuel**. I bless Him that all of our sins are forgiven through His sacrificial life, death and resurrection as a man, so there is nothing in the way of us having an intimate, love relationship with You. I am filled with joy as I read and receive Jesus' words to You in John 17:26, *"I have made you known to them, and will continue to make you known in order that the love you have for me may be in them and that I myself may be in them."* I pray these things for myself and for all of Your people, in **Immanuel's** glorious name. Amen.

What impacted me about Christ today...

_____

_____

_____

_____

_____

*Matthew 2:19-23 After Herod died, an angel of the Lord appeared in
a dream to Joseph in Egypt and said, "Get up, take the child and his
mother and go to the land of Israel, for those who were trying to take the
child's life are dead." So he got up, took the child and his mother and
went to the land of Israel. But when he heard that Archelaus was reigning
in Judea in place of his father Herod, he was afraid to go there. Having
been warned in a dream, he withdrew to the district of Galilee, and he
went and lived in a town called Nazareth. So was fulfilled what was said
through the prophets, that he would be called a **Nazarene**.*

Significance: The LORD JESUS CHRIST was identified by a place
of little human significance.

Dear Father,
I praise Jesus that He was willing to come to earth and live as a lowly **Nazarene**. I am grateful that His earthly father, Joseph, was part of Your grand
plan through his obedience to move his family to Nazareth. I am intrigued
that the origin of the word "**Nazarene**" refers to a weak branch, rather than a
strong tree. I marvel at how Jews from other parts of Israel thought that people from Nazareth were weaker or lesser than them. I honor Jesus that His
birth and upbringing as a **Nazarene** were a crucial part of fulfilling the Messianic prophecies that He would be "despised and rejected" by man. I grieve
that He had to endure so many difficult earthly circumstances, especially
His unsurpassed rejection and suffering to pay the penalty of sin for me and
all of mankind. But, because He is the **Nazarene**, I joyfully sing: "I Stand
Amazed In the Presence" by Charles Gabriel: (verse 1) "I stand amazed
in the presence of Jesus the Nazarene, And wonder how He could love
me, A sinner, condemned, unclean. (verse 4) He took my sin and my sorrows, He made them His very own; He bore the burden to Calvary, And
suffered and died alone. (verse 5) When with the ransomed in glory, His
face I at last shall see, 'Twill be my joy through the ages, To sing of His
love for me. (chorus) O how marvelous! O how wonderful! And my song
shall ever be: O how marvelous! O how wonderful! Is my Savior's love for
me!" In His precious name I pray these things. Amen.

What impacted me about Christ today...

My Son, Whom I Love

*Matthew 3:16-17 As soon as Jesus was baptized, he went up out of the water. At that moment heaven was opened, and he [John the Baptist] saw the Spirit of God descending like a dove and alighting on him. And a voice from heaven said, "This is my **Son, whom I love**; with him I am well pleased."*

Significance: **The LORD JESUS CHRIST has an eternal, perfect love relationship with God the Father.**

Dear Father,

I love to meditate on this extraordinary event between You, Your Son and the Holy Spirit. I am especially captivated by Your declaration that Jesus is Your **Son, Whom I Love**. I celebrate that this is an amazing fulfillment of the prophecy in Isaiah 42:1, where You said You would someday send Your servant, the *"chosen one in whom I delight,"* and *"put my Spirit on him."* I marvel at the relationship of immeasurable and infinite **love** that You, the Son and the Spirit (the Trinity) displayed in confirming Jesus as the long-awaited Messiah! I rejoice that You are well-pleased with Jesus, now and forever, as He fulfills all the plans and purposes You sent Him to earth to accomplish. I pray that You will pour into me, my family members and all other believers every bit of what You want us to know about the **Son, Whom I Love**, so we will **love** Him as You **love** Him, and submit ourselves entirely to His rule and reign. I pray also that You will remove all distractions and strongholds in the lives of the many people we know who do not yet have a relationship with the **Son, Whom I Love**, so they will eagerly seek Him as their Savior. I pray these things in Your beloved **Son's** name. Amen.

What impacted me about Christ today...

_____

_____

_____

_____

_____

_____

_____

*Matthew 9:35-38 Jesus went through all the towns and villages, teaching in their synagogues, proclaiming the good news of the kingdom and healing every disease and sickness. When he saw the crowds, he had compassion on them, because they were harassed and helpless, like sheep without a shepherd. Then he said to his disciples, "The harvest is plentiful but the workers are few. Ask the **Lord of the harvest**, therefore, to send out workers into his harvest field."*

Significance: The LORD JESUS CHRIST is the master of the fruit of the gospel.

Dear Father,

I praise You that it was Your perfect plan of the ages to send Jesus as the supreme **Lord of the Harvest**, during the past 2000 years and forever. I honor Him that He is in complete control of making salvation available to me and every other person in the world. I am forever grateful that He has the unlimited compassion, willingness to give His body and shed His blood, power to heal ills and forgive sins, absolute wisdom, authority over the powers of darkness, constant prayers for us, ability to plant and water the soil of our hearts, unconditional love, and servant spirit that are necessary for the **harvest** of all **harvests**. I give all glory to Him for myself and all the other people who have been **"harvested"** by Him so far. I pray that all the sowing, fertilizing and watering that He has done (and is still doing) for all the other people who have yet to be **harvested**, will continue flawlessly. I join the command He gave His disciples in asking that **all** the workers (including me and my family) that are necessary for the remaining plentiful **harvest** will be sent into His **harvest** field. May millions of believers join in this prayer, and in total dedication to the **Lord of the Harvest**, in Whose name I pray these things. Amen.

What impacted me about Christ today...

_____

_____

_____

_____

_____

_____

<u>Matthew 12:5-12</u> *[Jesus speaking] "Or haven't you read in the Law that the priests on Sabbath duty in the temple desecrate the Sabbath and yet are innocent? I tell you that* **something greater than the temple** *is here. If you had known what these words mean, 'I desire mercy, not sacrifice,' you would not have condemned the innocent. For the Son of Man is Lord of the Sabbath." Going on from that place, he went into their synagogue, and a man with a shriveled hand was there. Looking for a reason to bring charges against Jesus, they asked him, "Is it lawful to heal on the Sabbath?" He said to them, "If any of you has a sheep and it falls into a pit on the Sabbath, will you not take hold of it and lift it out? How much more valuable is a person than a sheep! Therefore it is lawful to do good on the Sabbath."*

Significance: **The LORD JESUS CHRIST is the ultimate and final place of worship.**

Dear Father,

I love to see how Jesus instructed the Jewish people (and His followers today) about His divinity. I marvel that in today's Scripture, Jesus very clearly told His listeners that the laws of the temple sometimes supersede the laws of the Sabbath, but that He is the **Something Greater Than the Temple**. I exalt Jesus that He knew that the people understood that only God is greater than the temple, so He was emphatically telling them that He is God. I bow before Jesus, as the great Creator and Lord of all justice, love, mercy, compassion, truth, power, righteousness and wisdom. I praise Him that He has no beginning and no end, and He is greater than all of man's religion, laws and customs. I worship Him that He is the undisputed Head of the Church. I pray that You will help me to hear and obey His commands first and foremost in every area of my life. I also pray that all His people will know Him so well and listen to Him so intently, that we will always follow Him without question. I ask that You will reveal to us any ways we are putting anything or anyone above Him in our lives, and compel us to repent. May we give all devotion, adoration and praise to **Something Greater Than the Temple**. In His great name I pray these things. Amen.

What impacted me about Christ today...

*<u>Matthew 12:6-12</u> [Jesus speaking] "I tell you that something greater than the temple is here. If you had known what these words mean, 'I desire mercy, not sacrifice,' you would not have condemned the innocent. For the Son of Man is **Lord of the Sabbath**." Going on from that place, he went into their synagogue, and a man with a shriveled hand was there. Looking for a reason to bring charges against Jesus, they asked him, "Is it lawful to heal on the Sabbath?" He said to them, "If any of you has a sheep and it falls into a pit on the Sabbath, will you not take hold of it and lift it out? How much more valuable is a person than a sheep! Therefore it is lawful to do good on the Sabbath."*

Significance: **The LORD JESUS CHRIST is the governor of all goodness and mercy in His kingdom.**

Dear Father,

I rejoice that Jesus, the divine Son of Man, reveals in today's Scripture that He is **Lord of the Sabbath**. I exalt Him that He is Lord of all that affects mankind, including our holiness and our rest. I am very grateful that all of Jesus' words and actions display Your wisdom and mercy to me and to all mankind. I am delighted that He ministers *"mercy not sacrifice,"* on the Sabbath and at all times. I pray that Your people will live in all of the sacrificial mercy of Christ that William Newell expresses so well in some of his hymn, "At Calvary": "Mercy there was great, and grace was free; Pardon there was multiplied to me; There my burdened soul found liberty, At Calvary." I pray that You will help me and multitudes of other believers respond to the **Lord of the Sabbath's** outpouring of mercy as Newell states later in the hymn: "Now I've giv'n to Jesus everything, Now I gladly own Him as my King, Now my raptured soul can only sing of Calvary." May we live wholly in the image of the **Lord of the Sabbath**, and do good, so that the mercy-starved world around us might be anxiously drawn to Him. I pray these things in His precious name. Amen.

What impacted me about Christ today...

_____

_____

_____

_____

*Matthew 13:24b, 36-43 [Jesus said] "The kingdom of heaven is like a man who sowed good seed in his field." . . . Then he left the crowd and went into the house. His disciples came to him and said, "Explain to us the parable of the weeds in the field." He answered, "The **one who sowed the good seed** is the Son of Man. The field is the world, and the good seed stands for the people of the kingdom. The weeds are the people of the evil one, and the enemy who sows them is the devil. The harvest is the end of the age, and the harvesters are angels. As the weeds are pulled up and burned in the fire, so it will be at the end of the age. The Son of Man will send out his angels, and they will weed out of his kingdom everything that causes sin and all who do evil. They will throw them into the blazing furnace, where there will be weeping and gnashing of teeth. Then the righteous will shine like the sun in the kingdom of their Father. Whoever has ears, let him hear."*

Significance: The **LORD JESUS CHRIST** broadcasts truth that leads to eternal life.

Dear Father,

I honor Jesus, the Son of Man, that You sent Him to earth as the **One Who Sowed the Good Seed**. I exalt Him that in Him dwells all the **goodness** (righteousness, truth, justice, love, mercy, compassion and much more) of the Godhead. I am exceedingly grateful that He alone has the authority to **sow** all of His **goodness** into the "***good seed***" (those who receive Him and become *"sons of the kingdom"*). Hallelujah, that I am one of those **good seed**! I pray that You will reveal more and more of the vast **goodness** of Jesus to the **good seed**, and help us to become increasingly consumed in Him, so that now, and at the end of the age when we are harvested, we will *"shine like the sun in the kingdom of their Father."* I pray also that You will do whatever is necessary in the lives of many millions of people around the world who are currently *"weeds,"* so that before it is too late, they will become **good seed** too. O Father, I pray that I and all of Christ's **good seed** will always hear Him. In the name of the **One Who Sowed the Good Seed** I ask these things. Amen.

What impacted me about Christ today...

_____

JUNE

*Matthew 13:44 [Jesus said] "The kingdom of heaven is like
treasure hidden in a field. When a man found it, he hid it again,
and then in his joy went and sold all he had and bought that field."*

Significance: The LORD JESUS CHRIST is like an unexpected discovery of the greatest value.

Dear Father,

I know that today's Scripture verse is focusing on the kingdom of heaven being like a **treasure hidden in a field**, but I am in awe that the kingdom of heaven is completely dependent upon Jesus. So, I delight in knowing that He is the ultimate **Treasure Hidden in a Field**. In fact, I praise Him that He is the greatest **Treasure** of all time. Thank You that You helped me find Him, and that Your Spirit is continually revealing the incomparable **treasure** of His Person and His kingdom to me. I want to **treasure** the Lord Jesus with all my heart as He instructed His followers in Matthew 6:21, *"For where your **treasure** is, there your heart will be also."* I confess that I often give my time and affections to "treasures" other than Jesus. I pray that You will help me, my family members and all other believers to joyfully sell (give up) all we have, so we can give ourselves wholly to the **Treasure Hidden in a Field**. At the same time, would You please admonish us to no longer hide the wonderful **Treasure** from the unsaved, but to proclaim all He is to everyone You bring into our lives. May the **Treasure** (that has been) **Hidden in a Field** up until now, be on the hearts, minds and lips of all people, here and around the world. I pray these things in the **treasured** name of Jesus. Amen.

What impacted me about Christ today...

_____

_____

_____

_____

_____

_____

_____

The One Of Great Value (Pearl Of Great Price)

Matthew 13:45-46 *[Jesus said] "Again, the kingdom of heaven is like a merchant looking for fine pearls. When he found **one of great value**, he went away and sold everything he had and bought it."*

Significance: The LORD JESUS CHRIST is worth far more than everything else we have or can imagine.

Dear Father,

I am filled with **great** joy as I also think about Jesus as the **One of Great Value** of the kingdom of heaven. I am delighted that in today's parable a merchant was very actively looking for fine pearls, when he found the **One of Great Value** (or the Pearl of **Great** Price). I rejoice that there is nothing which can compare to the unfathomable **value** of Jesus. Truly, He is of the **greatest value**. I exalt Him that the vastness of Your wisdom, beauty, righteousness, love, power, mercy, goodness, splendor, grace and much, much more dwells in Him. I marvel that He gave His precious life for me and for all of mankind, and that He is the Lord of all creation and the soon-coming King! I pray that You will put an intense longing in me and in great numbers of other believers to possess all of the **One of Great Value**. May we live in the passion of an old Swedish hymn, "Den Kostliga Parlan" ("O That Pearl of **Great** Price"): "O that Pearl of **great** price! Have you found it? Is the Savior supreme in your love? O consider it well, ere you answer, As you hope for a welcome above. Have you given up all for this Treasure? Have you counted past gains as but loss? Has your trust in yourself and your merits, Come to naught before Christ and His Cross?" I pray that unsaved people everywhere will soon become consumed with us in seeking the **One of Great Value**. I ask these things in His priceless name. Amen.

What impacted me about Christ today...

_____

_____

_____

_____

_____

_____

The Messiah, The Son Of The Living God

Matthew 16:13-19 When Jesus came to the region of Caesarea Philippi, he asked his disciples, "Who do people say the Son of Man is?" They replied, "Some say John the Baptist; others say Elijah; and still others, Jeremiah or one of the prophets." "But what about you?" he asked. "Who do you say I am?" Simon Peter answered, "You are the **Messiah, the Son of the living God.** *" Jesus replied, "Blessed are you, Simon son of Jonah, for this was not revealed to you by flesh and blood, but by my Father in heaven. And I tell you that you are Peter, and on this rock I will build my church, and the gates of Hades will not overcome it. I will give you the keys of the kingdom of heaven; whatever you bind on earth will be bound in heaven, and whatever you loose on earth will be loosed in heaven."*

S ignificance: **The LORD JESUS CHRIST is the ultimate and complete revelation of God to mankind.**

Dear Father,
I am in awe of Your strong revelation to Peter that Jesus is the **Messiah**, (the long-awaited Christ, Savior and Anointed One), **the Son of the Living God** (Your beloved, divine, One and Only Son)! I love how this combined name of **Messiah** and the **Son of the Living God** encompasses exactly what You and Christ wanted Peter and the rest of His disciples to understand about Him and about You. I praise Jesus that He builds His Church securely on the rock-solid foundation of all He is as the **Messiah, the Son of the Living God**. I pray that You will reveal to me and to many of His other followers today the vastness of Who He is, so that we too will build our lives entirely upon Him. Please help us to repent of all ways we have treated Him as less than the supreme **Messiah, the Son of the Living God**. Give us a burning passion to continually testify about His greatness to one another and to every unsaved person we can. I pray that a groundswell of the reality of Who Jesus is will be *"loosed"* into the hearts and minds of unsaved people of all ages, ethnic origins, languages, regions and social groups. May **Messiah's** Church be built for His honor in His name. Amen.

What impacted me about Christ today...

_____

_____

_____

*Matthew 20:25-28 Jesus called them [His disciples] together and said, "You know that the rulers of the Gentiles lord it over them, and their high officials exercise authority over them. Not so with you. Instead, whoever wants to become great among you must be your servant, and whoever wants to be first must be your slave—just as the Son of Man did not come to be served, but to serve, and to give his life as a **ransom for many**."*

Significance: The LORD JESUS CHRIST, the pure servant, paid the penalty to set men free from their sin.

Dear Father,
I rejoice that the redeeming purpose for the Son of Man's life on earth was to be a **Ransom for Many**. It is hard for me to comprehend that You and He loved me and all the billions of other people so much that He was willing to pay the ultimate price to liberate us from eternal captivity to sin. What an amazing way Jesus "practiced what He preached" in today's Scripture about being a servant (even a slave) of others! I know that I was 100% guilty of my sin, and so is every other person. But, I praise Him that He took our place, our suffering, our condemnation and our punishment on Himself. I thank Him with all my heart that I and the millions of other people who have received His gift of **ransom**, are gloriously alive in Him, now and forever! I shout "Hallelujah" for our certain assurance that Paul proclaims in Romans 8:1-2, *"Therefore, there is now no condemnation for those who are in Christ Jesus, because through Christ Jesus the law of the Spirit who gives life has set you free from the law of sin and death."* What a Savior Christ is! What a Servant! What a **Ransom for Many**! I pray that You will fill believers with a fresh, overflowing thanksgiving and praise to the **Ransom for Many**, and please put an intense longing for **ransom** from sin into the hearts and minds of lost people all around us. I pray these things in Jesus' serving name. Amen.

What impacted me about Christ today...

_____

_____

_____

_____

_____

*Matthew 21:6-9 The disciples went and did as Jesus had instructed them. They brought the donkey and the colt and placed their cloaks on them for Jesus to sit on. A very large crowd spread their cloaks on the road, while others cut branches from the trees and spread them on the road. The crowds that went ahead of him and those that followed shouted, "Hosanna to the **Son of David**! Blessed is he who comes in the name of the Lord! Hosanna in the highest heaven!"*

Significance: **The LORD JESUS CHRIST is the ultimate King of David's kingdom.**

Dear Father,
I exalt Jesus as He rode towards Jerusalem during the Passover season proclaiming that He was the promised Messiah. I can only imagine the pent-up longing the Jewish people had had for centuries that You would establish Your kingdom through a descendant of King David. I can imagine how fervently they believed that the Son of God coming in their time as the **Son of David** would free them from the tyranny of Roman rule and bless them again as a nation. I praise Jesus that He completely fulfilled all the ancient Messianic prophecies of Psalm 110:1, Zechariah 9:9 and others. I join the Jewish people in shouting, *"Hosanna ["Save now"] to the **Son of David**,"* and Psalm 118:25-26a, *"LORD, save us! LORD, grant us success! Blessed is he who comes in the name of the LORD."* But, I praise the **Son of David** that He transcends all the power and glory of King David and all other earthly kings, and His rule is of all heaven and earth, forever. I bow before Him, according to what You said about Him in Psalm 2:6-8, *"I have installed my King on Zion, my holy mountain. I will proclaim the LORD'S decree: He said to me, 'You are my **Son**; today I have become your father. Ask me, and I will make the nations your inheritance, the ends of the earth your possession.'"* I pray that believers today will worship Him as our Savior, King and Prince of Peace, and that His kingdom will come and His will be done in our lives and throughout the nations. All hail King Jesus, the **Son of David**, in Whose name I pray these things. Amen.

What impacted me about Christ today...

_____

_____

_____

Jesus, The Prophet From Nazareth In Galilee

Matthew 21:6-11 The disciples went and did as Jesus had instructed them. They brought the donkey and the colt and placed their cloaks on them for Jesus to sit on. A very large crowd spread their cloaks on the road, while others cut branches from the trees and spread them on the road. The crowds that went ahead of him and those that followed shouted, "Hosanna to the Son of David! Blessed is he who comes in the name of the Lord! Hosanna in the highest heaven!" When Jesus entered Jerusalem, the whole city was stirred and asked, "Who is this?" The crowds answered, "This is **Jesus, the prophet from Nazareth in Galilee."**

S ignificance: The LORD JESUS CHRIST is God's primary spokes-man to His people.

Dear Father,
I rejoice that when Jesus entered Jerusalem the whole city was stirred, and the people asked Who He was. I am glad that many of the people in the large crowd that traveled with Him to Jerusalem were from **Galilee**, and that they personally knew Him and could attest that He is **Jesus, the Prophet from Nazareth in Galilee**. I am in awe that they believed He was the prophet about Whom Moses stated in Deuteronomy 18:18, *"I will raise up for them a* **prophet** *like you from among their fellow Israelites, and I will put my words in his mouth. He will tell them everything I command him."* But, I am sorry they did not understand that You had sent Jesus as the **Prophet** Messiah to them to reveal Your majesty and love, give His life as a ransom for mankind, and rule His kingdom forever. I honor the great **Prophet from Nazareth in Galilee**, Who has all Your wisdom and knowledge. I pray that You will help me and the whole Church today to seek Him, know Him, listen to Him, obey Him and constantly speak of His greatness to one another, so that we will all be freshly awakened to all that He is. I pray that large crowds of unsaved people in our cities will be intensely *"stirred"* to know Him too. I pray these things in His **prophetic** name. Amen.

What impacted me about Christ today...

_____

_____

_____

*Matthew 23:8-12 But you are not to be called "Rabbi," for you have one Teacher, and you are all brothers. And do not call anyone on earth "father," for you have one Father, and he is in heaven. Nor are you to be called instructors, for you have one **Instructor**, the Messiah. The greatest among you will be your servant. For those who exalt themselves will be humbled, and those who humble themselves will be exalted.*

Significance: The LORD JESUS CHRIST is the one true teacher of all life.

Dear Father,

I thank You for one true **Instructor**, Jesus the Messiah (the Christ). I praise Him that He has always possessed all the understanding, truth, wisdom, knowledge and skill to be the perfect **Instructor** of all subjects, especially of all Who You are. I join in the amazement recorded in Matthew 7:28-29 of the people who heard His teaching: *"When Jesus had finished saying these things, the crowds were amazed at his teaching, because he taught as one who had authority, and not as their teachers of the law."* I pray that I, my family members and all of His followers in our day will clearly hear and obey all of His teachings and commands, since He taught only what You told Him to teach. I pray also that You will give us an insatiable desire to know all of His character, attributes, passions, burdens, prayers and deeds, so that we will worship and thank Him more, love Him more, serve Him more, give ourselves more to Him, and speak about Him with one another whenever we can. May we be so amazed with His authority that we are humbled before Him. I ask that You will draw many lost people to the **Instructor** too, and open their hearts and minds to His truth. I pray these things in His amazing name. Amen.

What impacted me about Christ today...

_____

_____

_____

_____

_____

_____

*Matthew 27:28-37 They stripped him and put a scarlet robe on him, and then twisted together a crown of thorns and set it on his head. They put a staff in his right hand. Then they knelt in front of him and mocked him. "Hail, **king of the Jews!**" they said. They spit on him, and took the staff and struck him on the head again and again. After they had mocked him, they took off the robe and put his own clothes on him. Then they led him away to crucify him. As they were going out, they met a man from Cyrene, named Simon, and they forced him to carry the cross. They came to a place called Golgotha (which means "the place of the skull"). There they offered Jesus wine to drink, mixed with gall; but after tasting it, he refused to drink it. When they had crucified him, they divided up his clothes by casting lots. And sitting down, they kept watch over him there. Above his head they placed the written charge against him: THIS IS JESUS, THE **KING OF THE JEWS**.*

Significance: **The LORD JESUS CHRIST is the divine ruler of Israel and the whole universe.**

Dear Father,

I am very grateful that Pilate directed his servants to unequivocally state on the sign above Jesus' head on the cross that Jesus is the **King of the Jews**. I rejoice that earlier Jesus had clearly told Pilate that He is the **King of the Jews**, and in John 18:36-37, He went even further in describing His **Kingly** stature: *"Jesus said, 'My **kingdom** is not of this world. If it were, my servants would fight to prevent my arrest by the Jewish leaders. But now my **kingdom** is from another place.' 'You are a **king**, then!' said Pilate. Jesus answered, 'You say that I am a **king**. In fact, the reason I was born and came into the world is to testify to the truth. Everyone on the side of truth listens to me.'"* Please help me and all followers of the **great** King to intently listen to Him, and to live in all of His truth. I pray that all people, including Jews, who have not yet received Jesus as their Messiah and King, will begin listening to and understanding the whole truth about Him. May we all exalt the **King of the Jews**, in Whose name I pray these things. Amen.

What impacted me about Christ today...

_____

_____

_____

_____

*Matthew 28:16-20 Then the eleven disciples went to Galilee, to the mountain where Jesus had told them to go. When they saw him, they worshiped him; but some doubted. Then Jesus came to them and said, "All authority in heaven and on earth has been given to me. Therefore go and make disciples of all nations, baptizing them in the name of the Father and of the **Son** and of the Holy Spirit, and teaching them to obey everything I have commanded you. And surely I am with you always, to the very end of the age."*

Significance: **The LORD JESUS CHRIST has all the life of the Father in Him; He is the divine descendant of the Father.**

Dear Father,

I love to focus on Your **Son**. I can only imagine how precious He is to You. I am in awe of Him as Your beloved **Son**, Your One and Only **Son**, Your co-eternal and co-equal **Son**, Your **Son** Who created all things, the **Son** You are well-pleased with, the **Son** Who is Your Heir of all things, the **Son** in Whom all of You dwells, the **Son** Whom You want to receive all glory, the **Son** Whom You have given all authority in heaven and on earth, the **Son** You have appointed as judge of all people, and unfathomably more. I exalt, worship, praise and adore Your **Son**. I give myself body, mind and spirit to Him alone. Oh, great Father, I pray that You will help me, my family members, and all of His followers to become immersed in, captivated by, and sold out to, Your **Son**, like You are. May we *"live and move and have our being"* in Your **Son** (Acts 17:28). What a joy it is that He sent His early disciples under His authority to do just that: *"make disciples of all nations."* I am forever grateful to be a recipient of that disciple-making process, including being baptized in the name of (or "into" a lifestyle of devotion to) all of the Father, **Son** and Holy Spirit. Hallelujah, that He is with His disciples to the very end of the age! I pray all these things in Your **Son's** wonderful name. Amen.

What impacted me about Christ today...

_____

_____

_____

*Mark 1: 21-24 They went to Capernaum, and when the Sabbath came, Jesus went into the synagogue and began to teach. The people were amazed at his teaching, because he taught them as one who had authority, not as the teachers of the law. Just then a man in their synagogue who was possessed by an evil spirit cried out, "What do you want with us, Jesus of Nazareth? Have you come to destroy us? I know who you are—the **Holy One of God!**"*

Significance: The LORD JESUS CHRIST is the personification of God's righteousness.

Dear Father,

I can well imagine that the people who heard Jesus teach in the synagogue were amazed by His authority. I am extremely amazed by His authority! I am very grieved that there were some Jews in His time of earthly ministry who wanted to discredit Him by suggesting that His authority came from demons (Matthew 12:24). But, I am very glad that the evil spirit written about in today's Scripture passage knew exactly Who Jesus is—the **Holy One of God**. I praise Jesus that He is the Messianic **One** Whom King David writes about in Psalm 16:10, *"Because you will not abandon me to the realm of the dead, nor will you let your faithful one [Holy One] see decay."* I exalt Jesus that in Him dwells the fullness of Your **holiness**. I worship Him that He alone is the **Holy One** You sent to earth to pay the penalty for mankind's sin, so that all who receive Him are forever set apart **(holy)** in Him! I pray that You will give us a passion to know every aspect we can of the **Holy One of God**. I pray also that we will live such radically **holy** lives that Jesus will receive much glory and honor, and that lost men, women, young people and children around us will be crying out to receive Him too. I ask these things in the righteous name of Jesus. Amen.

What impacted me about Christ today...

_____

_____

_____

_____

_____

*Mark 6:1-3 Jesus left there [His healing of Jairus' daughter] and went to his hometown, accompanied by his disciples. When the Sabbath came, he began to teach in the synagogue, and many who heard him were amazed. "Where did this man get these things?" they asked. "What's this wisdom that has been given him? What are these remarkable miracles he is performing? Isn't this the **carpenter**? Isn't this **Mary's son** and the brother of James, Joseph, Judas and Simon? Aren't his sisters here with us?" And they took offense at him.*

Significance: The LORD JESUS CHRIST was identified as an ordinary person to discredit the amazing wisdom and power He was displaying.

Dear Father,

I love it that Your perfect plan for Jesus included Him being a **Carpenter** and **Mary's Son**. I am in awe over what the **Carpenter** built with His skilled and mighty hands: objects of wood for everyday use by the people of His hometown, as well as His glorious kingdom through His amazing teaching and miraculous works. I marvel that even though Jesus was the **son** of a very ordinary woman, (who to some in Nazareth was scandalous because of Jesus' birth), that she was Your divine choice to be His mother, and she was totally faithful in her role for Him. I rejoice that You poured Your limitless wisdom, authority, righteousness and power into the humble upbringing of the Person of all persons. All praise and honor to Jesus, the **Carpenter** and **Mary's Son**, now and forevermore. I am sorry that His hometown residents took offense at Him, and even more so, I repent for the ways that I and any of His other followers today have failed to believe in His magnificent greatness, and to devote every part of our lives to Him. I pray that the burning passions of our lives will be to know more of the **Carpenter** and **Mary's Son**, and to tell everyone else about how excellent He is. I pray these things in His beloved name. Amen.

What impacted me about Christ today...

_____

_____

_____

_____

*Mark 10:42-45 Jesus called them [His disciples] together and said, "You know that those who are regarded as rulers of the Gentiles lord it over them, and their high officials exercise authority over them. Not so with you. Instead, whoever wants to become great among you must be your servant, and whoever wants to be first must be slave of all. For even the **Son of Man** did not come to be served, but to serve, and to give his life as a ransom for many."*

Significance: The **LORD JESUS CHRIST** is the fully-human Servant and Savior of mankind.

Dear Father,

I am very grateful that Your **Son** was willing to give up His heavenly glory to come to earth and become a **man**, so that He might experience all of human life, reveal all of You to **man**kind, and serve and suffer for our sins. I love a quote by Henry Gariepy in "100 Portraits of Christ": "The **Son** of God became the **Son of Man** that we might become sons of God. He was God clothed in the garb of humanity." I praise Jesus that as the **Son of Man**, He ultimately fulfills the glorious vision of His eternal dominion in Daniel 7:13a, *"In my vision at night I looked, and there before me was one like a **son of man**, coming with the clouds of heaven."* I am deeply impressed that the name, "**Son of Man**," so strongly describes Who Jesus is, that He called Himself the **Son of Man** more than any other name or title (80 or more times). I pray that I, my family members and millions of Jesus' other followers will dedicate ourselves to knowing all You want us to know about the **Son of Man**, and devote ourselves to being servants (even slaves) like Him. Please help us to pray continually that every lost person we know will find the **Son of Man** Who came to *"seek and save"* them. I ask these things in the name that is life for every person. Amen.

What impacted me about Christ today...

_____

_____

_____

_____

_____

*Mark 14:60-62 Then the high priest stood up before them and asked Jesus, "Are you not going to answer? What is this testimony that these men are bringing against you?" But Jesus remained silent and gave no answer. Again the high priest asked him, "Are you the Messiah [the Christ], the **Son of the Blessed One**?" "I am," said Jesus, "And you shall see the Son of Man sitting at the right hand of the Mighty One and coming on the clouds of heaven."*

Significance: The LORD JESUS CHRIST is the only offspring of the Heavenly Father.

Dear Father,
What an amazing interchange this was between Jesus and the high priest! I am surprised that Jesus answered this question, *"Are you the Christ, the **Son of the Blessed One**?"* I remember that in the Matthew 26:63 account, the high priest had given Jesus a solemn oath to answer it. Oh, I am so glad that He did answer! I give all praise to Jesus that here He unmistakably confirmed to the high priest and all the Jewish rulers in attendance His position as the Christ (Messiah and Anointed One) and His divinity as the One and Only **Son of the Blessed One** (Father and Almighty God). I would have loved to be there to hear Him speak two of the most monumental words of His earthly life: *"I am."* I am further filled with praise of Jesus that He then declared that one day they would see Him sitting at Your mighty right hand in heaven, then returning to earth as Lord of all. Truly, Jesus Christ is the supreme **Son of the Blessed One**! I join King David in His praise in Psalm 8:1 that is ultimately fulfilled in Christ: *"LORD, our Lord, how majestic is your name in all the earth. You have set your glory in the heavens."* I pray that You will help me and believers everywhere to hunger to know as much as we possibly can about His greatness, and to give ourselves to worshiping and adoring Him. I pray these things in the name of the **blessed** Christ. Amen.

What impacted me about Christ today...

_____

_____

_____

Luke 1:27b-35 The virgin's name was Mary. The angel went to her and said, "Greetings, you who are highly favored! The Lord is with you." Mary was greatly troubled at his words and wondered what kind of greeting this might be. But the angel said to her, "Do not be afraid, Mary; you have found favor with God. You will conceive and give birth to a son, and you are to call him Jesus. He will be great and will be called the **Son of the Most High***. The Lord God will give him the throne of his father David, and he will reign over Jacob's descendants forever; his kingdom will never end." "How will this be," Mary asked the angel, "since I am a virgin?" The angel answered, "The Holy Spirit will come on you, and the power of the Most High will overshadow you. So the holy one to be born will be called the Son of God."*

Significance: **The LORD JESUS CHRIST is the anointed Son of the great High God.**

Dear Father,

My spirit soars as I read in today's Scripture of Mary being told by an angel that she would have an immaculate **son**, Whom she was to name Jesus (the Savior). I highly exalt Jesus that the angel's additional pronouncement powerfully ties together His unbounded greatness as the One and Only **Son of the Most High**, and His assignment by You to reign on the throne of King David forever! Oh, **Most High** God, I thank You that once again You made it absolutely clear to all who are listening that You sent Your divine Son into the world as the great Savior and King. I love to think about the matchless depth of the Father/Son relationship that You and Jesus have always had, whether He was living on earth or by Your side in heaven. I love His testimony about Your relationship in John 10:30, *"I and the Father are one,"* and in John 17:21a, *"Father, just as you are in me and I am in you."* Please open the eyes, minds and spirits of me and all other believers to the supreme majesty of the **Son of the Most High**, and help us to worship and live in Him alone. In His spectacular name I pray these things. Amen.

What impacted me about Christ today...

_____

_____

_____

*<u>Luke 1:67-75</u> His [John the Baptist's] father Zechariah was filled with the Holy Spirit and prophesied: "Praise be to the Lord, the God of Israel, because he has come to his people and redeemed them. He has raised up a **horn of salvation** for us in the house of his servant David (as he said through his holy prophets of long ago), salvation from our enemies and from the hand of all who hate us—to show mercy to our ancestors and to remember his holy covenant, the oath he swore to our father Abraham: to rescue us from the hand of our enemies, and to enable us to serve him without fear in holiness and righteousness before him all our days."*

Significance: **The LORD JESUS CHRIST is the power of man's redemption.**

Dear Father,

I rejoice in Zechariah's proclamation (from the Holy Spirit) that in the incarnation of Jesus You were fulfilling ancient prophesies of raising up a **Horn of Salvation**, (a Mighty Savior or the "strength of **salvation**)," in the house of David to save His people from their physical and spiritual enemies. I praise Jesus that He is the great Protector (King) of His people, Who defends us from the destructive works of the enemy of our souls. I am eternally grateful that we are delivered by His mighty **salvation**. I remember Psalm 18:2, *"The Lord is my rock, my fortress and my deliverer; my God is my rock, in whom I take refuge, my shield and the **horn of my salvation**, my stronghold."* I praise Jesus that He alone fits all those characteristics, and exceedingly more. I pray that I and a groundswell of other believers will abandon our lives now to the **Horn of Salvation**, so that He will bring unprecedented revival, awakening, protection, righteousness and salvation to His Church and to all people. He is our Hope. May we *"serve him without fear in holiness and righteousness before him all our days."* I pray these things in His mighty name. Amen.

What impacted me about Christ today...

_____

_____

_____

_____

_____

*Luke 1:76-79 And you [John the Baptist], my child, will be called a prophet of the Most High; for you will go on before the Lord to prepare the way for him, to give his people the knowledge of salvation through the forgiveness of their sins, because of the tender mercy of our God, by which the **rising sun** will come to us from heaven to shine on those living in darkness and in the shadow of death, to guide our feet into the path of peace.*

Significance: The LORD JESUS CHRIST brings the day of salvation to a darkened world.

Dear Father,

I bless You for sending Jesus, the **Rising Sun**, from heaven to shine His saving light, truth and righteousness on all *"those living in darkness and in the shadow of death."* I am very grateful that You sent the **Rising Sun** because of Your tender mercy for me and all of mankind. I rejoice that Jesus' name of the **Rising Sun** is a fulfillment of the Messianic prophecy in Malachi 4:2: *"But for you who revere my name, the **sun of righteousness** will rise with healing in its rays."* I pray that the **Rising Sun** will shine all of His fullness on me, my family, all believers and unsaved people to the ends of the earth. O God, mankind has always needed His presence, but we desperately need Him now to flood into every person, place and situation in our darkened world. I pray that You will convict the Church of any ways we have diminished the **Rising Sun** in our personal lives and other spheres of influence Please help us to be vessels of His spiritual healing to every other person we can. I pray that the presence of the **Rising Sun** will be so pervasive here that great numbers of lost people will be crying out to receive Him. Please *"guide [all of] our feet into the path of peace."* I ask these things in His merciful name. Amen.

What impacted me about Christ today...

_____

_____

_____

_____

_____

_____

*Luke 2:8-12 And there were shepherds living out in the fields nearby, keeping watch over their flocks at night. An angel of the Lord appeared to them, and the glory of the Lord shone around them, and they were terrified. But the angel said to them, "Do not be afraid. I bring you good news that will cause great joy for all the people. Today in the town of David **a Savior** has been born to you; he is the Messiah [the Christ] the Lord. This will be a sign to you: You will find a baby wrapped in cloths and lying in a manger."*

Significance: The LORD JESUS CHRIST is the Deliverer of mankind from our sins.

Dear Father,

What great joy I have that Jesus was **born to be** the **Savior** of all mankind! I can understand some of what a **Savior** is from the dictionary's definition of **Savior**: "One who **saves**, delivers or rescues another person or a country." But, that is just a foretaste of the **Savior** You sent to earth to **save**, deliver and rescue me and countless other people from Your wrath for our sins. I praise Jesus that, while there have been many people who have claimed to be earthly saviors of the people under their rule, Jesus is the only Person Who has given Himself as the perfect sacrifice to once and for all **save** us from the guilt, power, condemnation and eternal death of our sin. Hallelujah! Jesus is our completely sinless, gracious, merciful, loving and sacrificial **Savior**. He is the perfect **Savior**, the complete **Savior**, the glorious **Savior**, the only **Savior**…my **Savior**. I pray that You will give me and all of the **Savior's** other followers such a consuming love and gratitude for Him that we will gladly follow John's testimony in 1 John 4:14 that: *"We have seen and testify that the Father has sent His Son to be the **Savior** of the world"* with everyone we know. I pray that the Holy Spirit will overcome ALL barriers to those people receiving Jesus as THEIR **Savior** before it is too late. All glory to the **Savior**, in Whose name I pray these things. Amen.

What impacted me about Christ today...

_____

_____

_____

_____

*Luke 2:25-28 Now there was a man in Jerusalem called Simeon, who was righteous and devout. He was waiting for the **consolation of Israel**, and the Holy Spirit was on him. It had been revealed to him by the Holy Spirit that he would not die before he had seen the Lord's Messiah [Christ]. Moved by the Spirit, he went into the temple courts. When the parents brought in the child Jesus to do for him what the custom of the Law required, Simeon took him in his arms and praised God.*

Significance: **The LORD JESUS CHRIST becomes for us, by His lordship over our lives, the comfort and relief to His people.**

Dear Father,

Thank You greatly for sending Jesus to the Jewish people more than 2000 years ago, as the **Consolation of Israel**. I honor Jesus that in every way He perfectly satisfies the definition of "**consolation**": "a source of comfort to somebody who is distressed or disappointed." I can only imagine the spiritual comfort and joy that flooded Simeon when he saw the baby Jesus and immediately knew that He was Your fulfillment for all the longings the people of Israel had had (and been disappointed about) for many centuries, beginning with the covenant You made with Abraham in Genesis 12:1-3: *"The LORD had said to Abram, 'Go from your country, your people and your father's household to the land I will show you. I will make you into a great nation and I will bless you; I will make your name great, and you will be a blessing. I will bless those who bless you, and whoever curses you I will curse; and all peoples on earth will be blessed through you.'"* I worship the matchless **Consolation of Israel** with Simeon and multitudes throughout the ages by gratefully singing the first verse of Phillips Brooks' "O Little Town of Bethlehem": "O little town of Bethlehem, How still we see thee lie! Above thy deep and dreamless sleep, The silent stars go by; Yet in thy dark streets shineth, The everlasting Light; The hopes and fears of all the years are met in thee tonight." I pray that the Church of today will put all our hopes and dreams in the **Consolation of Israel**. In His name I ask these things. Amen.

What impacted me about Christ today...

_____

_____

_____

*Luke 2:25-28 Now there was a man in Jerusalem called Simeon, who was righteous and devout. He was waiting for the consolation of Israel, and the Holy Spirit was on him. It had been revealed to him by the Holy Spirit that he would not die before he had seen the **Lord's Messiah** [Christ]. Moved by the Spirit, he went into the temple courts. When the parents brought in the child Jesus to do for him what the custom of the Law required, Simeon took him in his arms and praised God.*

Significance: The LORD JESUS CHRIST is the promised Anointed One from God.

~

Dear Father,

I am very pleased that the Holy Spirit revealed to Simeon that he would not die before he had seen Jesus, the **Lord's Messiah (Christ)**. I can imagine that Simeon must have been amazed that he would have the great privilege of seeing (not to mention holding) the **Messiah**, Who, the prophets had foretold for many centuries, would be sent by You to save their nation. I praise Jesus that He is God, the Lord of the universe, the One You said in Isaiah 9 would heal the sick, have the government on His shoulders, reign on King David's throne, and bring endless peace to Israel. I exalt Jesus, **Your** Chosen and Anointed **Messiah**. I thank You profusely that I and every person today can (before we die) see the **Lord's Messiah** by faith, and take Him into our arms (our lives). I rejoice that, like Jesus was physically known by Simeon, and later by His disciples and many other people of Israel, that He is present in Spirit for all people today to receive Him, know Him, love Him, be healed by Him, be forgiven and cleansed by Him, and be conformed to His image. Oh, Father, I pray that I and millions of believers today will be as desirous of seeing, holding and being sold out to the **Lord's Messiah** as Simeon was. As with Simeon, may You receive the highest praise. In Your Messiah's name I ask these things. Amen.

What impacted me about Christ today...

_____

_____

_____

_____

_____

A Light For Revelation To The Gentiles

*Luke 2:28-33 Simeon took him [Jesus] in his arms and praised God, saying: "Sovereign Lord, as you have promised, you may now dismiss your servant in peace. For my eyes have seen your salvation, which you have prepared in the sight of all nations, a **light for revelation to the Gentiles**, and the glory of your people Israel." The child's father and mother marveled at what was said about him.*

Significance: **The LORD JESUS CHRIST displays the whole truth of God for all people.**

Dear Father,

I continue rejoicing with Simeon that You allowed him to see the One Who would make salvation available to all people, and be a **Light for Revelation to the Gentiles**. I am deeply grateful that You did not send Jesus only to the Jewish people to **reveal** all You are. But, Hallelujah, You sent Your Son to also bring the full **light (revelation)** of Yourself to the Gentiles (all the people of the world), while He walked on the earth, now and forever! Oh, what glorious **light** Jesus **revealed** when He spoke and demonstrated Your limitless peace, righteousness, wisdom, justice, truth, grace, goodness, mercy, love, power, majesty, compassion, and exceedingly more! I marvel with Joseph and Mary at all their Son (and Your Son) is, as the divine **Light for Revelation to the Gentiles**. Truly, He is the magnificent *"glory of your people Israel."* I pray that You will open my eyes and the eyes of believers of all languages, tribes and nations (including the Jewish people), to see all that Jesus is, as the Savior of the world and as the **Light for Revelation to the Gentiles**. Please help us to see so much of His greatness that we will devote ourselves to knowing Him all we possibly can, honoring His holy name, submitting all our will to Him, and speaking with one another about the victorious hope we have in Him. I pray all these things in Jesus' brilliant name. Amen.

What impacted me about Christ today...

_____

_____

_____

_____

_____

*Luke 2:39-40 When Joseph and Mary had done everything required by the Law of the Lord, they returned to Galilee to their own town of Nazareth. And the **child** [Jesus] grew and became strong; he was filled with wisdom, and the grace of God was on him.*

Significance: **The LORD JESUS CHRIST was mature as a young boy according to the Father's perfect plan for Him.**

Dear Father,

I rejoice that while Jesus was a **Child** He grew and became strong, was filled with wisdom, and Your grace was upon Him. I am in awe how the fullness of the Godhead was poured into every part of Jesus' human upbringing, and that Your character and attributes were very evident in Him at an early age. The passage in Proverbs 22:6 applies to the godly influence of the earthly parents You gave Him: *"Start children off on the way they should go, and even when they are old they will not turn from it."* I praise You that as Jesus was developing as a **Child**, He received the best possible input from His family and community to fulfill His role as the Son of Man. I honor Jesus at every part of His life (including as a **child**), in everything He did and said. I pray that I and all other Christian parents today will be like the **Child's** parents in training our children (and grandchildren) in the Word, in righteousness, in worship, in prayer, and in obedience to You, so that they will grow as He did. I pray that many multitudes of children who do not have Christian parents or other Christian influences in their lives will miraculously be brought to Jesus, the **Child**, and open their hearts to salvation in Him. I pray these things in His dear name. Amen.

What impacted me about Christ today...

_____

_____

_____

_____

_____

_____

_____

*Luke 2:41-49 Every year Jesus' parents went to Jerusalem for the Festival of the Passover. When he was twelve years old, they went up to the festival, according to the custom. After the festival was over, while his parents were returning home, the **boy Jesus** stayed behind in Jerusalem, but they were unaware of it. Thinking he was in their company, they traveled on for a day. Then they began looking for him among their relatives and friends. When they did not find him, they went back to Jerusalem to look for him. After three days they found him in the temple courts, sitting among the teachers, listening to them and asking them questions. Everyone who heard him was amazed at his understanding and his answers. When his parents saw him, they were astonished. His mother said to him, "Son, why have you treated us like this? Your father and I have been anxiously searching for you." "Why were you searching for me?" he asked. "Didn't you know I had to be in my Father's house?"*

Significance: The LORD JESUS CHRIST displayed obedience to God even as a young person.

Dear Father,

I am impressed that the **Boy Jesus** at twelve years old (when by Jewish custom He became a "son of the law") was sitting with the teachers of the law, intently listening to what they said, asking questions, and answering their questions. I praise Jesus that **everyone** who heard Him was amazed at His understanding and answers, and that He clearly knew Who He was, Who You (His Father) were, and His mission from You as the Messiah. I honor Him that even at a young age, He was resolutely progressing towards fulfilling that mission. I am deeply impacted by His absolute devotion to You, as a **boy** and later as a man. I pray that multitudes of Christian boys and young men across America will become aware of the righteous character of the **Boy Jesus** and His devotion to You, and that the Holy Spirit will kindle a fire in them to radically live in all Jesus is. I pray the same for our girls and young women too. Please *"fix their eyes"* upon Jesus. I pray these things in His amazing name. Amen.

What impacted me about Christ today...

_____

_____

*Luke 3:3-6 He [John the Baptist] went into all the country around the Jordan, preaching a baptism of repentance for the forgiveness of sins. As is written in the book of the words of Isaiah the prophet: "A voice of one calling in the wilderness, 'Prepare the way for the Lord, make straight paths for him. Every valley shall be filled in, every mountain and hill made low. The crooked roads shall become straight, the rough ways smooth. And all people will see **God's salvation**.'"*

Significance: The **LORD JESUS CHRIST** is the unobstructed deliverer from heaven.

೩

Dear Father,

I am forever grateful that You have removed **all** the obstacles (prepared the way) for Jesus, **God's Salvation**, to come into the world to save me and the rest of mankind from our sins, and to rule and reign over our lives forever. I praise Jesus that He fulfills the Old Testament prophecy of Isaiah 40:5 that is quoted in today's Scripture, and another related prophecy in Isaiah 52:10, *"The LORD will lay bare his holy arm in the sight of all the nations, and all the ends of the earth will see the **salvation** of our God."* I desire to see and know all of Jesus, the blessed One Who brought Your **salvation** to me and to all people. I earnestly pray that You will help believers everywhere to see the greatness of our **Savior** as the Apostle Paul prays for the Church of Ephesus and us in Ephesians 1:17-19, *"I keep asking that the God of our Lord Jesus Christ, the glorious Father, may give you the Spirit of wisdom and revelation, so that you may know him [Jesus] better. I pray that the eyes of your heart may be enlightened in order that you may know the hope to which he has called you, the riches of his glorious inheritance in his holy people, and his incomparably great power for us who believe."* I further pray that You will do whatever is necessary in many millions of lost people that they might very soon see (with their eyes and with their spirits) and give their lives to **God's Salvation**. In His merciful name I pray these things. Amen.

What impacted me about Christ today...

_____

_____

_____

_____

*Luke 4:16-23 He [Jesus] went to Nazareth, where he had been brought up, and on the Sabbath day he went into the synagogue, as was his custom. He stood up to read, and the scroll of the prophet Isaiah was handed to him. Unrolling it, he found the place where it is written: "The Spirit of the Lord is on me, because he has anointed me to proclaim good news to the poor. He has sent me to proclaim freedom for the prisoners and recovery of sight for the blind, to set the oppressed free, to proclaim the year of the Lord's favor." Then he rolled up the scroll, gave it back to the attendant and sat down. The eyes of everyone in the synagogue were fastened on him. He began by saying to them, "Today this scripture is fulfilled in your hearing." All spoke well of him and were amazed at the gracious words that came from his lips. "Isn't this **Joseph's son**?" they asked. Jesus said to them, "Surely you will quote this proverb to me: 'Physician, heal yourself!' And you will tell me, ' Do here in your hometown what we have heard that you did in Capernaum.'"*

Significance: **The LORD JESUS CHRIST is the Messiah regardless of His earthly parentage.**

Dear Father,

I am saddened that while the people of Nazareth were amazed when Jesus read from Isaiah 61 about the Messiah and heard Him say He was the Messiah, they had such a limited understanding of Him that they could only believe Him to be the **son of Joseph**, a common local carpenter. Yes, Father, He was and is **Joseph's Son**, Who experienced all our human conditions, but, I praise Him that He is also the complete fulfillment of all of Isaiah 61 and of every other Messianic prophecy that is declared through Your ancient prophets! I worship **Joseph's Son**, the **Son** of Man and **Son** of God. I pray that I and all His followers today will repent of our lack of understanding of Him, and be cleansed of all disbelief. Please cause our eyes to be fastened on Him, and to speak well of Him as we become utterly amazed at all He is and does. May unprecedented numbers from all people groups and nations be gripped with the magnificence of Jesus. In His worthy name I pray these things. Amen.

What impacted me about Christ today...

Luke 7:11-17 Soon afterward, Jesus went to a town called Nain, and his disciples and a large crowd went along with him. As he approached the town gate, a dead person was being carried out—the only son of his mother, and she was a widow. And a large crowd from the town was with her. When the Lord saw her, his heart went out to her and he said, "Don't cry." Then he went up and touched the bier they were carrying him on, and the bearers stood still. He said, "Young man, I say to you, get up!" The dead man sat up and began to talk, and Jesus gave him back to his mother.

*They were all filled with awe and praised God. "A **great prophet** has appeared among us," they said. "God has come to help his people." This news about Jesus spread throughout Judea and the surrounding country.*

Significance: **The LORD JESUS CHRIST is the primary and most esteemed spokesman for God.**

Dear Father,

I can imagine how all the people who saw Jesus raise the dead man to life were filled with awe and praise. I can also imagine that those people thought Jesus was another **great prophet** like Elijah or Elisha who they knew had performed many powerful miracles and had great authority. I exalt Jesus that in Him all the promises, and prophecies and the law are summed up. I am grateful that the people knew they had seen a stunning display of Your divine power, so Jesus had undoubtedly come from You. I honor Jesus that He alone can be called the **Great Prophet** of all prophets. Please help me and many other believers today to have such awe of Jesus' astounding **greatness**, that news about Him spreads like wildfire throughout His Church and to all people. I pray again that very soon *"the earth will be filled with the knowledge of the glory of the LORD as the waters cover the sea"* (Habakkuk 2:14). I ask these things in the name and for the fame of the **Great Prophet**. Amen.

What impacted me about Christ today...

_____

_____

_____

_____

_____

A Friend Of Tax Collectors And Sinners

*Luke 7:33-34 For John the Baptist came neither eating bread nor drinking wine, and you say, "He has a demon." The Son of Man came eating and drinking, and you say, "Here is a glutton and a drunkard, a **friend of tax collectors and sinners**."*

Significance: The **LORD JESUS CHRIST** lovingly accepts and ministers to those whom others reject.

Dear Father,
I am very sorry that the people spoken about in today's Scripture passage were mocking Jesus by calling Him a **Friend of Tax Collectors and Sinners**. At the same time, I am eternally grateful that Jesus is the perfect, faithful, unconditional **Friend** to me and to all other **tax collectors and sinners** (all people), regardless of our status in life, the level of sin we have committed, or whether or not we receive His **friendship**. I praise Jesus, that in addition to Him having all the love and compassion of the very best **friend** all people could ever have, He also has all the power and authority to fulfill every act of **friendship** He knows we need. I am reminded of the first part of a hymn by Johnson Oatman, Jr.: (verse 1) "There's not a **Friend** like the lowly Jesus. No, not one! No, not one! None else could heal all our soul's diseases, No, not one! No, not one! (chorus) Jesus knows all about our struggles. He will guide 'til the break of day. There's not a **Friend** like the lowly Jesus. No, not one! No, not one!" I receive His all-encompassing **friendship**, give Him all my friendship, and earnestly pray that every person in my spheres of influence will soon awaken to the greatness of the **Friend of Tax Collectors and Sinners**, and gratefully choose to live in His redeeming **friendship** too. All honor and glory to the **Friend of Tax Collectors and Sinners**, in Whose name I pray these things. Amen.

What impacted me about Christ today...

_____

_____

_____

_____

_____

_____

*Luke 8:22-25 One day Jesus said to his disciples, "Let us go over to the other side of the lake." So they got into a boat and set out. As they sailed, he fell asleep. A squall came down on the lake, so that the boat was being swamped, and they were in great danger. The disciples went and woke him, saying, "**Master, Master**, we're going to drown!" He got up and rebuked the wind and the raging waters; the storm subsided, and all was calm. "Where is your faith?" he asked his disciples. In fear and amazement they asked one another, "Who is this? He commands even the winds and the water, and they obey him."*

Significance: The LORD JESUS CHRIST is the commander of all things.

Dear Father,

I am in awe as I think about how Jesus brought all of the heavens and earth into existence by the word of His mouth, and how He demonstrated that same **mastery** over the wind and the waves in this critical situation with His disciples on the lake. I can identify with the disciples crying *"**Master, Master**,"* because they knew Jesus was the only one Who had the authority to save them from being swamped. At the same time, I join the disciples as they were filled with fear and amazement at the unparalleled and unlimited power they were beginning to understand that Jesus possessed. I pray that You will help me, my family members and all other believers today to see the **Master** as clearly as those disciples did so that we too will be filled with fear and amazement of Him. I pray that You will help our faith in the **Master** to grow much deeper, so we will trust Him at all times, even when it seems like He is *"asleep."* Please convince us to give Him the command of **every** part of our lives. I pray too that the Holy Spirit will very soon reveal the power and majesty of the **Master** to all possible lost people around us, and they will cry out to Him to save them. In the **Master's** name I ask these things. Amen.

What impacted me about Christ today...

_____

_____

_____

_____

*Luke 9:37-42 The next day, when they came down from the mountain, a large crowd met him. A man in the crowd called out, "**Teacher**, I beg you to look at my son, for he is my only child. A spirit seizes him and he suddenly screams; it throws him into convulsions so that he foams at the mouth. It scarcely ever leaves him and is destroying him. I begged your disciples to drive it out, but they could not." "You unbelieving and perverse generation," Jesus replied, "how long shall I stay with you and put up with you? Bring your son here." Even while the boy was coming, the demon threw him to the ground in a convulsion. But Jesus rebuked the impure spirit, healed the boy and gave him back to his father.*

Significance: The LORD JESUS CHRIST instructs and leads His followers in how to live under His lordship.

Dear Father,

Thank You very much for the powerful demonstration of the lordship of Jesus in His cleansing of a young man from the control of a demon. I am confident that what Jesus **teaches** in this incident can apply to every part of our relationship with Him. I worship Him that He alone has the authority to overcome and cast out all forces of darkness. I praise Him that He is Lord of all the physical and spiritual kingdoms. I honor Him for being the divine **Teacher** of the people of Israel who encountered Him during His time with them on earth, and of me and countless other people throughout the ages who hear and read about His powerful, life-changing **teachings** and works. I can certainly understand how the many Jews whom He taught and miraculously healed were amazed with the authority of the great **Teacher**. I pray that I, my family members and all of His followers will devote ourselves to knowing all we possibly can about Him, so we will grow in trusting Him, obeying all He is **teaching** us, and speaking to everyone about His boundless wisdom and power. Please teach us to always follow the **Teacher**. I pray these things in His wise and worthy name. Amen.

What impacted me about Christ today...

_____

_____

_____

_____

Someone Stronger

*Luke 11:21-22 When a strong man, fully armed, guards his own house, his possessions are safe. But when **someone stronger** attacks and overpowers him, he takes away the armor in which the man trusted and divides up his plunder.*

S ignificance: The LORD JESUS CHRIST is always greater and stronger than His strong enemy, Satan.

Dear Father,

I rejoice that Jesus has always been (and will always be) **Someone Stronger** than the strong man, Satan! I praise Jesus that He is the omnipotent, omnipresent and omniscient One, and that when He attacks and overpowers Satan, He takes away all that has protected Satan's territory. I think of when You first declared to the serpent in Genesis 3:15 that Christ has divine authority over Satan: *"And I will put enmity between you and the woman, and between your offspring and hers; he will crush your head and you will strike his heel."* I also exalt **Someone Stronger** for what the Apostle Paul said about Him in Colossians 2:15, *"And having disarmed the powers and authorities, he made a public spectacle of them, triumphing over them by the cross."* I do not want to be under the influence of Satan (be one of his *"possessions"*) in any way. So, I again place **every part of my life**, and each of my family members, in the powerful hands of **Someone Stronger**. I pray that we and all other believers will live completely under His righteousness, love, majesty, justice, truth, authority and deliverance. I pray that **Someone Stronger** will overpower Satan's forces that have evil influence over any people or situations throughout the world. May great numbers of those people receive **Someone Stronger** as their Savior, and may individuals, families, neighborhoods, cities, states, regions, people groups and nations come under Christ's dominion. I ask these things in His mighty name, and for His glory. Amen.

What impacted me about Christ today...

_____

_____

_____

_____

_____

*Luke 13:22-27 Then Jesus went through the towns and villages, teaching as he made his way to Jerusalem. Someone asked him, "Lord, are only a few people going to be saved?" He said to them, "Make every effort to enter through the narrow door, because many, I tell you, will try to enter and will not be able to. Once the **owner of the house** gets up and closes the door, you will stand outside knocking and pleading, 'Sir, open the door for us.' But he will answer, 'I don't know you or where you come from.' Then you will say, 'We ate and drank with you, and you taught in our streets.' But he will reply, 'I don't know you or where you come from. Away from me, all you evildoers!'"*

Significance: **The LORD JESUS CHRIST is the One Who opens and closes the door to eternal life.**

Dear Father,

I praise Jesus, the **Owner of the House**. I am very thankful that, just as Jesus taught the Jewish people 2000 years ago the necessity of entering the **house** (coming into a saving relationship with Him) through the *"narrow door,"* He is still teaching all people who have eyes to see and ears to hear how to do so. I can imagine Him sitting in His **house** (His kingdom) inviting all people to do what He taught in Matthew 7:13-14, *"Enter through the narrow gate. For wide is the gate and broad is the road that leads to destruction, and many enter through it. But small is the gate and narrow the road that leads to life, and only a few find it."* I honor Jesus that You have given Him the total authority to *"get up and close the door"* at His chosen time to everyone who has not been willing to come to Him. I pray that I and all those who have come to the **Owner of the House** through the narrow door will worship Him continually for that gift, and will give every thought, passion, talent, moment, word and deed to Him. Please convict us to urgently pray that every obstacle that has been keeping all the lost people we know from entering into salvation through the narrow door will be overcome, before it is too late. I pray these things in the saving name of Jesus. Amen.

What impacted me about Christ today...

_____

_____

JULY

THE FRUIT OF THE LAND

SOURCE OF STRENGTH

A WALL OF FIRE

ANOINTED ONE

THE MESSIAH

SON OF THE LIVING GOD

OUR MIGHTY ONE

Savior, Prince of Peace

The eternal

the

HE SF

MY CHOSEN ONE

THE MOST HOLY THE DELIVERER

A GREAT LIGHT

guardian

IMMANUEL

THE SON OF MAN

THE ROCK OF ISRAEL

sign of the covenant

redeer

GOD WITH US

THE FOUNTAIN OF LIFE

MY HIDING PLACE

MY STRENG

WONDERFUL COUNSELOR

SON OF DAVID

HORN OF SALVA

THE COMMANDER

A STRONG TOWER

TEACHER

THE GREAT KING OVER ALL THE EAR

MY STRONG DELIVERER

PRINCE OF PEACE

THE KING OF GLORY

THE REFUGE FOR THE OPPRESSED

GOD, WHO RAISES THE DE

THE MAKER OF HEAVEN AND EAR

THE LORD THE KING

THE MIGHTY SCEPTER

A SHELTER FROM THE STORM

Bread of life

the Rock Their Savior

A Witness to

the People

*Luke 22:27-30 For who is greater, the one who is at the table or the one who serves? Is it not the one who is at the table? But I am among you as **one who serves**. You are those who have stood by me in my trials. And I confer on you a kingdom, just as my Father conferred one on me, so that you may eat and drink at my table in my kingdom and sit on thrones, judging the twelve tribes of Israel.*

Significance: The LORD JESUS CHRIST is the perfection of caring for and assisting others.

Dear Father,

I am deeply grateful that You sent Jesus, the Lord and Master of the whole universe, to earth as the **One Who Serves**. When Jesus talks about the greatness of one who sits at the table, compared to a person who serves, I cannot help but think of the immeasurable greatness of Jesus Himself. I exalt Him that He is the most revered and honored Person Who could ever sit at any table with any individual or group! Yet, I honor Him that He was willing to put aside His great authority to be the **Servant** of all servants, and the giver of all givers. I praise Him that all the attributes of a **servant** are maximized in Him: faithfulness, love, compassion, devotion, self-denial, patience, righteousness, grace, mercy, humility, tenderness, perseverance, wisdom and abundantly more. I especially remember what He did in John 13:5 with His disciples: *"He poured water into a basin and began to wash his disciples' feet, drying them with the towel that was wrapped around him."* I pray that You will help me and Jesus' other followers to eagerly know all we possibly can about the **One Who Serves**, and to die to our self-centered natures and live totally in Him. And, I pray that scores of unsaved people around us who desperately need to experience (see, touch, feel) Jesus' **servant** spirit will do so right away. I pray these things in His loving name. Amen.

What impacted me about Christ today...

_____

_____

_____

_____

*Luke 23:1-4 Then the whole assembly rose and led him [Jesus] off to Pilate. And they began to accuse him, saying, "We have found this man subverting our nation. He opposes payment of taxes to Caesar and claims to be **Messiah [Christ], a king**." So Pilate asked Jesus, "Are you the king of the Jews?" "You have said so," Jesus replied. Then Pilate announced to the chief priests and the crowd, "I find no basis for a charge against this man."*

Significance: The LORD JESUS CHRIST is the divine ruler of all rulers.

Dear Father,

I bow down before Jesus, Who does not just *"claim to be"* **Messiah (Christ) a King,** but Who unquestionably IS **Messiah a King** (Christ THE King)! I am in awe that before the beginning of time You determined that Jesus would be the **Messiah** (the Anointed One, the Christ, the Savior of the world), and the **King** (the Ruler and Lord) of all creation. I thank You that in Him is Your entire rule, saving power, healing, love, forgiveness, servant spirit, grace, revelation and wisdom. I exalt and adore the **Messiah King**. I devote every part of my life to Him and I proclaim His absolute supremacy. I pray that Your Spirit will cause *"the whole assembly"* (the whole Church) to become insatiably hungry to know the depths and riches of the **Messiah**, and to abandon ourselves to following Him above all else. I pray that rather than Jesus being charged with *"subverting our nation"* today, that great numbers of people will honor and revere Him as Lord of their lives and Lord of the nations. I especially pray that You will remove all obstacles for Jewish people around the world, to receive the **Messiah** as their king, now and forever. All glory to **Messiah a King**, Who alone is the reigning **King** of the Jews! In His majestic name I pray these things. Amen.

What impacted me about Christ today...

_____

_____

_____

_____

*<u>Luke 23:44-49</u> It was now about noon, and darkness came over the whole land until three in the afternoon, for the sun stopped shining. And the curtain of the temple was torn in two. Jesus called out with a loud voice, "Father, into your hands I commit my spirit." When he had said this, he breathed his last. The centurion, seeing what had happened, praised God and said, "Surely this was a **righteous man**." When all the people who had gathered to witness this sight saw what took place, they beat their breasts and went away. But all those who knew him, including the women who had followed him from Galilee, stood at a distance, watching these things.*

Significance: **The LORD JESUS CHRIST fulfills God's laws perfectly and finally.**

Dear Father,

I join the centurion in praising You and in proclaiming that surely Jesus is a **Righteous Man** (the Son of God in Whom all Your righteousness dwells). I marvel that Jesus, the spotless Lamb, was willing to suffer the excruciating death that I and every other person in the world deserves for our sins. Hallelujah, that His sacrifice tore the curtain of the temple to show that I and all who receive Him can have an intimate love relationship with You! Once again my heart cries out with Charles Wesley in a portion of his hymn, "And Can It Be": "And can it be that I should gain an interest in the Savior's blood! Died He for me who caused His pain. For me, who Him to death pursued? Amazing love! How can it be, that Thou, my God, should'st die for me?" I ask Your Spirit to cleanse me, my family members and all believers of everything that hinders us from fully abiding in the **Righteous Man**. May we be **righteous** as He is righteous, and commit ourselves (body, mind and spirit) entirely into His hands. I pray that multitudes of unsaved people today will be as startled by Who Christ is, as were the centurion and the others who witnessed His death in person. I pray these things in His **righteous** name. Amen.

What impacted me about Christ today...

_____

_____

_____

Powerful In Word And Deed Before God And All The People

---

*Luke 24:13a, 15b-17a, 18-21, 25-27, 32 Now that same day two of them were going to a village called Emmaus . . . Jesus himself came up and walked along with them; but they were kept from recognizing him. He asked them, "What are you discussing together as you walk along?" . . . One of them, named Cleopas, asked him, "Are you the only one visiting Jerusalem who does not know the things that have happened there in these days?" "What things?" he asked. "About Jesus of Nazareth," they replied. "He was a prophet, **powerful in word and deed before God and all the people**. The chief priests and our rulers handed him over to be sentenced to death, and they crucified him; but we had hoped that he was the one who was going to redeem Israel. And what is more, it is the third day since all this took place." . . . He said to them, "How foolish you are, and how slow to believe all that the prophets have spoken! Did not the Messiah have to suffer these things and then enter his glory?" And beginning with Moses and all the Prophets, he explained to them what was said in all the Scriptures concerning himself. . . . They asked each other, "Were not our hearts burning within us while he talked with us on the road and opened the Scriptures to us?"*

Significance: **The LORD JESUS CHRIST displays the true power and authority of God in everything He says and does.**

Dear Father,

I am in awe that Jesus is far greater than what the two disciples in today's Scripture passage understood when they spoke of Him as "**Powerful in Word and Deed Before God and all the People**." I praise Jesus, Who is **all-powerful** and **all-mighty** in **all** His words and deeds: driving out demons, healing the sick, teaching with wisdom and understanding, fulfilling all prophecies and promises, raising the dead, controlling the physical environment, forgiving sins, and astoundingly more. I am very sorry that even though He has always performed amazingly **powerful** words and deeds, billions of people have not known Who He really is. I repent that the Church has been *"foolish and slow"* in believing all that has been spoken about Him. I pray that millions of believers today will revere Him for His vast **power**, submit to His **power**, live in His **power**, and unreservedly speak of His **power**. In His glorious name I pray. Amen.

What impacted me about Christ today...

---

*John 1:1-4, 14a In the beginning was the **Word**, and the **Word**
was with God, and the **Word** was God. He was with God in the beginning. Through him all things were made; without him nothing was made
that has been made. In him was life, and that life was the light of all
mankind. . . . The **Word** became flesh and made his dwelling among us.*

Significance: The LORD JESUS CHRIST is God, and He communicates to all people the fullness of Who God is.

Dear Father,
I praise Jesus, the **Word**, that He has lived in intimate relationship with
You forever, and that He is God. I praise Him also that He is the Creator
of ALL things. All glory to Jesus that *"without him nothing was made that
has been made."* I am in awe that You have revealed Yourself through all
that the **Word** created, as affirmed in Hebrews 1:2, *"in these last days, he
[God] has spoken to us by his Son, whom he appointed heir of all things,
and through whom also he made the universe."* I exalt the **Word** that all
of the life of the Godhead is in Him, and that He *"became flesh and made
his dwelling among us."* I love Jesus' statement in John 10:10b of the
immeasurable authority and abundance that is in Him alone: *"I have come
that they may have life, and have it to the full."* I pray that I and an ever-
increasing number of other believers will set aside all other attractions and
passions we encounter, so that we can live *"to the full"* in the Lord Jesus,
the **Word**. I pray that as we know Him more and live in more of His fullness, we will be filled with so much joy and hope that we must tell others
about all that He is. Please give masses of lost men, women, young people
and children such a longing for all the **Word** is that they will stop at nothing to have Him in their lives very soon. In the life-giving name of Jesus I
pray these things. Amen.

What impacted me about Christ today...

_____

_____

_____

_____

_____

_____

*John 1:1-5, 14a In the beginning was the Word, and the Word was with God, and the Word was God. He was with God in the beginning. Through him all things were made; without him nothing was made that has been made. In him was life, and that life was the **light of all mankind**. The light shines in the darkness, and the darkness has not overcome it. . . . The Word became flesh and made his dwelling among us.*

Significance: The LORD JESUS CHRIST provides all enlightenment and victory for all people.

Dear Father,

I am very grateful for Jesus' powerful declaration in John 12:44-46, that strongly supports today's name of Him: *"Whoever believes in me does not believe in me only, but in the one who sent me. The one who looks at me is seeing the one who sent me. I have come into the world as a **light**, so that no one who believes in me should stay in darkness."* I exalt Jesus that He is the fullness of all the life and **light** of the Godhead for all people, and that there is no true **light** apart from Him. I rejoice that everything in mankind which is in the **light**—knowledge, integrity, truth, love, wisdom, holiness, purity, grace, mercy, joy, peace, gentleness, humility, forgiveness, self-control, and more—is from Jesus, Who is the **Light of all Mankind**. I worship Him and I want to live in all of His brilliance, cleansing, warmth and revelation. I am exceedingly glad that He cannot be overcome by the darkness. I pray that You will help me to be filled with the **Light of all Mankind** and be a messenger of Him to everyone You bring into my life. May the **Light** shine in all darkness in our region and to the ends of the earth. I pray these things in His holy name. Amen.

What impacted me about Christ today...

_____

_____

_____

_____

_____

_____

John 1:23-27, 29-30 John replied in the words of Isaiah the prophet, "I
am the voice of one calling in the wilderness, 'Make straight the way
for the Lord.'" Now the Pharisees who had been sent questioned him,
"Why then do you baptize if you are not the Messiah, nor Elijah, nor the
Prophet?" "I baptize with water," John replied, "but among you stands
one you do not know. He is the one who comes after me, the straps of
whose sandals I am not worthy to untie." . . . The next day John saw
Jesus coming toward him and said, "Look, the **Lamb of God***, who takes*
away the sin of the world! This is the one I meant when I said, 'A man
who comes after me has surpassed me because he was before me.'"

Significance: **The LORD JESUS CHRIST is God's sacrifice for**
man's sins.

Dear Father,
Thank You so much for sending Your beloved Son, the **Lamb of God**,
to earth. I praise Him that He is the only completely innocent, sacrificial offering that could pay the price of my sins and the sins of every
other person who receives Him as their Savior. Just as John the Baptist
announced when Jesus approached him, *"Look, the* **Lamb of God***,"* I pray
that millions of believers today will look at the **Lamb of God** and be overwhelmed with Your love, mercy, grace, peace, meekness, purity, and hope
in Him. I pray we will worship and love the **Lamb of God** for all He is,
and talk with one another about His greatness every chance You give us.
I pray we will be so filled with love and gratitude for the **Lamb of God**
that unsaved people will regularly ask us to tell them about Him. May the
whole world join in singing "Just As I Am" by Charlotte Elliott: (verse 1)
"Just as I am, without one plea, But that Thy blood was shed for me,
And that Thou bid'st me come to Thee, O Lamb of God, I come, I come!
(verse 2) Just as I am, and waiting not, To rid my soul of one dark blot;
To Thee whose blood can cleanse each spot, O Lamb of God, I come, I
come! (verse 5) Just as I am, Thou wilt receive, Wilt welcome, pardon,
cleanse, relieve; Because Thy promise I believe, O Lamb of God, I
come, I come!" In the sacrificial name of the **Lamb**. Amen.

What impacted me about Christ today...

*John 1:47-49 When Jesus saw Nathanael approaching, he said of him, "Here truly is an Israelite in whom there is no deceit." "How do you know me?" Nathanael asked. Jesus answered, "I saw you while you were still under the fig tree before Philip called you." Then Nathanael declared, "Rabbi, you are the Son of God; you are the **king of Israel**."*

Significance: The LORD JESUS CHRIST is the final leader of the chosen people.

Dear Father,

Thank You for the stunning way Jesus revealed to Nathanael that He was the Son of God and the **King of Israel**. I rejoice that Philip told Nathanael that Jesus was the Messiah and invited him to meet Jesus, and that when Jesus displayed the supreme knowledge that only Your divine Son possesses, Nathanael was assured that He was the **King** the people of Israel had been longing and praying for for centuries. I praise Jesus that He alone fulfills the Psalm 132:11 prophecy: *"The Lord swore an oath to David, a sure oath that He will not revoke: 'One of your descendants I will place on your throne.'"* I know that the people of Israel, and probably Nathanael too, were eagerly expecting that the Messiah would be a conquering earthly **King**, but I praise Him that He was then, and is forever, the eternal, **King** of Israel and **King** of the Universe, Who is far beyond what they could ask or imagine! All glory to the great **King**! I pray that You will reveal to me and to all other believers today exactly Who the Son of God and **King of Israel** is, and that we will worship Him, submit ourselves to Him entirely, and make His greatness known to one another and to all His potential subjects (currently unsaved people) we can. My heart cries out that many of those future subjects of the **King** will be Jews from around the world today. In the **King's** name I pray these things. Amen.

What impacted me about Christ today...

_____

_____

_____

_____

_____

John 3:16-17 *"For God so loved the world that he gave **his one and only Son**, that whoever believes in him shall not perish but have eternal life. For God did not send his Son into the world to condemn the world, but to save the world through him."*

Significance: The LORD JESUS CHRIST is The Beloved Gift the Father provided for mankind.

Dear Father,

When I imagine the depth of love You lavished on me and all mankind by completely giving Your precious, only-begotten, **One and Only Son**, no words can adequately express the wonder and gratitude that fills my heart. This sacrifice of Your **Son** reminds me of Genesis 22:1-2, 9b-12, where You directed Abraham to offer his beloved son as a sacrifice too: *"Some time later God tested Abraham. He said to him, 'Abraham!' 'Here I am,' he replied. Then God said, 'Take your son, your **only son**, whom you love— Isaac—and go to the region of Moriah. Sacrifice him there as a burnt offering on a mountain I will show you.' . . . He bound his son Isaac and laid him on the altar, on top of the wood. Then he reached out his hand and took the knife to slay his son. But the angel of the LORD called out to him from heaven, 'Abraham! Abraham!' 'Here I am,' he replied. 'Do not lay a hand on the boy,' he said. 'Do not do anything to him. Now I know that you fear God, because you have not withheld from me your son, your **only son**.'"* Thank You, Almighty God, for providing (not withholding) Your **One and Only Son**, as the **only** sacrifice/way through which we might have eternal life. I BELIEVE IN HIM! I pray that all other Christians will awaken now to unreserved belief in Christ for all He is! In the name of the **One and Only Son**. Amen.

What impacted me about Christ today...

_____

_____

_____

_____

_____

_____

*John 3:27-30 To this John [the Baptist] replied, "A person can receive
only what is given them from heaven. You yourselves can testify that
I said, 'I am not the Messiah but am sent ahead of him.' The bride
belongs to the **bridegroom**. The friend who attends the **bridegroom** waits
and listens for him, and is full of joy when he hears the **bridegroom's**
voice. That joy is mine, and it is now complete. He must become
greater; I must become less."*

Significance: The LORD JESUS CHRIST is the beloved and consummate groom for His Church.

Dear Father,

I am very grateful that I and all believers are part of the Bride, and the
Lord Jesus is our beloved **Bridegroom**. Hallelujah, we belong to Him.
He is the perfect lover, friend, protector, provider, strength, advocate and
redeemer. He is our all in all, and we are complete in Him alone. I eagerly
wait and listen for Him, and I am full of joy to hear His voice. Please help
me, my family members and the whole Church to be completely faithful
and devoted to Him, as He is completely faithful and devoted to us. I pray
that You will also help us to be prepared for Him like the five wise virgins
in Matthew 25 were ready with oil in their lamps when the **bridegroom**
arrived at the wedding banquet. I want more than anything else to attend
the banquet with Him, and to be with Him always. I pray, as John the
Baptist said, that Jesus, the **Bridegroom**, will increase in our lives, and
we would decrease, for His great glory. Will You please also do whatever
is necessary in the hearts and minds of great numbers of unsaved people
around us so that they will cry out for Him to be their **Bridegroom** too.
May they not be passed by at this urgent time in history. I ask all these
things in Jesus' lovely name. Amen.

What impacted me about Christ today...

_____

_____

_____

_____

_____

<u>*John 4:1-9*</u> *Now Jesus learned that the Pharisees had heard that he was gaining and baptizing more disciples than John—although in fact it was not Jesus who baptized, but his disciples. So he left Judea and went back once more to Galilee. Now he had to go through Samaria. So he came to a town in Samaria called Sychar, near the plot of ground Jacob had given to his son Joseph. Jacob's well was there, and Jesus, tired as he was from the journey, sat down by the well. It was about noon. When a Samaritan woman came to draw water, Jesus said to her, "Will you give me a drink?" (His disciples had gone into the town to buy food). The Samaritan woman said to him, "You are a **Jew** and I am a Samaritan woman. How can you ask me for a drink?" (For Jews do not associate with Samaritans).*

Significance: **The LORD JESUS CHRIST was a citizen of Israel, Who chose to associate with "outcasts" that His fellow Jewish citizens would not associate with.**

Dear Father,
I am very blessed that even though Jesus was definitely a **Jew** by birth and religious tradition (and was even a Jewish rabbi), in the encounter with the Samaritan woman He did what He typically did when there was a clash between culture/tradition and caring for people—He demonstrated Your great love. I honor Jesus that His position as a **Jew** was not diminished by reaching out to the Samaritan woman, but that He was wonderfully giving her all of Himself, as Lord of the **Jews** and Lord of all. I thank You that in Jesus, the **Jew** above all Jews, Your very Son, there is no prejudice, favoritism or conditional love. I rejoice that, as with the Samaritan woman, Jesus always reaches out to engage us in knowing Him and receiving the fullness of life in Him. I pray that I and all believers will be deeply grateful that the **Jew** reached out to us in love we could not possibly deserve. I ask that You will place all unsaved people in situations where He will reveal His life-transforming love to them. In His name I pray these things. Amen.

What impacted me about Christ today...

_____

_____

_____

John 4:9-10 The Samaritan woman said to him, "You are a Jew and I am a Samaritan woman. How can you ask me for a drink?" (For Jews do not associate with Samaritans.) Jesus answered her, "If you knew the **gift of God** *and who it is that asks you for a drink, you would have asked him and he would have given you living water."*

Significance: The LORD JESUS CHRIST is the Father's perfect present to mankind.

Dear Father,

I praise You that Jesus is the **Gift of God** (Your beloved Son, the One Who is most precious to You, the greatest **Gift** You could possibly give to mankind). As I think about Your **Gift**, I am reminded of Romans 6:23, *"For the wages of sin is death, but the* **gift of God** *is eternal life in Christ Jesus our Lord."* I am exceedingly grateful that Jesus, the **Gift of God**, has all of the power, love, righteousness, grace and wisdom to save us and keep us. I pray that You will freshly reveal to me and to all Christians how valuable Your free **Gift** is, and cause us to seek Him, love Him, worship Him, devote ourselves wholly to Him, and constantly speak of His great worth with each other. And, I pray that You will put an intense, desperate longing for the **Gift of God** into the hearts and minds of all unsaved people, and give them every opportunity to know and receive Him too. May the **Gift of God** become more precious to them than gold and silver and all of man's other aspirations, so that He will be their chief desire. In His name I ask these things. Amen.

What impacted me about Christ today...

_____

_____

_____

_____

_____

_____

_____

_____

*<u>John 4:9-15</u> The Samaritan woman said to him, "You are a Jew and I am a Samaritan woman. How can you ask me for a drink?" (For Jews do not associate with Samaritans.) Jesus answered her, "If you knew the gift of God and who it is that asks you for a drink, you would have asked him and he would have given you **living water**." "Sir", the woman said, "you have nothing to draw with and the well is deep. Where can you get this **living water**? Are you greater than our father Jacob, who gave us the well and drank from it himself, as did also his sons and his livestock?" Jesus answered, "Everyone who drinks this water will be thirsty again, but whoever drinks the water I give them will never thirst. Indeed, the water I give them will become in them a spring of water welling up to eternal life." The woman said to him, "Sir, give me this water so that I won't get thirsty and have to keep coming here to draw water."*

Significance: **The LORD JESUS CHRIST is the source of eternal refreshment.**

Dear Father,

I am very grateful that You sent Jesus, the ceaselessly abundant **Living Water** to the Samaritan woman, to me and to all mankind. I rejoice that only the **Living Water** is able to satisfy our deepest need: our spiritual thirst, now and for all of eternity. I marvel how Jesus knew everything about the Samaritan woman (and about me too), and that He uses the circumstances of our lives to offer His precious cleansing, sustaining, reviving, filling and healing life to us. I pray that You will put an insatiable thirst in me and every believer for the **Living Water**. I love to think of Him as our **Water of life**. I pray that You will immerse us in the **Living Water**. May we wholeheartedly live in Jesus' promise in John 7:37b-38, *"Let anyone who is thirsty come to me and drink. Whoever believes in me, as Scripture has said, rivers of **living water** will flow from within them."* May those rivers of **Living Water** overflow from us into the lives of all unsaved people we know, so they will very soon thirstily receive eternal **life** in Him. I pray these things in His name. Amen.

What impacted me about Christ today...

_____

_____

_____

*John 4:9-12 The Samaritan woman said to him, "You are a Jew and I am a Samaritan woman. How can you ask me for a drink?" (For Jews do not associate with Samaritans.) Jesus answered her, "If you knew the gift of God and who it is that asks you for a drink, you would have asked him and he would have given you living water." "Sir", the woman said, "you have nothing to draw with and the well is deep. Where can you get this living water? Are you **greater than our father Jacob**, who gave us the well and drank from it himself, as did also his sons and his livestock?"*

Significance: The LORD JESUS CHRIST outranks all of Israel's other patriarchs and all other great people of all time.

Dear Father,

I worship the Lord Jesus, Who is **Greater Than Our** (the Samaritan woman's) **Father Jacob**, and **greater** than all people who have ever lived or will ever live! I rejoice that the Samaritan woman was desirous of knowing about the power, authority and **greatness** of Jesus, and was willing to ask questions about Him. I say "Hallelujah," that Jesus is God and He was with You for all of eternity! I praise Him that He created all people and all things, including the water in the well and even the components of the bricks that made the well! I think of just a small portion of what You said in Job 38-42 about the greatness of the Creator of the world: *"Who shut up the sea behind doors when it burst forth from the womb, when I made the clouds its garment and wrapped it in thick darkness, when I fixed limits for it and set its doors and bars in place, when I said, 'This far you may come and no farther; here is where your proud waves halt?'"* I pray that I and all believers will constantly extol the **greatness** of Jesus, and that multitudes of the unsaved men, women, young people and children in our spheres of influence will urgently seek to discover the truth about His **greatness**. I pray these things in His majestic name. Amen.

What impacted me about Christ today...

_____

_____

_____

_____

*John 4:16-18, 21-26 He told her, "Go, call your husband and come back." "I have no husband," she replied. Jesus said to her, "You are right when you say you have no husband. The fact is, you have had five husbands, and the man you now have is not your husband. What you have just said is quite true." . . . "Woman," Jesus replied, "believe me, a time is coming when you will worship the Father neither on this mountain nor in Jerusalem. You Samaritans worship what you do not know; we worship what we do know, for salvation is from the Jews. Yet a time is coming and has now come when the true worshipers will worship the Father in the Spirit and in truth, for they are the kind of worshipers the Father seeks. God is spirit, and his worshipers must worship in the Spirit and in truth." The woman said, "I know that **Messiah (called Christ)** is coming. When he comes, he will explain everything to us." Then Jesus declared, "I, the one speaking to you—I am he."*

Significance: The LORD JESUS CHRIST is God's chosen vessel to bring God to mankind, and mankind to God.

Dear Father,

How powerful it was that the Samaritan woman had a strong confidence that the **Messiah (called Christ)** would be coming to the Jews, and that He was the One through Whom You had chosen to reveal Yourself. I honor the **Messiah** that all of Your fullness is in Him, and that He alone could tell the woman (and all people) of Your love, power, righteousness, mercy, grace, truth, justice and much more. As the Samaritan woman believed then, I believe now, that only the **Messiah** can restore hope and life to our desperate world. I am very grateful that I and all who believe in Him as our Savior can worship You in the Spirit and in truth. I bow down before the **Messiah**, and pray that His followers will hunger to know everything we possibly can about You and Him. I pray also that Your Spirit will remove all obstacles that have been keeping unbelievers today from the **Messiah**, so that very soon they will understand Who He is, like the Samaritan woman did when Jesus declared to her, *"I, the one speaking to—I am he."* In the matchless name of Jesus I pray all these things. Amen.

What impacted me about Christ today...

*John 4:39-42 Many of the Samaritans from that town believed in him because of the woman's testimony, "He told me everything I ever did" [said the woman]. So when the Samaritans came to him, they urged him to stay with them, and he stayed two days. And because of his words many more became believers. They said to the woman, "We no longer believe just because of what you said; now we have heard for ourselves, and we know that this man really is the **Savior of the world**."*

S ignificance: The LORD JESUS CHRIST is the One Who is able to deliver all people from their sins.

~

Dear Father,

What a glorious declaration when the people of Sychar said they *"know this man really is the **Savior of the World**."* Thank You that by just being with Jesus two days, these people became convinced that He was and is the Christ, the Promised One, the Anointed One, Your beloved Son, the Messiah, the Savior for the Jews, for them, **and for the whole world**! My spirit is thrilled to think how His presence must have been captivatingly strong, healing, freeing, convicting, comforting, revealing, righteous, hope-building, joyful, refreshing and much more! I think of words by Philip Bliss in his wonderful song of celebration, "Hallelujah, What A Savior": (verse 1) "Man of Sorrows! What a name. For the Son of God who came; Ruined sinners to reclaim. Hallelujah! What a Savior. (verse 3) Guilty, vile and helpless we; Spotless Lamb of God was He; Full atonement! Can it be: Hallelujah! What a Savior! (verse 5) When He comes, our glorious King. All His ransomed home to bring. Then anew His song we'll sing: Hallelujah! What a Savior!" I pray that today You will use whatever means are necessary to convincingly reveal the **Savior of the World** to all people and that they will receive Him as those in Sychar did. In His awesome name I pray these things. Amen.

What impacted me about Christ today...

_____

_____

_____

_____

_____

*<u>John 5:25-27</u> [Jesus said] "Very truly I tell you, a time is coming and has now come when the dead will hear the voice of the Son of God and those who hear will live. For as the Father has life in himself, so he has granted the Son also to have life in himself. And he has given him authority to **judge** because he is the Son of Man."*

Significance: The LORD JESUS CHRIST is the final administrator of justice for all mankind.

Dear Father,

I am in awe that as You **have** life (and **are** life), You have granted Your Son (Who is one with You) the fullness of life in Himself, and have given Him absolute authority to be the **Judge** of all creation, including mankind. I am very impressed that He possesses all the characteristics and abilities that are necessary to be the perfect **Judge**: the highest integrity, complete understanding of all truth, all wisdom and knowledge, total impartiality and fairness, a perfect understanding of justice, unmovable firmness coupled with pure mercy and love, sovereign rule over all punishment, and the power to forgive. I praise Him that His authority as ultimate **Judge** of me and all people is based upon the sacrifice He made for us as the Son of Man. I thank Him with all my heart for His sacrifice; I bow before Him in worship and adoration; and I submit to Him as righteous and holy **Judge**. I repent for the ways I have taken the supreme **Judge** for granted, and I pray that You will do whatever is necessary in my life and in all His followers to make us holy and obedient to Him, as He is holy and obedient to You. I pray that as the end of time draws quickly near, unprecedented numbers of lost people will also hear the **Judge's** voice, and immediately put their lives into His hands. In His just and righteous name I pray these things. Amen.

What impacted me about Christ today...

_____

_____

_____

_____

_____

*John 6:10-14 Jesus said, "Have the people sit down." There was plenty of grass in that place, and they sat down (about five thousand men were there). Jesus took the loaves, gave thanks, and distributed to those who were seated as much as they wanted. He did the same with the fish. When they had all had enough to eat, he said to his disciples, "Gather the pieces that are left over. Let nothing be wasted." So they gathered them and filled twelve baskets with the pieces of the five barley loaves left over by those who had eaten. After the people saw the sign Jesus performed, they began to say, "Surely this is the **Prophet** who is to come into the world."*

Significance: **The LORD JESUS CHRIST is the highest representative of God to man.**

Dear Father,

I join the people who saw this miraculous sign that Jesus did, in being profoundly amazed at Who He was (and still is today). I say with them: *"Surely [without a doubt] this is the **Prophet** who is to come into the world."* I give all glory to Jesus that the people realized the ancient prophecy which God had spoken through Moses in Deuteronomy 18:18 was being fulfilled in their presence: *"I will raise up for them a **prophet** like you from among their fellow Israelites, and I will put my words in his mouth. He will tell them everything I command him."* Oh, thank You, great Father, that Jesus fully spoke Your words and revealed Your attributes to the people 2000 years ago, and has continually revealed them since that time! I exalt Him that He is the **Prophet**—the Messiah, Son of Man, Savior, Christ—Hallelujah! I pray that Your Spirit will convict me and all believers in our day to know the vast words, attributes and deeds of the **Prophet**, so that we will devote ourselves to proclaiming His greatness to one another and to everyone else You bring into our lives. Please help us to focus our highest attention and passion upon Him. In His worthy name I pray these things. Amen.

What impacted me about Christ today...

_____

_____

_____

_____

_____

*John 6:32-38 Jesus said to them, "Very truly I tell you, it is not Moses who has given you the bread from heaven, but it is my Father who gives you the **true bread from heaven**. For the bread of God is the bread that comes down from heaven and gives life to the world." "Sir," they said, "always give us this bread." Then Jesus declared, "I am the bread of life. Whoever comes to me will never go hungry, and whoever believes in me will never be thirsty. But as I told you, you have seen me and still you do not believe. All those the Father gives me will come to me, and whoever comes to me I will never drive away. For I have come down from heaven not to do my will but to do the will of him who sent me."*

Significance: The LORD JESUS CHRIST is God's complete and satisfying provision for mankind.

Dear Father,

I bless Jesus that He is the **True Bread From Heaven**. I praise Him that He is THE **Bread** of God (Your only true **bread**), Whom You sent from heaven to give spiritual life to the world. I am glad that You sent the tempo-rary manna (bread) to physically feed the ancient people of Israel, but then 2000 years ago You sent the Person of Jesus to eternally feed and transform the souls of all people who receive Him as their Savior. What a magnificent gift You have given us in Him, as confirmed in 1 John 5:11-12, *"And this is the testimony: God has given us eternal life, and this life is in his Son. Whoever has the Son has life; Whoever does not have the Son of God does not have life."* I pray that You will give us a consuming longing to know all we can about the **True Bread from Heaven**, so we will never again try to be satisfied with any substitute "bread." This complete feeding of my soul with Jesus reminds me of some of Katherine Hankey's precious hymn: "I love to tell the story of unseen things above, Of Jesus and His glory, Of Jesus and His love; I love to tell the story, because I know 'tis true; It satisfies my longings as nothing else can do." I give all these things to You in the matchless name of Jesus. Amen.

What impacted me about Christ today...

_____

_____

_____

_____

*John 7:6-13 Therefore Jesus told them, "My time is not yet here; for you any time will do. The world cannot hate you, but it hates me because I testify that its works are evil. You go to the festival. I am not going to this festival, because my time has not yet fully come." After he said this, he stayed in Galilee. However, after his brothers had left for the festival, he went also, not publicly, but in secret. Now at the festival the Jewish leaders were watching for Jesus and asking, "Where is he?" Among the crowds there was widespread whispering about him. Some said, "He is a **good man**." Others replied, "No, he deceives the people." But no one would say anything publicly about him for fear of the leaders.*

Significance: The LORD JESUS CHRIST demonstrated a life of perfect goodness and righteousness.

Dear Father,

I am sorry that some of the people who were talking about Jesus at the festival had such a limited understanding of Jesus that they considered Him to be just a **good** "human being." I repent that that is the mindset which many people have of Him today. I love what Jesus said in Matthew 19:17a that only You are completely **good**: *"Why do you ask me about what is good?" Jesus replied. "There is only One who is good."* Then, I praise Jesus that as the Son of Man He possesses the fullness of Your boundless **goodness**, which is combined with all Your love, righteousness, mercy, kindness, compassion, justice, and infinitely more in Him! Truly, Jesus is the perfect **Good Man**. I want to taste and see all the **goodness** of Jesus, as 1 Peter 2:2-3 instructs us: *"Like newborn babies, crave pure spiritual milk, so that by it you may grow up in your salvation, now that you have tasted that the Lord is good."* I pray that my family members and all other believers will also crave to know and live in all of Jesus, the **Good Man**. I pray also that the Holy Spirit will convince masses of local unbelievers of their desperate need to give their lives to the **Good Man**. Oh, may there soon be a widespread awakening of all people to the wonders of the **Good Man**. In His name I pray these things. Amen.

What impacted me about Christ today...

_____

_____

*John 7:21-27 Jesus said to them, "I did one miracle, and you are all amazed. Yet, because Moses gave you circumcision (though actually it did not come from Moses, but from the patriarchs) you circumcise a boy on the Sabbath. Now if a boy can be circumcised on the Sabbath so that the law of Moses may not be broken, why are you angry with me for healing a man's whole body on the Sabbath? Stop judging by mere appearances, but instead judge correctly." At that point some of the people of Jerusalem began to ask, "Isn't this the **man they are trying to kill**? Here he is, speaking publicly, and they are not saying a word to him. Have the authorities really concluded that he is the Messiah? But we know where this man is from; when the Messiah comes, no one will know where he is from."*

Significance: The **LORD JESUS CHRIST** was known to be the man the Jewish leaders were trying to kill for using His authority beyond their religious laws.

Dear Father,

I praise Jesus that He had a complete understanding of the letter of the Law and the spirit of the Law, and, at the same time, He was filled with Your love and mercy for the many needy people He came in contact with. I honor Him that He did not come to earth to break the Law, but to fulfill it, and that He always obeyed Your highest will by speaking the truth and caring for people even if His words and actions caused the religious leaders to falsely judge Him. I am deeply grateful that Jesus was willing to become the **Man They are Trying to Kill**, for the sake of the Jewish people of His day, and for all people after that (including me). I pray that there will be no confusion among His followers today about Who He is. May Your Spirit very clearly reveal the majesty, righteousness, love, wisdom, power, grace, truth, justice and all the rest of the great Messiah's attributes to believers everywhere, so that we will wholeheartedly revere, honor, adore, obey and totally abandon ourselves to Him. I pray that ALL people will very soon experience the manifest presence of Christ. In His name I pray these things. Amen.

What impacted me about Christ today...

The Light Of The World

*<u>John 8:12</u> When Jesus spoke again to the people, he said, "I am the **light of the world**. Whoever follows me will never walk in darkness, but will have the **light** of life."*

Significance: The LORD JESUS CHRIST illumines mankind to all of God's truth and life.

Dear Father,

All my hope is in Jesus, the One and Only **Light of the World**. I rejoice that You sent Him to earth to reveal Your transforming truth and glory, illuminate and destroy the works of spiritual darkness, and provide eternal life for mankind. I worship the **Light of the World**, and I pray that all other believers will continually worship and adore Him. I earnestly pray that Your Spirit will help us to hear and wholly obey 1 John 1:5-7, *"This is the message we have heard from him [the Word] and declare to you: God is light; in him there is no darkness at all. If we claim we have fellowship with him and yet walk in the darkness, we lie and do not live out the truth. But if we walk in the light, as he is in the light, we have fellowship with one another, and the blood of Jesus, his Son, purifies us from all sin."* Please help us to put aside any other priorities that have been keeping us from knowing the depths of the **Light of the World** and following Him at all times, so that we will have all of the **light** of life! I pray that the Church today will walk so completely in the **Light of the World**, that unsaved people we know will urgently cry out to receive Him. I pray these things in His splendid name. Amen.

What impacted me about Christ today...

_____

_____

_____

_____

_____

_____

_____

_____

*John 8:54-59 Jesus replied [to the Jews], "If I glorify myself, my glory means nothing. My Father, whom you claim as your God, is the one who glorifies me. Though you do not know him, I know him. If I said I did not, I would be a liar like you, but I do know him and obey his word. Your father Abraham rejoiced at the thought of seeing my day; he saw it and was glad." "You are not yet fifty years old," they said to him, "and you have seen Abraham!" "Very truly I tell you," Jesus answered, "before Abraham was born, **I am**!" At this, they picked up stones to stone him, but Jesus hid himself, slipping away from the temple grounds.*

S**ignificance: The LORD JESUS CHRIST is the all-encompassing, eternal God.**

Dear Father,

I am especially in awe of Jesus' declaration of the truth ("very truly") that He is **I AM**. All glory to **I AM** because the Jews, who heard this declaration in person, clearly knew that He was not just claiming to have been born before their patriarch, Abraham, but that He is the eternal God. I am so grateful for the affirmation of this when You directed Moses in Exodus 3:14 to tell the Israelites that Your name is *"I AM WHO I AM."* I praise Jesus that He is all-powerful, all-wise, all-holy, all-present, all-sovereign and infinitely more (as You are). I pray that the Holy Spirit will continually remind all believers of the incomparable greatness of Jesus, the **I AM**, and that we will worship Him with our whole hearts, continually speak of His vastness to one another, devote every part of our lives to Him, and earnestly pray for His dominion over us. I pray that, as Jesus said in today's Scripture passage and in other places like John 17, that You will glorify **I AM** and He will glorify You. I fervently desire this to happen at this chaotic hour in history. I pray that masses of unsaved people will be so amazed with Who **I AM** is, that they will plead with Him to come into their lives. I ask all these things in the name of **I AM**. Amen.

What impacted me about Christ today...

_____

_____

_____

_____

*John 10:7-10 Therefore, Jesus said again, "Very truly I tell you, I am the **gate for the sheep**. All who come before me are thieves and robbers, but the sheep have not listened to them. I am the **gate**; whoever enters through me will be saved. They will come in and go out, and find pasture. The thief comes only to steal and kill and destroy; I have come that they may have life, and have it to the full."*

Significance: The LORD JESUS CHRIST is the only way to eternal salvation.

Dear Father,

I am exceedingly grateful that Jesus is the true **Gate** (or Door) **For The Sheep**. My heart is filled with praise that I and all other people can enter like sheep into a relationship with You (be saved) through Jesus. I love the wonderful confirmation in Acts 4:9-12 that we are able to come to You only through the **Gate**: *"If we are being called to account today for an act of kindness shown to a man who was lame and are being asked how he was healed, then know this, you and all people of Israel: It is by the name of Jesus Christ of Nazareth, whom you crucified but whom God raised from the dead, that this man stands before you healed. Jesus is 'the stone you builders rejected, which has become the cornerstone.' **Salvation is found in no one else**, for there is no other name under heaven given to mankind by which we must be saved."* I am so thankful that He is our complete protection from all who intend to harm us, **and** that we have the full abundance of life You created us to have, in Him. I pray that Your Spirit will remind me and all other believers how valuable the **Gate** is to each of us, so that we will worship, adore, trust and obey Him with all of our hearts. I pray also that Your Spirit will do whatever is necessary in all unsaved people to overcome all their resistance to entering through the **Gate For The Sheep**. I ask these things in the name of the Savior. Amen.

What impacted me about Christ today...

_____

_____

_____

_____

John 10:11, 14-15 "I [Jesus] am the **good shepherd**. The good shepherd lays down his life for the sheep. . . . I am **the good shepherd**; I know my sheep and my sheep know me—just as the Father knows me and I know the Father—and I lay down my life for the sheep."

Significance: The LORD JESUS CHRIST is the perfect pastor Who gives His life fully for His people.

Dear Father,

I thank You so much for Jesus, the eternal **Good Shepherd**. I am absolutely overwhelmed as I read about the limitless **goodness** of the Godhead throughout the whole Bible. I marvel that this **goodness** dwells in the Lord Jesus as He cares for me and all the rest of His beloved sheep. I love to think about how Jesus' great **goodness**, love, mercy, grace, righteousness, justice, and all of His other attributes work together perfectly in His **shepherding** of us. I worship the **Good Shepherd** that the greatest demonstration of His **goodness** was when He laid down His life for me and all of mankind as the sacrifice for our sins. I honor Him that He completely fulfills all the Biblical prophecies about **shepherding** His sheep, including Ezekiel 34:12, *"As a **shepherd** looks after his scattered flock when he is with them, so will I look after my sheep. I will rescue them from all the places where they were scattered on a day of clouds and darkness."* I am deeply blessed that He knows us intimately and that we can know Him intimately, just as You and Jesus know each other intimately! I place every part of my life under His care, and I pray that all believers will do so too. I pray that You make all of my friends, relatives, neighbors and work associates who have not yet received the **Good Shepherd** aware of how desperately they need Him too. I pray these things in His loving name. Amen.

What impacted me about Christ today...

_____

_____

_____

_____

_____

The Resurrection And The Life

*John 11:25-27, 41-43 Jesus said to her [Martha], "I am the **resurrection
and the life**. The one who believes in me will live, even though they die; and
whoever lives by believing in me will never die. Do you believe this?" "Yes,
Lord," she replied, "I believe that you are the Messiah, the Son of God, who
is to come into the world." . . . So they took away the stone [from Lazarus'
burial cave]. Then Jesus looked up and said, "Father, I thank you that you
have heard me. I knew that you always hear me, but I said this for the benefit
of the people standing here, that they may believe that you sent me." When
he had said this, Jesus called in a loud voice, "Lazarus, come out!"*

Significance: The **LORD JESUS CHRIST** is the source and
Spersonification of eternal life.

Dear Father,

Jesus' authority was amazing as He ministered to His dear friends Mary
and Martha in their grief over their brother Lazarus' death. I praise Jesus
that He had the power to **resurrect** Lazarus' physical body, and that much
more importantly, in Him, the spiritual **resurrection** and **life** of Lazarus,
and all people, is available. I exalt Him that He is the author and forerunner of **resurrected life** through His dying on the cross and being raised
to eternal life. Again, I am so grateful to Him for the **life**-giving and **life**-
sustaining truth He states about Himself in John 5:21, *"For just as the
Father raises the dead and gives them **life**, even so the Son gives **life** to
whom he is pleased to give it."* I honor Jesus that He is THE **Resurrection
and the Life**, Who is the certain Victor over Satan's darkness and death.
I believe that in Him I am living now, and that I will live forever spiritually, even though one day I will die physically. I DO believe that because
of Jesus' resurrection I will never be separated from You! I join Martha in
believing that Jesus is the Christ, Your Son. I pray that You will awaken
me, my family members and all other believers to the vastness of Who the
Resurrection and the Life is, and that our passion for Him and devotion
to Him will become uncontainable. May multitudes of unsaved people
become desperately hungry to know and receive the **Resurrection and
the Life**. In the victorious name of Jesus. Amen.

What impacted me about Christ today...

A Kernel Of Wheat

*John 12:23-28 Jesus replied, "The hour has come for the Son of Man to be glorified. Very truly I tell you, unless a **kernel of wheat** falls to the ground and dies, it remains only a single seed. But if it dies, it produces many seeds. Anyone who loves their life will lose it, while anyone who hates their life in this world will keep it for eternal life. Whoever serves me must follow me; and where I am, my servant also will be. My Father will honor the one who serves me. Now my soul is troubled, and what shall I say? 'Father, save me from this hour?' No, it was for this very reason I came to this hour. Father, glorify your name!" Then a voice came from heaven, "I have glorified it, and will glorify it again."*

Significance: The LORD JESUS CHRIST'S death produced the fruit of eternal life for all who believe in Him.

Dear Father,

I praise Jesus, the Son of Man, Who fulfills *"the truth"* of the **Kernel of Wheat** falling to the ground and dying so that many seeds (me and millions of other people receiving eternal life) might be produced from Him. I am eternally grateful that He was willing to come to earth to lose His life for our sake. I rejoice that You and the Son of Man are both glorified through His life and through His obedient death on the cross. I grieve that so many people who saw and heard the **Kernel of Wheat** in person rejected Him. I pray that those of us who are living now and have received Him will glorify Him, devote ourselves to knowing the depths of Who He is, die to ourselves, serve Him and others, and speak of His greatness and love to everyone. Please help us to say what the hymn, "Oh, To Be Like Thee" by Thomas Chisholm, says: (verse 1) "Oh, to be like Thee! Blessed Redeemer, This is my constant longing and prayer. Gladly I'll forfeit all of earth's treasures, Jesus, Thy perfect likeness to wear. (chorus) Oh, to be like Thee! Oh, to be like Thee, Blessed Redeemer, pure as Thou art; Come in Thy sweetness, come in Thy fullness; Stamp Thine own image deep on my heart." I pray that seeds from the **Kernel of Wheat's** death will fill the earth with the knowledge of the glory of the Lord. In His name I pray these things. Amen.

What impacted me about Christ today...

John 14:1-7 [Jesus said] "*Do not let your hearts be troubled. You believe in God; believe also in me. My Father's house has many rooms; if that were not so, would I have told you that I am going there to prepare a place for you? And if I go and prepare a place for you, I will come back and take you to be with me that you also may be where I am. You know the way to the place where I am going.*" *Thomas said to him, "Lord, we don't know where you are going, so how can we know the way?" Jesus answered, "I am the **way** and the truth and the life. No one comes to the Father except through me. If you really know me, you will know My Father as well. From now on, you do know him and have seen him.*"

Significance: **The LORD JESUS CHRIST is the one and only path-way to all of God.**

Dear Father,

I am deeply grateful that I and all mankind can know You through the Lord Jesus, the one and only **Way**. I am in awe that we can come to You for mercy and redemption through the merit of the **Way**. I rejoice that we can come to You for an intimate love relationship through the **Way**. I am humbled that we can come to You in prayer through the **Way**. I am delighted that we can come to You for provision, protection, wisdom, the gifts of the Spirit, the fruit of the Spirit and everything else we need as Your children through the **Way**. I give every part of my life to the **Way**. I join the Apostle Paul in his declaration to the Roman Governor Felix in Acts 24:14a that: *"I admit that I worship the God of our ancestors as a follower of the **Way**, which they call a sect."* I pray that Your Spirit will place an insatiable longing in all believers to know, love, serve and follow the **Way**. I pray all these things in His lovely name. Amen.

What impacted me about Christ today...

_____

_____

_____

_____

_____

_____

*John 14:1-7 [Jesus said] "Do not let your hearts be troubled. You believe in God; believe also in me. My Father's house has many rooms; if that were not so, would I have told you that I am going there to prepare a place for you? And if I go and prepare a place for you, I will come back and take you to be with me that you also may be where I am. You know the way to the place where I am going." Thomas said to him, "Lord, we don't know where you are going, so how can we know the way?" Jesus answered, "I am the way and the **truth** and the life. No one comes to the Father except through me. If you really know me, you will know My Father as well. From now on, you do know him and have seen him."*

Significance: **The LORD JESUS CHRIST is the personification and standard of all there is to know about God.**

Dear Father,

I worship Jesus and I believe in Him completely, because He is the whole **Truth**. Thank You for sending Him to earth to reveal the full **truth** about You and Your eternal kingdom: *"For the law was given through Moses; grace and **truth** came through Jesus Christ"* (John 1:17). My faith in Him becomes increasingly strong as I think about His teachings, commands and promises that begin with, *"Very truly I tell you,"* or *"I tell you the truth,"* and by Him saying that He only spoke what You told Him to speak. I joyfully receive Jesus' promise in John 8:31-32, *"To the Jews who had believed him, Jesus said, 'If you hold to my teaching, you are really my disciples. Then you will know the **truth**, and the **truth** will set you free.'"* Hallelujah. I pray that You will help me, my family and millions of other believers around the world to embrace all of Jesus, the **Truth**, so that we might abundantly know the **truth**, and be set free into all that You and He are. I pray these things in the abiding hope of Jesus' name. Amen.

What impacted me about Christ today...

_____

_____

_____

_____

_____

*John 14:1-7 [Jesus said] "Do not let your hearts be troubled. You believe in God; believe also in me. My Father's house has many rooms; if that were not so, would I have told you that I am going there to prepare a place for you? And if I go and prepare a place for you, I will come back and take you to be with me that you also may be where I am. You know the way to the place where I am going." Thomas said to him, "Lord, we don't know where you are going, so how can we know the way?" Jesus answered, "I am the way and the truth and the **life**. No one comes to the Father except through me. If you really know me, you will know My Father as well. From now on, you do know him and have seen him."*

Significance: **The LORD JESUS CHRIST is the essence of all true existence.**

Dear Father,

I praise Jesus for this final name He called Himself—the **Life**—in this declaration of three incomparable names that can only belong to Him. Thank You for reminding me again of John's statement in John 1:1-4 that Jesus was with You in the beginning, that He was and is You, and that in Him is **ALL LIFE** (for all eternity past, when He created all life in heaven and on earth, when He walked on the earth, this moment today, and for all eternity future). Again, I exalt You and I exalt Jesus that *"For as the Father has **life** in himself, so he has granted the Son also to have **life** in himself"* (John 5:26). Hallelujah, that there is nothing in **life** that is not from Him, for Him, to Him, by Him, about Him, in Him, with Him and through Him. I pray that I and all believers will commit to knowing everything there is to know about the **Life**, and giving up everything else so we can live in Him completely. I pray that Your Spirit will put a consuming longing for the **Life** in the hearts and minds of unbelievers around us, so that they will forsake everything else that has given them "life," and cry out to receive the real **Life**. In His living name I pray these things. Amen.

What impacted me about Christ today...

_____

_____

_____

_____

John 15:1-5 [Jesus said] "*I am the **true vine**, and my Father is the gardener. He cuts off every branch in me that bears no fruit, while every branch that does bear fruit he prunes so that it will be even more fruitful. You are already clean because of the word I have spoken to you. Remain in me, as I also remain in you. No branch can bear fruit by itself; it must remain in the vine. Neither can you bear fruit unless you remain in me. I am the vine; you are the branches. If you remain in me and I in you, you will bear much fruit; apart from me you can do nothing.*"

Significance: The LORD JESUS CHRIST is the source of all true fruitfulness.

Dear Father,

I love to think about all Jesus meant when He called Himself the **True Vine**. I praise Him that He is the completely **True** (genuine, perfect and legitimate) **Vine** (source of all life) for me and all other believers. I am deeply grateful that You sent Him to earth to reveal the fullness of **truth** about Your righteousness and justice, since the nation of Israel (Your early vineyard) had failed to do that. I am also grateful that all His followers (branches) have the priceless privilege of being grafted into Him. I rejoice that He is the source of all our peace, strength, protection, truth, hope, light, revelation, nourishment and all else. I am convinced that we cannot bear fruit for Him, or do anything, if we do not remain in Him. With all my heart and resolve, I give myself to remaining in Him alone, and I pray You will prune me to make me most fruitful. I pray that Your Spirit will focus more and more attention within the Church on all that the **True Vine** is, so that they will put aside every other **vine** they are attached to, and remain completely in Him. May we bear unprecedented fruit, for His pleasure and glory. I ask these things in Jesus' life-giving name. Amen.

What impacted me about Christ today...

_____

_____

_____

_____

_____

_____

AUGUST

*John 19:1-6 Then Pilate took Jesus and had him flogged. The soldiers twisted together a crown of thorns and put it on his head. They clothed him in a purple robe and went up to him again and again, saying, "Hail, king of the Jews!" And they slapped him in the face. Once more Pilate came out and said to the Jews gathered there, "Look, I am bringing him out to you to let you know that I find no basis for a charge against him." When Jesus came out wearing the crown of thorns and the purple robe, Pilate said to them, "Here is the **man**!" As soon as the chief priests and their officials saw him, they shouted, "Crucify! Crucify!" But, Pilate answered, "You take him and crucify him. As for me, I find no basis for a charge against him."*

Significance: **The LORD JESUS CHRIST suffered as a human being.**

Dear Father,

I praise Jesus that He is the Lord of the universe Who humbled Himself by descending from the glories of heaven to become an earthly **man**. My heart grieves that this pure, righteous, meek, loving and sacrificial God-**Man** and servant **Man**, had to suffer the incredible scorn and brutality of flogging, a crown of thorns on his head, being struck in His face and the agony of crucifixion. I am reminded of what Isaiah 53:3 says that the **Man** endured for my sins and the sins of mankind: *"He was despised and rejected by mankind, a **man** of suffering, and familiar with pain."* I honor Him for His absolute obedience to and dependency upon You. I bow before Him in my most heartfelt gratitude and adoration. All hail the **Man** Who was crucified on the cross, rose from the grave, ascended to Your right hand and rules from there forevermore! I pray You will often remind all of the **Man's** followers of the amazing love He has for us, so we will die to ourselves and live wholly in Him. I pray that the precious truth about the **Man** will capture the hearts and minds of many unsaved people here too, so they will very soon receive Him as their Savior. I ask these things in the beloved name of Jesus. Amen.

What impacted me about Christ today...

_____

_____

_____

*<u>John 20:11-12a, 13b-18</u> Now Mary [Magdalene] stood outside the tomb crying. As she wept, she bent over to look into the tomb and saw two angels in white, seated where Jesus' body had been . . . "They have taken my Lord away," she said, "and I don't know where they have put him." At this, she turned around and saw Jesus standing there, but she did not realize that it was Jesus. He asked her, "Woman, why are crying? Who is it you are looking for?" Thinking he was the gardener, she said, "Sir, if you have carried him away, tell me where you have put him, and I will get him." Jesus said to her, "Mary." She turned toward him and cried out in Aramaic, "**Rabboni!**" (which means "Teacher"). Jesus said, "Do not hold on to me, for I have not yet ascended to the Father. Go instead to my brothers and tell them, 'I am ascending to my Father and your Father, to my God and your God.'" Mary Magdalene went to the disciples with the news: "I have seen the Lord!" And she told them that he had said these things to her.*

Significance: **The LORD JESUS CHRIST is the honored teacher of teachers.**

Dear Father,

I cry out with Mary that Jesus is "**Rabboni**," which means Teacher, and even Great Master. I praise Jesus that this title was the most honorable the Jewish people could give their teachers, and that Mary is exuberantly expressing that He is her Lord and Master. I join Mary in joyfully declaring that **Rabboni** is my great Teacher, Master and Lord. I want to learn everything I can from Him, be under His lordship, submit to all His ways, abide with Him at all times and give Him glory from every part of my life. I also pray that multitudes of other Christians will be so desirous of knowing Jesus more and being with Him, that they will have the urgency and passion of Mary in seeking Him. I pray that, like Mary, when we see Him (or hear about Him or experience Him in any other ways), we will be eager to share the news with other followers that: *"I have seen the Lord!"* Please put a deep longing in the hearts of many unsaved people around us to hear the truth that only the **Rabboni** can give them. I ask all these things in His name. Amen.

What impacted me about Christ today...

John 20:26-29 A week later his disciples were in the house again, and Thomas was with them. Though the doors were locked, Jesus came and stood among them and said, "Peace be with you!" Then he said to Thomas, "Put your finger here; see my hands. Reach out your hand and put it into my side. Stop doubting and believe." Thomas said to him, "My Lord and my God." Then Jesus told him, "Because you have seen me, you have believed; blessed are those who have not seen and yet have believed."

Significance: **The LORD JESUS CHRIST deserves the highest reverence and belief of His people.**

Dear Father,

I say "Hallelujah" that Thomas did not need to put his hand in Jesus' side to immediately be certain of the divinity of Jesus when he was in Jesus' presence after His resurrection. I rejoice in the powerful revelation of the glory of Jesus that compelled Thomas to exclaim to Jesus, *"My Lord and My God."* I honor Jesus that He has always been **Lord and God** of all creation, and that You opened Thomas' understanding of that truth. I rejoice that Thomas finally believed in his heart and mind what John declared in John 1:14a, *"The Word became flesh and made his dwelling among us."* I pray that Your Spirit will so thoroughly reveal the greatness of Jesus to all the Body of Christ today that we too will exclaim **"My Lord and My God"** to Him. I pray also that You will cleanse us of all unbelief, and that an unprecedented groundswell of awakening, belief, awe and reverence of Jesus will fill us. I pray that with great hope we will tell the lost people around us that they too must know and believe in our **Lord** and our **God.** In His most worthy name I ask these things. Amen.

What impacted me about Christ today...

_____

_____

_____

_____

_____

_____

_____

Messiah (Christ) The Son Of God

*John 20:30-31 Jesus performed many other signs in the presence of his disciples, which are not recorded in this book. But these are written that you may believe that Jesus is the **Messiah,** [the Christ] **the Son of God,** and that by believing you may have life in his name.*

Significance: The LORD JESUS CHRIST is the anointed One from the heavenly Father.

Dear Father,

As I think of all the miraculous signs and works Jesus did, I join the Apostle John in conclusively believing that Jesus is the **Messiah, the Son of God**. I am in awe that these two majestic names for Him are brought together here: the **Messiah** (the Christ Who You promised from ancient times would come to earth to redeem people from their sins), and the **Son of God** (Your beloved co-eternal, co-equal Son; the Creator of the heavens and the earth). I pray that I and all others who have received Jesus as our Savior will believe in His supremacy like Martha (Lazarus' sister) stated in John 11:25-27, *"Jesus said to her, 'I am the resurrection and the life. The one who believes in me will live, even though they die; and whoever lives by believing in me will never die. Do you believe this?' 'Yes, Lord,' she replied, 'I believe that you are the **Messiah, the Son of God,** who is to come into the world.'"* And, I urgently pray You will use whatever miraculous signs are necessary to cause multitudes of unsaved people to believe that Jesus is the **Messiah, the Son of God**, so they will have life in Him too. In His excellent name I pray these things. Amen.

What impacted me about Christ today...

_____
_____
_____
_____
_____
_____
_____
_____

A Man Accredited By God

*Acts 2:22-23 Fellow Israelites, listen to this: Jesus of Nazareth was a **man accredited by God** to you by miracles, wonders and signs, which God did among you through him, as you yourselves know. This man was handed over to you by God's deliberate plan and foreknowledge; and you, with the help of wicked men, put him to death by nailing him to the cross.*

Significance: The LORD JESUS CHRIST is personally validated by the heavenly Father.

Dear Father,

I rejoice at yet another evidence of the abounding confidence we can have in Jesus! Thank You that He is a **Man Accredited by God** through the miracles, wonders and signs You did through Him! Hallelujah that there could be no greater **accreditation** or affirmation of Who Jesus is than by Your mighty works and deeds being fulfilled through Him! I am convinced that this is because of the total dependency upon You that He stated in John 5:19-21, *"Very truly I tell you, the Son can do nothing by himself; he can do only what he sees his Father doing, because whatever the Father does the Son also does. For the Father loves the Son and shows him all he does. Yes, and he will show him even greater works than these, so that you will be amazed. For just as the Father raises the dead and gives them life, even so the Son gives life to whom he is pleased to give it."* I pray that I and all other believers will continually worship and honor Jesus, the **Man Accredited by God**, and, as He is completely devoted and obedient to You, we will be likewise to Him. And, please also help the unsaved people we know to believe in Jesus. They need Him so much! I pray these things in His blessed name. Amen.

What impacted me about Christ today...

_____

_____

_____

_____

_____

_____

*Acts 2:24-28 But God raised him from the dead, freeing him from the agony of death, because it was impossible for death to keep its hold on him. David said about him: "I saw the Lord always before me. Because he is at my right hand, I will not be shaken. Therefore my heart is glad and my tongue rejoices; my body also will rest in hope, because you will not abandon me to the realm of the dead, you will not let your **Holy One** see decay. You have made known to me the paths of life; you will fill me with joy in your presence."*

Significance: The LORD JESUS CHRIST is the personification of what is sacred.

Dear Father,

I am very grateful for this bold declaration by Peter that Jesus is Your **Holy One**, Whom King David prophesied about in Psalm 16 (and Who has in other passages been called "Messiah, the Holy One of God, Son of God, King, Beloved Son and Anointed One"). I magnify Jesus, Who alone is completely holy—set apart for You—to reveal all of You to mankind, and to give His life as a ransom for us. I rejoice that You raised Your **Holy One** from the dead (not letting Him see decay), and that we can know the paths of life and be filled with joy in His presence. I pray that Your Spirit will put a consuming "burning" in the hearts of Christ's followers (especially me) to know everything we possibly can about Your **Holy One**, and to have an intimate love relationship with Him that overshadows all other passions in our lives. I especially pray You will cleanse us of anything that is keeping us from being **holy** as He is **holy**. I ask these things with all my heart, in Jesus' name. Amen.

What impacted me about Christ today...

_____

_____

_____

_____

_____

_____

Acts 3:11-15 While the man held on to Peter and John, all the people were astonished and came running to them in the place called Solomon's Colonnade. When Peter saw this, he said to them: "Fellow Israelites, why does this surprise you? Why do you stare at us as if by our own power or godliness we had made this man walk? The God of Abraham, Isaac and Jacob, the God of our fathers, has glorified his servant Jesus. You handed him over to be killed, and you disowned him before Pilate, though he had decided to let him go. You disowned the **Holy and Righteous One** *and asked that a murderer be released to you. You killed the author of life, but God raised him from the dead. We are witnesses of this."*

Significance: The LORD JESUS CHRIST is the standard of absolute purity.

Dear Father,

I can only imagine the indescribable **holiness** and **righteousness** that Jesus has had with You for all eternity. I am deeply grateful that You sent Him, the **Holy and Righteous** (just, true and upright) **One** to earth to pay the price for mankind's sins, so we can become **holy** and **righteous** in Him forever. I grieve that the people of Israel who saw His power and godliness dared to disown and kill Him. I equally grieve that I and so many other people today dare to disown Him. But, I am so very glad that You glorified the **Holy and Righteous One** through healing the crippled beggar, and Jesus' many other words and deeds! I pray You will do whatever is necessary in my life, in my family, in all other believers, and in great numbers of unsaved people around us that will cause us to be astonished with the **Holy and Righteous One** and "come running" directly to Him. Please convict us to repent for all ways we have disowned or dishonored Him. I pray these things in His righteous name. Amen.

What impacted me about Christ today...

_____

_____

_____

_____

_____

*Acts 3:11-15 While the man held on to Peter and John, all the people were astonished and came running to them in the place called Solomon's Colonnade. When Peter saw this, he said to them: "Fellow Israelites, why does this surprise you? Why do you stare at us as if by our own power or godliness we had made this man walk? The God of Abraham, Isaac and Jacob, the God of our fathers, has glorified his servant Jesus. You handed him over to be killed, and you disowned him before Pilate, though he had decided to let him go. You disowned the Holy and Righteous One and asked that a murderer be released to you. You killed the **author of life**, but God raised him from the dead. We are witnesses of this."*

Significance: **The LORD JESUS CHRIST is the source of all existence.**

Dear Father,

I praise Jesus, the wonderful **Author of Life**. Hallelujah, that in Him ALL life has always existed (John 1:4)! All honor and gratitude to Him that He created all life in heaven and on earth, including His breathing into mankind to give us physical and spiritual life. I am in awe that without Jesus we have no life, but in Him we have the endless abundance of His life! I thank Jesus that He not only creates and sustains all life, but He also restored the physical lives of Jairus' daughter, the Nain widow's son, and His dear friend Lazarus. Most of all, I am grateful that Jesus rose from the dead, so that I and all people can receive eternal life through Him, as Paul describes in Ephesians 2:4-5, *"But because of his great love for us, God, who is rich in mercy, made us alive with Christ even when we were dead in transgressions—it is by grace you have been saved."* I joyfully sing part of another Fanny Crosby hymn in celebration of my **life** in Jesus: "Blessed assurance, Jesus is mine! O what a foretaste of glory divine! Heir of salvation, purchase of God, born of His Spirit, washed in His blood. (chorus) This is my story, this is my song, Praising my Savior, all the day long; This is my story, this is my song, Praising my Savior, all the day long." I give myself totally to the **Author of Life**. All my hope is in Him. I pray these things in the name of **Life**. Amen.

What impacted me about Christ today...

*Acts 4:23-31 Peter and John . . . reported all that the chief priests and the elders had said to them. When they heard this, they raised their voices together in prayer to God. "Sovereign Lord," they said, "you made the heavens and the earth and the sea, and everything in them. You spoke by the Holy Spirit through the mouth of your servant, our father David: 'Why do the nations rage and the peoples plot in vain? The kings of the earth rise up and the rulers band together against the Lord and against his anointed one.' Indeed Herod and Pontius Pilate met together with the Gentiles and the people of Israel in this city to conspire against your **holy servant Jesus**, whom you anointed. They did what your power and will had decided beforehand should happen. Now, Lord, consider their threats and enable your servants to speak your word with great boldness. Stretch out your hand to heal and perform signs and wonders through the name of your holy servant Jesus." After they prayed, the place where they were meeting was shaken. And they were all filled with the Holy Spirit and spoke the word of God boldly.*

Significance: The LORD JESUS CHRIST is God's perfect messenger to the world.

Dear Father,

I love that today's Scripture brings together some Old and New Testament truths about Christ. All honor that He is Your Anointed One (Messiah) Whom King David prophesied about in Psalm 2, and Who the believers in Acts 4 knew was Your **Holy Servant Jesus**. I bless Jesus, the all-**Holy One** You sent to earth to perfectly **serve** mankind by revealing Who You are, and by giving His life as the Savior from our sins. I am very alarmed that today "*the kings of the earth band together against the Lord and against his anointed one*," in the same manner that Herod and Pilate "*met together with the Gentiles and the people of Israel to conspire against your **holy servant Jesus**.*" As Peter, John and the other early believers prayed, I pray You will compel believers today to speak boldly about His greatness. Please stretch out Your hand and perform miraculous signs and wonders through His name (including "shaking" anything that needs to be "shaken"). I pray that the Spirit will move so powerfully, that all who have been opposing Christ will be on their faces in humility before Him. In Jesus' name I ask these things. Amen.

What impacted me about Christ today...

The Prince And Savior

*Acts 5:29-32 Peter and the other apostles replied: "We must obey God rather than human beings! The God of our ancestors raised Jesus from the dead—whom you had killed by hanging him on a cross. God exalted him to his own right hand as **Prince and Savior** that he might bring Israel to repentance and forgive their sins. We are witnesses of these things, and so is the Holy Spirit, whom God has given to those who obey him."*

Significance: **The LORD JESUS CHRIST is the great king and deliverer of His people.**

Dear Father,

I am very glad You raised Jesus from the dead and exalted Him to Your right hand as **Prince and Savior**. I bow before Him Who rules forever as the great **Prince** of princes (Sovereign Lord, King and Ruler) and **Savior** (long-awaited Messiah) for all people. All dominion and glory to Him Who alone gives repentance and eternal forgiveness to me and all who confess our sins! I pray that Your Spirit will cause an increasing number of believers to be hungry (as King David expressed in Psalm 42:1-2) to know more about the **Prince and Savior**, and that we will be in utter amazement of all He is and all that He does. Please light a holy fire in us to worship Him, love and adore Him, speak continually to one another about His majesty, devote every part of our lives to Him, and pray for His manifest presence to saturate His whole Church, here and now. May widespread repentance and forgiveness of the lost be released. I pray these things in the exalted name of the Lord Jesus. Amen.

What impacted me about Christ today...

_____

_____

_____

_____

_____

_____

_____

_____

The Judge Of The Living And The Dead

Acts 10:39-43 *[Peter said] "We are witnesses of everything he did in the country of the Jews and in Jerusalem. They killed him by hanging him on a cross, but God raised him from the dead on the third day and caused him to be seen. He was not seen by all the people, but by witnesses whom God had already chosen—by us who ate and drank with him after he rose from the dead. He commanded us to preach to the people and to testify that he is the one whom God appointed as **judge of the living and the dead**. All the prophets testify about him that everyone who believes in him receives forgiveness of sins through his name."*

Significance: **The LORD JESUS CHRIST is the ultimate evaluator of the spiritual condition of every human being.**

Dear Father,
I praise You again for raising Jesus from the dead and for appointing Him as **Judge of the Living and the Dead**. I am in awe that all the wisdom, justice, righteousness and authority to **judge** all people dwells in Him. I am forever grateful that He gave His life as Savior/**Judge** to pardon all who receive Him while we are living, from the penalty of our sins. I can only imagine the day when all who have physically died will stand before Him to receive His final pronouncement of our eternal death or eternal life. I pray that Your Spirit will profoundly awaken me and many other Christ-followers everywhere to the fullness of Who the **Judge of the Living and the Dead** is, and compel us to boldly preach and testify about Him to one another and to the many unsaved people we know. I pray also that You will put a holy fear and reverence of the **Judge of the Living and the Dead** in the hearts of all those lost people, so that even the most resistant of them will very soon cry out to Him in repentance. I pray these things in Jesus' righteous and merciful name. Amen.

What impacted me about Christ today...

_____

_____

_____

_____

_____

_____

*Acts 17:6-7 But when they did not find them [Paul and Silas], they dragged Jason and some other believers before the city officials, shouting: "These men who have caused trouble all over the world have now come here, and Jason has welcomed them into his house. They are all defying Caesar's decrees, saying that there is **another king,** one called Jesus."*

Significance: The LORD JESUS CHRIST is the perfect choice over every other ruler in the universe.

Dear Father,

I praise You that there is **Another King** (or ruler) appointed by You before the beginning of time, and He is called Jesus. I praise Him that He stands alone, far greater and more majestic than all other kings combined. I bow before Him Who rules the heavens and the earth, and Whose kingdom shall never end. I exalt Him that He is the perfect **King**: all-loving, all-wise, all-gracious, all-just, all-mighty, all-holy, all-faithful, all-merciful, all-wealthy, unconquerable, a sacrificial servant, the giver of life, and infinitely more. Hallelujah that the kingdom of **Another King** is built on love, as He states in John 13:34, *"A new command I give you: Love one another. As I have loved you, so you must love one another."* I pray that I and many other believers will become so captivated by the greatness of **Another King** that we will give up all other allegiances, and live totally under His sovereign rule. And, please also give unsaved people from every background and mindset an intense dissatisfaction with whatever "king" they are serving, so they will urgently seek and surrender to **Another King**. I pray these things in His royal name. Amen.

What impacted me about Christ today...

_____

_____

_____

_____

_____

_____

_____

*Acts 17:22-28a Paul then stood up in the meeting of the Areopagus and said: "People of Athens! I see that in every way you are very religious. For as I walked around and looked carefully at your objects of worship, I even found an altar with this inscription: TO AN **UNKNOWN GOD**. So you are ignorant of the very thing you worship—and this is what I am going to proclaim to you. The God who made the world and everything in it is the Lord of heaven and earth and does not live in temples built by human hands. And he is not served by human hands, as if he needed any-thing. Rather, he himself gives everyone life and breath and everything else. From one man he made all the nations, that they should inhabit the whole earth; and he marked out their appointed times in history and the boundaries of their lands. God did this so that they would seek him and perhaps reach out for him and find him, though he is not far from any one of us. For in him we live and move and have our being."*

Significance: The LORD JESUS CHRIST is concealed until He is **S** revealed.

Dear Father,
I am so moved by Paul's message in this Scripture, that I want to pray parts of it back to You. Regardless of whether Jesus is the Unknown God to some people, I praise Him that He made the world and everything in it. I glorify Him that He is Lord of heaven and earth and does not live in temples built by human hands. I rejoice that He is not served by human hands, as if He needed anything, because He gives all men life and breath and everything else. All honor to Him that He made every nation of men, that they should inhabit the whole earth, and He determined the times set for them and the exact places where they should live. I thank Him that He did this so that I and all other people would seek Him and perhaps reach out for Him and find Him, though He is not far from each one of us. I pray that all of His followers will embrace the truth that we live and move and have our being in Him. I pray that Jesus' name will become **known** and received by masses of people who do not yet **know** Him. In His unrivaled name I pray these things. Amen.

What impacted me about Christ today...

*Acts 17:29-31 Therefore since we are God's offspring, we should not think that the divine being is like gold or silver or stone—an image made by human design and skill. In the past God overlooked such ignorance, but now he commands all people everywhere to repent. For he has set a day when he will judge the world with justice by the **man he has appointed**. He has given proof of this to everyone by raising him from the dead.*

Significance: The LORD JESUS CHRIST has been commissioned by the Father as the final judge of mankind.

Dear Father,
I thank You that Jesus is the **Man He Has** (You have) **Appointed** to one day judge the world with justice. I am deeply grateful that He has all Your wisdom, authority, righteousness and grace, and, at the same time, He knows through His life on earth what people are thinking, feeling, saying and doing. I rejoice that You raising the One Who suffered the most severe injustice (dying on the cross for people's sins) to the highest place of administering our justice, is absolute proof of His **appointment** by You. I pray that You will give me and all believers an intense desire to know all we can about the **Man He Has Appointed**. May we long to know His character, His love, His names, His teachings, His promises, His prayers, His passions and His burdens, so that we will understand more and more what it is to be Your offspring. Please help us to be so in awe of the **Man He Has Appointed** that we will tell every other Christian and unbeliever we know about all He is. And, I ask that a pervasive reverence of Jesus will rise up among the masses of people across our land who have not yet received Him as Savior, that causes them to fall on their faces in repentance before it is too late. I pray these things in His holy and just name. Amen.

What impacted me about Christ today...

_____

_____

_____

_____

_____

The Hope Of Israel

*Acts 28:17-20 Three days later he [Paul] called together the local Jewish leaders. When they had assembled, Paul said to them: "My brothers, although I have done nothing against our people or against the customs of our ancestors, I was arrested in Jerusalem and handed over to the Romans. They examined me and wanted to release me, because I was not guilty of any crime deserving death. The Jews objected, so I was compelled to make an appeal to Caesar. I certainly did not intend to bring any charge against my own people. For this reason I have asked to see you and talk with you. It is because of the **hope of Israel** that I am bound with this chain."*

Significance: The LORD JESUS CHRIST is the complete vindication for His people.

Dear Father,

I give glory to Jesus, Who is the true **Hope of Israel** and of all people and nations—2000 years ago, now and for all eternity. I am in awe that He fulfills every promise and prophecy of **hope** in the Bible from the beginning of time, including Psalm 62:5-8, *"Yes, my soul, find rest in God; my **hope** comes from him. Truly he is my rock and my salvation; he is my fortress, I will not be shaken. My salvation and my honor depend on God; he is my mighty rock, my refuge. Trust in him at all times, you people; pour out your hearts to him, for God is our refuge."* I pray that Your Spirit will reveal so much of the **Hope of Israel** to me, my family members and all other believers that we will acquire the same abounding **hope** in Him which the Apostle Paul had. May we resolutely devote every part of our lives to Him, even to the point of being bound with chains for Him. Please do whatever is necessary in the Jewish people around the world today so they will receive Him as their only **Hope** too. In His glorious name I pray these things. Amen.

What impacted me about Christ today...

_____

_____

_____

_____

_____

Romans 1:1-4 Paul, a servant of Christ Jesus, called to be an apostle and set apart for the gospel of God—the gospel he promised beforehand through his prophets in the Holy Scriptures regarding his Son, who as to his earthly life was a **descendant of David***, and who through the Spirit of holiness was appointed the Son of God in power by his resurrection from the dead: Jesus Christ our Lord.*

Significance: **The LORD JESUS CHRIST, as a human being, is in the lineage of King David.**

Dear Father,

Thank You for this affirmation that Your Son Jesus (as to His human nature) is the resurrected **Descendant of** (King) **David,** Who was promised in many Old Testament prophesies like Solomon's prayer in 2 Chronicles 6:16-17, *"Now LORD, the God of Israel, keep for your servant David my father the promises you made to him when you said, 'You shall never fail to have a successor to sit before me on the throne of Israel, if only your descendants are careful in all they do to walk before me according to my law, as you have done.' And now, LORD, the God of Israel, let your word that you promised your servant David come true."* I rejoice that as You called David *"a man after your own heart"* in 1 Samuel 13:14, truly Jesus is "a man after Your own heart" far more so. As David was chosen by You to rule Israel, Jesus is chosen by You, as Messiah, King and Lord, to rule all people. Please help me and all believers to submit completely to the rule of the **Descendant of David.** I pray these things in the name of our great king, Jesus. Amen.

What impacted me about Christ today...

_____

_____

_____

_____

_____

_____

_____

Romans 8:31b-39 If God is for us, who can be against us? He who did not spare his own Son, but gave him up for us all—how will he not also, along with him, graciously give us all things? Who will bring any charge against those whom God has chosen? It is God who justifies. Who then is the one who condemns? No one. Christ Jesus who died—more than that, who was raised to life—is at the right hand of God and is also interceding for us. Who shall separate us from the love of Christ? Shall trouble or hardship or persecution or famine or nakedness or danger or sword? As it is written: "For your sake we face death all day long; we are considered as sheep to be slaughtered." No, in all these things we are more than conquerors through him who loved us. For I am convinced that neither death nor life, neither angels nor demons, neither the present nor the future, nor any powers, neither height nor depth, nor anything else in all creation, will be able to separate us from the love of God that is in **Christ Jesus our Lord***.*

Significance: **The LORD JESUS CHRIST is our Savior and our God.**

Dear Father,
I am in awe of the Person of **Christ Jesus our Lord**. I rejoice in Peter's declaration about Him in Acts 2:36, *"Therefore let all Israel be assured of this: God has made this Jesus, whom you crucified, both Lord and Messiah* (Christ).*"* I worship, honor, praise and revere **Christ Jesus our Lord**, the Anointed One, Messiah, King, Son of God, One and Only, Light, Prince, Savior, Redeemer, Lord, Master, Ruler and substantially more. I exalt Him that He existed with You before time began, and that You sent Him to earth to reveal Your majesty and love, save mankind from our sins, and rule heaven and earth forever. I am eternally grateful that He is at Your right hand interceding for me and all other believers, and that **nothing** and **no one** can separate us from Your love in Him. Hallelujah! We are more than conquerors through Him! I pray that Your Spirit will deluge us now with the vastness of Who **Christ Jesus our Lord** is, so that our passion for Him and abandonment to Him will be like Peter's. I pray these things in Christ's splendid name. Amen.

What impacted me about Christ today...

*Romans 9:2-5 I have great sorrow and unceasing anguish in my heart. For I could wish that I myself were cursed and cut off from Christ for the sake of my people, those of my own race, the people of Israel. Theirs is the adoption to sonship; theirs the divine glory, the covenants, the receiving of the law, the temple worship and the promises. Theirs are the patriarchs, and from them is traced the human ancestry of the Messiah, who is **God over all**, forever praised! Amen.*

Significance: **The LORD JESUS CHRIST is the highest being in this universe.**

❧

Dear Father,
I grieve with Paul that the people of Israel, whom God had blessed so abundantly, had turned away from Christ, the supreme **God Over All**. I further grieve that they had forfeited the great honor they could have received as Your chosen people, to demonstrate to the world around them the majesty and love of the **God Over All**. I repent for the many ways I and other believers today are not living in the fullness of Who the **God Over All** is. I pray You will give us an insatiable desire to know everything we can about Him, so we will give up everything else to have an intimate love relationship with Him. Please help us to live in the full adoption as sons and daughters of Him. May the **God Over All**, be over all of our lives. I urgently pray that the men, women, young people and children all around us who are lost with many other gods over them, will very soon forsake all those gods, and invite the **God Over All** to save them. All praise, honor and glory to Jesus, in Whose name I pray these things. Amen.

What impacted me about Christ today...

A Stone That Causes People To Stumble, A Rock That Makes Them Fall

*Romans 9:30-33 What then shall we say? That the Gentiles, who did not pursue righteousness, have obtained it, a righteousness that is by faith; but the people of Israel, who pursued the law as the way of righteousness, have not attained their goal. Why not? Because they pursued it not by faith but as if it were by works. They stumbled over the stumbling stone. As it is written: "See, I lay in Zion a **stone that causes people to stumble** and a **rock that makes them fall**, and the one who believes in him will never be put to shame."*

Significance: The **LORD JESUS CHRIST** is an obstacle to unbelievers.

Dear Father,

I worship Jesus as the **Stone That Causes People to Stumble** and the **Rock That Makes Them Fall**. At the same time, I'm saddened that Who Jesus is and the lifestyle He calls His followers to live has caused so many people to stumble and fall from having faith in Him. My heart breaks that people are so ignorant about His greatness and love that they choose not to receive Him as Savior and Lord. I pray that You will compel me and the whole Church to seek to know the depths and riches of Jesus, so that we will worship Him continually, love Him with all our hearts, speak regularly of His greatness to one another and to the unsaved people we know, surrender every part of our lives to Him, and pray for His Lordship over us and all people and circumstances. May we be so awakened to all Christ is that those who have been stumbling and falling because of Him will convincingly *"know the truth, and the truth will set you free"* (John 8:32). And, I pray that Your promise in Isaiah 43:18-19 will come to pass in them: *"Forget the former things; do not dwell on the past. See, I am doing a new thing! Now it springs up; do you not perceive it? I am making a way in the wilderness and streams in the wasteland."* In Christ's name I pray these things. Amen.

What impacted me about Christ today...

_____

_____

_____

_____

The Righteousness Of God

*Romans 10:1-4 Brothers and sisters, my heart's desire and prayer to God for the Israelites is that they may be saved. For I can testify about them that they are zealous for God, but their zeal is not based on knowledge. Since they did not know the **righteousness of God** and sought to establish their own, they did not submit to God's righteousness. Christ is the culmination of the law so that there may be righteousness for everyone who believes.*

Significance: The LORD JESUS CHRIST is the source of true righteousness.

Dear Father,

I am forever glad that Jesus is the **Righteousness of God** (the Righteousness That Comes From God); He is the fullness of Your redeeming **righteousness**. I am so glad that His **righteousness** is for me, and for every other person of every status, ethnic origin, gender, age or geographic location. I pray that I and all who are already saved will abandon every part of our lives to the **Righteousness of God**, and continually grow in His matchless truth, holiness, purity, humility, grace, mercy, love, forgiveness, authority, suffering and all the other aspects of His **righteousness**. My heart's desire is like Paul's in today's Scripture. I pray that unsaved people everywhere who have been trying to live by their own understanding of righteousness will ache to know Jesus, the **Righteousness of God**, and will wholly submit to salvation in Him. I pray for a sweeping movement of what Paul describes in 1 Timothy 1:15-16 happened to him: *"Here is a trustworthy saying that deserves full acceptance: Christ Jesus came into the world to save sinners—of whom I am the worst. But for that very reason I was shown mercy so that in me, the worst of sinners, Christ Jesus might display his immense patience as an example for those who would believe in him and receive eternal life."* All praise to Jesus! I give all these things to You in His **righteous** name. Amen.

What impacted me about Christ today...

_____

_____

_____

The Culmination Of The Law

*Romans 10:1-4 Brothers and sisters, my heart's desire and prayer to God for the Israelites is that they may be saved. For I can testify about them that they are zealous for God, but their zeal is not based on knowledge. Since they did not know the righteousness of God and sought to establish their own, they did not submit to God's righteousness. Christ is the **culmination of the law** so that there may be righteousness for everyone who believes.*

Significance: **The LORD JESUS CHRIST fulfills the law of God completely in Himself.**

Dear Father,

I thank You that the law shows all people our unrighteousness and the impossibility of satisfying the curse of sin through our own works. I am so glad that You sent Jesus to earth to be the **Culmination** (end/fulfillment) **of the Law.** I think of His statement in Matthew 5:17, *"Do not think that I have come to abolish the Law or the Prophets; I have not come to abolish them but to fulfill them."* I rejoice that Jesus is completely pure, holy, righteous, just and obedient, and that He shed His blood on the cross for the total remission of our sins. I rejoice that I am fully cleansed and pardoned by You through Him. Hallelujah! My faith in Him is credited as righteousness, as Paul quoted King David in Romans 4:7-8, *"Blessed are those whose transgressions are forgiven, whose sins are covered. Blessed is the one whose sin the Lord will never count against them."* I pray that Your Spirit will remind me and all other believers of the incomparable price the **Culmination of the Law** paid for us, so that we will continually thank Him, praise Him and speak about all He is to the many lost people we know. May they become convicted of their urgent need for salvation through Jesus too, and steadfastly believe in Him. I praise Christ that He is ALL, and He is all we need. In the **Culmination of the Law's** name I pray these things. Amen.

What impacted me about Christ today...

_____

_____

_____

Romans 10:9-13 If you declare with your mouth, "Jesus is Lord," and believe in your heart that God raised him from the dead, you will be saved. For it is with your heart that you believe and are justified, and it is with your mouth that you profess your faith and are saved. As Scripture says, "Anyone who believes in him will never be put to shame." For there is no difference between Jew and Gentile—the same Lord is **Lord** *of all and richly blesses all who call on him, for, "Everyone who calls on the name of the Lord will be saved."*

Significance: The LORD JESUS CHRIST is the One Who all must call upon to be saved.

Dear Father,

I am in awe of Jesus, the **Lord of All**. I bow before Jesus, Who is One with You in all Your attributes, abilities and wisdom. All glory to Him that there is nothing He has not been **Lord** of, from eternity past, to now and forever. Hallelujah, that the **Lord of all** is the Creator of all, Sustainer of all, and Savior of all. Thank You for sending Him to reveal and demonstrate the fullness of Your **Lordship** to mankind, and to make His **Lordship** available to each of us without partiality. I confess with my mouth that Jesus is **Lord**, and I believe in my heart that You raised Him from the dead. I pray that my family and all other professing Christians will likewise confess and believe in the **Lord of all** with complete devotion. Please help us to be thirsty to know more of the amazing **Lord of all**, and to be as passionate about helping one another know Him as Paul stated he was in Galatians 4:19, *"My dear children, for whom I am again in the pains of childbirth until Christ is formed in you."* I plead that the teeming masses of broken, hurting, needy, sinful, fearful, shameful, desperate, deceived, angry, lost and dying people all around us who have not yet received Jesus, will call on the **Lord of all** today and be saved. I pray these things in the name above all names. Amen.

What impacted me about Christ today...

_____

_____

_____

Romans 11:25-27 *I do not want you to be ignorant of this mystery, brothers and sisters, so that you may not be conceited: Israel has experienced a hardening in part until the full number of the Gentiles has come in, and in this way all Israel will be saved. As it is written: "The **deliverer** will come from Zion; he will turn godlessness away from Jacob. And this is my covenant with them when I take away their sins."*

Significance: The LORD JESUS CHRIST is the eternal liberator of mankind.

Dear Father,

Thank You for this assurance that Jesus fulfills the covenant You made with the people of Israel to send a **Deliverer** to turn them (rescue them) from their godlessness. I am deeply grateful that the **Deliverer** of Your New Covenant came also for me and all Gentiles, as John said in John 1:12, *"Yet to **all** who did receive him, to those who believed in his name, he gave the right to become children of God."* I pray that we who have received the **Deliverer** as our Savior will regularly repent of any godlessness or hardness of our hearts that keeps us from completely submitting to His Lordship. May we constantly abide in the spirit of the Lord's prayer recorded in Matthew 6:13b, *"**deliver** us from the evil one."* I worship the **Deliverer** by singing some of "O Worship the King" by Robert Grant: (verse 1) "O worship the King, all glorious above, And gratefully sing His power and His love; Our Shield and Defender, the Ancient of Days, Pavilioned in splendor and girded with praise. (verse 2) O tell of His might, O sing of His grace, Whose robe is the light, Whose canopy space, His chariots of wrath the deep thunderclouds form, And dark is His path on the wings of the storm. (verse 5) Frail children of dust, and feeble as frail, In Thee do we trust, nor find Thee to fail; Thy mercies how tender! How firm to the end! Our Maker, Defender, Redeemer, and Friend." I pray the **Deliverer** will turn godlessness away from our cities and towns and whole nations. In His saving name I offer these things to You. Amen.

What impacted me about Christ today...

_____

_____

_____

_____

The Lord Of Both The Dead And The Living

*Romans 14:7-11 For none of us lives for ourselves alone, and none of us dies for ourselves alone. If we live, we live for the Lord; and if we die, we die for the Lord. So, whether we live or die, we belong to the Lord. For this very reason, Christ died and returned to life so that he might be the **Lord of both the dead and the living**. You, then, why do you judge your brother or sister? Or why do you treat them with contempt? For we will all stand before God's judgment seat. It is written: "As surely as I live," says the Lord, "every knee will bow before me; every tongue will acknowledge God."*

Significance: The LORD JESUS CHRIST'S rule extends to every era of history.

Dear Father,

I praise Jesus, Who died and returned to life, so that He might be **Lord of Both the Dead and the Living**. I worship Him that He has all power, authority, rule and dominion over my life, and all His followers' lives, now and forever. The words of Edward Perronet's glorious old hymn rise up within me as I meditate on Jesus' supreme lordship: (verse 1) "All hail the power of Jesus' Name! Let angels prostrate fall; Bring forth the royal diadem, and crown Him Lord of all. (verse 4) Let every kindred, every tribe, On this terrestrial ball, To Him all majesty ascribe, And crown Him Lord of all. (verse 5) O that with yonder sacred throng, We at His feet may fall! We'll join the everlasting song, and crown Him Lord of all." I pray that You will help me and all other believers be as sold out to Jesus as Paul stated in Philippians 1:21 that he was: *"For to me, to live is Christ and to die is gain."* Help us desire to know Jesus like Paul did, and to trust Jesus for our present and future like Paul did, and talk unceasingly about the greatness of Jesus like Paul did. Oh Father, may we live for the Lord Jesus, and when we die, may we die for Him as well. I pray that Your Spirit is opening the hearts of millions of spiritually lost people to cry out to the **Lord of Both the Dead and the Living** for mercy too. I pray these things in His exalted name. Amen.

What impacted me about Christ today...

Romans 15:7-13 *Accept one another [the weak and the strong in Jesus], then, just as Christ accepted you, in order to bring praise to God. For I tell you that Christ has become a servant of the Jews on behalf of God's truth, so that the promises made to the patriarchs might be confirmed and, moreover, that the Gentiles might glorify God for his mercy. As it is written: "Therefore I will praise you among the Gentiles; I will sing the praises of your name." Again, it says, "Rejoice, you Gentiles, with his people." And again, "Praise the Lord, all you Gentiles; let all the peoples extol him." And again, Isaiah says, "The **Root of Jesse** will spring up, one who will arise to rule over the nations; in him the Gentiles will hope." May the God of hope fill you with all joy and peace as you trust in him, so that you may overflow with hope by the power of the Holy Spirit.*

Significance: **The LORD JESUS CHRIST came from Jesse, the father of King David, to rule the nations.**

Dear Father,
I rejoice that Jesus, the **Root of Jesse** (the father of King David), was sent to earth for Your sovereign purposes to rule over the nations, and to become a servant of the Jews on behalf of Your truth. I am deeply grateful that every part of Jesus' life confirms the promises You made to the Old Testament patriarchs. I pray that Jews and Gentiles today who have put our trust in the **Root of Jesse** (the long-awaited Messiah) will glorify You for Your mercy, and will be filled with hope, joy and peace in Him. May we overflow with that great hope by the power of the Holy Spirit to all other Jews and Gentiles You bring into our lives. Please give us a deep passion to know the depths of the riches of Christ, so that we will continually seek Him and sing praises to His name. I pray that the kingdom of the **Root of Jesse** will expand beyond what we can ask or imagine, for His great glory. In His exalted name I ask these things. Amen.

What impacted me about Christ today...

_____

_____

_____

_____

_____

The Power Of God And The Wisdom Of God

*1 Corinthians 1:22-25 Jews demand signs and Greeks look for wisdom, but we preach Christ crucified: a stumbling block to Jews and foolishness to Gentiles, but to those whom God has called, both Jews and Greeks, Christ the **power of God and the wisdom of God**. For the foolishness of God is wiser than human wisdom, and the weakness of God is stronger than human strength.*

Significance: The LORD JESUS CHRIST personifies God's strength and understanding.

Dear Father,

I am very glad that even though the preaching of Christ crucified is a stumbling block to many Jews and foolishness to many Gentiles, He is truly the **Power of God** and the **Wisdom of God** to those who are called to Him. I rejoice that in Jesus dwells the fullness of Your **power** and Your **wisdom**, so He alone is worthy to be called the **Power of God** and the **Wisdom of God**. I praise Christ for the awesome manifestations of Your **power** through Him: He created all life, is Lord of all His creation, forgives sin and grants freedom to the lost, has authority over the powers of darkness, and fulfills Your prophecies and promises. I praise Christ for the awesome manifestations of Your **wisdom** through Him: He reveals Your infinite majesty and love to mankind, knows the hearts and minds of all people, disciples His followers in righteousness, judges His kingdom perfectly, and so much more. I pray that the consuming passion of believers will be to know the depths of the **Power of God** and the **Wisdom of God**, and that we will worship Him, trust Him, love Him, revere Him, abandon ourselves to Him and serve Him together. I pray these things in His mighty name. Amen.

What impacted me about Christ today...

_____

_____

_____

_____

_____

_____

Our Righteousness, Holiness And Redemption

*1 Corinthians 1:27-31 But God chose the foolish things of the world to shame the wise; God chose the weak things of the world to shame the strong. God chose the lowly things of this world and the despised things—and the things that are not—to nullify the things that are, so that no one may boast before him. It is because of him that you are in Christ Jesus, who has become for us wisdom from God—that is, our **righteousness, holiness and redemption**. Therefore, as it is written: "Let the one who boasts boast in the Lord."*

Significance: **The LORD JESUS CHRIST is the source of our salvation and godliness.**

Dear Father,
I thank You that I am in Christ Jesus, my **Righteousness, Holiness and Redemption**. I joyfully boast that there are no limits to His **righteousness, holiness and redemption**. I rejoice that Jesus is the fullness of **righteousness**: *"This **righteousness** is given through faith in Jesus Christ to all who believe. There is no difference between Jew and Gentile, for all have sinned and fall short of the glory of God, and are all justified freely by his grace through the redemption that came by Christ Jesus"* (Romans 3:22-24). And, I rejoice that Jesus is the fullness of **holiness**: *"But now that you have been set free from sin and have become slaves of God, the benefit you reap leads to **holiness**, and the result is eternal life. For the wages of sin is death, but the gift of God is eternal life in Christ Jesus our Lord"* (Romans 6:22-23). I rejoice also that Jesus is the fullness of **redemption**: *"In him [Jesus] we have **redemption** through his blood, the forgiveness of sins, in accordance with the riches of God's grace that he lavished on us. With all wisdom and understanding, he made known to us the mystery of his will according to his good pleasure, which he purposed in Christ"* (Ephesians 1:7-9). I pray that You will help me, my family members and all other believers to make every effort to live in the riches of Christ's **righteousness, holiness and redemption**. In His blessed name I ask these things. Amen.

What impacted me about Christ today...

*1 Corinthians 2:6-10a We do, however, speak a message of wisdom among the mature, but not the wisdom of this age or of the rulers of this age, who are coming to nothing. No, we declare God's wisdom, a mystery that has been hidden and that God destined for our glory before time began. None of the rulers of this age understood it, for if they had, they would not have crucified the **Lord of glory**. However, as it is written: "What no eye has seen, what no ear has heard, and what no human mind has conceived"—the things God has prepared for those who love him— these are the things God has revealed to us by his Spirit.*

Significance: The LORD JESUS CHRIST holds the greatest esteem and majesty of all beings.

Dear Father,
I worship Jesus, the **Lord of Glory** (the "glorious Lord"). I exalt Him in the **glory** that He has with You, expressed in John 17:1b-5, *"Father, the hour has come. Glorify your Son, that your Son may glorify you. For you granted him authority over all people that he might give eternal life to all those you have given him. Now this is eternal life: that they know you, the only true God, and Jesus Christ, whom you have sent. I have brought you glory on earth by finishing the work you gave me to do. And now, Father, glorify me in your presence with the glory I had with you before the world began."* I rejoice that He is the Messiah, the secret wisdom (mystery) that You destined before the beginning of time would be revealed one day by Your Spirit. I grieve that the Jewish rulers did not understand Who Jesus was, and they crucified Him. At the same time, I repent for the lack of understanding that so many people (believers and non-believers) in our world today have of the divinity of Jesus. I pray that You will clearly reveal to believers (me included) ALL the **Lord of Glory** is, so we will correctly conceive what You have prepared for those of us who love You and Him. All these things I pray in His **glorious** name. Amen.

What impacted me about Christ today...

_____

_____

_____

*1 Corinthians 3:10-11 By the grace God has given me [Paul], I laid a foundation as a wise builder, and someone else is building on it. But each one should build with care. For no one can lay any **foundation** other than the one already laid, which is Jesus Christ.*

Significance: The LORD JESUS CHRIST is the understructure upon which all spiritual life is built.

Dear Father,

I have an unshakable confidence that the **Foundation** of my life and the whole Church is the Person of Jesus. I rejoice that there is **no other foundation** upon which Your truth, justice, righteousness, strength and love for mankind can be built. I hold on to Jesus' words in Matthew 7:24-27, *"Therefore everyone who hears these words of mine and puts them into practice is like a wise man who built his house on the rock. The rain came down, the streams rose, and the winds blew and beat against that house; yet it did not fall, because it had its **foundation** on the rock. But everyone who hears these words of mine and does not put them into practice is like a foolish man who built his house on sand. The rain came down, the streams rose, and the winds blew and beat against that house, and it fell with a great crash."* I pray that You will reveal so much of the greatness of the **Foundation** to me and all Your people, that we will not dare to build our lives on anyone or anything but Him. I sing the first verse of Samuel Stone's song, "The Church's One Foundation," to praise Jesus for this attribute of Him: "The Church's one **foundation** is Jesus Christ, her Lord. She is His new creation, By water and the word. From heav'n He came and sought her, To be His holy bride; With His own blood He bought her, And for her life He died." In Jesus' sure and strong name I pray these things. Amen.

What impacted me about Christ today...

_____

_____

_____

_____

_____

_____

*1 Corinthians 5:6-8 Your boasting is not good. Don't you know that a little yeast leavens the whole batch of dough? Get rid of the old yeast, so that you may be a new unleavened batch—as you really are. For Christ, our **Passover lamb**, has been sacrificed. Therefore let us keep the Festival, not with the old bread leavened with malice and wickedness, but with the unleavened bread of sincerity and truth.*

S ignificance: The LORD JESUS CHRIST is God's substitute for our sins.

Dear Father,

I am eternally grateful that Christ is the **Passover Lamb** for me and all of sinful mankind. Thank You for sending Him to earth to sacrifice His spotless life once and for all for deliverance from the bondage of our sinful nature. I praise Him for what Paul declares in Romans 7:24-8:3a, *"What a wretched man I am! Who will rescue me from this body that is subject to death? Thanks be to God, who delivers me through Jesus Christ our Lord! So then, I myself in my mind am a slave to God's law, but in my sinful nature a slave to the law of sin. Therefore, there is now no condemnation for those who are in Christ Jesus, because through Christ Jesus the law of the Spirit who gives life has set you free from the law of sin and death. For what the law was powerless to do because it was weakened by the flesh, God did by sending his own Son in the likeness of sinful flesh to be a sin offering."* Hallelujah! I no longer have any condemnation for my sinful nature! I am free through Jesus' shed blood! I pray You will help me, my family members and a rapidly increasing number of other believers to live in the full freedom and hope of the **Passover Lamb**, and to constantly testify to one another of our devotion to Him. I pray these things in His life-giving name. Amen.

What impacted me about Christ today...

_____

_____

_____

_____

_____

*1 Corinthians 10:1-4 For I [Paul] do not want you be ignorant of the fact, brothers and sisters, that our ancestors were all under the cloud and that they all passed through the sea. They were all baptized into Moses in the cloud and in the sea. They all ate the same spiritual food and drank the same spiritual drink; for they drank from the **spiritual rock** that accompanied them, and **that rock** was Christ.*

Significance: **The LORD JESUS CHRIST is the source of all spiritual life.**

Dear Father,

I worship Christ that He has been the only **Spiritual Rock** (the sure spiritual provider) for our Jewish forefathers, and for me and all His people. I rejoice that He is completely righteous and true; He knows all of our spiritual needs; He is all-powerful to provide for those needs; and He *"accompanies"* us at all times. Thank You that the **Spiritual Rock** fulfills many Old Testament prophecies, including Lamentations 3:19-24, *"I remember my affliction and my wandering, the bitterness and the gall. I well remember them, and my soul is downcast within me. Yet this I call to mind, and therefore I have hope: Because of the LORD's great love we are not consumed, for his compassions never fail. They are new every morning; great is your faithfulness. I say to myself, 'The LORD is my portion; therefore I will wait for him.'"* I testify that Christ, the **Spiritual Rock,** is my portion. All my spiritual life comes from Him, now and for all eternity. Please remove every substitute for the **Spiritual Rock** that the enemy of our souls tries to convince us to drink from. I ask these things in Christ's all-sufficient name. Amen.

What impacted me about Christ today...

_____

_____

_____

_____

_____

_____

SEPTEMBER

THE FRUIT OF THE LAND
SOURCE OF STRENGTH
A WALL OF FIRE
ANOINTED ONE
THE MESSIAH
SON OF THE LIVING GOD
OUR MIGHTY ONE
Savior, Prince of Peace
The eternal
the
HE SP
MY CHOSEN ONE
THE MOST HOLY
THE DELIVERER
A GREAT LIGHT
IMMANUEL
guardian
THE ROCK OF ISRAEL
THE SON OF MAN
sign of the covenant
redeer
THE FOUNTAIN OF LIFE
GOD WITH US
MY HIDING PLACE
MY STRENG
WONDERFUL COUNSELOR
SON OF DAVID
HORN OF SALVA
THE COMMANDER
A STRONG TOWER
TEACHER
THE GREAT KING OVER ALL THE EAR
MY STRONG DELIVERER
PRINCE OF PEACE
THE KING OF GLORY
THE REFUGE FOR THE OPPRESSED
GOD, WHO RAISES THE DE
the Rock Their Savior
THE MAKER OF HEAVEN AND EART
THE LORD THE KING
THE MIGHTY SCEPTER
A SHELTER FROM THE STORM
A Witness to
the People
Bread of life

The Head Of Every Man

*1 Corinthians 11:3 But I want you to realize that the **head of every man** is Christ, and the head of the woman is man, and the head of Christ is God.*

Significance: **The LORD JESUS CHRIST is the leader of every man who is submitted to Him.**

Dear Father,

I worship You and Christ, that You are the **head** of Christ and He is the **Head of Every Man**. I rejoice that He came to earth to do Your will, say what You wanted Him to say, reveal Who You are, and give You all glory. I praise Jesus that His final words on the cross in John 19:30, *"It is finished,"* powerfully confirm that He submitted completely to You and finished all the work You assigned Him to do on earth. Hallelujah! I am also deeply grateful that Your **headship** of Christ is fully passed on to His **headship** of all men who give their lives to Him. I am amazed that His wisdom, power, authority and holiness are infinite, yet He loves the men, keeps them, never leaves them, forgives them, covers them with His grace, heals them, and infinitely more! I pray that multitudes of Christian men will repent for taking the **Head of Every Man** for granted, and for every part of their lives they have been unwilling to submit completely to His **headship**. Please help them from now on to worship, revere and obey Him as **Head** of every part of their lives. In accordance with the nature of **head-ship** You have directed in today's Scripture passage, I pray that women and children will submit to Christ's **headship** through their husbands and fathers. I pray these things in the name of Christ. Amen.

What impacted me about Christ today...

_____

_____

_____

_____

_____

_____

_____

_____

The Firstfruits Of Those Who Have Fallen Asleep

*1 Corinthians 15:20-26 But Christ has indeed been raised from the dead, the **firstfruits of those who have fallen asleep**. For since death came through a man, the resurrection of the dead comes also through a man. For as in Adam all die, so in Christ all will be made alive. But each in turn: Christ, **the firstfruits**; then, when he comes, those who belong to him. Then the end will come, when he hands over the kingdom to God the Father after he has destroyed all dominion, authority and power. For he must reign until he has put all his enemies under his feet. The last enemy to be destroyed is death.*

S**ignificance: The LORD JESUS CHRIST, risen from the dead, is the sure sign of a harvest of resurrected saints.**

Dear Father,

I join Paul in praising Christ that He has been raised from the dead, and is consequently the **Firstfruits of Those Who Have Fallen Asleep**. I am thrilled that Christ fulfills Your instructions to Moses in Leviticus 23:10-11, *"Speak to the Israelites and say to them: 'When you enter the land I am going to give you and you reap its harvest, bring to the priest a sheaf of the first grain you harvest. He is to wave the sheaf before the Lord so it will be accepted on your behalf; the priest is to wave it on the day after the Sabbath.'"* I rejoice that without question, Christ is like the wave offering from the **firstfruits** of the harvest, signifying a bountiful harvest to follow—a harvest of resurrected souls. I am very grateful that we who receive Him as our Savior are assured that even though we will one day die physically as He did, we will be resurrected in body and spirit to live with Him forever! I am in awe to think of the massive resurrection harvest that will usher believers into Christ's kingdom. I pray that You will help me and all believers to abandon ourselves to knowing the **Firstfruits of Those Who Have Fallen Asleep** more, loving Him with all our hearts, minds, souls and strength, and being used in His harvest however He directs. May He reign until He has put all His enemies under His feet and death is destroyed. I pray these things in His glorious name. Amen.

What impacted me about Christ today...

The Last Adam

*1 Corinthians 15:44b-49 If there is a natural body, there is also a spiritual body. So it is written: "The first man Adam became a living being"; the **last Adam,** a life-giving spirit. The spiritual did not come first, but the natural, and after that the spiritual. The first man was of the dust of the earth; the second man is of heaven. As was the earthly man, so are those who are of the earth; and as is the heavenly man, so also are those who are of heaven. And just as we have borne the image of the earthly man, so shall we bear the image of the heavenly man.*

Significance: **The LORD JESUS CHRIST is the source of a whole new race who are born again.**

Dear Father,
I am in awe of Jesus, the **Last Adam**, Whom You sent from heaven to make the life-giving Spirit available to me and all mankind. Thank You that only the **Last Adam** can free us from the burden of the sin nature the first Adam brought upon all people. I rejoice that I am free from the penalty of sin, and I have taken on all the characteristics of the **Last Adam** while I am in my earthly body. And, that one day soon I will share with the Apostle Paul in what he declared in Philippians 3:20-21, *"But our citizenship is in heaven. And we eagerly await a Savior from there, the Lord Jesus Christ, who, by the power that enables him to bring everything under his control, will transform our lowly bodies so that they will be like his glorious body."* I praise Jesus and submit every part of my life to Him. I want to bear His likeness completely, and I pray You will put a deep desire for that same relationship with Jesus in the hearts and minds of an increasing number of other believers. May unprecedented hope in Christ arise in us. I pray these things in His blessed name. Amen.

What impacted me about Christ today...

_____

_____

_____

_____

_____

_____

God, Who Raises The Dead

*2 Corinthians 1:8-11a We do not want you to be uninformed, brothers and sisters, about the troubles we experienced in the province of Asia. We were under great pressure, far beyond our ability to endure, so that we despaired of life itself. Indeed, we felt we had received the sentence of death. But this happened that we might not rely on ourselves but on **God, who raises the dead**. He has delivered us from such a deadly peril, and he will deliver us again. On him we have set our hope that he will continue to deliver us, as you help us by your prayers.*

Significance: The LORD JESUS CHRIST is God Who raises the dead to life.

Dear Father,

This incident powerfully affirms my confidence in Jesus, the **God Who Raises the Dead**. I praise Him for the power and authority He demonstrated when He raised Jairus' daughter, the widow of Nain's son, and Lazarus from the dead. I am gripped with today's Scripture passage about when Paul and some other disciples he was with believed they were certain to die—they had no power to save themselves nor could any other humans intervene for them. They were as powerless as if they were already dead. I rejoice that all they could do was cast themselves on the protection and deliverance of Jesus, the only One Who had sufficient power to **raise people from the dead**, and thus, sufficient power to save them from death. Thank You for this amazing lesson in Paul's and his companions' lives to trust the **God Who Raises the Dead** at all times, and in all situations. I pray You will help me and other believers to know Jesus as thoroughly as Paul did, to grow in that same reliance upon Him as Paul had, and to set our hope on Him as Paul did. I pray these things in the name of Jesus, our hope. Amen.

What impacted me about Christ today...

_____

_____

_____

_____

_____

*2 Corinthians 1:18-22 But as surely as God is faithful, our message to you is not "Yes" and "No." For the Son of God, Jesus Christ, who was preached among you by us—by me and Silas and Timothy—was not "Yes" and "No," but in him it has always been "Yes." For no matter how many promises God has made, they are "Yes" in **Christ**. And so through him the "Amen" is spoken by us to the glory of God. Now it is God who makes both us and you stand firm in **Christ**. He anointed us, set his seal of ownership on us, and put his Spirit in our hearts as a deposit, guaranteeing what is to come.*

Significance: **The LORD JESUS CHRIST is God's anointed and promised deliverer and king.**

Dear Father,

As the name **Christ** freshly sinks into my heart and mind, I am again in awe that all Who You are (and, thus, all that You want to communicate to mankind about Who You are) is in **Christ**! He is Your love; He is Your power; He is Your Son; He is Your life; He is Your truth; He is Your victory; He is Your glory; and infinitely more. All glory to **Christ** (the Anointed One and Messiah), Who the ancient prophets revealed You would send to redeem mankind from our sin and bondage. As I read today's Scripture passage, it makes perfect sense to me that only in **Christ** could ALL of the promises You have ever made in Genesis through Revelation be fulfilled! Oh Father, You are good and great beyond our imagination. I marvel at the vast goodness and greatness of Your promises that are being fulfilled in **Christ** (in the past, now and for all eternity)! My hope in **Christ** soars with the certainty of this "Yes" in Him. Please help me and all His people stand firm in Him. I pray these things in the name of Jesus, the glorious "Amen."

What impacted me about Christ today...

_____

_____

_____

_____

_____

_____

_____

The Light Of The Gospel

*2 Corinthians 4:4-6 The god of this age has blinded the minds of unbelievers, so that they cannot see the **light of the gospel** that displays the glory of Christ, who is the image of God. For what we preach is not ourselves, but Jesus Christ as Lord, and ourselves as your servants for Jesus' sake. For God, who said, "Let light shine out of darkness," made his light shine in our hearts to give us the light of the knowledge of God's glory displayed in the face of Christ.*

Significance: **The LORD JESUS CHRIST is the illumination and brilliance of the gospel.**

❧

Dear Father,

I want to live in the brilliance of the **Light of the Gospel** of the glory of Christ. I rejoice that He is the image of Your limitless brightness, excellence, truth, beauty, splendor, purity, wisdom and righteousness, which illuminates and overcomes the darkness of evil and sin in the world. I pray that I and all other believers will wholeheartedly let the fullness of the **Light of the Gospel** of the glory of Christ shine in our hearts. In fact, may we be consumed with the **Light of the Gospel**, worshiping Him and devoting ourselves to Him, speaking of His greatness continually to one another, and proclaiming Him with all our hearts to the many unbelievers all around us. Oh Father, may Your Spirit release this transforming message of Christ to overcome the pervasive blindness of the unbelievers' minds. Please awaken us all to the majesty of the **Light of the Gospel**. I pray these things in Christ's name and for His sake. Amen.

What impacted me about Christ today...

_____

_____

_____

_____

_____

_____

_____

_____

_____

The Treasure

*2 Corinthians 4:7-12 But we have this **treasure** in jars of clay to show that this all-surpassing power is from God and not from us. We are hard pressed on every side, but not crushed; perplexed, but not in despair; persecuted, but not abandoned; struck down, but not destroyed. We always carry around in our body the death of Jesus, so that the life of Jesus may also be revealed in our body. For we who are alive are always being given over to death for Jesus' sake, so that his life may also be revealed in our mortal body. So then, death is at work in us, but life is at work in you.*

Significance: **The LORD JESUS CHRIST is the true wealth in this universe.**

Dear Father,

I bless You for Jesus, the precious **Treasure** (of all treasures). I praise Jesus that there could be no more valuable and needed **Treasure**, now and for all eternity, than Him! I rejoice that all the truths, life, love, hope, grace, forgiveness and glory of Your gospel are in the **Treasure**. I also rejoice that You have put that invaluable **Treasure** in jars of clay (earthen vessels), which are weak and undependable people like me and all other men, women, young people and children who have received Him as our Savior. I pray You will strongly remind us how great Jesus our **Treasure**, is, and of our undeserved privilege of having Him in our lives, so we will constantly revere, adore, honor and give ourselves to Him. I pray that His life will powerfully be at work in us. Please compel us to tell everyone about Him. I pray also that very soon a groundswell of unsaved "jars of clay" will recognize that they too can have the **Treasure**, and will urgently cry out to Him for salvation. May all this work of the **Treasure** demonstrate Your surpassing power to all people. In Jesus' name I ask these things. Amen.

What impacted me about Christ today...

_____

_____

_____

_____

_____

The Indescribable Gift

*<u>2 Corinthians 9:12-15</u> This service [giving generously] that you perform is not only supplying the needs of the Lord's people but is also overflowing in many expressions of thanks to God. Because of the service by which you have proved yourselves, others will praise God for the obedience that accompanies your confession of the gospel of Christ, and for your generosity in sharing with them and with everyone else. And in their prayers for you their hearts will go out to you, because of the surpassing grace God has given you. Thanks be to God for his **indescribable gift**!*

Significance: The LORD JESUS CHRIST is the greatest gift the Father could ever give to mankind.

Dear Father,

I agree with Paul's overflowing heart in saying "Thank You" for Your **Indescribable Gift** of Jesus to me and to all people who receive Him as our Savior! Oh, the invaluable, unspeakable **gift** You have given us! No thoughts, words or songs can begin to convey the greatness of Who Jesus is, nor of the love You lavish on us by sacrificing Your beloved Son for us! I thoroughly delight in the incomparable benefits (current and eternal) that we receive through life in Him (His glorious strength, peace, hope, mercy, pardon, righteousness, love, wisdom, joy, deliverance, light and infinitely more). I think of the saying by Augustine that, "He who has Christ has everything. He who has everything but does not have Christ has nothing. And, he who has Christ plus everything else has no more than he who has Christ alone." Thank You that we have everything in Your **Indescribable Gift**! I repent for how I have often not treated Him as Your **Indescribable Gift**, and I pray that I, my family members and all other believers will, from now on, love Him, honor Him, cherish Him, worship Him, abandon ourselves to Him, abide in Him and speak continually about Him as Your blessed **Indescribable Gift**. I pray that Your Spirit will reveal the surpassing value of Jesus to unsaved people everywhere, so they will clamor to receive Him into their lives. I pray these things in the **indescribable** name of Jesus. Amen.

What impacted me about Christ today...

*2 Corinthians 11:2-3 I am jealous for you with a godly jealousy. I promised you to one **husband**, to Christ, so that I might present you as a pure virgin to him. But I am afraid that just as Eve was deceived by the serpent's cunning, your minds may somehow be led astray from your sincere and pure devotion to Christ.*

Significance: The LORD JESUS CHRIST is the bridegroom of the Church.

Dear Father,

Thank You that Christ is the one **Husband** You have promised to Your people, including in the prophecy in Isaiah 54:5, *"For your Maker is your **husband**—the LORD Almighty is his name—the Holy One of Israel is your Redeemer; he is called the God of all the earth."* What a joy it is to know You planned before the beginning of time that He would be the all-sufficient lover, caregiver, protector, provider, redeemer, servant, guide and much more for those who You have been preparing to receive Him as our perfect, eternal **Husband**. I repent for the ways my mind has been led astray from sincere and pure devotion to Christ, and I pray that many other Christians will similarly repent. Please help us strive to know everything there is to know about our **Husband**, to love Him with all our hearts and to submit ourselves completely to Him. May we be faithful to Him as He is absolutely faithful to us. My love for the **Husband** causes me to sing "Jesus the Very Thought of Thee," written centuries ago by Bernard of Clairvaux: (verse 1) "Jesus, the very thought of Thee, With sweetness fills my breast; But sweeter far Thy face to see, And in Thy presence rest. (verse 5) Jesus, our only joy be Thou, As Thou our prize wilt be. Jesus, be Thou our glory now, And thru eternity." I pray these things in His wonderful name. Amen.

What impacted me about Christ today...

_____

_____

_____

_____

_____

*Galatians 2:20 I have been crucified with Christ and I no longer live, but Christ lives in me. The life I now live in the body, I live by faith in the **Son of God**, who loved me and gave himself for me.*

Significance: **The LORD JESUS CHRIST possesses His Father's power to give eternal life to all who have faith in Him.**

Dear Father,

I am captivated by the precious truth of today's Scripture verse, that since I have received Jesus as my Savior, my "old spiritual man" is dead—crucified with Christ when He was crucified. I rejoice with all my heart, that because Christ rose from the grave and He lives in me, that my "new spiritual man" is alive in Him! I praise Christ that He is my life. I marvel at what Martin Luther said about a Christian's earthly life, "It is but the mask of life under which lives another, namely, Christ, Who is my true life." Hallelujah, that I and all believers live in all of this abundant life, *"by faith in the **Son of God**, who loved me and gave himself for me."* I exalt the **Son of God**, Your one and only **Son**, Whose divine **Sonship** with You is THE source of all the power through which all believers have life, now and for all eternity. I close this prayer with 1 John 5:11-13, *"And this is the testimony: God has given us eternal life, and this life is in his **Son**. Whoever has the **Son** has life; whoever does not have the **Son of God** does not have life. I write these things to you who believe in the name of the **Son of God** so that you may know that you have eternal life."* In His sacrificial name I place these things at Your feet. Amen.

What impacted me about Christ today...

_____

_____

_____

_____

_____

_____

_____

_____

The Seed

*<u>Galatians 3:16-19a, 21-24</u> The promises were spoken to Abraham and to his **seed** . . . who is Christ. What I mean is this: The law, introduced 430 years later, does not set aside the covenant previously established by God and thus do away with the promise. For if the inheritance depends on the law, then it no longer depends on the promise; but God in his grace gave it to Abraham through a promise. Why, then, was the law given at all? It was added because of transgressions until the **Seed** to whom the promise referred had come. . . . Is the law, therefore, opposed to the promises of God? Absolutely not! For if a law had been given that could impart life, then righteousness would certainly have come by the law. But Scripture has locked up everything under the control of sin, so that what was promised, being given through faith in Jesus Christ, might be given to those who believe. Before the coming of this faith, we were held in custody under the law, locked up until the faith that was to come would be revealed. So the law was our guardian until Christ came that we might be justified by faith.*

Significance: **The LORD JESUS CHRIST is the promised descendant of Abraham.**

Dear Father,

I worship Christ that He is the **Seed** (the Messiah) in Whom the covenant promises You made to Abraham are fulfilled, and through Whom all the nations of the earth will be blessed. Hallelujah, that the blessings (of salvation) in Jesus for all mankind are beyond what we can ask or imagine! I praise Jesus for resolutely stating to His disciples in Luke 24:44 after He rose from the grave: *"This is what I told you while I was still with you: Everything must be fulfilled that is written about me in the Law of Moses, the Prophets and the Psalms."* And, again, I delight in Paul's confirmation of Christ in 2 Corinthians 1:20a as the **Seed**, Messiah and Anointed One: *"For no matter how many promises God has made, they are 'Yes' in Christ."* I pray that I and all others who are "joint heirs with Christ," the **Seed,** will live in all His fullness, and will pass the **Seed** along to everyone else You bring into our lives. May the fruit of the **Seed** result in widespread renewal, transformation and harvest. I pray these things in the Promised One's name. Amen.

What impacted me about Christ today...

The One He [The Father] Loves

Ephesians 1:5-6 He [the Father] predestined us for adoption to sonship through Jesus Christ, in accordance with his pleasure and will— to the praise of his glorious grace, which he has freely given us in the ***One he loves.***

Significance: The LORD JESUS CHRIST is the One Who has the original love of the Father in Him.

Dear Father,

I worship Jesus Christ, Your dearly beloved Son, the **One He Loves** (the One You love). That name/attribute of Christ fills my spirit with the greatest joy and hope, since it captures the core of the Godhead: perfect love for one another! I am so grateful that out of that great love You predestined me and all others who would be adopted as Your sons and daughters through Jesus. I am humbled, honored, in awe and overwhelmingly thankful that You have freely given us Your **glorious grace** through the precious **One** You love. It is a grace we did not deserve and never could have earned. I rejoice at how John's testimony in 1 John 4:9-10 confirms that gift of grace: *"This is how God showed his love among us: He sent his one and only Son into the world that we might live through him. This is love: not that we loved God, but that he loved us and sent his Son as an atoning sacrifice for our sins."* I pray You will help us love Your Son as You love Him. I pray we will become deeply grateful for the glorious, life-giving grace You give us through Your Son. Help us to relinquish everything else in the world to live in that grace. I ask these things in the name of the **One He Loves**. Amen.

What impacted me about Christ today...

_____

_____

_____

_____

_____

_____

_____

*Ephesians 2:11-15 Therefore, remember that formerly you who are Gentiles by birth and called "uncircumcised" by those who call themselves "the circumcision" (which is done in the body by human hands)— remember that at that time you were separate from Christ, excluded from citizenship in Israel and foreigners to the covenants of the promise, without hope and without God in the world. But now in Christ Jesus you who once were far away have been brought near by the blood of Christ. For he himself is our **peace**, who has made the two groups one and has destroyed the barrier, the dividing wall of hostility, by setting aside in his flesh the law with its commands and regulations. His purpose was to create in himself one new humanity out of the two, thus making **peace**.*

Significance: **The LORD JESUS CHRIST is the sum total of peace.**

☙

Dear Father,

I give You glory that Jesus is my **Peace**, and the **Peace** of all who receive Him as our Savior. My heart is filled with joy that the only way Jews and Gentiles (all people) can have true, abundant, lasting **peace** between ourselves and You, and between one another, is through the cleansing blood of Jesus. I have marvelous hope about our **peace** from Scripture passages like Isaiah 53:4-5 that are fulfilled in Christ: *"Surely he took up our pain and bore our suffering, yet we considered him punished by God, stricken by him, and afflicted. But he was pierced for our transgressions, he was crushed for our iniquities; the punishment that brought us **peace** was on him, and by his wounds we are healed."* I pray that I, my family members and all other believers will devote ourselves to knowing Jesus our **Peace** more and more each day, and abandoning ourselves into all He is, so that we will be united **peacemakers** in Him. May the **peace** of Christ rule in our lives, in Your Church and across all nations. I pray these things in the reconciling name of Jesus. Amen.

What impacted me about Christ today...

_____

_____

_____

_____

_____

The Chief Cornerstone

*Ephesians 2:19-22 Consequently, you are no longer foreigners and strangers, but fellow citizens with God's people and also members of his household, built on the foundation of the apostles and prophets, with Christ Jesus himself as the **chief cornerstone**. In him the whole building is joined together and rises to become a holy temple in the Lord. And in him you too are being built together to become a dwelling in which God lives by his Spirit.*

S ignificance: The LORD JESUS CHRIST is the perfect foundation upon which His Church is built.

Dear Father,

I praise Christ Jesus that He is the **Chief Cornerstone**, upon Whom all of creation, including His Church and His kingdom, are being firmly built. I honor Jesus, the all-secure, all-solid, all-indestructible, all-strong, all-dependable, all-righteous **cornerstone** that supports and fulfills the promises and prophecies of our faith which were spoken about Him by the ancient apostles and prophets. I shout "Hallelujah" that I and all believers today are part of that building which is being joined together upon the **Chief Cornerstone** to become a dwelling in which You live by Your Spirit! I pray that You will help us reject all other influences that are enticing us to build our lives upon them. Please help us to build our lives (individually and together) solely upon the **Chief Cornerstone**. Oh, may we live in His supreme love, righteousness, truth, peace, strength, faith, joy, authority and all else that He is. I pray that our young people especially will not be satisfied unless their lives are built upon the **Chief Cornerstone**. In Jesus' strong and sure name I ask these things. Amen.

What impacted me about Christ today...

_____

_____

_____

_____

_____

_____

The Fullness Of God

*Ephesians 3:14-19 For this reason I kneel before the Father, from whom every family in heaven and on earth derives its name. I pray that out of his glorious riches he may strengthen you with power through his Spirit in your inner being, so that Christ may dwell in your hearts through faith. And I pray that you, being rooted and established in love, may have power, together with all the Lord's holy people, to grasp how wide and long and high and deep is the love of Christ, and to know this love that surpasses knowledge—that you may be filled to the measure of all the **fullness of God**.*

Significance: The LORD JESUS CHRIST is the totality of Who God is.

Dear Father,

I am in awe that Jesus is ALL You are, and that You sent Him to earth to **be** the **fullness of God**, to **reveal** the **fullness of God**, and to **make available** the **fullness of God** to all who seek Him. I praise Him that there is nothing lacking in Him of Your glory, majesty, power, love or wisdom. I am abounding in joy and hope that I and all believers can know You completely through Him! I am deeply grateful for the gift You have given us of Him dwelling in our hearts through faith, and that we are rooted and established in the wide, long, high and deep love of Christ. Truly, this is another confirmation of Christ's promise in John 10:10 that: *"I have come that they might have life, and have it to the full."* I pray that Your Spirit will give us an insatiable desire to know more and more of the **Fullness of God**. I think of the beautiful hymn by Eliza Hewitt that includes: (verse 1) "More about Jesus would I know, More of His grace to others show; More of His saving fullness see, More of His love Who died for me. (verse 2) More about Jesus let me learn, More of His holy will discern; Spirit of God, my Teacher be, Showing the things of Christ to me. (verse 3) More about Jesus in His Word, Holding communion with my Lord; Hearing His voice in every line, Making each faithful saying mine." May we be so captivated with Christ that we give ourselves body, mind and spirit to Him, and regularly exclaim of His greatness to one another. I pray these things in Jesus' glorious name. Amen.

What impacted me about Christ today...

*Ephesians 4:11-16 So Christ himself gave the apostles, the prophets, the evangelists, the pastors and teachers, to equip his people for works of service, so that the body of Christ may be built up until we all reach unity in the faith and in the knowledge of the Son of God and become mature, attaining to the whole measure of the fullness of Christ. Then we will no longer be infants, tossed back and forth by the waves, and blown here and there by every wind of teaching and by the cunning and craftiness of people in their deceitful scheming. Instead, speaking the truth in love, we will grow to become in every respect the mature body of him who is the **head**, that is, Christ. From him the whole body, joined and held together by every supporting ligament, grows and builds itself up in love, as each part does its work.*

Significance: **The LORD JESUS CHRIST is the Commander-in-Chief of all things, especially His Church.**

Dear Father,

I bow before Christ, the glorious **Head** of all creation, including the Body of Christ (His Church). I exalt Christ that everything comes from Him and is sustained by His perfect wisdom and authority. He is the **Head** of all languages, tribes, peoples, nations, kings, kingdoms, powers and generations. I rejoice that as **Head** of His Church He is the one and only sovereign King, Lord, Master, Leader, Ruler, Teacher, High Priest, Majesty, Shepherd, I AM and infinitely more over me and all His people. Glory to Jesus that all things in our lives are under Him, to Him, on Him, by Him, with Him, in Him, for Him and through Him. I pray You will help us speak the truth in love with each other, and **in all things** grow up unto our **Head**. May we all reach unity in the faith and in the knowledge of the Son of God and become mature, attaining to the whole measure of the fullness of Christ (our **Head**). Every part of my life is absolutely dependent upon Jesus, my **Head**. I pray these things in His name. Amen.

What impacted me about Christ today...

_____

_____

_____

The Fragrant Offering And Sacrifice To God

*Ephesians 5:1-2 Follow God's example, therefore, as dearly loved children and walk in the way of love, just as Christ loved us and gave himself up for us as a **fragrant offering and sacrifice to God**.*

Significance: The LORD JESUS CHRIST is the sweetest offering of all time to God.

Blessed Father,

I am very grateful that Christ loves me and all people so much that He was willing to come to earth and **offer** every part of His life for us, including **sacrificing** His body and His blood on the cross. I rejoice that His life is wonderfully **fragrant** ("sweet-smelling savor") to You. Truly, He is the beloved **Fragrant Offering and Sacrifice to God**. I pray that You will awaken me and many other followers of Christ to much more of Who the **Fragrant Offering and Sacrifice to God** is, so we will love, honor, revere, adore, imitate and abide in Him, for His great glory. I pray that You will especially help us to offer ourselves as **sacrifices** to You, as Paul says in Romans 12:1, *"Therefore, I urge you, brothers and sisters, in view of God's mercy, to offer your bodies as a living sacrifice, holy and pleasing to God—this is your true and proper worship."* As a part of wholly giving ourselves, I pray You will help us to obey Christ's command in John 13:34-35, *"A new command I give you: Love one another. As I have loved you, so you must love one another. By this all men will know that you are my disciples, if you love one another."* I pray all these things in Christ's fragrant name. Amen.

What impacted me about Christ today...

_____

_____

_____

_____

_____

_____

_____

_____

The Name That Is Above Every Name

<u>*Philippians 2:5-11*</u> *In your relationships with one another, have the same mindset as Christ Jesus: Who, being in very nature God, did not consider equality with God something to be used to his own advantage; rather, he made himself nothing by taking the very nature of a servant, being made in human likeness. And being found in appearance as a man, he humbled himself by becoming obedient to death—even death on a cross! Therefore God exalted him to the highest place and gave him the **name that is above every name**, that at the name of Jesus every knee should bow, in heaven and on earth and under the earth, and every tongue acknowledge that Jesus Christ is Lord, to the glory of God the Father.*

Significance: The LORD JESUS CHRIST has the greatest name of all names. One day, every knee will bow to His name.

Dear Father,

I worship Christ Jesus, the **Name That is Above Every Name**. All glory to Him, that He was willing to become a man and die on a cross in humble obedience to You. My amazement of Him soars as I think of His supreme rank, attributes, power, majesty, lordship, authority, rule, dominion and works. I joyfully acknowledge all He is called in Your Scriptures that are part of the **Name That is Above Every Name**: Emmanuel, Kinsman-Redeemer, Leader and Commander, Fortress, Shepherd, King of Glory, Help and Deliverer, Strong Tower, Anointed One, Savior, Master, Lord of lords, High Priest, Light of the World, Prince of Peace, Chief Cornerstone, Chosen One, Potter, Son of God, Spring of Living Water, Messenger of the Covenant, Servant, Bread of Life, Mediator, Pearl of Great Price, Indescribable Gift and countless more! At the **name** of Jesus, the **Name That is Above Every Name**, my knees bow now, and my tongue acknowledges now that He is Lord, to Your great glory! May His whole Church ardently love His **name**, and joyfully speak His **name** to everyone we know. I pray that You will cleanse us of everything that is keeping us from having the same attitude of humility as He does. In Christ's **name** I ask these things. Amen.

What impacted me about Christ today...

_____

_____

*Philippians 4:4-7 Rejoice in the **Lord** always. I will say it again: Rejoice! Let your gentleness be evident to all. The Lord is near. Do not be anxious about anything, but in every situation, by prayer and petition, with thanksgiving, present your requests to God. And the peace of God, which transcends all understanding, will guard your hearts and your minds in Christ Jesus.*

Significance: **The LORD JESUS CHRIST is the great ruler Who is completely able, and yet is very, very near to His people.**

Dear Father,

I worship Christ for what Paul declared in 1 Corinthians 8:6b, *"there is but one **Lord**, Jesus Christ, through whom all things came and through whom we live."* Hallelujah! The **Lord** is above all things; He created all things; He knows all things; He never changes; He is all-powerful; His promises are sure and steadfast; and **He is always near**! So, with all confidence, I can, *"Rejoice in the **Lord** always. I will say it again: Rejoice!"* I love to rejoice in the greatness of the **Lord** by singing the **Lord** is King" by Charles Wesley: (verse 1) "Rejoice, the **Lord** is King! Your **Lord** and King adore; Mortals give thanks and sing, and triumph evermore; Lift up your heart, lift up your voice; Rejoice, again I say, rejoice! (verse 2) Jesus, the Savior, reigns, the God of truth and love; When He had purged our stains He took His seat above; Lift up your heat, lift up your voice; Rejoice, again I say, rejoice!" I want to be completely submitted to Him, so I pray that You will help me and many other believers do what Paul said in Romans 13:14a, *"Clothe yourselves with the **Lord** Jesus Christ."* Please help us to trust Him regardless of what comes into our lives, so we will *"not be anxious about anything, but in everything, by prayer and petition, with thanksgiving, present our requests to God* (through Him)." May we receive the fullness of Your peace, which goes way beyond all our understanding, and guards our hearts and minds in Christ Jesus. I pray these things in His name. Amen.

What impacted me about Christ today...

_____

_____

_____

_____

Philippians 4:8-9 Finally, brothers and sisters, whatever is true, whatever is noble, whatever is right, whatever is pure, whatever is lovely, whatever is admirable—if anything is excellent or praiseworthy—think about such things. Whatever you have learned or received or heard from me, or seen in me—put it into practice. And the God of peace will be with you.

Significance: **The LORD JESUS CHRIST is the divine source of all true peace.**

Dear Father,

I am delighted that Jesus, the **God of Peace**, is with me at all times. I praise Him that He is the perfection of all the godly qualities in today's Scripture passage which lead to peace: He is noble, right, pure, lovely, admirable, excellent and praiseworthy. I marvel again that the heavenly host announced His birth as the "**peacegiver**" by saying, *"Glory to God in the highest, and on earth peace to men on whom his favor rests."* I hold on to some of the many other Scripture passages which affirm that Your peace is in Jesus, such as His own words in John 14:27, *"Peace I leave with you; my peace I give you. I do not give to you as the world gives. Do not let your hearts be troubled and do not be afraid,"* and in John 16:33, *"I have told you these things, so that in me you may have peace. In this world you will have trouble. But take heart! I have overcome the world."* I really want to experience what Paul says in Colossians 3:15, *"Let the peace of Christ rule in your hearts, since as members of one body you were called to peace. And be thankful."* I pray that You will help me, my family members and all other followers of Jesus to be increasingly desirous to know and live in the depths of the **God of Peace**. Oh, may we especially be messengers of His **peace** to one another. I ask all these things in His blessed name. Amen.

What impacted me about Christ today...

_____

_____

_____

_____

_____

The Son He Loves

*Colossians 1:13-14 For he [God the Father] has rescued us from the dominion of darkness and brought us into the kingdom of the **Son he loves**, in whom we have redemption, the forgiveness of sins.*

Significance: **The LORD JESUS CHRIST, God's only Son, is perfectly and infinitely loved by His Father.**

Dear Father,

What a precious name this is for Jesus—the **Son He Loves** (the Son of Your love). When I think of the all-encompassing, lavish **love** relationship that You and Your **Son** have had for each other for all eternity, I rejoice that Your mutual **love** is the foundation of Scripture and of the universe! I am exceedingly humbled that You **love** me and all people in the world so much that You were willing to give the **Son You love** for us. I joyfully return to a previous Scripture passage which ties all that **love** together: Ephesians 1:4b-6, *"In **love** he [the Father] predestined us for adoption to sonship through Jesus Christ, in accordance with his pleasure and will—to the praise of his glorious grace, which he has freely given us in the One he loves."* Thank You that You rescued us from the dominion of darkness into Your Son's kingdom. I pray that His followers throughout the world, including me, will fanatically love, honor, adore, cherish, obey, praise and speak to one another about the **Son He Loves**. May His love fill us now, and overflow as a tsunami onto the people around us who are spiritually lost and dying without Him. I pray these things in His beloved name. Amen.

What impacted me about Christ today...

_____

_____

_____

_____

_____

_____

_____

_____

_____

_____

The Image Of The Invisible God

*Colossians 1:15-20 The Son is the **image of the invisible God**, the firstborn over all creation. For in him all things were created: things in heaven and on earth, visible and invisible, whether thrones or powers or rulers or authorities; all things have been created through him and for him. He is before all things, and in him all things hold together. And he is the head of the body, the church; he is the beginning and the firstborn from among the dead, so that in everything he might have the supremacy. For God was pleased to have all his fullness dwell in him, and through him to reconcile to himself all things, whether things on earth or things in heaven, by making peace through his blood, shed on the cross.*

Significance: **The LORD JESUS CHRIST embodies all that the unseen God is.**

Dear Father,

I worship Christ, the one and only **Image of the Invisible God**. I rejoice that for all eternity, including when He came to earth as a man, He has possessed ALL Your exact qualities, characteristics, attributes and abilities (Your power, holiness, wisdom, love, mercy, peace and every other part of You). I love how Henry Gariepy stated this unique truth: "Christ was the visible manifestation of the **Invisible God**. He was God in human flesh and form." I bless Jesus for His powerful words about this with Philip in John 14:8-9a, *"Philip said, 'Lord, show us the Father and that will be enough for us.' Jesus answered: 'Don't you know me, Philip, even after I have been among you for such a long time? **Anyone who has seen me has seen the Father.**'"* I worship Christ for the Apostle John's declaration of His deity in John 1:18, *"No one has ever seen God, but the one and only Son, who is himself God and is in closest relationship with the Father, has made him known."* I pray that Your Spirit will put an insatiable hunger in me and multitudes of other believers to know everything we possibly can about the **Image of the Invisible God**. May He be our fondest passion. I pray these things in Christ's excellent name. Amen.

What impacted me about Christ today...

_____

_____

_____

_____

The Firstborn Over All Creation

Colossians 1:15-20 The Son is the image of the invisible God, the **firstborn over all creation**. *For in him all things were created: things in heaven and on earth, visible and invisible, whether thrones or powers or rulers or authorities; all things have been created through him and for him. He is before all things, and in him all things hold together. And he is the head of the body, the church; he is the beginning and the firstborn from among the dead, so that in everything he might have the supremacy. For God was pleased to have all his fullness dwell in him, and through him to reconcile to himself all things, whether things on earth or things in heaven, by making peace through his blood, shed on the cross.*

Significance: **The LORD JESUS CHRIST is the head and heir of all created order.**

Dear Father,
I am thrilled at Paul's revelation that Christ is the **Firstborn Over All Cre-ation**, *"For in him all things were created: things in heaven and on earth, visible and invisible, whether thrones or powers or rulers or authorities; all things have been created through him and for him."* Hallelujah! I know that Christ being **Firstborn Over All Creation** does **not** mean that He was the first created being, (since He has always existed), but that **He has always had the rank and preeminence of a firstborn related to all of His creation**. I praise Him that He is Head of all Creation, Heir of all Creation, Supreme over all Creation, Lord of all Creation, Ruler of all Cre-ation, Master of all Creation, King of all Creation, and far more than we can imagine! I love what St. Augustine wrote: "Christ is not valued at all unless He be valued above all." I pray that the Holy Spirit will continually make the **Firstborn Over All Creation's** spectacular greatness known to me and the whole Church, so we will value Him above all, and put all our hope in Him. I pray these things in His matchless name. Amen.

What impacted me about Christ today...

_____

_____

_____

_____

_____

Before All Things

*Colossians 1:15-20 The Son is the image of the invisible God, the firstborn over all creation. For in him all things were created: things in heaven and on earth, visible and invisible, whether thrones or powers or rulers or authorities; all things have been created through him and for him. He is **before all things**, and in him all things hold together. And he is the head of the body, the church; he is the beginning and the firstborn from among the dead, so that in everything he might have the supremacy. For God was pleased to have all his fullness dwell in him, and through him to reconcile to himself all things, whether things on earth or things in heaven, by making peace through his blood, shed on the cross.*

Significance: **The LORD JESUS CHRIST precedes and outranks everything in the universe.**

Dear Father,

I bless Jesus that He is **Before all Things**. I praise You and Jesus that before the beginning of time He was part of the Godhead. I think of what the Creation account says about God (in the Person of Jesus) in Genesis 1:1-3, *"In the beginning God created the heavens and the earth. Now the earth was formless and empty, darkness was over the surface of the deep, and the Spirit of God was hovering over the waters. And God said, 'Let there be light,' and there was light."* I marvel again how the Apostle John confirms Jesus' eternal nature and authority in John 1:1-3, *"In the beginning was the Word, and the Word was with God, and the Word was God. He was with God in the beginning. Through him all things were made; without him nothing was made that has been made."* I rejoice that the One Who is **Before all Things** created all things out of nothing, **and** that *"in him all things hold together"* (are sustained). I pray that You will continually remind me and countless other believers of Jesus' self-existent power, and help us to surrender our lives completely to His perfect wisdom, love, righteousness, order and lordship. I ask all these things in His superior name. Amen.

What impacted me about Christ today...

_____

_____

_____

The Head Of The Body

*Colossians 1:15-20 The Son is the image of the invisible God, the firstborn over all creation. For in him all things were created: things in heaven and on earth, visible and invisible, whether thrones or powers or rulers or authorities; all things have been created through him and for him. He is before all things, and in him all things hold together. And he is the **head of the body**, the church; he is the beginning and the firstborn from among the dead, so that in everything he might have the supremacy. For God was pleased to have all his fullness dwell in him, and through him to reconcile to himself all things, whether things on earth or things in heaven, by making peace through his blood, shed on the cross.*

Significance: **The LORD JESUS CHRIST is the ultimate head of the Church.**

Dear Father,

I praise Jesus that He is the undisputed **Head of the Body** (the Church), all the time, and in every way. Without Him we can do nothing! I bless Him that He knows everything about the **Body**, is all-wise and all-powerful to lead and care for the **Body**, created and totally sustains the **Body**, rules and governs the **Body**, loves and protects the **Body**, is the firstborn from among the dead for the **Body**, and in everything (for the **Body** and for all Creation), He is supreme. I rejoice that Your fullness dwells in and through the **Head of the Body**, and that I and all the other parts of His **Body** can live as one in that fullness. I pray You will convict me and all other members of the **Body** who have rejected, diminished, disobeyed, or rebelled against our **Head**, to repent of our wicked ways, and submit completely to His **Headship**. May what the Apostle Paul stated in Acts 17:28 become the consuming reality for us now: *"For in him [the **Head of the Body**] we live and move and have our being."* I pray these things in His supreme name. Amen.

What impacted me about Christ today...

_____

_____

_____

_____

_____

The Hope Of Glory

*<u>Colossians 1:25-27</u> I [Paul] have become its [the Church's] servant by the commission God gave me to present to you the word of God in its fullness—the mystery that has been kept hidden for ages and generations, but is now disclosed to the Lord's people. To them God has chosen to make known among the Gentiles the glorious riches of this mystery, which is Christ in you, the **hope of glory**.*

Significance: The LORD JESUS CHRIST is all of God's glorious hope.

Dear Father,
I think of a couple of definitions of **hope** that are so powerfully fulfilled in and through Christ: **Hope** is "confident expectation." **Hope** is "a firm assurance regarding things that are unclear and unknown." I am filled with amazement and gratitude that once I was without Christ and had no **hope**, but now, I have the glorious, unsearchable riches of Christ, my Savior and Lord, in me! All praise to Jesus for His glory-filled names, titles, attributes, works, powers, majesty and sacrifice. I am so grateful that I have abounding **hope**, now and forever, in the One and Only **Hope of Glory**! I pray for myself, my family and all other believers what Paul prayed in Ephesians 1:18-19a, *"I pray that the eyes of your heart may be enlightened in order that you may know the **hope** to which he has called you, the riches of his **glorious** inheritance in his holy people, and his incomparably great power for us who believe."* Oh, Father, I believe it is time for us to be consumed in Christ, the **Hope of Glory**! Please do whatever is necessary to strip all other attractions and affections from us. I pray these things with all **hope** in the name of Jesus, and for His **glory**. Amen.

What impacted me about Christ today...

_____

_____

_____

_____

_____

_____   _____

_____

*Colossians 2:1-3 I want you to know how hard I am contending for you and for those at Laodicea, and for all who have not met me personally. My goal is that they may be encouraged in heart and united in love, so that they may have the full riches of complete understanding, in order that they may know the **mystery of God**, namely, Christ, in whom are hidden all the treasures of wisdom and knowledge.*

Significance: The LORD JESUS CHRIST reveals the whole mystery of Who God is. To know Christ is to know God.

Dear Father,

Thank You that You have revealed the **Mystery of God**, namely, Christ, to me and to millions of others in the world and around the world. I rejoice that in Christ are hidden all the treasures of wisdom and knowledge. I confess that I am not able to comprehend the immensity of all wisdom and all knowledge. But, I am absolutely sure that Christ is big enough, vast enough, and supreme enough that all the treasures of Your wisdom and knowledge are hidden in Him. All majesty and glory to Him! As Paul struggled for the people of Colossae and Laodicea to have the full riches of complete understanding in order that they may know the **Mystery of God**, I struggle in prayer that all believers here and now may understand much, much more of Who Christ is. Please give us a thirst to know more about the **Mystery of God** whenever we read the Bible, see His creative works around us, experience His mighty deeds, and speak about Him with one another. I pray this thirst for the **Mystery of God** will penetrate the hearts of many unsaved people we know too. In Christ's awesome name I ask these things. Amen.

What impacted me about Christ today...

_____

_____

_____

_____

_____

_____

The Fullness Of The Deity

*Colossians 2:6-10 So then, just as you received Christ Jesus as Lord, continue to live your lives in him, rooted and built up in him, strengthened in the faith as you were taught, and overflowing with thankfulness. See to it that no one takes you captive through hollow and deceptive philosophy, which depends on human tradition and the elemental spiritual forces of this world rather than on Christ. For in Christ all the **fullness of the Deity** lives in bodily form, and in Christ you have been brought to fullness. He is the head over every power and authority.*

Significance: The LORD JESUS CHRIST is all that God is in a body.

Dear Father,

Thank You that in Christ is all the **Fullness** (completeness, entirety, totality) **of the Deity** in all the other names of Christ. I marvel that the whole **Deity** became incarnate in Christ in bodily form. My heart burns inside when I think about Him, like the hearts of the two disciples on the Road to Emmaus must have burned when Jesus revealed the **fullness** of Himself to them in the Old Testament. That incident reminds me of Jesus' wonderful words in John 10:10, *"I have come that they [His followers] may have life, and have it to the full."* I want to live in that fullness of the One Who is the **Fullness of the Deity**. I want to know all of Him, love all of Him, worship all of Him, depend upon all of Him, glorify all of Him, and speak about all of Him to other believers. I wholeheartedly agree with Frances Havergal's beautiful song of devotion to Jesus which begins, "Take my life and let it be, Consecrated Lord to Thee. Take my moments and my days. Let them flow in ceaseless praise." I pray that You will put a consuming burning for the **Fullness of the Deity** in the hearts of lost people that will cause them to cry out for Him to quench their desperate souls. I ask all these things in His inexhaustible name. Amen.

What impacted me about Christ today...

_____

_____

_____

_____

_____

The Head Over Every Power And Authority

---

*Colossians 2:6-10 So then, just as you received Christ Jesus as Lord, continue to live your lives in him, rooted and built up in him, strengthened in the faith as you were taught, and overflowing with thankfulness. See to it that no one takes you captive through hollow and deceptive philosophy, which depends on human tradition and the elemental spiritual forces of this world rather than on Christ. For in Christ all the fullness of the Deity lives in bodily form, and in Christ you have been brought to fullness. He is the **head over every power and authority**.*

Significance: **The LORD JESUS CHRIST is the absolute ruler of all kingdoms, visible and invisible.**

Dear Father,

I praise the Lord Jesus Christ, Who is the **Head Over Every Power and Authority**, now and forever. I marvel how all of Christ's names and attributes add to each other to describe His absolute **Headship**. I again marvel how many Scripture passages like Ephesians 1:19b-21 declare His authority too: *"That power is the same as the mighty strength he [God the Father] exerted when he raised Christ from the dead and seated him at his right hand in the heavenly realms, far above all rule and authority, power and dominion, and every name that is invoked, not only in the present age but also in the one to come."* I pray that I and all other believers will earnestly seek to know all we can about our supreme **Head**, and that we will humbly honor and obey Him, and submit every part of our lives to Him. I pray that all powers and authorities in the world will fear and revere the **Head Over Every Power and Authority**, and become subject to His rule and reign. For His is the kingdom and the power and the glory forever. Amen.

What impacted me about Christ today...

_____

_____

_____

_____

_____

*Colossians 3:1-4, 11, 16-17 Since, then, you have been raised with Christ, set your hearts on things above, where Christ is, seated at the right hand of God. Set your minds on things above, not on earthly things. For you died, and your life is now hidden with Christ in God. When Christ, who is your life, appears, then you also will appear with him in glory. . . . Here there is no Gentile or Jew, circumcised or uncircumcised, barbarian, Scythian, slave or free, but **Christ is all, and is in all**. . . . Let the message of Christ dwell among you richly as you teach and admonish one another with all wisdom through psalms, hymns and songs from the Spirit, singing to God with gratitude in your hearts. And whatever you do, whether in word or deed, do it all in the name of the Lord Jesus, giving thanks to God the Father through him.*

Significance: The LORD JESUS CHRIST surrounds everything, and, at the same time, He is the center of all there is.

Dear Father,

I am eternally grateful that **Christ is All, and is in All**. I can't comprehend the immensity of Him being **All** (totally surrounding and encompassing all creation) and at the same time being in the center/DNA/core of **All**. I worship Christ that there is nothing outside of His rule and reign and power. All things are by Him, for Him, through Him, to Him, in Him, and on and on. Nothing is too difficult for Him, and all things are possible through Him. His love never ends, never diminishes, is unconditional, and does not favor one person over another. All life, hope, peace, grace and mercy are in Him. He never leaves nor forsakes. He is all-holy, righteous and good. All glory is His. All majesty, honor, reverence, adoration, worship, devotion are due Him. He is light and revelation. Greater is He Who is in us than he who is in the world. I think of one of the phrases in Bishop Lockridge's poem-sermon about the greatness of Christ: "I wish I could describe Him to you! He is indescribable. He's irresistible, and He's invincible." I pray that the longing to know the depths of **Christ** (Who) **is All, and is in All** will be the greatest passion of my life, and the Church everywhere, and that You will help us abandon every other passion for Him. In the name of **Christ, my All**, I pray these things. Amen.

What impacted me about Christ today...

*1 Thessalonians 1:7-10 And so you [the Church of the Thessalonians] became a model to all the believers in Macedonia and Achaia. The Lord's message rang out from you not only in Macedonia and Achaia—your faith in God has become known everywhere. Therefore we do not need to say anything about it, for they themselves report what kind of reception you gave us. They tell how you turned to God from idols to serve the living and true God, and to wait for his **Son from heaven**, whom he raised from the dead—Jesus, who rescues us from the coming wrath.*

Significance: The LORD JESUS CHRIST is God's beloved Son Who will return to take His people to His Father.

Dear Father,

As I think about Christ, the **Son From Heaven**, my hope in Him is strengthened. I rejoice that You raised Your beloved **Son** from the dead to sit at Your right hand in heaven, and that one day soon He will return from heaven to earth in all His power and glory! Thank You that with all certainty He will rescue those who receive Him as their Savior from the wrath that will come upon all sinners. What a precious, undeserved privilege we believers have of waiting for the **Son From Heaven** to return. May we hold on to Paul's words in 1 Thessalonians 4:13-17, *"Brothers and sisters, we do not want you to be uninformed about those who sleep in death, so that you do not grieve like the rest of mankind, who have no hope. For we believe that Jesus died and rose again, and so we believe that God will bring with Jesus those who have fallen asleep in him. According to the Lord's word, we tell you that we who are still alive, who are left until the coming of the Lord, will certainly not precede those who have fallen asleep. For the Lord himself will come down from heaven, with a loud command, with the voice of the archangel and with the trumpet call of God, and the dead in Christ will rise first. After that, we who are still alive and are left will be caught up together with them in the clouds to meet the Lord in the air. And so we will be with the Lord forever."* In Christ's name I pray. Amen.

What impacted me about Christ today...

_____

_____

_____

The Lord Of Peace

*2 Thessalonians 3:16 Now may the **Lord of peace** himself give you peace at all times and in every way. The Lord be with all of you.*

Significance: **The LORD JESUS CHRIST is the source and supreme master of peace.**

Dear Father,

I worship Christ, Who is magnified in a variety of names and titles as **Lord** of His whole creation, including in Luke 2:11b, where an angel announced to local shepherds that a Savior had been born, proclaiming: *"He is the Messiah, [Christ] the **Lord**."* I again join the heavenly host in Luke 2:14, as they and the angel resoundingly praised You for sending Jesus, the **Lord of Peace**: *"Glory to God in the highest, and on earth **peace** to those on whom his favor rests."* I am exceedingly grateful that Your favor rests on those who receive Christ as their Savior, and that they receive His *"**peace** at all times and in every way."* Hallelujah, that Christ is the only One Who could die on the cross, to pay the price of mankind's sins, so that we can have eternal **peace** with You. I love to think of Him as the **Lord of Peace** (the Master, Ruler and Administrator of our peace). I pray that Your Spirit will reveal more and more of the vast powers and character of Jesus to me, my family members and many, many other believers, so that we will wholly trust Him and live in perfect **peace** in Him. Thank You that the **Lord of Peace** is always with us, as He promises in Matthew 28:20b, *"And surely I am with you always, to the very end of the age."* I pray these things in the name that is our certainty of **peace**, Jesus. Amen.

What impacted me about Christ today...

_____

_____

_____

_____

_____

_____

_____

_____

*1 Timothy 1:1-2 Paul, an apostle of Christ Jesus by the command of God our Savior and of **Christ Jesus our hope**, To Timothy my true son in the faith: Grace, mercy and peace from God the Father and Christ Jesus our Lord.*

Significance: The LORD JESUS CHRIST is the embodiment of all hope.

Dear Father,

I worship **Christ** (the Messiah, the Anointed One) **Jesus** (the Savior of the world), the blessed Son You sent to earth to reveal the depths of Who You are and to redeem us from our sins. I am in awe that **Christ Jesus** possesses and reveals all of the promises, attributes, nature, authority and glory of the Godhead. I am delighted that You have given Him all power in heaven and on earth. I praise Jesus that **all hope** for all time is in Him. He is the Solid Rock, the Secure Foundation, the Author and Finisher of our faith, our Constant Intercessor, our Advocate, our Good Shepherd, our Great High Priest and all else that comprises His supremacy. Truly, He is **Christ Jesus Our Hope!** I am exceedingly grateful that in **Christ Jesus**, I and all other believers have the unqualified assurance **(hope)** that the government of our lives and of this world are upon His all-sufficient shoulders (Isaiah 9:6), and that one day He will return for His people and establish His kingdom on earth. Please help us to know the fullness of **Christ Jesus Our Hope** and to live in all the **hope** we were meant to have in Him. I pray that we will be so filled with the Spirit of **Christ Jesus our Hope** that all lost people in our spheres of influence will ask us to share the reason for our **hope** with them. In Christ's name I pray these things. Amen.

What impacted me about Christ today...

_____

_____

_____

_____

_____

_____

The King Eternal, Immortal, Invisible, The Only God

*1 Timothy 1:15-17 Here is a trustworthy saying that deserves full acceptance: Christ Jesus came into the world to save sinners—of whom I am the worst. But for that very reason I was shown mercy so that in me, the worst of sinners, Christ Jesus might display his immense patience as an example for those who would believe in him and receive eternal life. Now to the **King eternal, immortal, invisible, the only God**, be honor and glory for ever and ever. Amen.*

Significance: **The LORD JESUS CHRIST is the only true King, possessing all the attributes of God forever.**

Dear Father,

I join Paul in giving honor and glory forever to Christ Jesus: the **King Eternal, Immortal, Invisible, the Only God**! What a powerful testimony of the limitless sovereignty of the eternal **King** and Ruler of the entire universe! I magnify Him that He has always been **King** of All, He is **King** now, and He will be **King** for all eternity. Hallelujah, that He fulfills many of the Psalms, including Psalm 10:16a: *"The Lord is **King** for ever and ever."* I am in awe that while all other kings have died, the **King Eternal, Immortal** lives forever and is worshipped and honored forever! I marvel that this is another evidence of what Paul says in Colossians 1:15, that Christ bears the full *"image of the **Invisible** God."* I am excited for the additional confirmation of the divinity of Christ in John 1:18, *"No one has ever seen God, but the One and **Only** Son, who is himself God and is in closest relationship with the Father, has made him known."* I pray that You will fill me and multitudes of other believers with the same overwhelming gratitude for our salvation as Paul had, so that we too will speak with all of our hearts of the patience, love, mercy, majesty, beauty and power of the **King Eternal, Immortal, Invisible, the Only God**. I pray these things in the merciful name of Christ our **King**. Amen.

What impacted me about Christ today...

_____

_____

_____

_____

*1 Timothy 2:1-6 I urge, then, first of all, that petitions, prayers, intercession and thanksgiving be made for all people—for kings and all those in authority, that we may live peaceful and quiet lives in all godliness and holiness. This is good, and pleases God our Savior, who wants all people to be saved and to come to a knowledge of the truth. For there is one God and one **mediator** between God and mankind, the man Christ Jesus, who gave himself as a ransom for all people. This has now been witnessed to at the proper time.*

Significance: The LORD JESUS CHRIST reconciles the relationship between God and man.

Dear Father,

I thank You that there is only one true **Mediator** ("go-between") that links holy You and sinful mankind. I am very grateful that the **Mediator** completely knows and loves You and all people, has the perfect solution to our spiritual conflict, and is completely qualified and willing to bridge the gap between all people and You. I bless Jesus that every person, regardless of race, color, gender, age, social class or any of man's other identifying categories, can receive His free gift of **Mediation**. Hallelujah, that my name and the names of every other person who have received the **Mediator** as our Savior are permanently written in the Lamb's Book of Life! I pray You will give believers a strong desire to know the **Mediator** more, and that any who are unsure of His complete work for them will receive full assurance in Him. May joyful thanksgiving, adoration, praise, honor and passion for the **Mediator** rise up among us. I pray these things in the name of Life, Jesus. Amen.

What impacted me about Christ today...

_____

_____

_____

_____

_____

_____

The Man Christ Jesus

*1 Timothy 2:1-6 I urge, then, first of all, that petitions, prayers, intercession and thanksgiving be made for all people—for kings and all those in authority, that we may live peaceful and quiet lives in all godliness and holiness. This is good, and pleases God our Savior, who wants all people to be saved and to come to a knowledge of the truth. For there is one God and one mediator between God and mankind, the **man Christ Jesus**, who gave himself as a ransom for all people. This has now been witnessed to at the proper time.*

Significance: The LORD JESUS CHRIST is both fully God and fully man Who alone is the ransom for mankind.

Dear Father,

I am very glad that the only Person Who could be the Mediator between God and men is the **Man Christ Jesus**. What a joy it is to think how Jesus was, and is, all that He designed mankind to be, with all the experiences, stages of life, feelings, thoughts, desires, needs and so on. Yet, He is the perfect, sinless man, with Your full attributes: wisdom, love, justice, mercy, knowledge, understanding, authority, holiness and infinitely more. I give all glory to Jesus, the one and only God-Man, Whom You sent from heaven to give Himself as a ransom for all men. I love how Philippians 2:5-8 again strongly declares this same truth about the nature and mission of the **Man Christ Jesus**: *"In your relationships with one another, have the same mindset as Christ Jesus: Who, being in very nature God, did not consider equality with God something to be used to his own advantage; rather, he made himself nothing by taking the very nature of a servant, being made in human likeness. And being found in the appearance as a **man**, he humbled himself by becoming obedient to death—even death on a cross!"* I pray that the Church of today will become increasingly enthralled with the **Man Christ Jesus**, and will unceasingly make requests, prayers, intercession and thanksgiving for everyone around us to be saved and come to the knowledge of the truth about Him. I pray these things in His obedient name. Amen.

What impacted me about Christ today...

_____

_____

_____

The Mystery From Which True Godliness Springs

*1 Timothy 3:16 Beyond all question, the **mystery from which true godliness springs** is great: He appeared in the flesh, was vindicated by the Spirit, was seen by angels, was preached among the nations, was believed on in the world, was taken up in glory.*

Significance: **The LORD JESUS CHRIST reveals all of God to mankind and makes His godliness available to all who are willing.**

Dear Father,

I praise Jesus that He is the long-awaited **Mystery From Which True Godliness Springs**. I marvel at the Apostle Paul's declaration that *"beyond all question"* the **mystery of godliness** is *"great!"* I am in awe that fulfilling the mystery required Your Son to leave His heavenly realm to: (1) reveal all You are (2) appear in a body (3) be vindicated by the Spirit (4) be seen by angels (5) be preached among the nations (6) be believed on in the world (7) be taken up in glory, and (8) be poised right now to return to earth as conquering King and Lord forever. I am deeply grateful that Your Son, Who was for many centuries "hidden" with You, was made manifest for my sake and for all of mankind! All glory and honor to Him! I am "blown away" by a number of other Scripture passages that powerfully state how Christ fulfills the **mystery**, including 2 Timothy 1:9b-10, *"This grace [of God] was given us in Christ Jesus before the beginning of time, but it has now been revealed through the appearing of our Savior, Christ Jesus, who has destroyed death and has brought life and immortality to light through the gospel."* Thank You, thank You, that Your great **godliness** has sprung into my life through Jesus, my Savior and Lord! I pray that I and a groundswell of other believers will give ourselves to knowing the depths of the **Mystery From Which True Godliness Springs**. I pray that You will remove all obstacles to great numbers of unsaved people understanding Who He is before it's too late. I ask these things in the liberating name of Jesus. Amen.

What impacted me about Christ today...

_____

_____

_____

*1 Timothy 4:9-10 This is a trustworthy saying that deserves full acceptance. That is why we labor and strive, because we have put our hope in the living God, who is the **Savior of all people**, especially of those who believe.*

Significance: The LORD JESUS CHRIST is the all-sufficient and only Savior for every human being.

Dear Father,
I join Paul in putting all my hope in the living God, Who is the **Savior of all People**. I rejoice that many Scripture passages (including Jesus' words in John 3:17) clearly state Jesus is the One and Only **Savior** You sent from heaven: *"For God did not send his Son into the world to condemn the world, but to save the world through him."* Another passage that resonates with me is found in Peter's message to the Sanhedrin in Acts 4:10-12: *"then know this, you and all the people of Israel: It is by the name of Jesus Christ of Nazareth, whom you crucified but whom God raised from the dead, that this man stands before you healed. Jesus is the stone you builders rejected, which has become the cornerstone. Salvation is found in no one else, for there is no other name under heaven given to mankind by which we must be saved."* I know that Jesus being the **Savior of all People** does not mean that all people are automatically saved; but I praise Him that it is **His desire** that all people be saved, and that we can only be saved through Him. I am grateful with all my heart that Jesus is my **Savior** and my eternal hope. I pray that I and all others who have received Him as our **Savior** will revere Him as our All in All, and constantly testify about His greatness to one another and to every unsaved person we know. I earnestly pray again that You will draw those lost people, and many millions more around the world, to the **Savior of all People**. In His precious name I ask these things. Amen.

What impacted me about Christ today...

_____

_____

_____

_____

_____

*2 Timothy 4:6-8 For I [Paul] am already being poured out like a drink offering, and the time for my departure is near. I have fought the good fight, I have finished the race, I have kept the faith. Now there is in store for me the crown of righteousness, which the Lord, the **righteous Judge**, very soon, will award to me on that day—and not only to me, but also to all who have longed for his appearing.*

Significance: **The LORD JESUS CHRIST is the absolute, final and perfect judge.**

Dear Father,

I honor Jesus as **judge** of **all** according to His words in John 5:22-23a, *"Moreover, the Father **judges** no one, but has entrusted all **judgment** to the Son, that all may honor the Son just as they honor the Father."* I honor Him that Your righteousness (holiness, purity, truth, blessedness, virtue, goodness, integrity and infinitely more) dwells in Him. Hallelujah! Our Lord Jesus is the **Righteous Judge**. I am very grateful that He does not **judge** me and all other people as earthly judges do, but in His perfect wisdom and **righteousness**. I am very grateful that one day, all who sincerely desire His return will receive a crown of **righteousness**. I want to live now and for all eternity completely under His rule, and I say with all my heart, as John did in Revelation 22:20b, *"Amen. Come, Lord Jesus."* I pray that that same eager longing for the **Righteous Judge** will very soon rise up within the whole Church. In His holy name I pray these things. Amen.

What impacted me about Christ today...

_____

_____

_____

_____

_____

_____

_____

_____

_____

_____

The Blessed Hope

*Titus 2:11-14 For the grace of God has appeared that offers salvation to all people. It teaches us to say "No" to ungodliness and worldly passions, and to live self-controlled, upright and godly lives in this present age, while we wait for the **blessed hope**—the appearing of the glory of our great God and Savior, Jesus Christ, who gave himself for us to redeem us from all wickedness and to purify for himself a people that are his very own, eager to do what is good.*

Significance: The LORD JESUS CHRIST is all the hope His people are eagerly waiting for.

Dear Father,

I bow before Jesus, the **Blessed** Lord of the universe. He supremely exceeds all the synonyms of the word "**blessed**": revered, venerated, holy, hallowed, divine, heavenly, sacred, godlike, supernatural and more. I love to meditate on His triumphal entry into Jerusalem, especially John 12:13, *"They [the great crowd] took palm branches and went out to meet him, shouting, 'Hosanna! **Blessed** is he who comes in the name of the Lord! **Blessed** is the King of Israel!'"* Truly, Jesus is the One You blessed before the beginning of time to be the **Hope** of the world, the fullness of the **Hope** You have always had for mankind, now and forever. As Paul said in Romans 8:22-25, one day Jesus, the **Blessed Hope**, will return and consummate that hope: *"We know that the whole creation has been groaning as in the pains of childbirth right up to the present time. Not only so, but we ourselves, who have the firstfruits of the Spirit, groan inwardly as we wait eagerly for our adoption to sonship, the redemption of our bodies. For in this **hope** we were saved. But hope that is seen is no hope at all. Who hopes for what they already have? But if we hope for what we do not yet have, we wait for it patiently."* I pray that I, my family members and all other believers will live now in all Jesus is, and eagerly wait for His return. I ask these things in His **blessed** name. Amen.

What impacted me about Christ today...

_____

_____

_____

_____

*Titus 2:11-14 For the grace of God has appeared that offers salvation to all people. It teaches us to say "No" to ungodliness and worldly passions, and to live self-controlled, upright and godly lives in this present age, while we wait for the blessed hope—the appearing of the glory of our **great God and Savior**, Jesus Christ, who gave himself for us to redeem us from all wickedness and to purify for himself a people that are his very own, eager to do what is good.*

Significance: The LORD JESUS CHRIST is the fullness of both God and Savior.

↬

Dear Father,

I rejoice that Paul clearly proclaims Jesus Christ is the great **God,** the one Who is co-equal with You, existing for all eternity with You, the fullness of Who You are, and sent by You to reveal You to mankind. He is surely the **Savior**. I am in awe of how Paul ties "**Great God and Savior**" and "Jesus Christ" together to abundantly emphasize the breadth and depth of Christ's majesty, glory, rule, mission, sacrifice, divinity, lordship and more. Christ is ALL and is in ALL! I am extremely grateful that I and millions of other believers in our region and throughout the world have absolute certainty that, on the day You have appointed, Jesus Christ, our **Great God and Savior**, will return in all His glory from Your right hand in heaven to gather us unto Himself forever! I fervently pray that today You will compel me and many, many other believers to consecrate ourselves to knowing and loving our **Great God and Savior**, so we will be *"His very own"* with all our hearts. I pray these things in Jesus' great name. Amen and Amen.

What impacted me about Christ today...

_____

_____

_____

_____

_____

_____

Philemon 1:3, 25 *Grace and peace to you from God our Father and the* **Lord Jesus Christ**. *. . . The grace of the* **Lord Jesus Christ** *be with your spirit.*

Significance: **The LORD JESUS CHRIST, in one Person, is Master, Savior and Messiah.**

Dear Father,

I love this introduction and conclusion of Philemon, where Paul prays that the limitless grace of our **Lord** (the Ruler and Governor of all His people) **Jesus** (our perfect and absolute Savior) **Christ** (the Messiah) would envelop Philemon, me and all people who have given our lives to Him. I rejoice that Your grace (and all of the Godhead) resides in the **Lord Jesus Christ**, as the Apostle John confirms in John 1:17, *"For the law was given through Moses; grace and truth came through Jesus Christ."* Truly, His grace is perfect and all-sufficient, as the Lord told Paul in 2 Corinthians 12:8-9a, *"Three times I pleaded with the Lord to take it [the thorn in his flesh] away from me. But he said to me, 'My grace is sufficient for you, for my power is made perfect in weakness.' Therefore I will boast all the more gladly about my weaknesses so that Christ's power may rest on me."* I want to know and live in all of the **Lord Jesus Christ**, especially in His grace. He is far more than sufficient for me. I pray that multitudes of His followers will increasingly seek to know the divine all-sufficiency of the **Lord Jesus Christ**, and will grow significantly as ministers of all He is to one another and to the world around us that desperately needs Him. I pray these things in the name of the Lord. Amen.

What impacted me about Christ today...

_____

_____

_____

_____

_____

_____

_____

_____

The Heir Of All Things

Hebrews 1:1-4 _In the past God spoke to our ancestors through the prophets at many times and in various ways, but in these last days he has spoken to us by his Son, whom he appointed_ **heir of all things**_, and through whom also he made the universe. The Son is the radiance of God's glory and the exact representation of his being, sustaining all things by his powerful word. After he had provided purification for sins, he sat down at the right hand of the Majesty in heaven. So he became as much superior to the angels as the name he has inherited is superior to theirs._

S ignificance: The LORD JESUS CHRIST is the creator and God's appointed heir of all things.

Dear Father,

I rejoice that Jesus is Your One and Only Son. I am in awe that through Him the whole universe was made. Everything You have wanted to reveal to me and all people is made known by Him. My mind can only comprehend a little bit of the vast universe Your Son made, and the boundless wisdom, truth, righteousness, commands, promises and immeasurably more He has spoken (which is far beyond what the forefathers and prophets were able to speak of). Truly, Your Son is worthy of Your appointing Him **Heir of All Things**. All glory to You, and all glory to Jesus for His declaration of this in John 16:15, _"All that belongs to the Father is mine. That is why I said the Spirit will receive from me what he will make known to you."_ I wholeheartedly want the Spirit to make all of the **Heir of All Things** known to me and my family, and for us to live in all of Him. I rejoice in Romans 8:16-17, _"The Spirit himself testifies with our spirit that we are God's children. Now if we are children, then we are heirs—heirs of God and co-heirs with Christ, if indeed we share in his sufferings in order that we may also share in his glory."_ I pray these things in Christ's blessed name. Amen.

What impacted me about Christ today...

_____

_____

_____

_____

*Hebrews 1:1-4 In the past God spoke to our ancestors through the prophets at many times and in various ways, but in these last days he has spoken to us by his Son, whom he appointed heir of all things, and through whom also he made the universe. The Son is the **radiance of God's glory** and the exact representation of his being, sustaining all things by his powerful word. After he had provided purification for sins, he sat down at the right hand of the Majesty in heaven. So he became as much superior to the angels as the name he has inherited is superior to theirs.*

Significance: **The LORD JESUS CHRIST is the perfect display of God's glory.**

Dear Father,
I bow before You, the God of **glory**, and before Your Son, the **Radiance** (splendor, brightness, excellence, perfection, dazzling light) **of God's** (Your) **Glory**. I am deeply grateful that through Christ You fully answered Moses' request in Exodus 33:18, *"Now show me your glory."* I rejoice that in the incarnate Christ, Your magnificent **glory** (the full display of Who You are) radiates to us as John says in John 1:14, *"The Word became flesh and made his dwelling among us. We have seen his **glory**, the **glory** of the one and only Son, who came from the Father, full of grace and truth."* I want to know all of **the Radiance of God's Glory** that I can. I pray that You will help me know much more of Him, grow in my love relationship with Him, experience the depths of His power and **glory**, and speak continually of Him to many other believers. I join in the Doxology found in Jude 1:24-25, *"To him who is able to keep you from stumbling and to present you before his **glorious** presence without fault and with great joy—to the only God our Savior be glory, majesty, power and authority, through Jesus Christ our Lord, before all ages, now and forevermore! Amen."*

What impacted me about Christ today...

_____

_____

_____

_____

_____

The Exact Representation Of His Being

<u>Hebrews 1:1-4</u> *In the past God spoke to our ancestors through the proph-ets at many times and in various ways, but in these last days he has spo-ken to us by his Son, whom he appointed heir of all things, and through whom also he made the universe. The Son is the radiance of God's glory and the **exact representation of his being**, sustaining all things by his powerful word. After he had provided purification for sins, he sat down at the right hand of the Majesty in heaven. So he became as much superior to the angels as the name he has inherited is superior to theirs.*

Significance: The LORD JESUS CHRIST exactly represents Who God is.

Dear Father,

It is amazing to conceive that Your Son is the **Exact Representation of His (Your) Being**. I rejoice that this name ties back to His being the *"Image of the Invisible God"* in Colossians 1:15. I marvel that Your Son's words **exactly represent** Your words to mankind; His righteousness **exactly rep-resents** Your righteousness; His power **exactly represents** Your power; His majesty **exactly represents** Your majesty; His love **exactly repre-sents** Your love; His grace **exactly represents** Your grace; His servant heart **exactly represents** Your servant heart; His promises **exactly rep-resent** Your promises; His prayers **exactly represent** Your prayers; His rule and judgment **exactly represent** Your rule and judgment; His forgive-ness **exactly represents** Your forgiveness; and on and on. Hallelujah! I KNOW YOU THROUGH YOUR SON, and I praise Your Son and You. I pray You will give me, my family members and all believers a devout pas-sion to know all there is to know about the **Exact Representation of His Being**, and, thus, to know You more and more. I pray these things in His superior name. Amen.

What impacted me about Christ today...

_____

_____

_____

_____

_____

His (God's) Firstborn

*<u>Hebrews 1:6</u> And again, when God brings his **firstborn** into the world, he says, "Let all God's angels worship him."*

Significance: The LORD JESUS CHRIST is the most highly valued Person in God's kingdom.

Dear Father,

I again honor the Lord Jesus Christ, **His** (Your) **Firstborn**, Your Heir, Your divine Son, the Creator of heaven and earth, including the angels. I rejoice that Your **Firstborn** is superior to all He has created, and that He sustains all things by His powerful word. He alone is worthy of all praise. As You direct all the angels and all the rulers of the world to worship Your **First-born**, I worship Him too with all that is within me. I pray that You will continually remind all His followers of the greatness of Your **Firstborn**, so that we will unite in ceaselessly worshiping, loving, adoring, honoring, glorifying, cherishing, serving and obeying Him. All of these magnificent truths about Jesus cause me to want to express my reverence and affection for Him by singing "Tis So Sweet To Trust in Jesus" by Louisa Stead: (verse 1)"Tis so sweet to trust in Jesus, Just to take Him at His word; Just to rest upon His promise, Just to know, 'Thus saith the Lord!' (verse 4) I'm so glad I learned to trust Thee, Precious Jesus, Savior, Friend; And I know that Thou art with me, Wilt be with me to the end. (chorus) Jesus, Jesus, how I trust Him! How I've proved Him o'er and o'er! Jesus, Jesus, precious Jesus! Oh, for grace to trust Him more!" I pray that You will reveal the preeminence of the **Firstborn** to vast num-bers of people who have never wanted Him to be involved in their lives, so that they will realize how urgently they need Him. I pray all these things in His exalted name. Amen.

What impacted me about Christ today...

_____

_____

_____

_____

_____

_____

_____

*Hebrews 1:8-12 But about the Son he [God, the Father] says, "Your throne, O **God**, will last for ever and ever; a scepter of justice will be the scepter of your kingdom. You have loved righteousness and hated wickedness; therefore God, your God, has set you above your companions by anointing you with the oil of joy." He also says, "In the beginning, Lord, you laid the foundations of the earth, and the heavens are the work of your hands. They will perish, but you remain; they will all wear out like a garment. You will roll them up like a robe; like a garment they will be changed. But you remain the same, and your years will never end."*

Significance: **The LORD JESUS CHRIST is the one true God in every respect.**

Dear Father,

I rejoice that the writer of Hebrews quoted this passage from Psalm 45, which clearly foretells that Your Son, the magnificent Messiah and King, is fully **God**. I love how Paul's glorious statement in Philippians 2:5b-6 confirms Christ's complete divinity: *"Have the same mindset as Christ Jesus: Who, being in very nature **God**, did not consider equality with God something to be used to his own advantage."* I honor Your Son, that He was with You in the beginning, and that He laid the foundation of the heavens and the earth with His hands. I praise Your Son, the divine **God**, Who rules from His righteous throne for ever and ever. Glory to Him that He will remain the same, and His years will never end. I bow my heart and mind in utmost reverence of Your Son, and say to Him, "O **God**, O **God**, O **God**." I pray that You will cause great numbers of believers everywhere to become as convinced as Paul was that Jesus is totally God. May an awe of Him and an adoration of Him fill His Church as never before. May we all live under His scepter. May ungodly leaders around the world fear Him. In His excellent name I pray these things. Amen.

What impacted me about Christ today...

_____

_____

_____

_____

_____

*Hebrews 2:9-10 But we do see Jesus, who was made lower than the angels for a little while, now **crowned with glory and honor** because he suffered death, so that by the grace of God he might taste death for everyone. In bringing many sons and daughters to glory, it was fitting that God, for whom and through whom everything exists, should make the pioneer of their salvation perfect through what he suffered.*

Significance: The LORD JESUS CHRIST is exalted above all things through His suffering.

Dear Father,

I am in awe that You made Jesus, the Son of Man, a little lower than the angels; but, because He suffered death for all people, He is **Crowned With Glory and Honor** (the highest honor). I am again amazed at Paul's description in Ephesians 1:20-23 of what Jesus being **crowned with glory and honor** partially consists of: *"he [God] raised Christ from the dead and seated him at his right hand in the heavenly realms, far above all rule and authority, power and dominion, and every name that is invoked, not only in the present age but also in the one to come. And God placed all things under his feet and appointed him to be head over everything for the church, which is his body, the fullness of him who fills everything in every way."* I pray that I and multitudes of other followers of the **One** Who is **Crowned With Glory and Honor** will devote our lives to worshiping Him, yielding ourselves to Him, serving Him, obeying Him and speaking of His greatness to one another. May we heartily sing more of "Crown Him With Many Crowns" by Matthew Bridges: (verse 3)"Crown Him the Lord of Life! Who triumphed o'er the grave; Who rose victorious in the strife, For those He came to save. His glories now we sing, Who died and rose on high, Who died eternal life to bring, And lives that death may die." I pray these things in Christ's **glorious** name. Amen.

What impacted me about Christ today...

_____

_____

_____

_____

_____

*Hebrews 2:9-10 But we do see Jesus, who was made lower than the angels for a little while, now crowned with glory and honor because he suffered death, so that by the grace of God he might taste death for everyone. In bringing many sons and daughters to glory, it was fitting that God, for whom and through whom everything exists, should make the **pioneer of their salvation** perfect through what he suffered.*

Significance: The LORD JESUS CHRIST is the architect and maker of salvation.

Dear Father,

I agree with the writer of Hebrews that it is fitting that You made the **Pioneer of Their** (Our) **Salvation** perfect (complete) through suffering. I rejoice with all my heart that You sent Him to earth to suffer and die on the cross so that I and all mankind might have eternal life. Truly, He is our **Pioneer** (Author, Firstborn, Leader, Perfector) and the One and Only through Whom we can have salvation. I exalt and thank Him that He makes the way and He leads those who believe in Him into glorious **salvation**. Hallelujah! I praise the **Pioneer of Their Salvation** that He makes believers in Him holy, and that we are now in His family! I am grateful that day to day He is helping us grow into the fullness of our salvation (becoming His disciples). I pray that You will put a deep gratitude in the hearts of all believers for the priceless gift the **Pioneer of Their Salvation** is to us, and convict us to repent of everything else that has been more precious than Him in our lives. Please build in us an intimate love relationship with the **Pioneer of Their Salvation**, that we cannot wait to talk about with everyone else You bring into our lives. I ask these things in Jesus' life-giving name. Amen.

What impacted me about Christ today...

_____

_____

_____

_____

_____

_____

A Merciful And Faithful High Priest

*Hebrews 2:14-18 Since the children have flesh and blood, he [Christ] too shared in their humanity so that by his death he might break the power of him who holds the power of death—that is, the devil—and free those who all their lives were held in slavery by their fear of death. For surely it is not angels he helps, but Abraham's descendants. For this reason he had to be made like them, fully human in every way, in order that he might become a **merciful and faithful high priest** in service to God, and that he might make atonement for the sins of the people. Because he himself suffered when he was tempted, he is able to help those who are being tempted.*

Significance: The LORD JESUS CHRIST perfectly presents man's need for God to the Father.

Dear Father,

I worship Jesus that He came to earth and was like people in every way, in order that He might become our **Merciful and Faithful High Priest**. I am deeply grateful that He knows how we think and feel, and what our trials, temptations, fears, sufferings and needs are, so He has immense mercy and compassion for us. Thank You also that He was completely **faithful** to Your mission for Him by saying all You told Him to say, and doing all You told Him to do. And, that He **faithfully** prayed to You, revered You, served You and revealed You to the world. I praise Him with all my heart that as our **High Priest** He **faithfully** offers the sacrifice and intercession that makes atonement for our sins. Please urge me, my family members and many other believers to give ourselves to knowing, adoring and living in our **Merciful and Faithful High Priest**. Finally, I pray Your Spirit will open the hearts and minds of multitudes of unsaved people all around us to the **Merciful and Faithful High Priest's** transforming mercy and **faithfulness** too. I ask all these things in His name. Amen.

What impacted me about Christ today...

_____

_____

_____

_____

_____

*Hebrews 3:1-2, 6 Therefore, holy brothers and sisters, who share in the heavenly calling, fix your thoughts on Jesus, whom we acknowledge as our **apostle and high priest**. He was faithful to the one who appointed him, just as Moses was faithful in all God's house. . . . But Christ is faithful as the Son over God's house. And we are his house, if indeed we hold firmly to our confidence and the hope in which we glory.*

Significance: The **LORD JESUS CHRIST** is both God's ambassador to man and man's representative to God.

Dear Father,

I join the writer of Hebrews in fixing my thoughts on Jesus, the only **Apostle and High Priest**. I praise Jesus that He is faithful to the One (You) Who sent Him to earth as **apostle** (ambassador) to proclaim all You are (like Moses was to the Old Testament Jewish people, but far superior to Moses). I also praise Jesus that He is completely faithful as **high priest** in all ways of pleading our causes before You (like Aaron, the Old Testament high priest, but far superior to Aaron). I rejoice that Jesus, the **Apostle and High Priest**, perfectly combines and fulfills both of those offices. I pray You will help me and all His other followers today to learn all we can from, and submit wholly to, the blessed **Apostle and High Priest**. And, please compel us to continually confess His greatness to one another, and hold on to our courage and the hope of which we boast in Him. I pray these things in His holy name. Amen.

What impacted me about Christ today...

_____

_____

_____

_____

_____

_____

_____

_____

_____

_____

A Son Over God's House

*Hebrews 3:1-2, 6 Therefore, holy brothers and sisters, who share in the heavenly calling, fix your thoughts on Jesus, whom we acknowledge as our apostle and high priest. He was faithful to the one who appointed him, just as Moses was faithful in all God's house. . . . But Christ is faithful as the **Son over God's house**. And we are his house, if indeed we hold firmly to our confidence and the hope in which we glory.*

Significance: The LORD JESUS CHRIST perfectly stewards His inheritance from the Father.

Dear Father,

What a joyful assurance it is that Christ is the **Son Over God's** (Your) **House**! I rejoice that He is the sole Heir with all rights and authority over Your whole house, now and forever. I worship Christ that He is completely faithful in honoring and obeying You, and in perfectly caring for all Your house. I am so grateful that I and all others who have received Your Son as our Savior are the house over which You have placed Him. There is nothing better I can imagine than to be His family (His people) under His loving, wise, graceful, strong, righteous, merciful, just and protective care. Please help us to be as devoted to the **Son Over God's House** as He is to You: obeying Him, loving Him, serving Him, worshiping Him, knowing Him, communicating with Him, and boasting of His wonders to one another at all times. May Your Son be our great delight, as we *"hold firmly to our confidence and the hope in which we glory"* in Him. I pray these things in Your Son's faithful name. Amen.

What impacted me about Christ today...

_____

_____

_____

_____

_____

_____

_____

_____

The Builder Of Everything

*Hebrews 3:3-4 Jesus has been found worthy of greater honor than Moses, just as the builder of a house has greater honor than the house itself. For every house is built by someone, but God is the **builder of everything**.*

Significance: The LORD JESUS CHRIST has conceived and constructed everything into existence.

Dear Father,

I give highest honor to God, the Son, Who is the supreme **Builder of Everything** (and the Creator and Maker of everything). I remember with great awe that the **Builder of Everything** was with You in the beginning, and that He has all wisdom and understanding, is all-powerful, and is Lord of all the resources of His kingdom. I praise Him that He did a perfect job of **building everything** just by speaking His mighty word. Hallelujah, that nothing is lacking in Him, and that He rules with all glory and majesty over all He has **built**. I pray that I and all believers in Christ will praise Him as the exalted **Builder of Everything**, and that we will live every part of our lives upon Him. I am delighted when I consider what wonderful workmanship He has put into us! Please convict us to repent from giving our allegiance to any other influences that falsely claim to be builders without Him. I pray You will compel us to urgently share the true hope we have in the **Builder of Everything** with the huge numbers of lost people all around us, and that You will open their hearts to receive Him as their **Builder** very soon too. I pray these things in the name that gives all life—Jesus. Amen.

What impacted me about Christ today...

_____

_____

_____

_____

_____

_____

_____

The Great High Priest

*Hebrews 4:14-16 Therefore, since we have a **great high priest** who has ascended into heaven, Jesus the Son of God, let us hold firmly to the faith we profess. For we do not have a high priest who is unable to empathize with our weaknesses, but we have one who has been tempted in every way, just as we are—yet he did not sin. Let us then approach God's throne of grace with confidence, so that we may receive mercy and find grace to help us in our time of need.*

Significance: **The LORD JESUS CHRIST, knowing man's weakness, is the perfect mediator between God and man.**

Dear Father,

I earnestly desire to hold firmly to the faith I possess in Jesus the Son of God, the **Great High Priest**. I rejoice that all the high priests (including Aaron and Levi) that preceded the **Great High Priest** are fulfilled in Him. I praise Him that He has gone into heaven to sprinkle His own blood on the mercy seat to permanently cleanse the sins of His people, and that He intercedes continually to You for our needs. I think an even more appropriate title for Him than **Great High Priest**, is **Greatest High Priest**! I am deeply grateful that, though He was without sin, He can sympathize with my weaknesses and care for me and all His followers with unconditional mercy and grace. I pray that You will help us to submit our lives wholly to the **Great High Priest** and become completely dependent upon Him. I ask these things in His gracious and holy name. Amen.

What impacted me about Christ today...

_____

_____

_____

_____

_____

_____

_____

_____

_____

The Source Of Eternal Salvation

Hebrews 5:7-10 During the days of Jesus' life on earth, he offered up prayers and petitions with fervent cries and tears to the one who could save him from death, and he was heard because of his reverent submission. Son though he was, he learned obedience from what he suffered and, once made perfect, he became the **source of eternal salvation** *for all who obey him and was designated by God to be high priest in the order of Melchizedek.*

Significance: The LORD JESUS CHRIST is the foundation of total deliverance for all Who believe in Him.

Dear Father,

I praise Jesus that He offered up prayers and petitions with loud cries to You to save Him from death, and that You heard Him because of His reverent submission to You. I grieve that He had to learn obedience through suffering, but I rejoice that His suffering made Him perfect (complete) as the Savior of the world. I bow before Him, the One and Only **Source** (Author) **of Eternal Salvation** for me and all who obey Him by believing on Him. I marvel that Jesus, the Creator and Source of **all** physical life, is also the **Source of Eternal Salvation** (Life). Hallelujah! He is the Redeemer, Savior, Mediator, Advocate, Blessed Hope, Deliverer, Chosen One, Living Water and many more names and titles that declare His salvation power! I am again very grateful that Peter's declaration in Acts 2:21 is absolutely true today: *"And everyone who calls on the name of the Lord will be saved."* I pray that a consuming gratitude to Jesus for our eternal life will rise up within my spirit and within all believers everywhere, to the point that we must tell each other about His greatness and about our growing love for, and devotion to, Him. May we submit to Him as He submits to You. In the name of the **Source of Eternal Salvation** I ask these things. Amen.

What impacted me about Christ today...

_____

_____

_____

_____

_____

The High Priest In The Order Of Melchizedek

*Hebrews 5:7-10 During the days of Jesus' life on earth, he offered up prayers and petitions with fervent cries and tears to the one who could save him from death, and he was heard because of his reverent submission. Son though he was, he learned obedience from what he suffered and, once made perfect, he became the source of eternal salvation for all who obey him and was designated by God to be **high priest in the order of Melchizedek.***

S ignificance: The LORD JESUS CHRIST'S priesthood is like Melchizedek's, but far greater and eternal.

Dear Father,
I honor Jesus that in addition to becoming the source of eternal salvation for all who obey Him, He was designated by You as **High Priest in the Order of Melchizedek**. I note that **Melchizedek** was King of Salem (King of Peace), priest of the Most High God, a special gift from You, superior to Abraham, and had an unknown beginning and end. Yes, Jesus was "in the order of" (resembled) **Melchizedek**, but I exalt Him that He is the **High** Priest, the King of kings Whose kingdom will never end, the "I Am" before Abraham and all people were created, the Beginning and the End, the full indwelling of the Godhead, and far greater than **Melchizedek** in all ways. I rejoice that Jesus is the **High Priest That Completes the Order of Melchizedek**. I repent for all the ways I have taken the great Priest and King Jesus for granted, and have not revered and adored Him. Please help me to *"seek first his kingdom and his righteousness"* (Matthew 6:33a), and *"remain in"* Him (John 15:4a) at all times. All glory to Jesus. I pray these things in His holy name. Amen.

What impacted me about Christ today...

_____

_____

_____

_____

_____

_____

*Hebrews 6:4-6 It s impossible for those who have once been enlightened, who have tasted the **heavenly gift**, who have shared in the Holy Spirit, who have tasted the goodness of the word of God and the powers of the coming age and who have fallen away, to be brought back to repentance. To their loss they are crucifying the Son of God all over again and subjecting him to public disgrace.*

Significance: **The LORD JESUS CHRIST is the ultimate gift from the heavenly Father.**

Dear Father,

I thank You that I have definitely tasted Jesus, the **Heavenly Gift**. As I continue to taste Your most blessed **Heavenly Gift** to mankind, I cannot help but think of what King David says in Psalm 34:8a, *"Taste and see that the LORD is good."* Oh, the incomparable, boundless goodness of the Godhead that You sent to us in Your Son, the **Heavenly Gift**! I think again of Jesus telling the Samaritan woman in John 4:10 that He is THE **gift** from You: *"Jesus answered her, 'If you knew the **gift of God** and who it is that asks you for a drink, you would have asked him and he would have **given** you living water.'"* I never tire of the testament of Your **gift** of love that Jesus pledges in John 3:16-17, *"For God so loved the world that he **gave** his one and only Son, that whoever believes in him shall not perish but have eternal life. For God did not send his Son into the world to condemn the world, but to save the world through him."* I pray that You will continually help me and all others who have tasted Your **Heavenly Gift**, to feast on Him and to consciously *"live and move and have our being"* in Him. (Acts 17:28a). Please do whatever is necessary to keep us from falling away from Him. I pray these things in His priceless name. Amen.

What impacted me about Christ today...

_____

_____

_____

_____

_____

_____

The Guarantor Of A Better Covenant

*Hebrews 7:21-26 But he [Jesus] became a priest with an oath when God said to him: "The Lord has sworn and will not change his mind: 'You [Jesus] are a priest forever.'" Because of this oath, Jesus has become the **guarantor of a better covenant**. Now there have been many of those priests, since death prevented them from continuing in office; but because Jesus lives forever, he has a permanent priesthood. Therefore he is able to save completely those who come to God through him, because he always lives to intercede for them. Such a high priest truly meets our need—one who is holy, blameless, pure, set apart from sinners, exalted above the heavens.*

S ignificance: **The LORD JESUS CHRIST is the absolute pledge that God's new covenant will be fulfilled.**

Dear Father,
I am very grateful that You swore the oath to Jesus that He is a priest forever (the permanent priest), thus becoming THE **Guarantor of a Better** (New) **Covenant** between You and mankind. I praise Jesus that as the **Guarantor of a Better Covenant** He is the everlasting, total security and pledge that all the penalties of the law have been satisfied for those who receive Him as Savior. Hallelujah! I magnify Jesus that He is the only One Who is able to completely save all who come to You through Him, because He always lives to intercede for us! I pray that You will give me and many other believers an intense hunger to know the **Guarantor of a Better Covenant** more, and that as we know Him more we will increase in our awe of, and gratitude to, Him. Please help us to totally yield to Him and overflow with a deep passion to tell others of His greatness. I pray these things in the sacrificial name of Jesus. Amen.

What impacted me about Christ today...

_____

_____

_____

_____

_____

_____

*Hebrews 7:23-26 Now there have been many of those priests, since death prevented them from continuing in office; but because Jesus lives forever, he has a permanent priesthood. Therefore he is able to save completely those who come to God through him, because he always lives to intercede for them. Such a high priest truly meets our need—one who is holy, blameless, pure, set apart from sinners, **exalted above the heavens.***

Significance: The LORD JESUS CHRIST holds the highest rank in this universe—greater than all His creation.

Dear Father,

I rejoice that the Lord Jesus is the high priest Who completely meets my needs and those of all others who have accepted Him as our Savior. I praise Him that He is not only superior to all other earthly priests by being eternal, but He is perfectly holy and righteous, has never done wrong to anyone, is undefiled and pure from any sinful desire or deed, and has never taken part with sinners in their ways of life. All glory to Jesus, Who alone is **Exalted Above the Heavens** (greater than the whole universe He created). He is worthy to be **exalted** throughout all ages as He is in all Scripture, such as Paul's declaration in Ephesians 1:20-21 that You: *"raised Christ from the dead and seated him at his [Your] right hand in the heavenly realms, far above all rule and authority, power and dominion, and every name that is invoked, not only in the present age but also in the one to come."* I pray that You will reveal more and more of Jesus' greatness to me and multitudes of other believers, so we will trust Him with every part of our lives, and speak boldly about the One Who is **Exalted Above the Heavens** to all others You bring into our lives. May **exaltation** of Jesus fill the Church in this present age. I pray these things in His glorious name. Amen.

What impacted me about Christ today...

_____

_____

_____

_____

_____

_____

A Ransom To Set Them Free

Hebrews 9:11-15 _But when Christ came as high priest of the good things that are now already here, he went through the greater and more perfect tabernacle that is not made with human hands, that is to say, is not a part of this creation. He did not enter by means of the blood of goats and calves; but he entered the Most Holy Place once for all by his own blood, thus obtaining eternal redemption. The blood of goats and bulls and the ashes of a heifer sprinkled on those who are ceremonially unclean sanctify them so that they are outwardly clean. How much more, then, will the blood of Christ, who through the eternal Spirit offered himself unblemished to God, cleanse our consciences from acts that lead to death, so that we may serve the living God! For this reason Christ is the mediator of a new covenant, that those who are called may receive the promised eternal inheritance—now that he has died as a **ransom to set them free** from the sins committed under the first covenant._

S**ignificance: The LORD JESUS CHRIST is both the payment and payer to redeem sinners.**

Dear Father,
I am very grateful that Christ is the **Ransom to Set Them Free**, for me and all other people who have received eternal freedom from the penalty of our sins through His blood shed on the cross. I exalt Jesus, Who alone possesses Your love, power, righteousness, authority, humility, grace and mercy to **ransom**, liberate, rescue, emancipate, redeem and deliver us. Thank You with all my heart for this glorious truth that Paul states in 1 Timothy 2:5-6, _"For there is one God and one mediator between God and mankind, the man Christ Jesus, who gave himself as a **ransom** for all people. This has now been witnessed to at the proper time."_ I pray that You will reveal to all people who have received the **Ransom to Set Them Free,** how great and gracious He is, and compel us to repent for all ways we have put Him in second, or lower, place in our lives. Oh God, we owe everything to Jesus. Please make Him our Life, our All. I pray that as He **ransomed** Himself for us, we will give ourselves wholly to Him. In His blessed name I pray these things. Amen.

What impacted me about Christ today...

One Sacrifice

*Hebrews 10:8-14 First he [Jesus] said, "Sacrifices and offerings, burnt offerings and sin offerings you did not desire, nor were you pleased with them"—though they were offered in accordance with the law. Then he said, "Here I am, I have come to do your will." He sets aside the first to establish the second. And by that will, we have been made holy through the sacrifice of the body of Jesus Christ once for all. Day after day every priest stands and performs his religious duties; again and again he offers the same sacrifices, which can never take away sins. But when this priest had offered for all time **one sacrifice** for sins, he sat down at the right hand of God, and since that time he waits for his enemies to be made his footstool. For by **one sacrifice** he has made perfect forever those who are being made holy.*

Significance: **The LORD JESUS CHRIST is the once-for-all sacrifice for all sins.**

Dear Father,

All glory to Jesus Christ, Your beloved Son, Who came to earth to do Your will, by offering His body as the **One Sacrifice**. Thank You that the **One Sacrifice** is the only complete, perfect, total **Sacrifice**—given once for man's sins, for all time. How marvelous His **sacrifice** is, as written in Hebrews 9:26b-28, *"But he has appeared once for all at the culmination of the ages to do away with sin by the **sacrifice** of himself. Just as people are destined to die once, and after that to face judgment, so Christ was sacrificed once to take away the sins of many; and he will appear a second time, not to bear sin, but to bring salvation to those who are waiting for him."* I praise Jesus that when His **sacrifice** was completed, He sat down at Your right hand and is waiting for His enemies to soon be made His footstool. I pray that Your Spirit will continually remind me and all other believers of the absolute greatness that only the **One Sacrifice** possesses, and the immeasurable love and grace He has for us, so that we will gladly die to self in order to live wholly (and holy) in Him. I pray these things in His name. Amen.

What impacted me about Christ today...

_____

_____

November

*<u>Hebrews 10:19-23</u> Therefore, brothers and sisters, since we have confidence to enter the Most Holy Place by the blood of Jesus, by a **new and living way** opened for us through the curtain, that is, his body, and since we have a great priest over the house of God, let us draw near to God with a sincere heart with the full assurance that faith brings, having our hearts sprinkled to cleanse us from a guilty conscience and having our bodies washed with pure water. Let us hold unswervingly to the hope we profess, for he who promised is faithful.*

Significance: **The LORD JESUS CHRIST is the only pathway to eternal life.**

Dear Father,

I know that the "old way" of the High Priest once a year bringing the blood of sacrificed animals into the Most Holy Place only temporarily cleansed the people of Israel's sins. So, I heartily rejoice that You sent Jesus to earth as the only way, the **New and Living Way**, through Whom I and all mankind can receive permanent forgiveness of the penalty of our sins. I am immediately reminded of what Jesus said about Himself in John 14:6, *"I am the **way** and the truth and the life. No one comes to the Father except through me."* I praise Jesus that He is not only the **new** (and perfectly improved) **way** for our eternal redemption, but He is the **living** way: He is alive forevermore; in Him is abundant life; He came that all people might be saved; and His blood is ever-flowing and limitless. Please often remind me and all other believers of John 1:4, *"In **him** was **life**, and that **life** was the light of all mankind,"* and cause us to thank and praise the **New and Living Way** constantly for all He is and for the confidence we have to enter the Most Holy Place by His blood. I pray these things in His life-assuring name. Amen.

What impacted me about Christ today...

_____

_____

_____

_____

_____

A Great Priest Over The House Of God

*Hebrews 10:19-23 Therefore, brothers and sisters, since we have confidence to enter the Most Holy Place by the blood of Jesus, by a new and living way opened for us through the curtain, that is, his body, and since we have a **great priest over the house of God**, let us draw near to God with a sincere heart with the full assurance that faith brings, having our hearts sprinkled to cleanse us from a guilty conscience and having our bodies washed with pure water. Let us hold unswervingly to the hope we profess, for he who promised is faithful.*

Significance: **The LORD JESUS CHRIST is the royal mediator through Whom His people have access to God.**

Dear Father,

I am very thankful You have given me and all other believers a **Great Priest Over the House of God** (His whole Church on earth). I worship Him as He was foretold in Zechariah 6:12-13, *"Tell him [Joshua] this is what the LORD Almighty says: 'Here is the man whose name is the Branch, and he will branch out from his place and build the temple of the LORD. It is he who will build the temple of the LORD, and he will be clothed with majesty and will sit and rule on his throne. And he will be a priest on his throne. And there will be harmony between the two.'"* I praise Jesus that as the **Great Priest Over the House of God**, He is the greatest and most royal Priest and King over His people. I rejoice that His righteous blood opened the curtain (veil) for us to draw near to You *"with a sincere heart in full assurance of faith."* Please help us, Lord, to *"hold unswervingly to the hope we profess, for he who promised is faithful."* This hope causes me to sing the wonderful words written in "My Hope is Built" by Edward Mote: "My hope is built on nothing less, Than Jesus' blood and righteousness. I dare not trust the sweetest frame, But wholly lean on Jesus' name. (chorus) On Christ the solid Rock I stand, All other ground is sinking sand. All other ground is sinking sand. (verse 3) His oath, His covenant, His blood, Support me in the whelming flood. When all around my soul gives way, He then is all my Hope and Stay." I pray all these things in the name of the **Great Priest Over the House of God**. Amen.

What impacted me about Christ today...

_____

_____

*<u>Hebrews 10:36-38</u> You need to persevere so that when you have done the will of God, you will receive what he has promised. For, "In just a little while, **he who is coming** will come and will not delay." And, "But my righteous one will live by faith. And I take no pleasure in the one who shrinks back."*

Significance: The LORD JESUS CHRIST, Who is the grand and ultimate subject of all prophetic vision, will soon come and fulfill all prophecy.

Dear Father,

This name of Christ gives me abounding hope. I rejoice that Jesus is **He Who is Coming**, Who alone ultimately fulfills Your prophecy in Habakkuk 2:3, *"For the revelation awaits an appointed time; it speaks of the end and will not prove false. Though it linger, wait for it; it will certainly come and will not delay."* I hold on to a number of related New Testament Scriptures including Christ's promise in Luke 21:25-28 that seems increasingly appropriate to our time in history: *"There will be signs in the sun, moon and stars. On the earth, nations will be in anguish and perplexity at the roaring and tossing of the sea. People will faint from terror, apprehensive of what is coming on the world, for the heavenly bodies will be shaken. At that time they will see the Son of Man coming in a cloud with power and great glory. When these things begin to take place, stand up and lift up your heads, because your redemption is drawing near."* Glory to Jesus that He will soon come back to earth from heaven with power to judge the world and give His people our final deliverance. Please help me and all other believers to devote ourselves to knowing all about **He Who is Coming** so that we will be able to persevere in righteous faith. *"Amen. Come, Lord Jesus"* (Revelation 22:20).

What impacted me about Christ today...

_____

_____

_____

_____

_____

_____

The Pioneer (Author) And Perfector (Finisher) Of Faith

*Hebrews 12:1-2 Therefore, since we are surrounded by such a great cloud of witnesses, let us throw off everything that hinders and the sin that so easily entangles. And let us run with perseverance the race marked out for us, fixing our eyes on Jesus, the **pioneer and perfector of faith**. For the joy set before him he endured the cross, scorning its shame, and sat down at the right hand of the throne of God.*

Significance: The LORD JESUS CHRIST initiates and completes our entire relationship with God.

Dear Father,

There is nothing I want more than to join the great cloud of faithful witnesses in fixing my eyes upon Jesus, the **Pioneer (Author) and Perfector (Finisher) of Faith**. I honor Him that, as the **Author** of our faith, He is the supreme source, leader and prince of our faith, Who has always demonstrated absolute confidence and faith in You. As the **Finisher** of our faith there cannot possibly be anyone Who has a greater faith in You than He does—He has the finished (fully completed) relationship of faith with You. I rejoice that *"for the joy set before him he endured the cross, scorning its shame, and sat down at the right hand of the throne of God."* With all my heart, I want to know all I possibly can about the **Pioneer and Perfector of Faith**, so that I will surrender my life completely to Him, and live in abandoned faith in Him and in You. I earnestly pray that You will help me and scores of other believers to very soon *"throw off everything that hinders and the sin that so easily entangles, and run with perseverance the race marked out for us."* I pray these things in the **faithful** name of Jesus. Amen.

What impacted me about Christ today...

_____

_____

_____

_____

_____

_____

The Mediator Of A New Covenant

*Hebrews 12:22-24 But you have come to Mount Zion, to the city of the living God, the heavenly Jerusalem. You have come to thousands upon thousands of angels in joyful assembly, to the church of the firstborn, whose names are written in heaven. You have come to God, the Judge of all, to the spirits of the righteous made perfect, to Jesus the **mediator of a new covenant**, and to the sprinkled blood that speaks a better word than the blood of Abel.*

Significance: The LORD JESUS CHRIST fulfills God's new covenant with His people.

Dear Father,

I am overwhelmingly grateful that I am already a citizen with You in heaven (the city of the living God), as well as with tens of thousands of angels, the many other people who have previously died as believers in Christ, and, most importantly, Jesus the **Mediator of a New Covenant**. I rejoice that the old covenant and its mediator, Moses, are passed away, and that the new and immeasurably superior covenant is now in force forever because of the sprinkled blood of Jesus. Thank You for the powerful confirmation of this in Hebrews 8:6, *"But in fact the ministry Jesus has received is as superior to theirs as the covenant of which he is mediator is superior to the old one, since the new covenant is established on better promises."* I praise Jesus, Who is superior as Your Son, the Creator of the heavens and earth, the Savior, the Redeemer and Messiah of all people, and also the **Mediator of the New Covenant**. I pray that Your Spirit will continually remind me and all believers of the greatness of Who the **Mediator of a New Covenant** is, and of the great value of our citizenship in heaven through Him. May we speak of His wonders with every breath You give us. I pray these things in His name. Amen.

What impacted me about Christ today...

_____

_____

_____

_____

_____

<u>Hebrews 13:5-6</u> *Keep your lives free from the love of money and be content with what you have, because God has said, "Never will I leave you; never will I forsake you." So we say with confidence, "The Lord is my* **helper***; I will not be afraid. What can mere mortals do to me?"*

Significance: The LORD JESUS CHRIST is the truest companion to mankind.

Dear Father,

Thank You that Jesus completely fulfills this promise of Yours (found also in Psalm 118) to be the **Helper** (provider, protector, guide, encourager and refuge) of all who trust in Him. I am very grateful there is nothing in my life that is too big or too small for His help. I praise Jesus that He has **ALL** power, wisdom, understanding, goodness, mercy, grace, and love, and is always with me. I rejoice that not only will He not forsake me, but that He **cannot** forsake me. Again, I am reminded of His promise in Mathew 28:20b, *"And surely I am with you always, to the very end of the age."* I pray that I and all other followers of Christ will devote ourselves to knowing Him **so well** that we completely trust Him in all circumstances, thank Him at all times, and worship Him continually. Thank you that His perfect love drives out all fear (1 John 4:18). I also pray that we will give every part of our lives to Him, pray regularly for His rule and reign over our lives, and always speak to each other about His magnificence. Please help us to constantly abide in Jesus, the **Helper**. I pray these things in the powerful name of Jesus. Amen.

What impacted me about Christ today...

_____

_____

_____

_____

_____

_____

_____

_____

_____

The Same Yesterday And Today And Forever

*Hebrews 13:7-8 Remember your leaders, who spoke the word of God to you. Consider the outcome of their way of life and imitate their faith. Jesus Christ is the **same yesterday and today and forever**.*

S ignificance: The LORD JESUS CHRIST, as God, never changes.

☙

Dear Father,

I rejoice that Your Spirit directed the writer of Hebrews to combine the words "Jesus" and "Christ" when stating that He is the **Same Yesterday and Today and Forever**. Truly, Jesus (His Person) Christ (His Office) is the One and Only Who can be the **Same Yesterday and Today and Forever**. I am in awe as I think of the majestic greatness of Who He was **Yesterday** with You before the foundation of the world. I praise Him that after He created the heavens and the earth, He revealed the fullness of Who You are by performing mighty works in Your name, redeeming mankind from our sins, and finally ascending to heaven to rule at Your right hand and intercede for His people. As David Bryant says in "Tribute to Christ," "All of Scripture, all of creation, all of history, all of the purposes and prophecies and promises of God are summed up in You (Christ) alone." I am amazed that He has been **all** life and **all** hope to men and women for over 2000 years since He walked on earth as a man, including **Today**, and that He remains unchangeable, immovable, undiminished and all-supreme every moment. I honor Jesus Christ that He will unquestionably have the same preeminence when He returns to earth to exercise final justice on earth, and when He rules and reigns over His kingdom **Forever**. I pray You will compel me and all other believers to know the One Who is the **Same Yesterday and Today and Forever**, trust Him, live in His fullness, and continually declare His greatness. I pray these things in the name of Jesus Christ. Amen.

What impacted me about Christ today...

_____

_____

_____

_____

*Hebrews 13:20-21 Now may the God of peace, who through the blood of the eternal covenant brought back from the dead our Lord Jesus, that **great Shepherd of the sheep**, equip you with everything good for doing his will, and may he work in us what is pleasing to him, through Jesus Christ, to whom be glory for ever and ever. Amen.*

Significance: The LORD JESUS CHRIST is the great protector and guardian of our souls.

Dear Father,

I exalt the Lord Jesus, the **Great Shepherd of the Sheep**. I know that only He Who is Lord of all and Emmanuel, could be the **Great Shepherd of the Sheep** (His sheep), because He gave His blood and fulfilled the eternal covenant. I am humbled by the first word in today's name, "**Great,**" as it applies to Hebrews 4:14, *"Therefore, since we have a **great high priest** who has ascended into heaven, Jesus the Son of God, let us hold firmly to the faith we profess."* I am in awe that ALL of Jesus' great high priestly ability is **also** part of Him as the **Great Shepherd of the Sheep**. At the same time, I am greatly strengthened and comforted by several Scripture passages where Jesus explains His role as **shepherd** of His beloved sheep (followers), including John 10:2-4, *"The one who enters by the gate is the **shepherd of the sheep**. The gatekeeper opens the gate for him, and the sheep listen to his voice. He calls his own sheep by name and leads them out. When he has brought out all his own, he goes on ahead of them, and his sheep follow him because they know his voice."* I pray that I and all other believers will know the **Great Shepherd of the Sheep** so well that we will submit ourselves wholly to Him and follow wherever He leads. Glory to Jesus forever and ever. In His great name I pray these things. Amen.

What impacted me about Christ today...

_____

_____

_____

_____

_____

_____

Our Glorious Lord Jesus Christ

*James 2:1-4 My brothers and sisters, believers in our **glorious Lord Jesus Christ** must not show favoritism. Suppose a man comes into your meeting wearing a gold ring and fine clothes, and a poor man in filthy old clothes also comes in. If you show special attention to the man wearing fine clothes and say, "Here's a good seat for you," but say to the poor man, "You stand there," or "Sit on the floor by my feet," have you not discriminated among yourselves and become judges with evil thoughts?*

S ignificance: The LORD JESUS CHRIST, the One deserving all glory, fosters respect among people.

Dear Father,

I am in awe as I think of the majesty of our **Glorious Lord Jesus Christ**. I bow before the **Lord** (Ruler, Master) **Jesus** (Savior) **Christ** (Anointed One) Who has had all **glory**, and will have all **glory** for all eternity! Truly, there is none other than He Who is the magnificent Radiance of Your **glory**. I take today's Scripture passage very seriously because in combining **Lord**, **Jesus** and **Christ**, then emphasizing that He is **glorious**, James is declaring the infinite and unmatched power, glory, authority, lordship and supremacy of the Person of persons. I pray that You will do whatever is necessary to convince me, my family members and multitudes of other believers, to bow our knees and confess with our tongues (Philippians 2) from this moment on, how great the **Glorious Lord Jesus Christ** is. I pray that one way we will honor and submit to our **glorious Lord** is to sincerely respect, honor and care for one another, regardless of each other's race, social status, possessions, color, age, gender and so on. Please put in our hearts a conviction to help each other grow in our devotion to Jesus. I ask these things in the **Glorious Lord Jesus Christ's** name. Amen.

What impacted me about Christ today...

_____

_____

_____

_____

_____

_____

*James 4:11-12 Brothers and sisters, do not slander one another. Anyone who speaks against a brother or sister or judges them speaks against the law and judges it. When you judge the law, you are not keeping it, but sitting in judgment on it. There is only one **Lawgiver and Judge**, the one who is able to save and destroy. But you—who are you to judge your neighbor?*

Significance: **The LORD JESUS CHRIST is both the maker and administrator of God's laws.**

Dear Father,

Thank You that Jesus is the ultimate **Lawgiver and Judge** for me and all mankind. I praise Him that He is the great Legislator of the Church, Who alone has the right to give laws (precepts, teachings, commands and promises) for His people to live by. I rejoice that in and through Him is all Your truth, justice, wisdom, knowledge, righteousness, repentance, discipline and revelation necessary for **guiding and blessing** our lives. I am grateful for other Scripture passages that clearly confirm Jesus is the One Who is able to save and destroy, like it says in Matthew 10:28, *"Do not be afraid of those who kill the body but cannot kill the soul. Rather, be afraid of the One who can destroy both soul and body in hell."* I especially love King David's devotion to Your laws in all of Psalm 119, and I pray that You will help me and Your whole Church to obey the spirit of verses 1-2, *"Blessed are those whose ways are blameless, who walk according to the law of the LORD. Blessed are those who keep his statutes and seek him with all their heart."* I pray that as we know the **Lawgiver and Judge** more, we will not judge our brothers and sisters, but will help each other live in His ways. I ask these things in the name of Jesus, the giver and perfector of all justice and truth. Amen.

What impacted me about Christ today...

_____

_____

_____

_____

_____

A Lamb Without Blemish Or Defect

*1 Peter 1:18-21 For you know that it was not with perishable things such as silver or gold that you were redeemed from the empty way of life handed down to you from your ancestors, but with the precious blood of Christ, a **lamb without blemish or defect**. He was chosen before the creation of the world, but was revealed in these last times for your sake. Through him you believe in God, who raised him from the dead and glorified him, and so your faith and hope are in God.*

Significance: The LORD JESUS CHRIST is the perfect sacrifice for the sins of mankind.

Dear Father,

Thank You profusely that Christ gave His most precious blood, as the *"Lamb of God, who takes away the sin of the world"* (John 1:29b)! I praise Christ that since He is totally pure in Himself (without **blemish**) and untouched by any form of sin (without spot or **defect**), His blood, which has inestimable value, pays the entire penalty for my sin and the sin of all people. All glory to the beloved **Lamb Without Blemish or Defect**. I pray You will give me an unceasing desire to know everything I possibly can about the **Lamb Without Blemish or Defect** and all the other names, attributes, characteristics and works of Christ. Please help me to value Him with all my heart, soul, mind and strength, and to speak of His wonders to all other believers You bring into my life. He is our blessed hope! I pray Your Spirit will open the hearts of throngs of unbelievers to their crucial need to know and receive the **Lamb Without Blemish or Defect** as their Savior and Lord. I ask these things in His redemptive name. Amen.

What impacted me about Christ today...

_____

_____

_____

_____

_____

_____

Chosen Before The Creation Of The World

*1 Peter 1:18-21 For you know that it was not with perishable things such as silver or gold that you were redeemed from the empty way of life handed down to you from your ancestors, but with the precious blood of Christ, a lamb without blemish or defect. He was **chosen before the creation of the world**, but was revealed in these last times for your sake. Through him you believe in God, who raised him from the dead and glorified him, and so your faith and hope are in God.*

Significance: The LORD JESUS CHRIST'S role as Savior was predetermined before time began.

Dear Father,

I rejoice that You predetermined before the creation of the world that Jesus would be the atoning Sacrifice for my sin and all other people. Thank You that Your beloved Son is the only One Who could be **Chosen Before the Creation of the World**, not as an afterthought or as a way to resolve something that went wrong with people after creation, but as a part of Your original plan for us. I don't fully understand all this "mystery," but I am very glad You have always had a perfect plan (through the perfect Person) for our redemption, and that You revealed Him, and raised Him from the dead and glorified Him *"in these last times"* for our sake. I think of what Paul says in Ephesians 1:4-6, *"For he [God] chose us in him before the creation of the world to be holy and blameless in his sight. In love he predestined us for adoption to sonship through Jesus Christ, in accordance with his pleasure and will—to the praise of his glorious grace, which he has freely given us in the One he loves."* Thank You, Father, for choosing Him to be our Savior. I pray that You will continually remind me and all other believers of the greatness of the One Who was **Chosen Before the Creation of the World**, so our faith and hope in Him will always be growing and unwavering. I ask these things in the name of the **Chosen** One. Amen.

What impacted me about Christ today...

_____

_____

_____

_____

*1 Peter 2:4-5 As you come to him [Jesus], the **living Stone**—rejected by humans but chosen by God and precious to him—you also, like living stones, are being built into a spiritual house to be a holy priesthood, offering spiritual sacrifices acceptable to God through Jesus Christ.*

Significance: The LORD JESUS CHRIST is the strong foundation upon which spiritual life is built.

Dear Father,

What a privilege it is to come to Jesus, the **Living Stone**. I praise Him that He is the Son of the **Living** God, and *"In him was [and is all] **life**"* (John 1:4) from before the beginning of time. Oh, how grateful I am that You raised Him from the dead and He **lives** so that I and all mankind may have life in Him now and forever. I am reminded again of the wonderful truth Jesus revealed to the Samaritan woman about His **life**-giving power in John 4:10, *"If you knew the gift of God and who it is that asks you for a drink, you would have asked him and he would have given you **living** water."* I am in awe that Jesus gives **life** to an object which is not normally considered alive, a **stone**. I rejoice that I and all who receive Jesus as our Savior are like *"living stones"* being built upon Him, the **Living Stone** (foundation) *"into a spiritual house to be a holy priesthood."* I repent for all the times I have rejected Him or tried to build my life upon any other **"stone"** than the **Living Stone**, and I pray that You will keep me absolutely dependent upon Him. I pray these things in the name of life, Jesus. Amen.

What impacted me about Christ today...

_____

_____

_____

_____

_____

_____

*1 Peter 2:6-9 For in Scripture it says: "See, I lay a stone in Zion, a **chosen and precious cornerstone**, and the one who trusts in him will never be put to shame." Now to you who believe, this stone is precious. But to those who do not believe, "The stone the builders rejected has become the cornerstone," and, "A stone that causes men to stumble and a rock that makes them fall." They stumble because they disobey the message—which is also what they were destined for. But you are a chosen people, a royal priesthood, a holy nation, God's special possessions, that you may declare the praises of him who called you out of darkness into his wonderful light.*

Significance: The LORD JESUS CHRIST is God's perfect beginning point of spiritual development.

Dear Father,

I am deeply grateful that going back to Isaiah 28:16, You declared You were going to lay the foundation of the Church in Jerusalem. I praise Jesus, that He gave His life in Jerusalem for our sins and completely fulfills this prophecy as the **Chosen** (Chief, Elect) **and Precious Cornerstone** of the Church. I worship Jesus that only in Him does the fullness of the Godhead dwell, and thus only He is acceptable to be **chosen** by You as the **cornerstone** of the foundation of the Church. I also worship Jesus that only He is absolutely **precious** to You, and to me and all others who have accepted Him as our Savior and the **Chosen and Precious Cornerstone** upon which to build our lives. When I think of the attributes that the **precious** Person of Jesus possesses, I marvel at His super-abundant love, grace, mercy, humility, righteousness, truth, excellence, peace, strength and so much more. I trust the **Chosen and Precious Cornerstone**; I love Him; I need Him; I put my life totally upon Him; I belong to Him; and I *"declare the praise of him who called me out of darkness into his wonderful light."* I pray these things in His solid name. Amen.

What impacted me about Christ today...

_____

_____

_____

_____

An Example

*1 Peter 2:19-22 For it is commendable if someone bears up under the pain of unjust suffering because they are conscious of God. But how is it to your credit if you receive a beating for doing wrong and endure it? But if you suffer for doing good and you endure it, this is commendable before God. To this you were called, because Christ suffered for you, leaving you an **example**, that you should follow in his steps. "He committed no sin, and no deceit was found in his mouth."*

Significance: The LORD JESUS CHRIST is the perfect, unfailing model Who will never disappoint.

Dear Father,

I am in awe that Jesus, the Son of God, is the only Person Who is the perfect **Example**, Whose steps I and all people should follow. I honor Him that His unjust suffering and death for us is His highest demonstration as the **Example** for us. I rejoice that He is our complete **Example** in all other aspects of His life. All glory to Him that I and all His followers can know and live in all His character, teachings, deeds, promises, prayers and passions. I think of what Paul instructs us in 1 Corinthians 11:1, *"Follow my example, as I follow the **example** of Christ."* I pray You will compel me to follow Paul in his wholehearted commitment to this in Philippians 3:7-11, *"But whatever were gains to me I now consider loss for the sake of Christ. What is more, I consider everything a loss because of the surpassing worth of knowing Christ Jesus my Lord, for whose sake I have lost all things. I consider them garbage, that I may gain Christ and be found in him, not having a righteousness of my own that comes from the law, but that which is through faith in Christ—the righteousness that comes from God on the basis of faith. I want to know Christ—yes, to know the power of his resurrection and participation in his sufferings, becoming like him in his death, and so, somehow, attaining to the resurrection from the dead."* I pray these things in the name of the blessed **Example**. Amen.

What impacted me about Christ today...

_____

_____

_____

_____

_____

The Shepherd And Overseer
Of Your Souls

*1 Peter 2:24-25 He [Christ] himself bore our sins in his body on the cross, so that we might die to sins and live for righteousness; by his wounds you have been healed. For you were like sheep going astray, but now you have returned to the **Shepherd and Overseer of your souls**.*

Significance: **The LORD JESUS CHRIST cares perfectly for His sheep.**

Dear Father,

I thank You profusely that Jesus bore on the cross my sins and the sins of all people so we can be healed of the penalty of those sins and live for righteousness. I know that each one of us was like sheep going astray from the true fold before *"the Son of Man [the great **Shepherd**] came to seek and to save the lost"* (Luke 19:10). I praise Jesus that there could only be one **Shepherd** Whom You sent to seek and save our souls, as He said in John 10:11, *"I am the good **shepherd**. The good **shepherd** lays down his life for the sheep."* I am in awe that the **Shepherd** has all power and all love to lay down His life for us, and to protect and guide us for our best good and for His glory. I say, "Hallelujah" that He is not only our **Shepherd**, but also the perfect **Overseer** (Universal Bishop, Superintendent, Guardian) of our souls, Who has all Your wisdom, authority, lordship, majesty, understanding, and infinitely more to govern our souls, now and for all eternity. I am deeply grateful to You and to Jesus that my soul is so very precious to You. As I think of Psalm 23:1, *"The LORD is my shepherd, I lack nothing."* I pray that You will help me and all other believers know much more of His vastness so we will turn/return wholly to the **Shepherd and Overseer of Your Souls**, in Whom we lack nothing. In His faithful name I ask these things. Amen.

What impacted me about Christ today...

_____

_____

_____

_____

_____

_____

The Righteous For The Unrighteous

*1 Peter 3:15-18 But in your hearts revere Christ as Lord. Always be pre-pared to give an answer to everyone who asks you to give the reason for the hope that you have. But do this with gentleness and respect, keeping a clear conscience, so that those who speak maliciously against your good behavior in Christ may be ashamed of their slander. For it is better, if it is God's will, to suffer for doing good than for doing evil. For Christ also suffered once for sins, the **righteous for the unrighteous**, to bring you to God. He was put to death in the body but made alive in the Spirit.*

Significance: **The LORD JESUS CHRIST embodies the perfect exchange of good for evil.**

Dear Father,

The name/attribute of Christ, **Righteous for the Unrighteous**, seems to clearly capture His character and purpose for coming to earth. I revere Him that He Who is all-righteous (completely just, holy, clean, pure and innocent) came to suffer humiliation, rejection and scorn, including dying on the cross in the place of me and all other people who are unrighteous, unholy, impure and evil. I love how Paul confirms this in 2 Corinthians 5:21 by stating: *"God made him [Christ] who had no sin to be sin for us, so that in him we might become the righteousness of God."* I think also of what Paul said in Romans 5:8: *"But God demonstrates his own love for us in this: While we were still sinners, Christ died for us."* I pray that I and multitudes of other believers will become so devoted to Christ for His willingness to suffer for us that we will praise Him continually for all He is, thank Him continually for His mercy and love, and become willing to suffer in all ways He directs us—for His magnificent glory. May we always be ready nd willing to give an answer to everyone who asks us why we have this hope in Him. I pray these things in the **righteous** name of Jesus. Amen.

What impacted me about Christ today...

_____

_____

_____

_____

_____

*1 Peter 4:14-19 If you are insulted because of the name of Christ, you are blessed, for the Spirit of glory and of God rests on you. If you suffer, it should not be as a murderer or thief or any other kind of criminal, or even as a meddler. However, if you suffer as a Christian, do not be ashamed, but praise God that you bear that name. For it is time for judgment to begin with God's household; and if it begins with us, what will the outcome be for those who do not obey the gospel of God? And, "If it is hard for the righteous to be saved, what will become of the ungodly and the sinner?" So then, those who suffer according to God's will should commit themselves to their **faithful Creator** and continue to do good.*

Significance: The LORD JESUS CHRIST, Who made His people, also sustains them in all situations.

Dear Father,

I worship Jesus, the **Faithful Creator** of heaven and earth. I marvel that at all times throughout Scripture He demonstrates His absolute **faithfulness** and devotion to You, to all people, to His teachings, and to the prophecies and promises about Him, including Hebrews 3:6, *"But Christ is **faithful** as a Son over God's house. And we are his house, if indeed we hold firmly to our confidence and the hope in which we glory."* I rejoice that His **faithfulness** is an integral part of His being our **Creator** and the **Creator** of all things, Who has all Your power, wisdom, authority, creativity, righteousness, understanding and boundless other attributes to fulfill His will in us. Once more, I am deeply strengthened by His promise in Matthew 28:20b, *"And surely I am with you always, to the very end of the age."* I am also grateful that our **Creator** is so **faithful** to sustain us in times of tribulation. I pray You will pour into me, my family members and all believers an increasing understanding of the magnificence of our **Faithful Creator,** so we will commit ourselves totally to Him, and trust Him regardless of what comes into our lives. May we **faithfully** proclaim the name of Christ and do good for His glory at all times. I pray these things in the **faithful** name of Jesus. Amen.

What impacted me about Christ today...

*1 Peter 5:1-4 To the elders among you, I appeal as a fellow elder and a witness of Christ's sufferings who also will share in the glory to be revealed: Be shepherds of God's flock that is under your care, watching over them—not because you must, but because you are willing, as God wants you to be; not pursuing dishonest gain, but eager to serve; not lording it over those entrusted to you, but being examples to the flock. And when the **Chief Shepherd** appears, you will receive the crown of glory that will never fade away.*

Significance: The LORD JESUS CHRIST is the supreme guardian of His sheep.

Dear Father,

I worship Christ, the **Chief Shepherd** of His whole flock. All glory and honor to Him that He is the Prince, Leader, Head, Overseer and Superintendent of all His undershepherds (pastors). I am grateful that the **Chief Shepherd** of shepherds has always had, and will always have, all authority, wisdom and grace to provide His undershepherds with all they need to care for the flock. I take great confidence in Paul's declaration in Philippians 4:19, *"And my God will meet all your needs according to the riches of his glory in Christ Jesus."* So, I pray You will help me and all other leaders within the Church to abandon ourselves to knowing the depths of the **Chief Shepherd**, loving Him with all our hearts, abiding in Him, following Him, worshiping Him, and talking continually about His greatness to the flocks He gives us. When He appears, may we *"receive the crown of glory that will never fade away."* I pray these things in the name of our wonderful, beautiful, mighty, beloved and glorious **Chief Shepherd**. Amen.

What impacted me about Christ today...

_____

_____

_____

_____

_____

*2 Peter 1:1-2 Simon Peter, a servant and apostle of Jesus Christ, To those who through the righteousness of our **God and Savior Jesus Christ** have received a faith as precious as ours: Grace and peace be yours in abundance through the knowledge of God and of Jesus our Lord.*

S**ignificance: The LORD JESUS CHRIST is both God and Savior in one Person.**

Dear Father,

I delight that I and all people who receive the most precious gift of faith do so through the righteousness of our blessed **God and Savior Jesus Christ**. I am in awe thinking of all those names of Him combined: **God** (the Word Who was with God, and is God for all time), **Savior** (our Redeemer and Mediator), **Jesus** (the One Who saves) and **Christ** (Messiah and Anointed One). I worship our **God and Savior Jesus Christ,** the only One through Whom the fullness of Your righteousness is possible. I pray that You will help me and all believers devote ourselves completely to knowing all we possibly can of Him, and to living like Paul testified in Romans 1:16-17, *"For I am not ashamed of the gospel, because it is the power of God that brings salvation to everyone who believes: first to the Jew, then to the Gentile. For in the gospel the righteousness of God is revealed—and righteousness that is by faith from first to last, just as it is written: 'The righteous will live by faith.'"* Please help us to grow as servants of our **God and Savior Jesus Christ** with unwavering faith in Him. May *"grace and peace be ours in abundance through the knowledge of God and of Jesus our Lord."* I pray these things in the most precious name of Jesus. Amen.

What impacted me about Christ today...

_____

_____

_____

_____

_____

_____

*2 Peter 1:16-18 For we did not follow cleverly devised stories when we told you about the coming of our Lord Jesus Christ in power, but we were eyewitnesses of his **majesty**. He received honor and glory from God the Father when the voice came to him from the Majestic Glory, saying, "This is my Son, whom I love; with him I am well pleased." We ourselves heard this voice that came from heaven when we were with him on the sacred mountain.*

Significance: The LORD JESUS CHRIST displays the royalty of the Godhead.

Dear Father,

I rejoice that the Apostle Peter had the immense privilege of being an eye-witness (with James and John) of His **Majesty**, the Lord Jesus Christ, receiving honor and glory from You on the Mount of Transfiguration. What an incredible display of Your fullness dwelling in Jesus, the great Messiah and **Majesty**! I strongly believe that what You said about Him at that time: *"This is my son, whom I love; with him I am well pleased,"* were the words Your beloved Son most wanted to hear, and were the strongest pos-sible confirmation that He was fulfilling the purposes for which You sent Him to earth. I believe that His transfiguration was irrefutable proof of His exceeding greatness now, and that one day He will return with power and glory to consummate His eternal kingdom as He has promised. I pray that You will reveal His **Majesty** so profoundly to me, my family and mul-titudes of other believers around the world that we will be gripped with the same awe of Him and trust in Him that Peter had. I join Charles Wesley in praising the **majestic** Jesus through some additional verses of "Rejoice, the Lord is King": (verse 3) "His kingdom cannot fail, He rules o'er earth and Heav'n, The keys of death and hell are to our Jesus giv'n; Lift up your heart, lift up your voice; Rejoice, again I say, rejoice! (verse 4) He sits at God's right hand, Till all His foes submit, And bow to His command, and fall beneath His feet: Lift up your heart, lift up your voice; Rejoice, again I say, rejoice!" In His exalted name I pray these things. Amen.

What impacted me about Christ today...

_____

_____

*1 John 1:1-4 That which was from the beginning, which we have heard, which we have seen with our eyes, which we have looked at and our hands have touched—this we proclaim concerning the **Word of life**. The life appeared; we have seen it and testify to it, and we proclaim to you the eternal life, which was with the Father and has appeared to us. We proclaim to you what we have seen and heard, so that you also may have fellowship with us. And our fellowship is with the Father and with his Son, Jesus Christ. We write this to make our joy complete.*

Significance: **The LORD JESUS CHRIST embodies and communicates eternal life to the world.**

Dear Father,

I praise Jesus that He was with You from the beginning, and that as the **Word of Life,** He is the complete source and fountain of all **life**. This again reminds me of what John said in John 1:1-4 about Who Christ is: *"In the beginning was the **Word**, and the **Word** was with God, and the **Word** was God. He was with God in the beginning. Through him all things were made; without him nothing was made that has been made. In him was **life**, and that **life** was the light of mankind."* I exalt the **Word of Life** that He is Your incarnate Son, Whom You sent to earth to reveal to mankind Who You are, and to fulfill all Your prophecies and promises. What an amazing privilege John and the other disciples had to hear the **Word of Life** with their physical ears, see Him with their eyes and touch Him with their hands. My heart leaps when I again read in John 1:14 what the disciples experienced in the Person of Jesus, the blessed Messiah: *"The **Word** became flesh and made his dwelling among us. We have seen his glory, the glory of the one and only Son, who came from the Father, full of grace and truth."* I pray You will enable me to hear and see and touch the breadth and depth of the **Word of Life**, and to boldly proclaim Him to everyone You bring into my life. I ask these things in the name of **Life**, Jesus. Amen.

What impacted me about Christ today...

_____

_____

_____

_____

*1 John 1:1-4 That which was from the beginning, which we have heard, which we have seen with our eyes, which we have looked at and our hands have touched—this we proclaim concerning the Word of life. The life appeared; we have seen it and testify to it, and we proclaim to you the **eternal life**, which was with the Father and has appeared to us. We proclaim to you what we have seen and heard, so that you also may have fellowship with us. And our fellowship is with the Father and with his Son, Jesus Christ. We write this to make our joy complete.*

Significance: **The LORD JESUS CHRIST is Himself eternal life, not a period of time, but a Person.**

Dear Father,

Again, I thank You that the Apostle John, and the rest of the early apostles and disciples, could definitely agree and testify that He Who is Life, Jesus Christ, **did appear** (was incarnate, manifested His presence) and dwelt among them. I rejoice that those followers could boldly proclaim that the Word of Life is the **Eternal Life**, the eternal Son of God, Who had always been with You before He came to earth! I am deeply, deeply grateful that I and all who receive Him as our Savior have **eternal life** in the One Who is **Eternal Life!** I bless Jesus that through Him we have fellowship with You and with Him, as He prayed in John 17:3, *"Now this is **eternal life**: that they know you, the only true God, and Jesus Christ, whom you have sent."* My joy is magnificently complete! I believe with all my heart that it is time now for me and masses of other believers to give everything to Jesus so we can live in John 17 fellowship with You and with Him. Please help us to do that. I pray these things in the name of Jesus, our precious **Eternal Life**. Amen.

What impacted me about Christ today...

_____

_____

_____

_____

_____

*1 John 2:1-3 My dear children, I write this to you so that you will not sin. But if anybody does sin, we have an advocate with the Father—**Jesus Christ, the Righteous One**. He is the atoning sacrifice for our sins, and not only for ours but also for the sins of the whole world. We know that we have come to know him if we keep his commands.*

Significance: The LORD JESUS CHRIST is the only one Who is wholly righteous.

Dear Father,

I am filled with gratitude that when I and other believers sin, we have One Who speaks to the Father in our defense. Without a doubt, He is **Jesus** (the Savior) **Christ** (the Messiah)**, the Righteous One**. I praise **Jesus Christ** that He is our **righteous** defender and advocate: the only sinless and totally **Righteous One**, Who gave His life for us, sits at Your right hand, and constantly intercedes with You for us. All glory to **Jesus**! I am deeply in awe that He does not try to conceal our sins or claim we have not sinned, but He fully admits our guilt before You, then pleads for and obtains our full pardon based upon His **righteousness**. I rejoice that **Jesus Christ, the Righteous One** is Your Son in Whom You are well pleased. I pray that I and a rapidly growing number of Christians in all cities and nations today will become as Peter, John and the other disciples were when they recognized that **Jesus** is "the **Christ,** the Son of the Living God," and submitted themselves to living in His **righteousness**. Oh, may we come to know Him so well that we always keep his **righteous** commands. I pray these things with all hope in the name of **Jesus**. Amen.

What impacted me about Christ today...

_____

_____

_____

_____

_____

_____

_____

The Atoning Sacrifice For Our Sins

*1 John 2:1-3 My dear children, I write this to you so that you will not sin. But if anybody does sin, we have an advocate with the Father—Jesus Christ, the Righteous One. He is the **atoning sacrifice for our sins**, and not only for ours but also for the sins of the whole world. We know that we have come to know him if we keep his commands.*

S ignificance: The LORD JESUS CHRIST'S sacrifice was the necessary payment for our sins.

Dear Father,

I am extremely grateful that Jesus Christ, the Righteous One is the **Atoning Sacrifice for our Sins** and the sins of the whole world. I honor Jesus that He is the only One Who is completely holy, and Whose sacrifice could atone for, or appease, the offense of our sins against You. I praise Him that only the shedding of His blood is sufficient to satisfy Your justice. Oh, I thank You so much that You initiated this **sacrificial atoning**, as 1 John 4:10 says: *"This is love: not that we loved God, but that he loved us and sent his Son as an **atoning sacrifice for our sins**."* I also think of Romans 3:25-26 about You choosing Christ for the **atonement** for Your justice: *"God presented Christ as a **sacrifice of atonement**, through the shedding of his blood—to be received by faith. He did this to demonstrate his righteousness, because in his forbearance he had left the sins committed beforehand unpunished—he did it to demonstrate his righteousness at the present time, so as to be just and the one who justifies those who have faith in Jesus."* I pray that You will flood me and all Christians with thanksgiving and praise for the **Atoning Sacrifice for our Sins**, so that we will overflow with love for and adoration of Him as we speak to one another. In His **atoning** name I pray these things. Amen.

What impacted me about Christ today...

_____

_____

_____

_____

_____

_____

_____

The Son Jesus Christ

*1 John 5:20 We know also that the Son of God has come and has given us understanding, so that we may know him who is true. And we are in him who is true by being in his **Son Jesus Christ**. He is the true God and eternal life.*

S ignificance: The LORD JESUS CHRIST reveals the complete understanding of God.

Dear Father,

I praise You again for sending Your beloved **Son Jesus** (the Savior) **Christ** (Messiah) to the earth 2000+ years ago. I never cease to be amazed and filled with hope that I and all other people who want to understand You *"Who are true,"* can do so completely through knowing Your **Son Jesus Christ!** It is especially thrilling to me that some of Christ's names like, *"Exact Representation of his Being"* (Hebrews 1:3), *"Son of God"* (John 1:34), and *"Image of the Invisible God"* (Colossians 1:15), confirm very clearly and powerfully the full revelation of You in Christ. As I read and meditate on Christ's love, character, nature, attributes, authority, works, servant heart, majesty, words, sacrificial obedience, abiding presence and constant intercession, I marvel that I am knowing, feeling, understanding, tasting and enjoying all of You through Him! I am reminded of the book by Henry Blackaby called "Experiencing God." I love the assurance I have that I am "experiencing" You through "experiencing" Your **Son Jesus Christ!** I pray that You will help all believers to eagerly devote our energies and passions to knowing Him and making Him known. May lost people cry out to the **Son Jesus Christ** as never before! In His indescribable name I ask these things. Amen.

What impacted me about Christ today...

_____

_____

_____

_____

_____

_____

> *1 John 5:20 We know also that the Son of God has come and has given us understanding, so that we may know him who is true. And we are in him who is true by being in his Son Jesus Christ. He is the **true God** and eternal life.*

Significance: **The LORD JESUS CHRIST is the true God as much as the Father is the true God.**

Dear Father,

I am delighted with the multiple declarations in this Scripture passage that You are the **True God**, and Your Son Jesus Christ is also the **True God**. I am reminded of John 10:30 where Jesus says: *"I and the Father are one,"* and that all of Scripture (and the entire universe) are filled with affirmations that the Father, Son and Spirit are God, and that all other gods and idols are false gods. I want to again pray John 17:3, which says: *"Now this is eternal life: that they know you, the only true God, and Jesus Christ, whom you have sent."* I am exceedingly grateful that we can know everything we need to know about You by knowing everything we possibly can about Jesus, the **True God**. I pray that You will hold nothing back in helping me, my family and all other Christians who are hungry for Jesus, to know the manifold riches of His character, power, will, sacrificial love, servant spirit, promises, teachings, prayers and immeasurably more, so that we will become increasingly devoted to the **True God**. Thank You that in Christ, the **True God**, we can have the fullness of eternal life, now and forever. I pray that the **fact** that Jesus is the **True God** will burn in the hearts and minds of millions of unbelievers, and all obstacles to giving their lives to Him will be overcome. I pray these things in His absolutely **true** name. Amen.

What impacted me about Christ today...

_____

_____

_____

_____

_____

_____

*2 John 1:3, 9 Grace, mercy and peace from God the Father and from
Jesus Christ, the **Father's Son**, will be with us in truth and love. . . .
Anyone who runs ahead and does not continue in the teaching of Christ
does not have God; whoever continues in the teaching has both the
Father and the Son.*

Significance: **The LORD JESUS CHRIST is the only Son of our
Heavenly Father.**

Dear Father,
I love it that John calls Jesus Christ the **Father's Son**. What a precious
affirmation of the relationship You and Your Son have. I remember a number of places in the Bible where You are referred to as the *"Father of our
Lord Jesus Christ."* I praise You and Your **Son** that there has never been
a more perfect example of the statement "Like **Father**, like **Son**," since
Your **Son** is the perfect likeness of His **Father**. This reminds me of the
many ways Jesus refers to the intimacy You have with each other, including John 10:37-38, *"Do not believe me unless I do the works of my Father.
But if I do them, even though you do not believe me, believe the works,
that you may know and understand that the **Father** is in me, and I in the
Father."* I rejoice that You and Jesus have had that wonderful **Father/
Son** relationship for all eternity: with the highest love, respect, oneness,
trust, truth, submission, obedience, adoration and all the other categories
He expresses in John 17. With all my heart, I want to live in all the grace,
mercy and peace from You and Your **Son**, and be with You in all truth and
love. And, please help me to live in all of Jesus' teaching, so that I have all
of the **Father** and the **Son**. I pray these things in the name of the **Father's
Son**. Amen.

What impacted me about Christ today...

_____

_____

_____

_____

_____

_____

_____

*3 John 1:5-8 Dear friend, you are faithful in what you are doing for the brothers and sisters, even though they are strangers to you. They have told the church about your love. Please send them on their way in a manner that honors God. It was for the sake of the **Name** that they went out, receiving no help from the pagans. We ought therefore to show hospitality to such people so that we may work together for the truth.*

Significance: **The LORD JESUS CHRIST'S rank and authority is above all others in the universe.**

Dear Father,

I worship and praise the Lord Jesus Christ, Who is the **Name** above every name, to Whom one day very soon every knee in heaven and on earth and under the earth will bow, and every tongue will confess that He is Lord to Your glory. I rejoice that all Your power, authority, righteousness, grace and wisdom are in the **Name**, that kings and nations rise and fall under the **Name**, and for the sake of the **Name** millions of followers have gone out to proclaim the new life that is in Him alone. I pray You will build in me a consuming love for the **Name**, so I will speak of His wonders with great delight to every other believer I can. May He become the center of the thoughts, discussions, prayers, affections, praises and amazement of His people. May Your Spirit give us an unquenchable passion to spread the fame of the **Name** to many multitudes of men, women, young people and children all around us who are currently lost without Him. I pray these things in the name of the **Name**. Amen.

What impacted me about Christ today...

_____

_____

_____

_____

_____

_____

_____

_____

Our Sovereign And Lord

*Jude 1:3-4 Dear friends, although I was very eager to write to you about the salvation we share, I felt compelled to write and urge you to contend for the faith that was once for all entrusted to God's holy people. For certain individuals whose condemnation was written about long ago have secretly slipped in among you. They are ungodly people, who pervert the grace of our God into a license for immorality and deny Jesus Christ our only **Sovereign and Lord**.*

Significance: The LORD JESUS CHRIST is the absolute Ruler of the universe.

Dear Father,
I worship Jesus Christ, our Savior and Redeemer, the only true **Sovereign and Lord**. I love to go through the Bible and find many places that acknowledge Jesus Christ as the **Sovereign** (monarch and preeminent ruler) and **Lord** (master and head), of all His creation, now and forever. I am in awe that Your **sovereign** wisdom, power, authority, benevolence, righteousness and grandeur dwells within Him. I am reminded of Daniel 4:24-26 where the prophet speaks to King Nebuchadnezzar about the supreme sovereignty of God (which is fulfilled in Jesus): *"This is the interpretation [of the king's dream], Your Majesty, and this is the decree the Most High has issued against my lord the king: 'You will be driven away from people and will live with the wild animals; you will eat grass like the ox and be drenched with the dew of heaven. Seven times will pass by for you until you acknowledge that the Most High is **sovereign** over all kingdoms on earth and gives them to anyone he wishes. The command to leave the stump of the tree with its roots means that your kingdom will be restored to you when you acknowledge that Heaven rules.'"* I pray that You will saturate me so completely with the knowledge of the greatness of our **Sovereign and Lord** that I will never deny Him, but will proclaim all He is with all my heart. I pray these things in His majestic name. Amen.

What impacted me about Christ today...

_____

_____

_____

_____

DECEMBER

*<u>Revelation 1:4b-6</u> Grace and peace to you from him who is, and who was, and who is to come, and from the seven spirits before his throne, and from Jesus Christ, who is the **faithful witness**, the firstborn from the dead, and the ruler of the kings of the earth. To him who loves us and has freed us from our sins by his blood, and has made us to be a kingdom and priests to serve his God and Father—to him be glory and power for ever and ever! Amen.*

Significance: **The LORD JESUS CHRIST is the living testimony of Who God is.**

Dear Father,

I bow before Jesus Christ, Who is the true **Faithful Witness**, and I try to imagine the unfathomable vastness of His **faithfulness**. I think of His being the Way and the Truth and the Life, of His being One with You for all eternity, of His being all holiness and wisdom, and of the limitless other characteristics of Jesus that demonstrate His absolute knowledge of You. I praise Jesus that He is entirely reliable, so His followers and all people can totally believe what He says about You and what He does in Your name. I rejoice that Jesus is the **Faithful Witness**, or **Faithful** Testimony, of You through all His names, teachings, promises, prayers and prophecies. I love to meditate on what He said in John 8:28-29, *"So Jesus said, 'When you have lifted up the Son of Man, then you will know that I am he and that I do nothing on my own but speak just what the Father has taught me. The one who sent me is with me; he has not left me alone, for I always do what pleases him.'"* I pray that I and many other believers will give ourselves to constantly growing in our knowledge of, and abandonment to, the **Faithful Witness** so we will become increasingly **faithful witnesses** to one another of all He is and all You are. I pray these things in the **faithful** name of Jesus. Amen.

What impacted me about Christ today...

_____

_____

_____

_____

Revelation 1:4b-6 Grace and peace to you from him who is, and who was, and who is to come, and from the seven spirits before his throne, and from Jesus Christ, who is the faithful witness, the **firstborn from the dead**, and the ruler of the kings of the earth. To him who loves us and has freed us from our sins by his blood, and has made us to be a kingdom and priests to serve his God and Father—to him be glory and power for ever and ever! Amen.

Significance: The LORD JESUS CHRIST, raised from the dead, is the proof an I promise of a resurrection of all saints.

Dear Father,

I am grateful that Jesus Christ is the **Firstborn From the Dead**. I praise You that while other people, like Lazarus, rose from the dead to die again, You raised Christ from His death on the cross to die no more. I am thankful for the powerful explanation of this truth in Acts 13:32-37, *"We tell you the good news: What God promised our ancestors he has fulfilled for us, their children, by raising up Jesus. As it is written in the second Psalm: 'You are my son; today I have become your Father.' God raised him from the dead, so that he will never be subject to decay. As God has said, 'I will give you the holy and sure blessings promised to David.' So it is also stated elsewhere: 'You will not let your holy one see decay.' Now when David had served God's purpose in his own generation, he fell asleep; he was buried with his ancestors and his body decayed. But the one whom God raised from the dead did not see decay."* I rejoice that because Jesus Christ, Your Son, is the **Firstborn From the Dead**, I and all people who receive Him as our Savior are Your sons and daughters and will one day rise from the dead with Him. Please strongly convict us to share this good news very soon with the many people in our lives who are currently lost and dying without Him. In His name I pray these things. Amen.

What impacted me about Christ today...

_____

_____

_____

_____

_____

*Revelation 1:4b-6 Grace and peace to you from him who is, and who was, and who is to come, and from the seven spirits before his throne, and from Jesus Christ, who is the faithful witness, the firstborn from the dead, and the **ruler of the kings of the earth**. To him who loves us and has freed us from our sins by his blood, and has made us to be a kingdom and priests to serve his God and Father—to him be glory and power for ever and ever! Amen.*

Significance: The LORD JESUS CHRIST is the ruler over every earthly ruler for all time.

Dear Father,

As I meditate on this mighty name of Jesus Christ, the **Ruler of the Kings of the Earth**, I humble myself and worship Him in all His glory and majesty. I magnify Jesus, the supreme **Ruler**, Leader and Prince, as He exercises dominion over all the rulers of the people of the earth! I am in awe that the fullness of Your power, authority, wisdom, lordship, grandeur and rights dwells in Him. I think of Psalm 99:1-3 which points to Christ as **Ruler**: *"The Lord reigns, let the nations tremble; he sits enthroned between the cherubim, let the earth shake. Great is the LORD in Zion; he is exalted over all the nations. Let them praise your great and awesome name—he is holy."* I pray You will convict all kings and rulers throughout the earth to fear and submit to Christ's rule. All praise and gratitude to the **Ruler of the Kings of the Earth**, Who loves me and all His people, *"and has freed us from our sins by his blood, and has made us to be a kingdom and priests to serve his God and Father—to him be glory and power for ever and ever! Amen."*

What impacted me about Christ today...

_____

_____

_____

_____

_____

_____

Revelation 1:8 *"I am the Alpha and the Omega," says the Lord God, "who is, and who was, and who is to come, the **Almighty**."*

Significance: The **LORD JESUS CHRIST** is the omnipotent, supreme being.

Dear Father,

I honor Jesus, Who possesses all Your power, might and omnipotence. I think of the announcement of the Messiah in Isaiah 9:6b, *"And he will be called Wonderful Counselor, **Mighty** God, Everlasting Father, Prince of Peace."* I praise Jesus that from eternity to eternity He is the **Almighty**. I am "blown away" when I think again about the vast **almightiness** of Christ, Who Paul says in Colossians 3:11, *"Is all and is in all!"* I give the highest praise of Jesus that He "is **All**" (above and beyond all He has created), and, at the same time, "is **in All**" (the core or DNA of all He has created)! I am deeply grateful that: He knows all things; He is everywhere; He has all grace and mercy; His love never fails, and is enduring forever; He has all wisdom and understanding; nothing is too difficult for Him; He is completely secure and unchanging; He is entirely faithful; and He is completely pure and holy. He is **Almighty** in all ways! I pray that You will give me and many other believers a persistent craving to know the **Almighty**, so we will trust Him and give ourselves wholly to His lordship. I earnestly plead that Your Spirit will open the understanding of millions of lost people to see the **Almighty** and tremble before Him. I pray these things in His incomparable, **almighty** name. Amen.

What impacted me about Christ today...

_____

_____

_____

_____

_____

_____

_____

_____

*Revelation 1:17-18 When I saw him [Jesus Christ], I fell at his feet as though dead. Then he placed his right hand on me and said: "Do not be afraid. I am the First and the Last. I am the **Living One**; I was dead, and now look, I am alive for ever and ever! And I hold the keys of death and Hades."*

Significance: The LORD JESUS CHRIST is the self-existent being, the source of all life.

Dear Father,
I can only imagine the depth of awe and fear the Apostle John experienced when he was face-to-face with the glorified Lord Jesus Christ, Who had been crucified and raised from the dead 50 years before, and is now the blazing **Living One**. Oh, what brilliance and authority the **Living One** possesses! I join John in profound awe of Jesus as I realize how the **Living One** supremely fulfills what Jesus declared about Himself in John 10:10b, *"I have come that they might have **life**, and have it to the full."* Thank You so much that all life, **ALL THE FULLNESS OF LIFE**, is in the **Living One** alone. I rejoice also to recall the great fulfillment of Jesus' revelation to Martha in John 11:25-26, *"I am the resurrection and the **life**. The one who believes in me will live, even though they die; and whoever lives by believing in me will never die. Do you believe this?"* I pray that You will help me, my family members and all Christ's followers to have a **living faith** in the incomparable **Living One**, and be on our faces (in body and spirit) in His holy presence. I pray these things in the **living** name of Jesus. Amen.

What impacted me about Christ today...

Alive For Ever And Ever

*Revelation 1:17-18 When I saw him [Jesus Christ], I fell at his feet as though dead. Then he placed his right hand on me and said: "Do not be afraid. I am the First and the Last. I am the Living One; I was dead, and now look, I am **alive for ever and ever**! And I hold the keys of death and Hades."*

Significance: **The LORD JESUS CHRIST, even in His humanity, lives forever.**

Dear Father,

I again praise Jesus Christ, Who, though He was once dead, He is **Alive For Ever and Ever**! I rejoice that He **lived** with You for all eternity past, gave **life** and light to all creation at the beginning of time, was born to earthly **life** as the Son of Man, rose from death to **life** while He was still a man, and is **Alive For Ever and Ever** now in heaven and when He returns to earth one day. Hallelujah! I praise Jesus that none of the prophecies, promises and plans about Him will ever be cut short or unfulfilled, because He is absolutely **Alive For Ever and Ever**. I exalt the **Alive For Ever and Ever** that He will never change, never diminish, never waver and never die again. Glory to Jesus, Who *"holds the keys to death and Hades,"* which completely assures me and all His other followers that we too will not be prisoners of death, but will experience eternal **life** with Jesus. I pray that You will continually remind us that Jesus is **Alive For Ever and Ever**, so that we will trust Him with every part of our lives and overflow with abounding hope. I pray that the many people I know who have no true hope of eternal life, will become convinced that **Jesus is Alive For Ever and Ever**, and intently put their lives in His hands. I pray these things in the victorious name of Jesus. Amen.

What impacted me about Christ today...

_____

_____

_____

_____

_____

_____

The Hidden Manna

*Revelation 2:14-17 Nevertheless, I have a few things against you: There are some among you who hold to the teaching of Balaam, who taught Balak to entice the Israelites to sin so that they ate food sacrificed to idols and committed sexual immorality. Likewise, you also have those who hold to the teaching of the Nicolaitans. Repent therefore! Otherwise, I will soon come to you and will fight against them with the sword of my mouth. Whoever has ears, let them hear what the Spirit says to the churches. To the one who is victorious, I will give some of the **hidden manna**. I will also give that person a white stone with a new name written on it, known only to the one who receives it."*

Significance: The LORD JESUS CHRIST is the invisible, super-natural provision of God for His people.

Dear Father,

I am very grateful You have provided Jesus, the blessed **Hidden Manna**, to me and all others who have received Him as our Savior. This name wonderfully strengthens and encourages me, and reminds me of Jesus' response in John 6:32-35 to people's questions about why they should believe in Him: *"Jesus said to them, 'Very truly I tell you, it is not Moses who has given you the bread from heaven, but it is my Father who gives you the true bread from heaven. For the bread of God is the bread that comes down from heaven and gives life to the world.' 'Sir,' they said, 'always give us this bread.' Then Jesus declared, 'I am the bread of life. Whoever comes to me will never go hungry, and whoever believes in me will never be thirsty.'"* Thank You that although Christ is **"hidden"** in heaven from those who have not yet received Him, we believers are wholly nourished spiritually (as through a feast) in Him, now and forever. I pray that You will help me and all other believers to become hungry to consume only the **Hidden Manna**, and refuse all other pleasures of the world with which we have tried to satisfy our longings. May Jesus no longer be **"hidden"** to many lost people we know, so they will become ravishingly hungry for Him too. I pray these things in Jesus' name. Amen.

What impacted me about Christ today...

_____

_____

_____

*Revelation 3:7 To the angel of the church in Philadelphia write: "These are the words of him who is **holy and true**, who holds the key of David. What he opens no one can shut, and what he shuts no one can open."*

Significance: The LORD JESUS CHRIST is the ultimate expression of holiness and truth.

Dear Father,
I bow in awe of the only One Who has ever been, or will ever be, absolutely **Holy and True**—the Lord Jesus Christ. I love the discussion that includes Jesus' holiness between the virgin Mary and the angel in Luke 1:34-35, *"How will this be," Mary asked the angel, "since I am a virgin?" The angel answered, "The Holy Spirit will come on you, and the power of the Most High will overshadow you. So the **holy one** to be born will be called the Son of God."* I also remember Peter's statement in Acts 3:13-14, *"The God of Abraham, Isaac and Jacob, the God of our fathers, has glorified his servant Jesus. You handed him over to be killed, and you disowned him before Pilate, though he had decided to let him go. You disowned the **Holy** and Righteous One and asked that a murderer be released to you."* I exalt the most **holy** Jesus! I honor Him also for the many declarations throughout the Bible that He is the **True** God, in the midst of many other gods and idols which relentlessly vie for man's devotion. Hallelujah, that in the book of John alone it is said of Jesus, *"For the law was given through Moses; grace and **truth** came through Jesus Christ"* (1:17); *"Jesus answered, 'I am the way and the **truth** and the life'"* (14:6); *"You are a king, then!" said Pilate. Jesus answered, "You say that I am a king. In fact, the reason I was born and came into the world is to testify to the **truth**. Everyone on the side of **truth** listens to me"* (18:37). All glory to Jesus, the **Holy and True**, Who, as the heir of the throne of David, has sole authority to decide who enters His kingdom. I pray these things in His mighty name. Amen.

What impacted me about Christ today...

_____

_____

_____

_____

*Rev. 3:11-13 I am coming soon. Hold on to what you have, so that no one will take your crown. The one who is victorious I will make a pillar in the temple of my God. Never again will they leave it. I will write on them the name of my God and the name of the city of my God, the new Jerusalem, which is coming down out of heaven from my God; and I will also write on them my **new name**. Whoever has ears, let them hear what the Spirit says to the churches.*

Significance: The LORD JESUS CHRIST will receive a new title when the Father makes all things new.

Dear Father,

Words cannot adequately express my delight that Jesus is returning to earth soon, and that for those of us who overcome the deceptions of this world, He will write Your name on us, as well as the name of Your city, the new Jerusalem, and His **New Name!** I am very anxious to know that exalted name that only You now know, and I imagine it will complement or summarize His spectacular names which have already been made known to us: Savior, Light of the World, Lord, King of kings, Bread of Life, Image of the Invisible God, Immanuel, Word, Author of Life, Messiah, and infinitely more. I marvel that Christ has earned the **New Name** by His humiliation as the Son of Man, and that it will one day confirm His pledge to believers that we will dwell with Him forever. Although I do not know what the **New Name** is yet, I praise Christ with all my being! I pray that I and all His followers will hear what the Spirit is saying to us now about the supremacy of Christ, and we will earnestly devote ourselves to worshiping Him, loving Him, revering Him, yielding everything to Him, heartily speaking to one another about His worthiness, and praying for His rule and reign over us and His entire kingdom. I pray these things in the fullness of His **New Name**. Amen.

What impacted me about Christ today...

_____

_____

_____

_____

_____

Revelation 3:14-16, 18-20 *"To the angel of the Church in Laodicea write: These are the words of the **Amen**, the faithful and true witness, the ruler of God's creation. I know your deeds, that you are neither cold nor hot. I wish you were either one or the other! So, because you are lukewarm—neither hot nor cold—I am about to spit you out of my mouth. . . . I counsel you to buy from me gold refined in the fire, so you can become rich; and white clothes to wear, so you can cover your shameful nakedness; and salve to put on your eyes, so you can see. Those whom I love I rebuke and discipline. So be earnest and repent. Here I am! I stand at the door and knock. If anyone hears my voice and opens the door, I will come in and eat with that person, and they with me."*

Significance: The LORD JESUS CHRIST is all there is of God's truth. There can be no more of truth than what He says and Who He is.

Dear Father,
I exalt Christ that He gave Himself the title, the **Amen**, in this last letter to the churches. I praise Him for His pledge that all His words and revelations are the most true and trustworthy that can possibly be, especially compared to the lukewarmness and other deficiencies of those churches. I am so grateful that there is nothing more that can be said about You and Your kingdom beyond what He says and reveals. I again marvel at the authority and faithfulness of the **Amen** that Paul wrote about in 2 Corinthians 1:18-22, *"But as surely as God is faithful, our message to you is not 'Yes' and 'No.' For the Son of God, Jesus Christ, who was preached among you by us—by me and Silas and Timothy—was not 'Yes' and 'No,' but in him it has always been 'Yes.' For no matter how many promises God has made, they are 'Yes' in Christ. And so through him the 'Amen' is spoken by us to the glory of God. Now it is God who makes both us and you stand firm in Christ. He anointed us, set his seal of ownership on us, and put his Spirit in our hearts as a deposit, guaranteeing what is to come."* I pray You will help me and all believers become on fire to know all the **Amen is**, and to *"stand firm"* in Him. In His name I pray these things. Amen.

What impacted me about Christ today...

Revelation 3:14-16, 18-20 "*To the angel of the Church in Laodicea write:-These are the words of the Amen, the faithful and true witness, the* **ruler of God's creation**. *I know your deeds, that you are neither cold nor hot. I wish you were either one or the other! So, because you are lukewarm—neither hot nor cold—I am about to spit you out of my mouth. . . . I counsel you to buy from me gold refined in the fire, so you can become rich; and white clothes to wear, so you can cover your shameful nakedness; and salve to put on your eyes, so you can see. Those whom I love I rebuke and discipline. So be earnest and repent. Here I am! I stand at the door and knock. If anyone hears my voice and opens the door, I will come in and eat with that person, and they with me.*"

Significance: The LORD JESUS CHRIST is the reigning King over all of God's creation.

Dear Father,

Thank You for the great hope all believers have in Jesus, the sovereign **Ruler of God's Creation**. I honor Jesus again as the Word, Who created and **rules** all things. I fondly go back to Paul's strong declaration in Colossians 1:15-18, "*The Son is the image of the invisible God, the firstborn over all creation. For in him all things were created: things in heaven and on earth, visible and invisible, whether thrones or powers or rulers or authorities; all things have been created through him and for him. He is before all things, and in him all things hold together. And he is the head of the body, the church; he is the beginning and the firstborn from among the dead, so that in everything he might have the supremacy.*" I praise Jesus that He **rules** in total righteousness. I honor His boundless qualifications to tell the Church of Laodicea, as well as the Church of our day, of our lukewarmness and all our other sins. I pray that You will convict us to repent of all our sins. I am deeply grateful that the **Ruler of God's Creation** is standing at the door of our lives and knocking. Please help us to clearly hear His voice and throw open the door of our hearts, for Him to dwell in and **rule** every part of us. I pray these things in His wise name. Amen.

What impacted me about Christ today...

_____

_____

_____

Worthy

*Revelation 4:9-11 Whenever the living creatures give glory, honor and thanks to him who sits on the throne and who lives for ever and ever, the twenty-four elders fall down before him who sits on the throne and worship him who lives for ever and ever. They lay their crowns before the throne and say: "You are **worthy**, our Lord and God, to receive glory and honor and power, for you created all things, and by your will they were created and have their being."*

Significance: The LORD JESUS CHRIST has all the excellence and merit to deserve all of our praise.

Dear Father,
I join the living creatures and the twenty-four elders in giving Christ, our Lord and God, all glory and honor. He alone created all things by the authority of His will, and He is most **Worthy**. I am continually in awe of the glorious Lord Jesus Christ as I remember Paul's proclamation in Colossians 1:16-17, *"For in him all things were created: things in heaven and on earth, visible and invisible, whether thrones or powers or rulers or authorities; all things have been created through him and for him. He is before all things, and in him all things hold together."* When I think of the immeasurable qualities, powers and attributes that comprise the Person of Christ, I again join John in bowing before Him: He is the same for all eternity, infinite in power, all holy and righteous, omniscient and omnipresent, the great ruler and sustainer of all He created, all life and light, the Son of the Most High God and Son of Man, victorious over death and sin, the exact representation and fullness of You, the suffering servant, the peace that passes all understanding, and much more than I or anyone can imagine. I pray that You will help me and all of Christ's followers to give our lives to knowing and living in the vastness of the One Who is **Worthy**, so we will lay our crowns before His throne and proclaim His **worthiness** without restraint. I pray these things in the name of our Lord and God. Amen.

What impacted me about Christ today...

_____

_____

_____

_____

The Lion Of The Tribe Of Judah

*Revelation 5:4-5 I wept and wept because no one was found who was worthy to open the scroll or look inside. Then one of the elders said to me, "Do not weep! See, the **Lion of the tribe of Judah**, the Root of David, has triumphed. He is able to open the scroll and its seven seals."*

Significance: **The LORD JESUS CHRIST is the unconquerable King Who will lead His people to ultimate victory.**

Dear Father,
I exalt the Lord Jesus, the only One Who could be the **Lion of the Tribe of Judah**. I rejoice that He has always possessed all the power, authority, majesty, strength, dominion and wisdom of the supreme **Lion** to rule all of His kingdom. I praise Him that He is the Messiah of the **Tribe of Judah**, and the **Lion of the Tribe of Judah,** Who conquered suffering and death forever and ever! I bow before the sovereign **Lion of the Tribe of Judah** Who is absolutely worthy to break the seals and open the scrolls of the Revelation of the future! I join Charles Rolls in acknowledging the greatness of the **Lion** in "Time's Noblest Name": "The insuperable strength of Christ in His Lordship as the **Lion of Judah** enables Him to save to the uttermost, subdue all things to Himself, stabilize His kingdom eternally, and satisfy His redeemed forevermore. No force flourishes that He cannot frustrate; there is no might He cannot master, no strength He cannot subdue, and no power exists over which He cannot prevail. The position He holds and the power He wields entitle Him to coordinate the nations by gathering them together in one, to consummate an eternal union and to consolidate the everlasting Kingdom." I pray that I and all His subjects will submit our bodies, minds and spirits to the **Lion of the Tribe of Judah**, in Whose name I pray these things. Amen.

What impacted me about Christ today...

_____

_____

_____

_____

_____

_____

_____

*Revelation 5:6a, 7-8a, 9-11a, 12 Then I saw a **Lamb**, looking as if it had been slain, standing at the center of the throne, encircled by the four living creatures and the elders. . . . He went and took the scroll from the right hand of him who sat on the throne. And when he had taken it, the four living creatures and the twenty-four elders fell down before the **Lamb**. . . . And they sang a new song, saying: "You are worthy to take the scroll and to open its seals, because you were slain, and with your blood you purchased for God persons from every tribe and language and people and nation. You have made them to be a kingdom and priests to serve our God, and they will reign on the earth." Then I looked and heard the voice of many angels, numbering thousands upon thousands, and ten thousand times ten thousand. . . . In a loud voice they were saying: "Worthy is the **Lamb**, who was slain, to receive power and wealth and wisdom and strength and honor and glory and praise!"*

Significance: **The LORD JESUS CHRIST, God's sacrificial creature, was slain for our sins and now possesses ALL authority.**

Dear Father,

I exalt the perfect, sinless **Lamb** Who bears the marks of having been sacrificially slain (and is also the Lion of the Tribe of Judah). All glory to this Redeemer **Lamb** Whose life provides full atonement for my sins and the sins of all mankind. This awesome scene powerfully reminds me of the account John had recorded about Jesus decades earlier, in John 1:29, *"The next day John [the Baptist] saw Jesus coming toward him and said, 'Look, the **Lamb** of God, who takes away the sin of the world!'"* I praise the **Lamb** that He has the full authority and dominion that is portrayed in the seven horns, and the full intelligence to see and know all things that is portrayed in the seven eyes, which are part of Your Spirit being sent out into all the earth. I join the vast worship of the Lamb that will one day erupt in heaven when the Lamb takes the scroll and opens its seals: *"Worthy is the **Lamb**, who was slain, to receive power and wealth and wisdom and strength and honor and glory and praise."* May such resounding praise of the worthy **Lamb** burst forth among His people everywhere today! I pray these things in His victorious name. Amen.

What impacted me about Christ today...

Sovereign Lord, Holy And True

*Revelation 6:9-11 When he [the Lamb] opened the fifth seal, I saw under the altar the souls of those who had been slain because of the word of God and the testimony they had maintained. They called out in a loud voice, "How long, **Sovereign Lord, holy and true**, until you judge the inhabitants of the earth and avenge our blood?" Then each of them was given a white robe, and they were told to wait a little longer, until the full number of their fellow servants, their brothers and sisters, were killed just as they had been.*

Significance: **The LORD JESUS CHRIST is the absolute ruler of this universe, perfect in all His attributes.**

Dear Father,

I honor the Lamb for the willingness of His followers' to be slain because of their testimony of Him. I know that in our Scripture today those slain saints are calling out to Him, the **Sovereign Lord, Holy and True**, to judge those who have inflicted suffering and death on them. I rejoice that He is the Judge Who created all people, knows all people's hearts and deeds, is all wise and just, and is now and forever the completely **Sovereign Lord** (Ruler and Master) of all. I am again deeply grateful for the assurance of Jesus' unlimited authority (**sovereign lordship**) that He confirmed to His disciples in Matthew 28:18b, *"All authority in heaven and on earth has been given to me."* I exalt Jesus that, while He is fully the **Sovereign Lord**, He is also fully the **Holy and True** One. I praise Jesus that **all** holiness and truth originate in Him, and that **all** holiness and truth His people have are through Him, by Him and for Him! I pray that Your Spirit will put an intense desire in me and multitudes of other believers to know all we possibly can of the **Sovereign Lord, Holy and True**, so we will trust Him with our lives, as those who have been slain are trusting Him to avenge their blood. I pray these things in Christ's holy name. Amen.

What impacted me about Christ today...

_____

_____

_____

_____

_____

*Revelation 15:1-4 I saw in heaven another great and marvelous sign: seven angels with the seven last plagues—last, because with them God's wrath is completed. And I saw what looked like a sea of glass glowing with fire and, standing beside the sea, those who had been victorious over the beast and its image and over the number of its name. They held harps given them by God and sang the song of God's servant Moses and of the Lamb: "Great and marvelous are your deeds, **Lord God Almighty**. Just and true are your ways, King of the nations. Who will not fear you, Lord, and bring glory to your name? For you alone are holy. All nations will come and worship before you, for your righteous acts have been revealed."*

Significance: **The LORD JESUS CHRIST is astoundingly victorious in every realm forever.**

Dear Father,

What an incomparable scene this is of the seven angels with the last seven plagues and those who had been victorious over the beast joining together to sing the song of Moses and the song of the Lamb, beginning with: *"Great and marvelous are your deeds, **Lord God Almighty**!"* All glory to Jesus, the One Who is **Lord** and Monarch of all, **God** in Whom all the fullness of the Godhead dwells among us, and the **Almighty**, as Jesus said of Himself in Revelation 1:8, *"I am the Alpha and the Omega," says the* **Lord God**, *"who is, and who was, and who is to come, the **Almighty**."* I join those heavenly beings in singing that *"Great and marvelous"* are the deeds of Jesus Christ Who alone is the **Lord God Almighty**. I praise Him with my whole being that His deeds have always been great and marvelous. I am thrilled that the more I know of Him and His greatness, the more I want to know of Him. I pray that Your Spirit will now awaken the Church of all nations to the vast storehouse of the **Lord God Almighty's** greatness, so that we will fall on our faces in worship of and submission to Him. I pray these things in Christ's **almighty** name. Amen.

What impacted me about Christ today...

_____

_____

_____

*Revelation 15:1-4 I saw in heaven another great and marvelous sign: seven angels with the seven last plagues—last, because with them God's wrath is completed. And I saw what looked like a sea of glass glowing with fire and, standing beside the sea, those who had been victorious over the beast and its image and over the number of its name. They held harps given them by God and sang the song of God's servant Moses and of the Lamb: "Great and marvelous are your deeds, Lord God Almighty. Just and true are your ways, **King of the nations**. Who will not fear you, Lord, and bring glory to your name? For you alone are holy. All nations will come and worship before you, for your righteous acts have been revealed."*

Significance: The LORD JESUS CHRIST is the universal King over all people in every era of history.

Dear Father,

I rejoice with the transfigured saints in heaven who will one day proclaim that the beast is not the king of the earth, but that Jesus, the Lord God Almighty, is the One Who has always been, and always will be, just and true in all His ways. He is THE **King of the Nations**! As I think of some of the other terms that, throughout the ages, have been associated with **kingly** authority and dominion--Majesty, Monarch, Lord, Sovereign, Emperor, Magistrate, Governor, Ruler and many more--I exalt Jesus that He is the completeness of all those names, titles and ranks! I pray that as it will happen at the end of the ages, Your Spirit will clearly reveal the **King of the Nations'** many righteous acts and judgments today, so that I, the Church and countless numbers of unbelievers will acknowledge His authority, fear Him, submit to His holiness, and give all glory to Him. May all who are proud and in rebellion of the great **King**, repent and humble themselves before Him. All hail **King** Jesus! I pray these things in His holy name. Amen.

What impacted me about Christ today...

_____

_____

_____

_____

_____

_____

Revelation 19:11-15 *I [John] saw heaven standing open and there before me was a white horse, whose rider is called **Faithful and True**. With justice he judges and wages war. His eyes are like blazing fire, and on his head are many crowns. He has a name written on him that no one knows but he himself. He is dressed in a robe dipped in blood, and his name is the Word of God. The armies of heaven were following him, riding on white horses and dressed in fine linen, white and clean. Coming out of his mouth is a sharp sword with which to strike down the nations. "He will rule them with an iron scepter." He treads the winepress of the fury of the wrath of God Almighty.*

S ignificance: The LORD JESUS CHRIST is unwaveringly dependable in all of His deeds.

Dear Father,

I exalt the white horse's rider, Who is called **Faithful and True**. I rejoice that He is the victorious Messiah, in Whom dwells all the **faithfulness** and **truth** of the Godhead. I watch in eager anticipation that He will soon go forth to conquer the beast and the false prophet, and subject the whole world to Himself. Hallelujah! Jesus alone is **faithful** and worthy of the confidence of His whole Church in delivering us from all our enemies; and He is **true** to all the Biblical promises that have been made about Himself! I marvel that, with perfect justice, the **Faithful and True** judges and makes war, His eyes are like all-consuming, blazing fire, and on His head are the many crowns which testify to His holy character and deeds. I think of the many Scripture declarations of His might in battle, including Psalm 45:3-4, *"Gird your sword on your side, you mighty one; clothe yourself with splendor and majesty. In your majesty ride forth victoriously in the cause of **truth**, humility and justice; let your right hand achieve awesome deeds."* I pray that You will impress upon me and many other believers the renowned **faithfulness** and **truth** of Jesus, so we will die to all of self and live in all of Him. Please convince us that all our hope is in Him, in Whose name I pray these things. Amen.

What impacted me about Christ today...

_____

_____

*Revelation 19:11-15 I [John] saw heaven standing open and there before me was a white horse, whose rider is called Faithful and True. With justice he judges and wages war. His eyes are like blazing fire, and on his head are many crowns. He has a name written on him that no one knows but he himself. He is dressed in a robe dipped in blood, and his name is the **Word of God**. The armies of heaven were following him, riding on white horses and dressed in fine linen, white and clean. Coming out of his mouth is a sharp sword with which to strike down the nations. He will rule them with an iron scepter. He treads the winepress of the fury of the wrath of God Almighty.*

Significance: The LORD JESUS CHRIST is the perfect declaration of all God is.

Dear Father,

I wonder what glorious name is written on the Lord Jesus Christ that only You and He know. I can only imagine how great and expansive that name is. I am eager to know it and to worship Christ accordingly. At the same time, I delight in focusing today on His name, the **Word of God** ("Logos of God"). I praise Him that He is Your divine Son, Who was with You for all eternity. I honor Him for speaking the whole world into existence out of nothing, and for coming to earth to speak and demonstrate all that You want mankind to know about Yourself and Your kingdom. I exalt Him that He gave His life on the cross to fulfill Your Messianic word, then rose from death and ascended to heaven as eternal Conqueror. As I think about the robe the **Word of God** is dressed in, I am intrigued that the blood on it is what He shed for sinners, but it is also a foreshadowing of the colossal amount of blood that will be shed by the ungodly on the day that He and his army execute final judgment. I worship the **Word of God** that He will fulfill Isaiah 63:1-5 when He *"treads the winepress"* to satisfy Your wrath. I pray that You will reveal His supreme majesty to believers everywhere, so we will devote our highest attention and affection to Him. Urge us to fervently tell every lost person we know about Him before it's too late. In His name I humbly pray these things. Amen.

What impacted me about Christ today...

Revelation 19:11-16 I [John] saw heaven standing open and there before me was a white horse, whose rider is called Faithful and True. With justice he judges and wages war. His eyes are like blazing fire, and on his head are many crowns. He has a name written on him that no one knows but he himself. He is dressed in a robe dipped in blood, and his name is the Word of God. The armies of heaven were following him, riding on white horses and dressed in fine linen, white and clean. Coming out of his mouth is a sharp sword with which to strike down the nations. He will rule them with an iron scepter. He treads the winepress of the fury of the wrath of God Almighty. On his robe and on his thigh he has this name written: "KING OF KINGS AND LORD OF LORDS."

Significance: The LORD JESUS CHRIST is the incomparably supreme ruler over every king and kingdom.

Dear Father,

I am in great anticipation as I read about the Lord Jesus Christ one day leading the armies of heaven with a sharp sword coming out of His mouth to strike down nations, and of His ruling the nations with an iron scepter, and inflicting Your wrathful judgments on the evil of the earth. I praise Christ that those who have received Him as their Savior will unite under His leadership, be strengthened and protected by Him, and be cleansed by His righteousness and truth, as they march with Him into His great and final conquest of the forces of evil! All glory to Him that in this war He will demonstrate ALL the attributes and powers of the incomparable, unprecedented, unconquerable and forever-ruling, supreme **KING OF KINGS**! I bow before the **KING OF KINGS** that this name will be on His robe and thigh, as the name that most boldly proclaims His glorious conquests (like earthly kings often have done when they conquered their adversaries). I pray that **right now** You will convince me and all other believers of the matchless majesty of the **KING OF KINGS**, so we will worship Him and devote ourselves to His rule over every part of our lives. I pray these things in the name of my **King**. Amen.

What impacted me about Christ today...

_____

_____

_____

Lord Of Lords

*Revelation 19:11-16 I [John] saw heaven standing open and there before me was a white horse, whose rider is called Faithful and True. With justice he judges and wages war. His eyes are like blazing fire, and on his head are many crowns. He has a name written on him that no one knows but he himself. He is dressed in a robe dipped in blood, and his name is the Word of God. The armies of heaven were following him, riding on white horses and dressed in fine linen, white and clean. Coming out of his mouth is a sharp sword with which to strike down the nations. He will rule them with an iron scepter. He treads the winepress of the fury of the wrath of God Almighty. On his robe and on his thigh he has this name written: "KING OF KINGS AND **LORD OF LORDS.**"*

S ignificance: **The LORD JESUS CHRIST outranks every other authority in every aspect.**

Dear Father,
As I was in awe of Christ's supreme authority as KING OF KINGS, I am in awe of Him as **LORD OF LORDS**! I understand that lordship pertains to those who have the right to administrate one or more spheres of influence, and I marvel that the Lord Jesus Christ administrates and predominates ALL other administrators of ALL spheres of influence. He is Lord of all leaders, rulers, magistrates, warriors, legislators, judges, mediators, authorities, managers and every other imaginable lordship! I am reminded of Peter's statement at Cornelius' house in Acts 10:36, *"You know the message God sent to the people of Israel, announcing the good news of peace through Jesus Christ, who is **Lord** of all."* Glory to Jesus Christ that He is **Lord** of all—in war and in peace! I agree with Charles Rolls in worshiping Christ about His lordship: "The ultimate of His unlimited lordship is inevitable, for all conflicts must cease, all fetters fall, all persecutors perish, all tyrannies terminate, all evils end, and even death itself must be destroyed. Whenever we dwell on the capabilities of Christ, the very foresight of His prescience, the vast insight of His providence, and the vital oversight of His preeminence assure the mind forever that He is really and truly **Lord of lords**." I pray that I and the whole Church of today will submit ourselves completely to the oversight of the **LORD OF LORDS**, in Whose name I pray these things. Amen.

What impacted me about Christ today...

Revelation 21:1-3, 5a, 6-7 Then I saw a new heaven and a new earth, for the first heaven and the first earth had passed away, and there was no longer any sea. I saw the Holy City, the new Jerusalem, coming down out of heaven from God, prepared as a bride beautifully dressed for her husband. And I heard a loud voice from the throne saying, "Look! **God's dwelling place** *is now among the people, and he will dwell with them. They will be his people, and God himself will be with them and be their God." . . . He who was seated on the throne said, "I am making everything new!" . . . He said to me: "It is done. I am the Alpha and the Omega, the Beginning and the End. To the thirsty I will give water without cost from the spring of the water of life. Those who are victorious will inherit all this, and I will be their God and they will be my children."*

Significance: The LORD JESUS CHRIST is the permanent tabernacle of God.

Dear Father,

I remember that, in ancient times, Your glory "tabernacled" or **dwelled** with Your people. I rejoice that, for more than the past 2000 years, all of Your fullness has **dwelt** in Your precious Son, Jesus. I delight that the Person of Jesus is **God's Dwelling Place**. I can only imagine how marvelous it will be on the day (and forever after) when those of us who have received Him as our Savior will live with Him face-to-face. How wonderful it already is that the all-sufficient, all-mighty, all-majestic **God's Dwelling Place** acknowledges us as His people today, and that soon there will be no time or space between us living totally in His presence, protection, provision and care. I pray that Your Spirit will reveal the vastness of **God's Dwelling Place** to me and His other followers everywhere, so that we will give ourselves to knowing Him more, cherishing Him, honoring Him, exalting Him, revering Him, abiding in Him, speaking constantly of Him to one another, and praying for His kingdom to come and His will to be done. I pray these things in the name of the One through Whom I intimately know You. Amen.

What impacted me about Christ today...

_____

_____

_____

Revelation 21:1-3, 5a, 6-7 Then I saw a new heaven and a new earth, for the first heaven and the first earth had passed away, and there was no longer any sea. I saw the Holy City, the new Jerusalem, coming down out of heaven from God, prepared as a bride beautifully dressed for her husband. And I heard a loud voice from the throne saying, "Look! God's dwelling place is now among the people, and he will dwell with them. They will be his people, and God himself will be with them and be their God." . . . **He who was seated on the throne** *said, "I am making everything new!"* . . . *He said to me: "It is done. I am the Alpha and the Omega, the Beginning and the End. To the thirsty I will give water without cost from the spring of the water of life. Those who are victorious will inherit all this, and I will be their God and they will be my children."*

Significance: **The LORD JESUS CHRIST presides over God's kingdom.**

Dear Father,

Thank You for the grand unfolding of Your plan, where Your Son, **He Who was Seated on the Throne**, will *"make everything new"* for His kingdom and for all the people He has redeemed. I exalt Him that He has been seated on the throne at Your right hand since He rose from the dead and ascended into heaven. My spirit is filled with gratitude, awe and hope that You have given Him all authority to judge mankind, as is powerfully evidenced in the impending judgment of the dead recorded in Revelation 20:11-12, *"Then I saw a great white throne and him who was seated on it. The earth and the heavens fled from his presence, and there was no place for them. And I saw the dead, great and small, standing before the throne, and books were opened. Another book was opened, which is the book of life. The dead were judged according to what they had done as recorded in the books."* I worship **He Who was Seated on the Throne** because all His judgments and all the words He says to make things new are absolutely *"trustworthy and true!"* Please soon awaken Your people to the spectacular greatness of **He Who was Seated on the Throne**, and to the increasing fulfillment of these Revelations about Him, so our consuming passion will be to know Him for all He is. In His exalted name I pray. Amen.

What impacted me about Christ today...

*Revelation 21:1-3, 5a, 6-7 Then I saw a new heaven and a new earth, for the first heaven and the first earth had passed away, and there was no longer any sea. I saw the Holy City, the new Jerusalem, coming down out of heaven from God, prepared as a bride beautifully dressed for her husband. And I heard a loud voice from the throne saying, "Look! God's dwelling place is now among the people, and he will dwell with them. They will be his people, and God himself will be with them and be their God." . . . He who was seated on the throne said, "I am making everything new!" . . . He said to me: "It is done. I am the **Alpha and the Omega**, the Beginning and the End. To the thirsty I will give water without cost from the spring of the water of life. Those who are victorious will inherit all this, and I will be their God and they will be my children."*

Significance: The LORD JESUS CHRIST is the full spectrum of godliness.

Dear Father,

I rejoice that although what Jesus says in this passage and in all of Revelation is for the future, it will **all happen** with **all certainty** because You and Jesus have said it will happen. Thus, *"It is done!"* Hallelujah, that You and Jesus are trustworthy, true and unchangeable (Godly)! I also rejoice that today's name of Jesus, the **Alpha and the Omega**, uses the first and last letters of the Greek alphabet, which confirms that He has been God for all eternity past, and will be God for all eternity future. I praise Jesus that there is nothing before Him, beyond Him, after Him or in addition to Him, so that I and all people who believe in Him as Savior can be certain that we will soon inherit all He is and all of His kingdom. It is so reassuring to know that all Your promises to the thirsty, including in Isaiah 55:1, are ultimately fulfilled in the **Alpha and Omega**: *"Come, all you who are thirsty, come to the waters; and you who have no money, come, buy and eat! Come, buy wine and milk without money and without cost."* Please convince me and all other believers today to wholeheartedly delight in Jesus, *"the richest of fare,"* in Whose name I pray these things. Amen.

What impacted me about Christ today...

_____ _____

_____ _____

The Beginning And The End

Revelation 21:1-3, 5a, 6-7 Then I saw a new heaven and a new earth, for the first heaven and the first earth had passed away, and there was no longer any sea. I saw the Holy City, the new Jerusalem, coming down out of heaven from God, prepared as a bride beautifully dressed for her husband. And I heard a loud voice from the throne saying, "Look! God's dwelling place is now among the people, and he will dwell with them. They will be his people, and God himself will be with them and be their God." . . . He who was seated on the throne said, "I am making everything new!" . . . He said to me: "It is done. I am the Alpha and the Omega, the **Beginning and the End**. To the thirsty I will give water without cost from the spring of the water of life. Those who are victorious will inherit all this, and I will be their God and they will be my children."

S ignificance: The LORD JESUS CHRIST encompasses every part of history, which is "His story."

Dear Father,

I am so grateful that I can _"fix my eyes upon Jesus"_ (Hebrews 12), the matchless **Beginning and the End**, from Whom all things have originated, and Who sums up all things. I rejoice with the heavenly host that there is nothing and no one before Him, and there will be nothing and no one after Him. I praise Jesus that **He is limitless**, and that all my life, now and beyond the end of time, is spiritually new and absolutely secure in His authority and power! I hold onto the powerful phrase in today's Scripture, _"It is done,"_ and I pray You will constantly remind me that all of creation is "DONE" (finished, completed, fulfilled) in Him! I repent for the times I have not had faith in the **Beginning and the End**, and have not trusted Him as Lord of my life and of the universe. I pray You will give me the hunger to intimately know the **Beginning and the End** that King David, Paul, John, Mary, Martha, Isaiah, Daniel, Peter and our other godly ancestors had, that caused them to love and obey Him with all their beings. May the Church today resoundingly proclaim to one another and to all flesh that He is THE "Joy to the World." I pray these things in His blessed name. Amen.

What impacted me about Christ today...

_____

_____

_____

*Revelation 21:22-27 I did not see a temple in the city, because the Lord God Almighty and the Lamb are its **temple**. The city does not need the sun or the moon to shine on it, for the glory of God gives it light, and the Lamb is its lamp. The nations will walk by its light, and the kings of the earth will bring their splendor into it. On no day will its gates ever be shut, for there will be no night there. The glory and honor of the nations will be brought into it. Nothing impure will ever enter it, nor will anyone who does what is shameful or deceitful, but only those whose names are written in the Lamb's book of life.*

Significance: **The LORD JESUS CHRIST is the living and final place of worship.**

Dear Father,

My words are inadequate to express even the glimpse I already have of the **Temple**. But, I am exceedingly grateful that there will not be a separate religious facility in the Holy City of Jerusalem, because You and Your Son are the **Temple** of the new city! What a wonderful revelation this passage is that the new city is all **Temple**, where You and the Lamb are present everywhere in all Your holiness and oneness! I marvel as I envision everyone in the New Jerusalem focused in praise on You and Your Son. This seems to be a glorious fulfillment of Psalm 22:3 where You inhabit the praise of Your people. I give all worship to the **Temple** like King David gave to You in his praise in Psalm 34:1, *"I will extol the LORD at all times; his praise will always be on my lips."* I am exceedingly delighted that every other praise uttered by saints throughout the ages will be brought to the **Temple** and woven there into continuous, eternal praise. Oh my Father, please prepare me and all Your people today for eternity with the **Temple**, by revealing to us much more of Christ than we have ever known. In His holy name I pray these things. Amen.

What impacted me about Christ today...

_____

_____

_____

_____

*Revelation 21:22-27 I did not see a temple in the city, because the Lord God Almighty and the Lamb are its temple. The city does not need the sun or the moon to shine on it, for the glory of God gives it light, and the Lamb is its **lamp**. The nations will walk by its light, and the kings of the earth will bring their splendor into it. On no day will its gates ever be shut, for there will be no night there. The glory and honor of the nations will be brought into it. Nothing impure will ever enter it, nor will anyone who does what is shameful or deceitful, but only those whose names are written in the Lamb's book of life.*

Significance: **The LORD JESUS CHRIST is the source of everlasting light.**

Dear Father,

How great it is that the New City of Jerusalem does not need the sun or moon to shine on it, because Your glory gives the entire city ALL of its light, and Jesus Christ the Lamb, the Son of God, the Messiah, is its **Lamp**. I think back to the all-encompassing splendor of this Light that is prophesied in Isaiah 60:19, *"The sun will no more be your light by day, nor will the brightness of the moon shine on you, for the LORD will be your everlasting light, and your God will be your glory."* How wonderful that the **Lamp** directs, displays and radiates the inexhaustible brilliance, revelation, luminescence, heat and all-sufficiency of the Light. I rejoice with everything in me that the nations will walk by the Light of the **Lamp**, and their kings will bring their splendor unto it. Hallelujah! He is the Light of lights, Lamp of lamps, Splendor of splendors, and Glory of glories! I worship You and I worship Jesus that total freedom, security, purity and truth will prevail where there is no night, and the gates of the city never need to be shut. I pray that I and all others whose names are written in the Lamb's book of life will right now awaken to all the **Lamp** is, and never turn away from His brilliance. I pray these things in His glorious name. Amen.

What impacted me about Christ today...

_____

_____

_____

_____

*Revelation 22:1-4, 12a, 13-14 Then the angel showed me the river of the water of life, as clear as crystal, flowing from the throne of God and of the Lamb down the middle of the great street of the city. On each side of the river stood the **tree of life** . . . And the leaves of the tree are for the healing of the nations. No longer will there be any curse. The throne of God and of the Lamb will be in the city, and his servants will serve him. They will see his face, and his name will be on their foreheads. . . . [Jesus said] "Look, I am coming soon! . . . I am the Alpha and the Omega, the First and the Last, the Beginning and the End. Blessed are those who wash their robes, that they may have the right to the **tree of life** and may go through the gates into the city."*

Significance: **The LORD JESUS CHRIST bears life-giving fruit.**

ॐ

Dear Father,

I worship the Lamb, Who is the **Tree of Life**. I rejoice that He is the totality of **Life**! I am in awe that He is the **Life** (John 14:6), the Light of **Life** (John 8:12), the Bread of **Life** (John 6:35), the Word of **Life** (Philippians 2:16), the Fountain of **Life** (Psalm 36:9), the Promise of **Life** (2 Timothy 1:1), the Resurrection and the **Life** (John 11:25), and the Author of **Life** (Acts 3:15). I am grateful that as the **Tree of Life**, He completely provides for the healing and other needs of the inhabitants of the City. I am thrilled that the **Tree of Life** is the ultimate fulfillment of Paul's prayer in Ephesians 3:14-19, *"For this reason I kneel before the Father, from whom every family in heaven and on earth derives its name. I pray that out of his glorious riches he may strengthen you with power through his Spirit in your inner being, so that Christ may dwell in your hearts through faith. And I pray that you, being rooted and established in love, may have power, together with all the Lord's holy people, to grasp how wide and long and high and deep is the love of Christ, and to know this love that surpasses knowledge—that you may be filled to the measure of all the fullness of God."* I give all my **life** to the One Who is all **Life**. In His name I pray. Amen.

What impacted me about Christ today...

_____

_____

_____

Revelation 22:7-9a, 9b-10, 12-13 [Jesus said], "Look, I am coming soon! Blessed is the one who keeps the words of the prophecy written in this scroll [Revelation]." [John said] "I, John, am the one who heard and saw these things. And when I had heard and seen them, I fell down to worship at the feet of the angel who had been showing them to me. But he said to me, 'Don't do that! I am a fellow servant with . . . all who keep the words of this scroll. Worship God!' Then he told me, 'Do not seal up the words of the prophecy of this scroll, because the time is near." . . . [Jesus said again] "Look, I am coming soon! My reward is with me, and I will give to each person according to what they have done. I am the Alpha and the Omega, the First and the Last, the Beginning and the End."

S ignificance: The LORD JESUS CHRIST is the originator and completer of all good for all time.

Dear Father,

As I think about Jesus stating that He is the **First and the Last** (as well as the Alpha and the Omega and the Beginning and the End), my hope in Him abounds, and my joy that He is *"coming soon"* abounds. Through the name of Jesus, the **First and the Last**, I understand His supremacy more clearly, and I am compelled to do what the angel commanded John: *"Worship God!"* I rejoice that there are no limitations on what Christ is the **First and the Last** of. I can barely imagine the divine authority He has always had, and will always have as the **First and the Last**. I praise Him for the vast ways He is **First**: **First** to know, love and communicate with You; **First** in mastery over death and darkness; **First** in righteousness, sacrifice and obedience to You; **First** in unconditional love; **First** in expressing the fullness of the Godhead; **First** as Your Exact Representation; **First** as the creator of the universe; **First** as the forgiver of sins; **First** as judge of all mankind; **First** to give His life as a servant; **First** to make disciples; and, **First** to rule the heavens and the earth. I worship Christ that He is **The Last** (the conclusion, final) of ALL He is **First** of! May all His people exalt the Lord Jesus Christ that He is the sum-total of all good! In His all-surpassing name I pray these things. Amen.

What impacted me about Christ today...

The Root And Offspring Of David

Revelation 22:16-17 *"I, Jesus, have sent my angel to give you this testimony for the churches. I am the **Root and the Offspring of David**, and the bright Morning Star." The Spirit and the bride say, "Come!" And let the one who hears say, "Come!" Let the one who is thirsty come; and let the one who wishes take the free gift of the water of life.*

Significance: The LORD JESUS CHRIST is both the divine ancestor and the human descendant of David.

Dear Father,

I am very grateful that Jesus sent His angel to give me and His whole Church the testimony about Him in the Book of Revelation. I am further grateful that Genesis through Revelation testifies Who Christ has always been, is right now, and will be throughout all eternity to come. I rejoice that Jesus declares in today's passage that He is the **Root and the Offspring of David**, which confirms He is divinely qualified to guarantee that everything in Revelation is absolutely true. I am in awe that Jesus resolutely declared Himself to be the Fulfillment of the prophecy that the Messiah would come, and, that not only is He the promised descendant or **Offspring** of David, but that He is the eternal source or **Root** of David! I worship the majestic King Jesus, the **Root and the Offspring of David**. I repent for all the times I have lacked faith in Him, and for all the ways I have treated Him as less than the Sovereign, Lord, Ruler, Master, King, Overseer, Governor and Shepherd that He is. I pray that You will do whatever is needed in me, my family and the Church of the nations to convince us that the **Root and the Offspring of David** is our All in All, so that we will give our all to Him. I pray these things in His exalted name. Amen.

What impacted me about Christ today...

_____

_____

_____

_____

_____

_____

_____

Revelation 22:16-17 *"I, Jesus, have sent my angel to give you this testi-mony for the churches. I am the Root and the Offspring of David, and the* **Bright Morning Star**.*" The Spirit and the bride say, "Come!" And let the one who hears say, "Come!" Let the one who is thirsty come; and let the one who wishes take the free gift of the water of life.*

Significance: **The LORD JESUS CHRIST is the radiant light that precedes His return.**

Dear Father,

What a spectacular finale the **Bright Morning Star** is to the past year of focusing on the greatness of Christ through His names! I say "Hallelujah" that the **Bright Morning Star** is the last "I am" that Jesus calls Himself! I think about how the celestial morning star in the sky is the light that can be seen before the sunrise of each day. I am enthralled that the divine **Morning Star**, Who most **brightly** (most brilliantly) shines in the spiritual darkness, will soon usher in His return to earth and His eternal kingdom. My imagination can only begin to fathom the radiant **brightness** and beauty that Jesus possesses. I exalt Him that all the authority and attributes of the Godhead are manifested in His inexhaustible and all-consuming **brightness**! I am forever grateful that one day He will lead all who have called upon Him into His blessed presence. I praise the **Bright Morning Star** that He merits being called the "**Star** of Eternal Hope" for me and all of His people. I revere and adore the One Who is our All, and is in All. I pray that I and His entire bride worldwide will join Your Spirit in fervently praying for the **Bright Morning Star** to *"Come!"* I pray also that You will give many millions of unsaved people an unbearable thirst for the Savior, and that they will fervently invite Him to come into their lives. I ask all these things in Jesus' **bright** name. Amen.

What impacted me about Christ today...

_____

_____

_____

_____

_____

References used for the names and attributes of Christ and Scripture passages:

"*100 Portraits of Christ*", Henry Gariepy, Victor Books, 1987

"*640 Names and Attributes of Christ: Exalting the Name of YESHUA, Jesus the Christ*", Pastor Ted Corley, 2008

"*CHRIST Is All! A Joyful Manifesto on The Supremacy of God's Son*" David Bryant, New Providence Publishers, 2004

"*Names of Jesus*", William Brent Ashby, Rose Publishing

"*Praying the Names of Jesus*", Ann Spangler, Zondervan, 2006

"*The Holy Bible, New International Version*", Zondervan Bible Publishers, Grand Rapids, Michigan, 1984

"*The Bible Illustrator*", Joseph S. Excell, Baker Book House, Grand Rapids, MI, May 1977, Library of Congress Catalog Number: 54-11086, ISBN: 0-8010-3280-6

"*The Incredible Christ, The Names and Titles of Jesus Christ A-G*", Charles J. Rolls, Loixeau Brothers, Inc., October 1988

"*The World's Greatest Name, The Names and Titles of Jesus Christ H-K*", Charles J. Rolls, Loixeau Brothers, Inc., May 1989

"*Time's Noblest Names, The Names and Titles of Jesus Christ L-O*", Charles J. Rolls, Loixeau Brothers, Inc., September 1988

"*The Name Above Every Name, The Names and Titles of Jesus Christ P-S*", Charles J. Rolls, Loixeau Brothers, Inc., January 1987

"*His Glorious Name, The Names and Titles of Jesus Christ T-Z*", Charles J. Rolls, Loixeau Brothers, Inc., May 1989

"*The Words and Works of Jesus Christ, A Study of the Life of Christ,* J. Dwight Pentecost, Zondervan Publishing House, Grand Rapids, Michigan, 1981

I pray that God will soon give His people a widespread CHRIST-awakening, which David Bryant defines as: **"*whenever God's Spirit uses God's Word to re-convert God's people back to God's Son for ALL that He is.*"**

Bibliography

"I Want to Know More of Christ"

Ashby, William Brent, *Names of Jesus*. Torrance, CA: Rose Publishing, 2008.

Bryant, David, *Christ Is All*. New Providence, NJ: New Providence Publishers, 2005.

Bryant, David, "Tribute 1." Christ Alone Study Guide. 2010.

Corley, Pastor Ted, "640 Names and Attributes of Christ: Exalting the Name of YESHUA, Jesus

the Christ." *Stone Cut Without Hands*. 2008. Cornerstone.

http://www.stonecutwithouthands.com/chanukah.html

Excell, Joseph S., *The Bible Illustrator*. Grand Rapids, MI: Baker Book House, 1977.

Gariepy, Henry, *100 Portraits of Christ*. Wheaton, Illinois: Victor Books, 1987.

Havergal, Frances Ridley, "Looking Unto Jesus." c. 1870.

Lockridge, Bishop S.M., "That's My King." Detroit sermon, 1976.

Pentecost, J. Dwight, *The Words and Works of Jesus Christ,--A Study of the Life of Christ*. Grand

Rapids, MI: Zondervan, 1981.

Rolls, Charles J., *The Names and titles of Jesus Christ. Neptune*, NJ:

Loixeau Brothers, Inc., 1987-1989.

Spangler, Ann, *Praying the Names of Jesus*. Grand Rapids, MI: Zondervan, 2006.

The Holy Bible (New International Version). Grand Rapids, MI: Zondervan, 2011.

About Steve

 Steve's consuming passion is to know the depths of the matchless Christ, and to speak about Christ's greatness with as many other believers as he can. Steve is an ordained minister, and the representative for International Renewal Ministries in Washington State. IRM wants to see a move of God initiated and sustained in as many communities as possible. As an IRM representative, Steve networks with the pastors in Washington in various streams of prayer. He actively visits pastors' prayer groups, works alongside other prayer ministries in the area, and facilitates Prayer Summits. Steve and his wife, Johnnie, have two children and reside greater Seattle Area.

If you want to contact Steve Hall about speaking at a retreat, seminar, small group gathering or congregation about the greatness of Christ, or if you want to order more "I Want to Know More of Christ" books, please go to our website at www.KnowingMoreOfChrist.com.

APPENDIX

ALPHABETICAL NAMES/ATTRIBUTES OF CHRIST BY DATE OF APPEARANCE

NAME/ATTRIBUTE	DATE
Alive For Ever And Ever	December 6
Almighty, The	December 4
Alpha And The Omega, The	December 24
Amen, The	December 10
Ancient Of Days, The	May 7
Angel Of His Presence, The	April 26
Anointed One, Your (God's)	February 23
Another King	August 12
Apostle And High Priest, The	October 21
Arm Of The Lord, The	April 17
Atoning Sacrifice For Our Sins, The	November 25
Author Of Life, The	August 8
Balm In Gilead, The	April 28
Banner For The Peoples, A	March 27
Beautiful Wreath, A	April 3
Before All Things	September 24
Beginning And The End, The	December 25
Blessed Hope, The	October 10
Boy Jesus, The	June 22
Branch Of The Lord, The	March 17
Bridegroom, The	July 10
Bright Morning Star, The	December 31
Builder Of Everything, The	October 23
Canopy, A	March 19
Capstone, The	May 17
Carpenter/Mary's Son, The	June 11
Chief Cornerstone, The	September 14
Chief Shepherd, The	November 19
Child, The	June 21

NAME/ATTRIBUTE	DATE
Chosen And Precious Cornerstone, A	November 14
Chosen Before The Creation Of The World	November 12
Chosen One, My	April 14
Christ	September 5
Christ Is All And Is In All	September 30
Christ Jesus Our Hope	October 3
Christ Jesus Our Lord	August 17
Close To The Brokenhearted	February 5
Commander Of The Army Of The Lord, The	January 13
Consolation Of Israel, The	June 18
Creator Of The Ends Of The Earth, The	April 13
Crowned With Glory And Honor	October 18
Culmination Of The Law, The	August 21
Defense, My	March 28
Deliverer, The	August 23
Descendant Of David, A	August 16
Despised By The People,	January 28
Dwelling Place, Our	February 25
Eternal God, The	January 11
Eternal Life, The	November 23
Everlasting Father, The	March 24
Everlasting God, The	April 12
Everlasting Light, Your	April 25
Everlasting To Everlasting	February 26
Ever-Present Help In Trouble, An	February 11
Exact Representation Of His Being, The	October 15
Exalted Above The Heavens	October 29
Example, An	November 15
Faithful And True	December 18
Faithful Creator, The	November 18
Faithful Witness, The	December 1
Father's Son, The	November 28
First And The Last, The	December 29

NAME/ATTRIBUTE	DATE
Firstborn From The Dead, The	December 2
Firstborn Over All Creation, The	September 23
Firstfruits Of Those Who Have Fallen Asleep, The	September 2
Fortress, My	January 24
Foundation, The	August 29
Fountain Of Life, The	February 6
Fragrant Offering And Sacrifice To God, The	September 17
Friend Of Tax Collectors And Sinners, A	June 26
Friend Who Sticks Closer Than A Brother, The	March 16
Fruit Of The Land, The	March 18
Fullness Of God, The	September 15
Fullness Of The Deity, The	September 28
Gate For The Sheep, The	July 24
Gift Of God, The	July 12
Glorious Crown, A	April 2
Glorious Lord Jesus Christ, Our	November 9
Glorious Sword, The	January 12
Glory Of Israel, The	January 15
God	October 17
God And Savior Jesus Christ, Our	November 20
God For Ever And Ever, Our	February 13
God My Savior	January 26
God Of Heaven, The	March 13
God Of Justice, A	April 8
God Of My Ancestors	May 5
God Of My Life, The	February 9
God Of Peace, The	September 20
God Of The Hebrews, The	January 3
God Over All, The	August 18
God Who Avenges Me, The	January 27
God Who Made Them, The	January 9
God Who Performs Miracles, The	February 22
God, Who Raises The Dead	September 4

NAME/ATTRIBUTE	DATE
God's Dwelling Place	December 22
God's Salvation	June 23
Good And Upright	February 1
Good Man, A	July 20
Good Shepherd, The	July 25
Great And Mighty God, The	May 1
Great God And Savior, Our	October 11
Great High Priest, The	October 24
Great High Priest Over The House Of God, A	November 2
Great Light, A	March 21
Great Prophet, A	June 25
Great Shepherd Of The Sheep, The	November 8
Greater Than Our Father Jacob	July 14
Guarantor Of A Better Covenant, The	October 28
Guardian (Kinsman)-Redeemer, The	January 14
Guide Even To The End, Our	February 14
He Who Is Coming	November 3
He Who Touches The Earth And It Melts	May 10
He Who Was Seated On The Throne	December 23
He Who Watches Over Israel	March 11
Head, The	September 16
Head Of Every Man, The	September 1
Head Of The Body, The	September 25
Head Over Every Power And Authority, The	September 29
Heavenly Gift, The	October 27
Heir Of All Things, The	October 13
Help And Deliverer, My	February 7
Helper, My	November 6
Helper Of The Fatherless, The	January 22
Hidden Manna, The	December 7
Hiding Place, My	February 4
High And Exalted One, The	April 23
High Priest In The Order Of Melchizedek, The	October 26

NAME/ATTRIBUTE	DATE
His (God's) Firstborn	October 16
His (God's) One And Only Son	July 9
His Majesty	November 21
His Son From Heaven	October 1
Holy	April 24
Holy And Awesome	March 7
Holy And Righteous One, The	August 7
Holy And True	December 8
Holy One, The	August 6
Holy One Of God, The	June 10
Holy One Of Israel, The	February 24
Holy Servant Jesus, The	August 9
Hope, My	February 18
Hope Of Glory, The	September 26
Hope Of Israel, The	August 15
Horn Of Salvation, A	June 15
Husband, The	September 9
I Am, The	July 23
Image Of The Invisible God, The	September 22
Immanuel (God With Us)	May 25
Indescribable Gift, The	September 8
Instructor, The	June 7
Jealous	January 5
Jesus	May 24
Jesus Christ The Righteous One	November 24
Jesus, The Prophet From Nazareth In Galilee	June 6
Jew, A	July 11
Joseph's Son	June 24
Judge, The	July 17
Judge Of The Living And The Dead, The	August 11
Kernel Of Wheat, The	July 27
King Eternal, Immortal, Invisible, The Only God, The	October 4
King From Long Ago, My	February 21

NAME/ATTRIBUTE	DATE
King Of Glory, The	January 30
King Of Heaven, The	May 6
King Of Israel, The	July 8
King Of Kings	December 20
King Of The Jews, The	June 8
King Of The Nations (Ages)	December 17
Lamb, A	December 14
Lamb Of God, The	July 7
Lamb Without Blemish Or Defect, A	November 11
Lamp	December 27
Last Adam, The	September 3
Life, The	July 30
Light For Revelation To The Gentiles, The	June 20
Light For The Gentiles, A	April 15
Light Of All Mankind, The	July 6
Light Of The Gospel, The	September 6
Light Of The World, The	July 22
Lion Of The Tribe Of Judah, The	December 13
Living God, The	March 3
Living One, The	December 5
Living Stone, The	November 13
Living Water, The	July 13
Lord, The	September 19
Lord And My God, My	August 3
Lord God Almighty	December 16
Lord Jesus Christ, The	October 12
Lord Most High, Great King Over All The Earth, The	February 12
Lord My Faithful God	February 3
Lord Of All, The	August 22
Lord Of All The Earth, The	March 2
Lord Of Both The Dead And The Living, The	August 24
Lord Of Glory, The	August 28
Lord Of Lords	December 21

NAME/ATTRIBUTE	DATE
Lord Of Peace, The	October 2
Lord Of The Harvest, The	May 28
Lord Of The Sabbath, The	May 30
Lord Strong And Mighty, Lord Mighty In Battle, The	January 31
Lord The King, The	February 8
Lord Who Heals You, The	January 4
Lord's Messiah (Christ), The	June 19
Maker Of Heaven And Earth, The	March 10
Man, The	August 1
Man Accredited By God, A	August 5
Man Christ Jesus, The	October 6
Man He Has Appointed, The	August 14
Man Of Suffering, A	April 18
Man They Are Trying To Kill, The	July 21
Man Who Is Close To Me (The Father), The	May 19
Master, The	June 27
Mediator, The	October 5
Mediator Of A New Covenant, The	November 5
Merciful And Faithful High Priest, A	October 20
Messenger Of The Covenant, The	May 20
Messiah (Called Christ), The	July 15
Messiah (Christ) A King	July 2
Messiah (Christ) The Son Of God	August 4
Messiah, The Son Of The Living God, The	June 3
Mighty God, The	March 23
Mighty One, Our	April 9
Mighty One Of Jacob, The	April 16
Mighty Scepter, The	March 5
Mighty Warrior Who Saves, The	May 14
Most Excellent Of Men, The	February 10
Most Holy, The	May 8
Mystery From Which True Godliness Springs, The	October 7
Mystery Of God, The	September 27

NAME/ATTRIBUTE	DATE
Name, The	November 29
Name That Is Above Every Name, The	September 18
Nazarene, A	May 26
New And Living Way, A	November 1
New Name	December 9
One He [The Father] Loves, The	September 12
One Lawgiver And Judge	November 10
One Of Great Value (Pearl Of Great Price), The	June 2
One Sacrifice	October 31
One They Have Pierced, The	May 18
One Who Gives Victory To Kings, The	March 15
One Who Serves, The	July 1
One Who Sowed The Good Seed, The	May 31
Our Righteousness, Holiness And Redemption	August 27
Our Sovereign And Lord	November 30
Owner Of The House, The	June 30
Passover Lamb, The	August 30
Peace, Our	September 13
Peg Into A Firm Place, A	March 30
Pierced For Our Transgressions	April 19
Pioneer (Author) And Perfector (Finisher) Of Faith, The	November 4
Pioneer Of Their Salvation, The	October 19
Portion, My	March 9
Portion Of Jacob, The	May 4
Potter, The	April 27
Power Of God And The Wisdom Of God, The	August 26
Powerful In Word And Deed Before God And All The People	July 4
Priest Forever In The Order Of Melchizedek, A	March 6
Prince And Savior, The	August 10
Prince Of Peace, The	March 25
Prophet, The	July 18
Rabboni	August 2

NAME/ATTRIBUTE	DATE
Radiance Of God's Glory, The	October 14
Rain Falling On A Mown Field	February 20
Ransom For Many, A	June 4
Ransom To Set Them Free, A	October 30
Redeemer, My	January 19
Refiner And Purifier Of Silver, A	May 21
Refuge For The Needy In Their Distress, A	March 31
Refuge For The Oppressed, The	January 21
Refuge In Times Of Trouble, A	May 13
Resting Place, The	May 2
Resurrection And The Life, The	July 26
Righteous For The Unrighteous, The	November 17
Righteous God, My	January 20
Righteous Judge, The	October 9
Righteous Man, A	July 3
Righteous Servant, My	April 20
Righteousness Of God, The	August 20
Rising Sun, The	June 16
Rock In Whom I Take Refuge, The	February 27
Rock Of Israel, The	January 16
Rock Of Our Salvation, The	February 28
Rock That Is Higher Than I, The	February 15
Rock Their Savior, The	January 10
Root And Offspring Of David, The	December 30
Root Of Jesse, The	August 25
Royal Son, The	February 19
Ruler And Commander Of The Peoples, A	April 22
Ruler Of All Things, The	January 17
Ruler Of God's Creation, The	December 11
Ruler Of The Kings Of The Earth, The	December 3
Ruler Over Israel, The	May 12
Same Yesterday And Today And Forever, The	November 7
Savior, A	June 17

NAME/ATTRIBUTE	DATE
Savior Of All People, The	October 8
Savior Of The World	July 16
Scapegoat, The	January 6
Scepter, The	January 8
Seed, The	September 11
Servant, The Branch, My	May 16
Shade At Your Right Hand, Your	March 12
Shelter From The Storm, A	April 1
Shepherd, My	January 29
Shepherd And Overseer Of Your Souls, The	November 16
Shoot . . . From The Stump Of Jesse, A	March 26
Sign, A	March 20
Sign Of The Covenant, The	January 1
Someone Stronger	June 29
Something Greater Than The Temple	May 29
Son, The	June 9
Son He Loves, The	September 21
Son Jesus Christ, The	November 26
Son Of Abraham, The	May 23
Son Of David, The	June 5
Son Of God, The	September 10
Son Of Man, The	June 12
Son Of The Blessed One, The	June 13
Son Of The Most High, The	June 14
Son Over God's House, A	October 22
Son, Whom I Love, My	May 27
Source Of Eternal Salvation, The	October 25
Source Of Strength, A	April 5
Sovereign Lord, The	April 30
Sovereign Lord, Holy And True	December 15
Spirit Of Justice, A	April 4
Spiritual Rock, The	August 31
Splendor Of His Holiness, The	March 1

NAME/ATTRIBUTE	DATE
Splendor Of Our God, The	April 10
Spring Of Living Water, The	April 29
Stairway, The	January 2
Star, The	January 7
Stone That Causes People To Stumble, A Rock That Makes Them Fall, A	August 19
Stone The Builders Rejected, The	March 8
Strength, My	January 23
Strong Deliverer, My	March 14
Strong Tower Against The Foe, A	February 16
Stronghold For The People Of Israel, A	May 9
Stronghold Of My Life, The	February 2
Sun Of Righteousness, The	May 22
Support, My	January 25
Sure Foundation, A	April 7
Teacher	June 28
Temple	December 26
Tested Stone, A	April 6
Thunders With Mighty Voice	February 17
Treasure, The	September 7
Treasure Hidden In A Field, A	June 1
Tree Of Life, The	December 28
True Bread From Heaven, The	July 19
True God, The	November 27
True Vine, The	July 31
Truth, The	July 29
Unknown God, The	August 13
Verdant Pasture, The	May 3
Very Great	March 4
Wall Of Fire, A	May 15
Watchtower Of The Flock, The	May 11
Way, The	July 28
Way Of Holiness, The	April 11

NAME/ATTRIBUTE	DATE
Wells Of Salvation, The	March 29
Witness, My	January 18
Witness To The Peoples, The	April 21
Wonderful Counselor, The	March 22
Word, The	July 5
Word Of God, The	December 19
Word Of Life, The	November 22
Worthy	December 12

AUDIO Ink
PUBLISHING

AudioInk Publishing was founded on the principle that
"everyone has a story to tell".

"YOU TELL THE STORY, WE TELL
THE WORLD"

AudioInk, a division of Made For Success, Inc., is dedicated to providing authors and speakers the opportunity to "Tell their story" through the different mediums available; Key Note Speeches, audiobooks, eBooks and Physical Books, both online and at retail. We provide generous royalties and light costs to authors and speakers in an effort to extend the greatest opportunity to all we have the honor of serving.

There are many ways we can assist you with your project. Please review the list of services that AudioInk Publishing offers and let us know how we can help you.

1. From Manuscript editing to Ghostwriting, we can help you get your manuscript to print. Contact our publishing office at support@AudioInk.com

2. Want a best-seller? Our SnowBall campaign can take you there. Contact our sales office at sales@AudioInk.com

3. Book Trailer videos and author videos: are becoming an integral part of promoting your book and yourself as an author. Want to check out a few? Go to www. AudioInk.com. If you have questions or are ready to get started please contact Bryan at bheathman@AudioInk.com

4. Want to turn your book into an eBook or other book derivative? Contact bheathman@AudioInk.com

5. Once you choose AudioInk Publishing, you become part of a team. Need coaching or consulting? contact bheathman@AudioInk.com

6. Author or Book Website? If you don't promote you, who will? Let us help with a book and/or author website. Contact bheathman@AudioInk.com

You can also Visit our Website: www.AudioInk.com read our testimonials, send us an email, request more information.

Get Quantity Discounts

AudioInk Published Print books are available at quantity discounts for orders of 10 copies or more. Please call us toll free at (888)-884-8365 x 5 or email us at support@AudioInk.com